$\mathcal{R}$eligion in America

THIRD EDITION

Julia Mitchell Corbett

Ball State University

Prentice Hall, Upper Saddle River, New Jersey 07458

Library of Congress Cataloging-in-Publication Data
Corbett, Julia Mitchell.
    Religion in America / Julia Mitchell Corbett.—3rd ed.
        p. cm.
    Includes bibliographical references and index.
    ISBN 0-13-476029-8
    1. United States—Religion—1960–   2. United States—Religion.
I. Title.
BL2525.C67 1997
200′.973—dc20   97-7870
                                                           CIP

Editorial/production supervision and interior design: *Barbara DeVries*
Acquisitions editor: *Angela Stone*
Prepress and Manufacturing buyer: *Lynn Pearlman*
Editorial Assistant: *Meg McGuane*
Cover design director: *Jayne Conte*

This book was set 11/12 Adobe Garamond by The Composing Room of Michigan, Inc. and was
printed by Courier Companies, Inc. The cover was printed by Phoenix Color Corp.

© 1997, 1994, 1990 by Prentice-Hall, Inc.
Simon & Schuster/A Viacom Company
Upper Saddle River, New Jersey 07458

Printed in the United States of America
10 9 8 7 6 5 4 3 2 1

ISBN 0-13-476029-8

Prentice-Hall International (UK) Limited, *London*
Prentice-Hall of Australia Pty. Limited, *Sydney*
Prentice-Hall Canada Inc. *Toronto*
Prentice-Hall Hispanoamericana, S.A., *Mexico*
Prentice-Hall of India Private Limited, *New Delhi*
Prentice-Hall of Japan, Inc., *Tokyo*
Simon & Schuster Asia Pte. Ltd., *Singapore*
Editoria Prentice-Hall do Brasil, Ltda., *Rio de Janeiro*

To Our First Grandchild,
Courtney Elizabeth Arbogast,
with the hope that she will have
both the strength of her own convictions
and appreciation for the convictions of others.

Contents

4   Consensus Protestantism   54

5   Catholics in the United States   88

6   Consensus Religion in the Jewish Framework   112

Preface

Far too often, when people discuss religion, the discussion becomes an unproductive and unpleasant argument about who is right and who is wrong. This does not have to be the case. The approach taken in this book is the academic study of religion as a part of the humanities. I will introduce this approach in the first chapter. It offers a unique opportunity to learn about American communities of faith in an atmosphere free of both judgment and partisan advocacy. It focuses on what each group believes and does and on what these beliefs and practices mean to those who are a part of it. It does not evaluate whether those beliefs and practices are right or wrong, nor does it make judgments about whether a religion is true or false. The academic study of religion does not judge and it does not advocate. It does not present religion as preferable to nonreligion, nor does it favor secularity over religiousness. It does not attempt to make converts to or from any particular community of faith. Each community of faith speaks for itself, without its beliefs and practices being judged favorably or unfavorably.

Although religious beliefs and practices are presented impartially in this book, it is important that you know from the outset that this book is not value-free. I believe that religion is an important part of humanity's story. I also believe that nothing in the entire spectrum of human religiousness can be completely strange to any of us, because we are all human. I believe firmly in the freedom of religion that is guaranteed by the Constitution. In the climate of pluralism that we have in the United States, toleration and understanding of those who are different from ourselves are vitally important. We must move beyond toleration, however. I believe in the community of neighbors, not strangers. This is a community of dialogue, based on respect and the appreciation of differences. It is a community based on every individual's commitment to freedom of belief and freedom of religious practice within the boundaries of the law.

Several things are on my mind as I write this Preface to the third edition. First, and you should be aware of this as you begin to read, there is a vast distinction between religion as it is described in books—as I describe it in *this* book, for example—and religion as people actually live it. Jacob Neusner makes this point forcefully in a recent book.[1] A majority of both Jews and Christians do not attend corporate worship with any regularity. Nor do they pray with the constancy their holy books instruct. Catholics do not necessarily follow their church's teachings about such personal matters as birth control and abortion. Some American Buddhists drink wine with dinner, in violation of a prohibition on intoxicants (which some read as a prohibition on intoxication). So do some Muslims, in the face of a similar prohibition. What are we to make of all this? Do we dismiss these followers as "bad" members of their respective communities of faith? As "lax," as "backslidden"? I think not. The Protestant religious heritage, as Neusner suggests, has given people in the United States a legacy that says religion is private, very much subject to individual conscience. As a people, we choose from our religions' teachings those things that are personally meaningful to us and feel perfectly free to leave the rest alone. Not "bad" or "lax," but *different* in our way of being religious than what the books describe. So when you meet actual Methodists or Hindus or Jews, they won't conform completely to what you have read. Their lives, however, *will* be informed at some level by their religious faith.

Second, I've been pondering two distinctly different visions about religion in the United States. One reflects the devastation of the Branch Davidian compound at Waco, Texas. There is concern, in some quarters, at least, that the approach of the year 2000 may produce an increase in these kinds of activities. "This is only the beginning as the year 2000 approaches," says one author. "We're in for a helluva ride with these millennial groups."[2] The director of the Centre for the Study of Terrorism and Political Violence at the University of Saint Andrews states, "Religion provides justification and context. If God's telling you to do it, anything goes."[3] This vision also reflects the list of hate crimes compiled annually by the Southern Poverty Law Center. 1994 was not an atypical year, and the figures are both depressing and frightening. Hate crimes based on religion, either perpetrated by persons with religious motives or enacted against people because of their religion, have increased again.

The other vision comes from a statement of purpose written by the Assembly of Metropolitan Religious, Spiritual, and Civic Leaders in Chicago, Illinois, in connection with the 1993 World's Parliament of Religions held in that city.[4]

The first is a vision of religious conflict, a situation in which religion fuels hatred—fanaticism that occasionally even erupts into criminal activity. Religion can be a force that leads to disruption and fear. The second is a vision in which

[1] Jacob Neusner, *Introduction to American Judaism: What the Books Say, What the People Do* (Minneapolis, MN: Fortress Press, 1994).
[2] Hal Mansfield, in *Newsweek*, April 3, 1995, p. 40.
[3] *Newsweek*, April 3, 1995, p. 40.
[4] Used with permission.

Figure P-1

We are persons of all races, cultures, faiths, and traditions. Although we often find ourselves living among strangers, we have the opportunity to encounter and know each other as neighbors. For in the midst of this rich tapestry of religious and cultural diversity, we share the joys and struggles of everyday life. . . .

Our diversity also presents challenges. Overcoming barriers of language and custom is hard work. Truly listening to others rather than simply viewing them through our own lenses is a conscious choice. Being secure enough in our own identities to "live and let live" is no small accomplishment. . . .

In a spirit of mutual respect and appreciation, affirming our common humanity and celebrating our diversity of experience and tradition, we commit ourselves:

> To respect, understand, learn and benefit from the religious, spiritual, and cultural traditions of our neighbors;
> To share the wisdom and vision of our own precious, unique religious and spiritual traditions, building toward a more peaceful, interdependent and interactive . . . community;
> To join together in this way in order that we may defeat racism and sexism, alleviate poverty, reduce hostilities and tensions, empower the disenfranchised, preserve and nurture the Earth.

In the process of interreligious dialogue and cooperation, we pledge:

> To forgive each other when we fail to be sensitive to one another's feelings and needs;
> To trust each other enough to keep trying;
> To look deeply into our own traditions for inspiration, guidance, and strength;
> To never lose sight of a future characterized by common cause and hope.

compassion and wisdom promote understanding and harmony. It is up to each of us to help decide which kind of a world we will live in.

We have in the United States a commitment to and a history of cooperation and tolerance among a vast diversity of religious groups. We have never seen the bitter religious wars that have marred the histories of some nations. From the very beginning of the colonial period, diversity of religious thought and practice has meant that no single religion would ever would ever have an exclusive claim on American hearts and minds. The freedom of religion guaranteed in our Constitution has provided a safe haven in which both pluralism and tolerance have flourished. Legal disestablishment helps to limit rancor between religious groups by lessening the mixing of religious issues with political issues and by ensuring that all religious perspectives have similar legal standing. It prevents the criminalization of religious dissent.

Other factors contribute to the religious harmony that we enjoy. Most of us believe that people's religions are their own business and not subject to the interference of others. The level of education in the United States is higher than it is in many other countries. With education comes greater tolerance in matters of religion, as well as in other things. America was—and, in a cultural sense, continues to be—the "new world." There is an abiding sense of not being tied to time-honored cultural (including religious) patterns and habits. Experimentation and being willing to try out new approaches are accepted and often regarded as virtues. Morality has always been an important focus of religion in the United States, going back even to the colonial period of our history. Within a broad range, the common moral ground shared by most religions encourages peaceful coexistence.

Third, I hope you will enjoy your study of religion in the United States. Religion, along with families and friends, work and creative endeavors, school and leisure time, helps to make life meaningful and good for most Americans. It is a fascinating and rewarding subject for study. Fundamentally, this is a book about people, because religion is about people. For most people in the United States, religion is also about something that transcends people, such as God or another higher reality. But it is always about people, what people believe and how they act in response to those beliefs. So this is a book about us, all of us.

Finally, I hope you will come to appreciate and value the vast diversity of American religion. Religion in the United States is more diverse than religion anywhere else on earth. Each of us has the opportunity to meet many people who are different from ourselves. They are our neighbors, roommates, coworkers, friends, classmates, dating partners, and spouses. The United States is an ideal place to learn about religion, not only in books, but as it is embodied in the people with whom we come into contact every day.

A note to teachers: Some of the questions for review that follow each chapter suggest that students write essays. Many more of the questions could be used, or adapted for use, in this way by those teachers who want to have their students do more writing.

Books are always the product of far more people than just the author, and this book is no exception. I am grateful to all the clergy and religious laypeople who provided information and encouragement. Department Chair David B. Annis and my colleagues in the Department of Philosophy at Ball State University have been, as always, unfailingly helpful and supportive. Meg McGuane and Angela Stone, Religion Editors at Prentice Hall, and Barbara DeVries, Production Editor, were a pleasure to work with. As always, my husband's unwavering love and encouragement make my life a daily joy.

Julia Mitchell Corbett
Ball State University

1

*S*tudying Religion: Points of Departure

Before you read this chapter, think about how and where you have learned about religion so far. What kinds of things did you study? What was the purpose of your study? Also, think about how *you* define religion. All of us have some idea of what religion is. What does the word *religion* mean to you?

STUDYING RELIGION AS A PART OF THE HUMANITIES

The study of religion has many dimensions. Studying religion as a part of a course of study in the humanities may involve attitudes and methods that are new to you.

Most of us who think about religion first learned to do so in a religious organization or a community of faith, or perhaps within our families. Maybe it was in preparation to become a member of a church or synagogue.[1] Perhaps it was learning about our own religion in Sunday school or Hebrew day school classes. For some, it was probably learning the prayers of our faith from our parents. We can call this method of studying religion a **devotional** approach. This is study undertaken by members of a community of faith when they study their own religion. Therefore, we can call it an "inside" perspective. It usually involves the personal faith commitments of both teachers and students. It takes as its beginning point the faith of the community, the "givens" accepted as a part of their tradition. For Christians, for example, the uniqueness of Jesus and Jesus' special role in God's plan for the world is such a given. For Jews, the oneness of God has

---

[1]A *synagogue* is a Jewish house of worship and center for study.

a similar role. Buddhists[2] take the early teachings of the Buddha as foundational. These starting points are often found in or derived from the group's sacred writings.

The word **theology** is sometimes used for this type of study. Theology takes faith as its starting point. It is, in Saint Anselm's classic definition, "faith seeking understanding."[3] Theology uses intellectual concepts to understand a particular religious tradition and to express its relevance for the present.

The goal of such devotional study is that those who engage in it will become more knowledgeable about and more committed to their faith. It does not necessarily involve attempting to show that one's own faith is superior or correct, although it is sometimes used in this way. Devotional study is an important part of educating people in their faith and helping them to mature as religious persons. It is a significant aspect of the growth and development of any religion. A firm understanding of one's own faith is also one foundation for dialogue with others.

The **academic study of religion** differs from the devotional approach in that it makes no assumptions about the beliefs, or lack of beliefs, of the scholar. Religious studies teachers and students alike may be believers, nonbelievers, or agnostics (people who believe that we cannot be certain whether God exists or not) in their personal religious lives.

Rather than concentrating on one religion, the academic study of religion promotes a lively awareness of the diversity of religious beliefs, practices, and experiences that people have. It encourages open-minded acceptance of that diversity. It investigates religions in their historical and cultural settings and examines a broad range of materials to provide the most balanced treatment possible. It distinguishes between historical fact and things that are taken as true only by a particular community of faith.

In studying religion from an academic standpoint, we may try to *explain* religious behavior and beliefs, as well as simply *describe* them. You will see a number of examples of this in Chapter 12. However, such explanations must never become *reductionistic*. Reductionism is an oversimplification that claims to exhaust the meaning of a phenomenon by explaining it in terms of some other, external factor. For example, saying that people are religious because economic deprivation in their earthly lives makes "pie in the sky by-and-by" attractive, is a case of reductionism. While there may be some truth to this for some persons, it does not exhaust the meaning of religion.

When we study religion academically, the study takes place in an atmosphere that is free of advocacy. It promotes neither religion nor nonreligion. It educates about all religions and neither favors nor belittles any. It is loyal first of all

---

[2]Buddhism is an Eastern religion found in the United States.

[3]Saint Anselm was a Christian theologian who lived between 1033 and 1109 C.E. The abbreviations C.E. for Common Era and B.C.E. for Before the Common Era have replaced A.D. (*Anno Domini*, the year of our Lord) and B.C. (Before Christ) in most scholarly writing.

to the guidelines of public scholarship. Its commitments are to knowledge and understanding for their own sake and to religion as a vigorous dimension of humanity's story (Figure 1–1). It does not involve the personal beliefs of its teachers and students. It is especially important to keep the distinction between the devotional study of religion and the academic study of religion clear in public, tax-supported schools, colleges, and universities. An institution supported by taxes paid by people of all faiths and by those who are not religious cannot favor one religion over others. Nor can it favor either religion or secularity. To do so clearly violates the disestablishment clause of the First Amendment to the Constitution. Our personal religious views *might* change when we study religion academically, but, if that happens, it is a personal by-product of the study and not its goal.

The **academic study of theology** itself occupies something of a "borderland" between the devotional study of religion and the academic study of religion. Especially at the graduate level, and, to a lesser extent in seminary education, the academic study of theology uses the same scholarly methods—literary, philosophical, comparative—as does the academic study of religion. In its use of these methods, it makes itself subject to the same criteria of public verifiability that apply in other academic disciplines. Its assumptions, however, may not be subject to the same kind of verifiability. For example, the very basic Christian assumption of the simultaneous divinity and humanity of Jesus cannot be so verified.

As an example, let us consider how someone might study a particular biblical passage. A Christian or Jew engaged in the devotional study of the Bible would turn to it as a believer studying the Word of God, trying to understand it more fully and grasp its contemporary meanings. Questions about the passage's exact authorship, date, and various translations of the original language would

Figure 1–1   The study of religion is an integral part of education in the humanities. (*Photo by the author.*)

be important. People involved in the study of the Bible as literature (an academic class) have commitments, as scholars, to scholarship, whatever their personal religious beliefs may be. They look at the passage as literature, not as the Word of God. In a similar way, religious studies professionals might engage in a comparative study of the sacred writings of several religions. These would be viewed as examples of sacred writings, but not as divine revelation.

The 1963 United States Supreme Court decision in *Abington* v. *Schempp* has particular relevance for the academic study of religion. The Court ruled that schools and school personnel could not mandate devotional activities in their schools and classrooms. For example, teachers cannot lead their students in saying grace before lunch. The Bible cannot be read as a morning devotional exercise. People who favored such exercises in the public schools charged that the Court had, in effect, supported the religion of secularism (nonreligion). Justice Clark, in replying to this charge, distinguished between the practice of religion, such as devotional exercises, and study about religion. He went on to say that study about religion as a part of human culture and the humanities is well within the guidelines established by the First Amendment to the Constitution. This Supreme Court decision allows for the academic study of religion at all levels of public education.

Religious groups cannot be barred from using public school facilities or other public buildings, however. If secular groups can use these facilities, then religious groups must have the same privilege. This is the result of the **Equal Access Act**. The Equal Access Act was passed by the 98th Congress in 1984 and upheld by the Supreme Court in *Board of Education of Westside Community School District* v. *Mergens* (1990). For example, if a school board permits such noncurricular clubs as a chess club or Boy or Girl Scouts to use their facilities for meetings, then a Bible study club must have the same right. Usually, interpretation holds that teachers or other school personnel may not be officially involved in such groups. If a city-county building has a public meeting room, then religious groups must be allowed to use it on the same basis as secular groups. The net effect of *Abington* v. *Schempp* and *Mergens* is that schools cannot actively promote religious activities, but neither can they prohibit them.

You may be wondering whether religious studies is defined by having a distinctive method or a distinctive subject matter. Religious studies scholars do not agree on the answer. In my opinion, religious studies is a distinct and identifiable academic discipline because it investigates the subject of religion in all its forms. Its *subject matter* is distinctive. In its investigation of its subject, it uses many methods. Human religious behavior is a very complex phenomenon and calls for many investigative tools.

There is no single best way to study religion. The method used will depend on many things, such as the scholar's training and personal preferences and what aspect of religion is being investigated. Just as a hammer is best for certain tasks and a paintbrush for others, some methods work better than others for answering specific questions. A variety of methods is necessary, and no one of them can claim primary authority.

Within the academic study of religion, we can distinguish two interrelated types of inquiry. The **social-scientific study of religion** is very much an "outside" point of view. It focuses on observation and on data that are quantifiable. Its goal is to be wholly objective. The data that it provides make a crucial contribution to our understanding of religion. Psychologists and sociologists who study human religious behavior often use social-scientific methods. The widespread use of computers for data processing and analysis has greatly enhanced this branch of the academic study of religion.

People **study religion as a part of the humanities** to understand a religious group, belief, or practice from the standpoint of what it is like for those who follow it. This approach encourages students and teachers to enter empathically into the life and experience of the religious "other." It seeks imaginative participation, developing what can be described as an "inside-outside" point of view. We can, with practice, become increasingly able to see religions other than our own *as if* from the inside, while remaining on the outside. We do not become participants, but we learn to value and appreciate the meaning that the religion has for those who are participants in it.

Such study is not completely value-neutral. It remains academic in that it does not advocate for religion or nonreligion generally, or for or against any particular religion. It encourages such values as appreciation for diversity and respect for the religious choices that individuals make. It refrains from judging the rightness or wrongness of those choices, and instead tries to grasp their meaning.

The academic study of religion may come under attack from either of two sides. On one side are traditional believers who are threatened by any viewpoint that refuses to judge the truth or falsity of religious beliefs and takes the position that there is no one true religion. On the other side are those who refuse to take religion seriously and think that it must be "explained away" in terms of social, psychological, or economic factors. As philosopher of religion Ninian Smart writes, in either case, people "forget that religions are what they are and have the power they have regardless of what we may think about their value, truth, or rationality. They also forget that . . . we have to listen to one another"[4] in a nation that is as religiously diverse as is the United States.

Perhaps you have felt one of these two ways at times, or perhaps you do now. You might occasionally find yourself feeling threatened by some of the material studied, by the way it is studied, or by your classmates' comments. Remember that the study of religion from an academic viewpoint allows everyone ideological space in which to exist. All that is required is that you extend to the beliefs of others the same respect that you wish for your own.

---

[4]Ninian Smart, *Worldviews: Crosscultural Explorations of Human Beliefs* (New York: Charles Scribner's Sons, 1983), p. 17.

WHY STUDY RELIGION?

Many, perhaps most, of you reading this are studying religion to receive academic credit for a course. But there are other reasons for studying religion. We study our own religion to learn more about a significant dimension of our lives. Our commitment to it matures as we base our devotion to it on greater knowledge and understanding.

Why study other people's religions? Doing so can help us to understand other people. Religion is an important, even essential, part of many people's lives, and by understanding and appreciating it, we come to know them better. Prejudice often results in part from a simple lack of knowledge and information. While knowledge and understanding do not guarantee freedom from prejudice, a lack of knowledge greatly increases the likelihood of prejudice.

It is also important that we understand religion because it has had an important role in history and continues to have a significant impact on contemporary events. Religion has had and continues to have an impact on cultural forms such as literature, art, and music. Finally, because all religions have deeply human roots, to understand anyone's religion can help us understand ourselves and our culture better.

Writing in the *Journal of the American Academy of Religion*, Jacob Neusner evocatively summarizes the significance of religious studies in the humanities:

> The importance of learning about a religion other than our own is to prepare us for the confrontation with difference, to educate our sympathies to welcome diversity, to discover what we can be in what we are not. . . . In finding out things we did not know, we learn. In encountering and entering into worlds we did not make, we discover. In the learning and discovery, we uncover in ourselves things we did not know were there. We find out we can be more than we are.[5]

DEFINING RELIGION

Religion is an ambiguous word. People use it to mean various things. Even scholars in religious studies cannot agree on its meaning. The beginning point of understanding its meaning can be ordinary usage. That is, we do have some idea of what religion is. If someone asks, for example, "What religion do you practice?" we know how to answer the question. If someone mentions a religious service, we have a general idea of what sort of activity is meant.

By itself, our everyday, unreflective definition is inadequate. It is probably limited to our own experiences with religion. Our definition might be biased in some way, based on what we have been taught is "true" religion. Different peo-

---

[5]Jacob Neusner, "Why Religious Studies in America? Why Now?" *Journal of the American Academy of Religion*, 52, no. 4 (Winter 1984), 740.

ple have different everyday definitions, and the same person may use different definitions at different times.

For purposes of study, we must have a good working definition. A **working definition** is one that is useful and adequate, but it is not necessarily the only possible one. It should meet the following three criteria:

1. **A good working definition of religion is broad enough to include all religions.** It should not define religion in a way that leaves out some manifestations of religion. Nor should it leave out any specific religion. For example, if we say that *religion* means belief in God (having in mind God as Jews and Christians think about God), we will leave out those people who worship many *deities* (a general word meaning "gods or goddesses") and those who worship none at all. This definition also focuses on belief and excludes other important dimensions of religion.
2. At the same time, **it must be sufficiently specific to distinguish religion from other similar things,** such as a nonreligious philosophy of life or a deeply held and passionate commitment to a social or political cause.
3. **It also needs to be as free of prejudice or bias as we can make it.** Definitions that state what true or genuine religion is often fall into the trap of imposing one person's or group's bias on their definition of religion generally.

In sum, then, our working definition of religion needs to be broad enough to include all religions, yet specific enough to allow us to distinguish religion from other, similar things. It also must not define religion in terms of our own prejudices.

We will use the working definition given in Figure 1–2. It is important to know and understand this definition, since it underlies everything that follows throughout the book.

Religions are also *communities of faith.* They are groups of people knitted together by their shared commitment to a common worldview and their participation in shared experiences. The nature of religious commitment and experience means that it often claims its adherents' greatest, most intense loyalties. The ties within communities of faith are frequently among the strongest and most meaningful of human relationships.

Figure 1–2

WORKING DEFINITION OF RELIGION

A *religion* is an integrated system of belief, lifestyle, ritual activities, and institutions by which individuals give meaning to (or find meaning in) their lives by orienting themselves to what they take to be holy, sacred, or of the highest value.

Let's discuss this definition of religion in detail. A religion is an **integrated system**. Ideally, all the dimensions in a religion hold together to make a comprehensive, coherent whole. Its various parts work together without conflict and with mutual support. The extent to which this is the case varies from one religion to another and from one person to another. But ideally, a religion does have coherence among its various dimensions. These dimensions include beliefs, a lifestyle, rituals, and institutions.

Belief takes many forms. Beliefs are the ideas of a religion. For example, most religions have an idea about what the purpose of human life is. Most have beliefs concerning how the world came into being and what happens to people after death. These beliefs are found in scripture, statements of faith, creeds (official written statements), hymns, stories, and handbooks of belief, to name but a few locations. The beliefs of a community of faith also exist in the minds of its members, although these may not be as well worked out as those found in official statements.

Nearly all religions have guidelines for their members' daily **lifestyle**. These include codes of conduct and standards of behavior, as well as carefully worked out ethical systems. They involve both formal requirements and customs and less formal folkways and habits. Examples include dietary regulations followed by Jews and by Seventh-day Adventists, and dress codes followed by certain Christian groups and many Muslims.

Religions also include **ritual activities**. These are the ceremonial actions, usually repetitive in nature, that people perform as a part of their religious behavior. The word *worship* suggests that there is a divine being or beings who are being worshiped. Not all religious people worship such a being, although they do participate in other rituals. So *worship* is too narrow a term for our use. Religious rituals include worship, however, along with prayer, chanting, meditation, the lighting of candles, pilgrimages, and the devotional reading of religious books, to name but a few examples. There are religious rituals that are public and corporate, and there are those that individual people and families do privately. For many religious people, the rhythm of regular participation in the ritual life of their religion is more important than is reflection on religious beliefs.

Finally, although religion has to do with individual people, it also develops **institutions and organizations**. Like-minded people join together for instruction, for rituals, and for fellowship. Structures for governance and decision making are necessary. Other things in this category are arrangements for admitting members to the group and expelling them from it, educational functions, and arrangements for the selection, training, and support of leaders.

Religion is one way that **people give meaning to or find meaning in their lives**. A religion is a human creation or development. Its beliefs, lifestyle, rituals, and institutions are the products of human thought and activity. It is continuous with the many other ways that we either create or find meaning in our lives, such as through the personal relationships that are dear to us, the work that we do, and the values, ideals, and causes to which we give our loyalty. Religion is continuous with these other structures of meaning and shares their profoundly human roots.

Religion involves that which people take to be **sacred, holy, or of the highest value.** Although religion is continuous with other structures of meaning, it is also unique. Most interpretations of religion hold that its uniqueness is in its reference to the sacred or to the highest value. It reaches beyond the individual and the ordinary concerns of day-to-day living. Religion puts us in touch with the sense of mystery that shines through the cracks of our common world. It has to do with the most comprehensive, fullest expression or embodiment of reality.

TALKING ABOUT RELIGION IN THE UNITED STATES: THE "MAINSTREAM" AND "MARGINS" PROBLEM

From the earliest beginnings of what would become the United States, there has been both consensus in religion and considerable variation from that consensus. The words "mainstream" or "mainline" are often used to refer to this consensus. They indicate the central tendency, the religious affiliations, beliefs, and practices of the majority. Mainstream religious groups not only reflected the majority culture; they had a large role in shaping that culture. Their values and standards became those of the society as a whole. Earlier studies of religion in the United States often assumed that mainstream religions were the only ones worthy of consideration.

There have also always been "marginal" groups that departed from the mainline in various ways. These groups are often called "sects" or "cults." If they were included at all in surveys of religion, they were treated as though they were less important than the mainstream. Sometimes, they have been treated as if they were not only different but deviant. The mainstream-sectarian-marginal designation is not satisfactory. Although it does show how these religious categories relate to the larger culture, the word "mainstream" has a normative ring, and "sectarian" and "marginal" have correspondingly negative overtones.

When we name the various styles of religion, we must recognize both the formative and continued status of the mainstream and the genuine differentness of the margins, without making the mainstream normative and without delegitimizing the margins. In the discussion that follows, I have chosen the term **consensus religion** as a way of talking about the central tendency that shows its role in the culture without making it normative. Similarly, I have chosen to use simply **alternatives to the consensus** to describe the genuine differentness of the nonconsensus religions without marginalizing or delegitimizing their existence.

QUESTIONS AND ACTIVITIES FOR REVIEW, DISCUSSION, AND WRITING

1. Write a paragraph in which you explain what you hope to gain from your study of religion in the United States. Are your goals academic, personal, or a combination of both? Compare your answer with those of other people.

2. What are some classroom activities that would be prohibited by the *Abington* v. *Schempp* ruling? What kinds of activities are allowed?
3. Do you think that religious clubs (such as student Bible study clubs or prayer groups) should have the same opportunities to use classroom space before or after school hours as nonreligious groups do? Why or why not? You might want to organize a debate on this topic.
4. Ask several of your friends how they define religion, and compare their answers. How are they alike? Different?
5. Look up the definition of *religion* in any standard dictionary and write an essay in which you evaluate it based on what you have learned in this chapter.
6. If you are a part of a religious group, think about how the four dimensions of religion we discussed apply to it.

FOR FURTHER READING

Ellwood, Robert, *Introducing Religion.* Englewood Cliffs, NJ: Prentice Hall, Inc., 1994. A brief introduction to what religion is and what its roles are, from the perspectives of several of the disciplines that make up the academic study of religion.

2

Overview of Religion in the United States

The United States has become known for its freedom of religion. People decide for themselves whether they will be a part of a religious group, and, if so, which one. Before reading this chapter, stop and think about what freedom of religion means to you personally. How important is it to you? In what specific ways does it affect your life? Do you think there should be limits on religious freedom? If so, what should they be, and why do you think they are necessary?

DISESTABLISHMENT AND THE CONSTITUTION

Prior disillusionment with established religion and the existence of religious pluralism worked against the continued existence of established religion in the United States. The American experience with established churches was influenced by the experience of European settlers who were forced to flee from establishments of religion in their home countries. It was also influenced by the experiments with pluralism and freedom of religion that had been carried out in Rhode Island and Pennsylvania. Many people concluded that civil power and privilege for churches led to problems, while toleration and equality under the law was good for both the churches and society at large.[1] In addition, no single religious group had enough support throughout the original thirteen states to make its belief and practice the law of the land. Furthermore, the framers of the

[1]Henry Steele Commager, *The Empire of Reason* (Garden City, NY: Anchor Press, 1977), pp. 210–11.

Constitution held several views of religion. Some were Protestant and Catholic Christians. Others were advocates of naturalistic religion based on rationality and morality and still others were nonbelievers or atheists. Freethinkers either questioned or rejected traditional Christianity, and their views helped to bring about the official separation of church and state that we have now. Still others came from those strands of Protestant Reformation thought that advocated strict separation of church and state.

Matters pertaining to religion are found in three places in the Constitution: Article 6, the First Amendment, and the Fourteenth amendment.

1.   Article 6 prohibits religious requirements for holding public office.

> The Senators and Representatives . . . , and the Members of the several State Legislatures, and all executive and judicial offices, both of the United States and the several States, shall be bound by Oath or Affirmation, to support this Constitution; but **no religious Test shall ever be required as a Qualification to any Office or public Trust under the United States** [emphasis added].

In other words, someone's religion or lack of religion cannot legally be a qualification for holding public office. In a pluralistic culture in which religion and government are separate functions, affirmations about religion cannot be requirements for holding public office.

2.   The First Amendment to the Constitution contains some of the most important religious liberty legislation in our nation's history. It is part of the Bill of Rights, prepared under the leadership of James Madison. It reads as follows:

> **Congress shall make no law respecting an establishment of religion, or prohibiting the free exercise thereof;** or abridging the freedom of speech, or of the press; or the right of the people peaceably to assemble, and to petition the Government for a redress of grievances [emphasis added].

Let us look at these two religion clauses separately. The "establishment clause" says that the United States Congress cannot make any one religion the official religion of the United States. It cannot act in a way that gives preferential treatment or support to one religion above others. Nor can it support religion or nonreligion generally, one over the other. Insofar as possible, it must maintain a neutral stance toward religion.

The second clause is often called the "free exercise" clause. It states that the government cannot interfere with any person's religion. A significant distinction was made in the interpretation of this clause and has remained a part of judicial precedent. In *Reynolds* v. *United States* (1878), Reynolds held that a law against marriage to more than one person at the same time violated his religious freedom, because he was a member of a religion that advocated that practice. The Supreme Court did not agree with Reynolds. In a landmark opinion, the Court held that the free exercise clause applied to religious beliefs, but not necessarily to the actions arising from those beliefs. It held that "actions which are in violation of social duties or subversive of good order" cannot be tolerated, even when they are done in the name of religion.

This is a dilemma that cannot be fully resolved. Since religion is an intimate joining of belief and action, it may seem odd to tell people that they may believe what they please but prevent them from acting on those beliefs. Yet there are actions that no reasonable human being would condone, such as the torture of people or animals. There are actions that, if permitted, would utterly disrupt the social order, such as the refusal to be bound by any laws. These sorts of actions cannot be tolerated, even in the hallowed name of religious freedom.

Freedom of speech, the press, and assembly also contributes to religious freedom. These freedoms mean that people may speak and write openly about their views on religious questions. They may gather peaceably to listen to speakers or to worship in whatever ways they choose.

These two clauses account for most of the freedom of religion cases to come before the Court. The framers of the Bill of Rights could not possibly have known the range of circumstances these first ten amendments might be required to cover. The provisions of the bill are necessarily very broad, both allowing for and requiring constant reinterpretation. The majority opinion in *Walz v. Tax Commission of the City of New York* (1970) summarizes the role of the Supreme Court:

> The general principle deducible from the First Amendment and all that has been said by the Court is this: That we will not tolerate either governmentally established religion or governmental interference with religion. Short of those expressly proscribed governmental acts there is room for play in the joints productive of a benevolent neutrality which will permit religious exercise to exist without sponsorship and without interference.

Over the years, the applications of the First Amendment have illustrated considerable "play in the joints" as the Court has struggled with the meaning of freedom of religion in a culture in which religious pluralism continues to be a major feature.

3.   The Fourteenth Amendment is the final Constitutional reference to religious liberty. Added in 1868, this long amendment touches on several issues. The crucial point for religious liberty is in Section 1:

> **No State shall make or enforce any law which shall abridge the privileges or immunities of citizens of the United States**; nor shall any State deprive any person of life, liberty, or property without due process of law; nor deny to any person within its jurisdiction the equal protection of the laws [emphasis added].

Both Article 6 and the religion clauses in the First Amendment deal with what the federal government may not do. The Fourteenth Amendment holds that the states as well are not to "abridge the privileges" of their citizens, including the privilege of religious freedom. When the Constitution was originally written, several of the states did have establishments of religion. Such state interference with religion is prohibited under the Fourteenth Amendment.

LEGISLATIVE EFFORTS

The **Religious Freedom Restoration Act** was signed into law in November 1993. In the early 1990s, freedom of religion for smaller and less popular religions appeared to have been jeopardized by certain United States Supreme Court decisions. To cite a well-known example, *Employment Division of the State of Oregon v. Smith* (1990) overturned the principle that the government's interest had to be "compelling" to justify restricting freedom of religion. In *Smith*, the Court upheld the denial of unemployment benefits to Native Americans who lost their jobs because they used the illegal drug peyote as a sacrament in religious ceremonies. In its majority opinion, the Court held that the free exercise of religion deserves no special protection, as long as the law applies to nonreligious groups also. This line of argument lays the groundwork for the restriction of any unpopular religious practice.

In response to the perceived threats to religious liberty, a diverse coalition of religious leaders and groups came together to support the passage of the Act. This bill protects the free exercise of religion through a legislative act rather than by judicial means, enhancing protection especially for the lesser-known and less-understood religions.

Section 3, which spells out the core of the Act, states:

> Government shall not substantially burden a person's exercise of religion, even if the burden results from a rule of general applicability, except as provided in subsection (b). . . .
>
> (b) . . . Government may substantially burden a person's exercise of religion only if it demonstrates that application of the burden to the person—(1) is in furtherance of a compelling governmental interest; and (2) is the least restrictive means of furthering that compelling governmental interest.

In other words, if the government does infringe on a person's religious freedom, the government must have a serious reason for doing so and must then do so in a way that gives the least interference possible.

INSTITUTIONAL AND POPULAR RELIGION

We defined **religion** in Chapter 1 in a way that emphasizes religions as structured social systems, institutions, or organizations. This aspect of religion can be called **institutional religion**. The word **ecclesial** is sometimes used to describe this aspect of religion. There is another aspect of religion in the United States that is at least as significant as ecclesial religion. This is **popular religion**—religion that occurs outside the formal boundaries of religious institutions.

Popular religion encompasses a wide range of religious activities that take place outside the boundaries of formal religious organizations and that are not directly provided by them. It is a "dimension of religious life that is elusive and difficult to describe," as a recent study of the phenomenon puts it.[2] There is no one agreed-upon definition of popular religion, but we can describe it.

Popular religion is the religious belief and practice of ordinary people rather than of theologians and religious leaders. It is transmitted through various channels outside of ecclesial institutions.[3]

It exists alongside ecclesial religion as a complement to it. It is a supplement to participation in ecclesial religion for some people, and a substitute for it for others.

It offers people simpler, more direct access to the sacred than they have through the mediation of formal religious groups.

It draws on the core religious institutions of the culture (in the United States, primarily Christianity) but blends this with other sources and traditions. It often reflects both mainstream and alternative values.

Formal religious organizations impose order and structure on religion. Popular religion is distinguished by a lively sense of the supernatural without the imposition of formal structure. It does not have the "conceptual coherence" of organized religion. People do not abandon formal religion for popular religiosity, but use the latter to develop their own personal worldview.

It is not limited to the United States nor to modern times, nor is it dependent on "modernization, industrialization, or urbanization." Examples can be found in all cultures in all times.

In summarizing the importance of popular religion for understanding religion in the United States, the author writes:

[For] the vast majority of Americans, a sense of the supernatural so lively that it cannot be contained in creed and doctrine permeates life. . . . [O]rdinary men and women have sought and continue to seek direct access to the realm of the supernatural in order to use its power to give them control over their lives and to endow their lives with meaning. . . . Sometimes they gain that access through religious traditions and institutions, but more often [they do so] through fusing together an array of beliefs and practices to construct personal and very private worlds of meaning. If we would understand the dynamics of being religious, American style, we must explore the phenomenon of popular religiosity.[4]

Examples of popular religion abound. Some people place statues of Jesus, Mary, Saint Francis, or the Buddha in their yards. There is religious music (even

---

[2]Charles H. Lippy, *Being Religious, American Style: A History of Popular Religiosity in the United States.* (Westport, CT: Greenwood Press, 1994), p. 1.

[3]This section draws loosely on Lippy, *Being Religious,* chap. 1.

[4]Lippy, *Being Religious,* pp. 18–19.

in heavy metal format in the form of *Heaven's Metal* and *Gospel Metal*) and a wide array of religious television programming. Two popular musicals include "Jesus Christ, Superstar" and "Godspell." There are a number of Christian theme parks, such as Christus Gardens in Gatlinburg, Tennessee. "Precious Moments" figurines feature religious themes, as do several lines of greeting cards. Religious bookstores are located in most cities. There are religious-theme computer games and educational software to help children learn about the Bible. A number of catalogs offer a variety of items for people devising their own spirituality. One such catalog has an umbrella that features the eight major symbols of Tibetan Buddhism, as well as items reflecting Native American (and other) religions. In another catalog, those of Jewish faith can choose from a vast assortment of Jewish religious items such as prayer shawls, menorahs, Passover plates, and mezzuzahs (all of which are described in Chapter 6).

Two other examples of popular religion in action will round out our discussion of this important topic. One is religious activism around the controversy over abortion rights. Although there is organized support from religious groups on all sides of the issue, other activists are motivated as individuals by their religious beliefs (Figure 2.1).

Another example is a "March for Jesus" held in Elkhart, Indiana. An intergenerational and interracial group of more than 2,000 Christians marched in the rain, carrying banners, clutching balloons, singing hymns, and clapping. About 120 similar marches took place across the United States. "Drench this land with your awesome presence," the crowd prayed as dark clouds gave way to torrential rain. "Let grace and mercy flood this land." The purpose of the marches was to praise Jesus and increase Christian visibility in the communities in which they took place.[5]

Figure 2–1   The conflict over abortion rights often includes a religious dimension. (*Paul Conklin/Monkmeyer Press.*)

[5]Thanks to former student Kathryn Neighbours for calling this event to my attention.

DATA AND OBSERVATIONS

Statistical data about religion are important because they can help us form an overall picture of religion in the United States. Information about religion has not been collected as a part of the U.S. Census since the 1930s. To do so is held to be a violation of the separation of church and state. This lack of "official" data means that our two main sources for data about religion are the reports of religious organizations themselves and the results of national polls and surveys. Caution is called for in interpreting either kind of data.

The accuracy of reports from religious organizations varies widely. Membership rolls may be computerized and be reasonably accurate. Or they may be kept by hand and seldom updated. Too, religious organizations differ in whom they count as members. Some include the children of parents who are members, for example, while others include only full members. Nor do membership rolls distinguish between the faithful weekly attender and the person whose name remains on the list but who never attends. Most congregations also have faithful participants who are not actual members and are therefore not included in the official number. Membership statistics usually do not give us other significant data about the people in a community of faith.

Polls and surveys have their pitfalls, too. Even though questionnaires are sent to a probability sample,[6] differential return rates may bias the results. In face-to-face or telephone interviews, respondents sometimes try to please the interviewer or give the answer that they believe is socially correct. This phenomenon affects even anonymous written questionnaires. Not all people interpret a question in the same way, again eroding the accuracy of the response.

All of this is not to say that statistical data are meaningless or hopelessly inaccurate. They do give us valuable information about who we are, what we think, and how we act religiously, as a nation. They are approximations that are sufficiently accurate to be very useful.

We will look at some data about religion in the United States. Before we do so, stop and ask yourself how *you* would answer the following questions. What percentage of the population do you think is Protestant? Catholic? Jewish? What percentage claims no religion? What percentage of us believes in God? How frequently do we pray? How often do we attend religious services? These are a few of the questions that we will answer by analyzing the data available to us.

Several general observations can be made about religion in the United States:

1.   **It is characterized by vast diversity**. There is an almost overwhelming variety of religious groups, organizations, and activities. The most recent edition of *The Encyclopedia of American Religions* includes 1,730 religious organizations, divided into 19 distinct families. Ten of these families are Christian and nine are

---

[6]A *probability sample* is one that, because of the sampling procedures used, ensures that each person in the population being sampled has an equal chance of being selected for the sample, at least at some stage of the process. This means that the sample accurately reflects the characteristics of the population being sampled.

not. There are some 900 Christian denominations discussed.[7] Independent congregations that do not belong to a specific family are not included unless very large, so there are even more groups than the *Encyclopedia* indicates. Many of these religious organizations have a great deal of internal diversity as well. There are significant differences among congregations within the same denomination, as well as major differences of opinion among members of the same congregation. The United States might well be thought of as a living laboratory of religious diversity.

The Immigration Reform Act of 1965 brought about "a significant fast-forwarding in the globalization of American life," especially in urban areas. This tide of immigrants did not come from Europe, as had been the case in the past. They are Hispanics, Africans, Middle Easterners, and Asians.[8] Their presence has greatly diversified religion in the United States in both quantity and quality, bringing with it dramatically increased opportunities for both interreligious dialogue and conflict.

2.   **There is also consensus in American religion.** As we saw in the discussion of popular religion, most people in the United States believe in God, in life after death, and they pray. About two-thirds are Protestants. And, the ideas and ideals that people hold about what the United States is and ought to be are often expressed in language that reminds us of religion.

There is consensus in institutional religion as well. As you will learn in Chapter 3, there is a cluster of communities of faith that has been at the heart of the religious enterprise in the United States historically, and whose members continue to make up the majority of organized religion's members. This consensus has played and continues to play an important role in religion and in the culture.

3.   While there have been gradual changes and occasional shifts in religious belief and practice over the past half-century, survey data reveal that **religion in the United States is a remarkably stable phenomenon.** "Basic religious beliefs, even religious practice, today differs relatively little from the levels recorded 50 years ago."[9]

4.   **Religion has become much more visible in recent years.** Christian radio and television stations abound. Songs by popular Christian vocalists such as Sandi Patti and Amy Grant are played on secular stations. A public television report on the Christian hymn "Amazing Grace" demonstrated its impact far beyond the walls of churches. Christian bookstores can be found in most cities. Bumper stickers and window decals on cars proclaim the driver's faith. Religious news is

---

[7]J. Gordon Melton, *The Encyclopedia of American Religions*, 4th ed. (Detroit, MI: Gale Research, Inc., 1993).

[8]Wade Clark Roof, "Toward the Year 2000: Reconstructions of Religious Space," *Religion in the Nineties: The Annals of the American Academy of Political and Social Science,* ed. Wade Clark Roof, vol. 527. (Newbury Park, CA: Sage Publications, 1993), pp. 157–60.

[9]George Gallup, Jr., and Jim Castelli, *The People's Religion: American Faith in the 90s* (New York: Macmillan Publishing Company, 1989), p. 4.

no longer restricted to the religion page of the Saturday newspaper, and analyses of religious events appear regularly in weekly news magazines.

5. **People in the United States are largely traditional in their approach to religion.** That is, they hold to the established teachings of their faith without desiring to modify them very much. The decade of the 1960s was a time of liberalization and modernization. Many people wanted their religion to be compatible with the latest findings of science. They wanted it to be in tune with the surrounding culture. Beginning in the 1970s, there was a definite turn to conservatism and a renewal of interest in preserving the historical essentials of Christianity. A similar interest arose in Judaism. The recovery of traditional Jewish life has become important for many people of Jewish faith.

The distinctions between religious fundamentalism, conservatism, and liberalism cut across most of the religious groups in the United States. The distinction is sometimes expressed in terms of fundamental, moderate, and liberal religious attitudes as well. Currently, about half of the people in the United States are moderate in their religious views. Approximately one-third are fundamentalist. The remainder are liberal in their religious outlook (Figure 2–2).

There is no completely agreed upon way of defining any of these three perspectives. The categories also apply best to Protestant Christianity, although they have limited usefulness in other contexts. One useful approach is to use people's attitude toward the Bible itself. Which of the following comes closest to describing *your* view of the Bible?

The Bible is the actual Word of God, to be taken literally, word for word, and it is without error.

The Bible is the inspired Word of God, but not everything in it should be taken literally, and it may contain human errors. These errors do not, however, invalidate its truth about God.

Figure 2–2 About half of the people in the United States are religious conservatives. About one-third are fundamentalist, and the remainder are liberals.

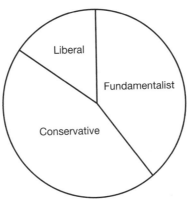

The Bible is an ancient book of stories, legends, and precepts written by human beings.

Fundamentalism is distinguished by its militant emphasis on correct *belief.* The emphasis on belief distinguishes it from the *holiness movement* (lifestyle emphasis), *pentecostalism* (religious experience), and from *evangelicalism* (communicating the Christian Gospel to everyone). Fundamentalists want to defend traditional Christian teachings in their most traditional form, against all challenges. They believe that the most threatening of these challenges comes from theological liberalism or modernism within Christianity and from secular humanism. George Marsden, one of the foremost scholars of the American fundamentalist movement, describes it this way:

> Fundamentalists. . . . are Bible-believers who take absolutely seriously the understanding of the Gospel message that proclaims that God sent his son into the world to die for sinners and that the only hope for eternal salvation, and to avoid an eternity in Hell, is to believe that Jesus died for one's sins and to make him the Lord of one's life. The only ultimately important question for humans is "What must I do to be saved?"[10]

It is the importance of human salvation that animates the fundamentalists' insistence on biblical "inerrancy." If there can be any errors in the Bible, then what guarantees that its basic message of sin and salvation is not in error as well? Nothing, say the fundamentalists. Taking the Bible as the literal Word of God safeguards it from the intrusion of human sinfulness.

The life of the fundamentalist is one in which the way that leads to salvation is clearly spelled out and grounded in the absolute authority of God's inerrant Word. Fundamentalism offers certainty when the stress of living in a perpetual gray area becomes too much to bear. Fundamentalism assures its adherents that they are right, and that God guarantees that they are right. Its adherents believe that fundamentalism is free of the ambiguity that characterizes so much of our modern life.

Conservatism takes the position that historic faith ought to be preserved insofar as possible, with only minimal regard for changes in the secular world. It is of greater concern that belief be right than relevant; or, better put, only right belief has any hope of being relevant. Tradition judges modernity in matters of faith, even though modernity may have the final word in matters of science and history. Conservatives hold that the Bible is the inspired Word of God, without believing that everything in it must be taken literally. While human errors may have crept in matters not directly related to human sin and salvation, divine in-

[10]George Marsden, "Fundamentalism," in *Encyclopedia of the American Religious Experience: Studies of Traditions and Movements*, ed. Charles H. Lippy and Peter W. Williams (New York: Charles Scribner's Sons, 1988), p. 947.

spiration safeguards the Bible's basic message. Religious conservatism offers its followers a pattern of belief and a way of life that mediates between the historic tradition and life in the modern world. It upholds that tradition while allowing for the discoveries of science and human reason in their appropriate spheres of activity. It gives firm guidance for how life is to be lived, without being rigid and dogmatic. It makes allowance for some degree of change and accommodation, while maintaining its deep concern for the tradition.

Religious **liberals** want to accommodate the historic faith to the realities of the modern world. If there is a conflict, the demands of modernity take precedence over the tradition. Liberals want to bring faith into line with human progress as reflected in science and reason. Faith and reason are partners on a common quest. One scholar describes liberalism this way: "The defining mark of liberalism [in its heyday] was neither creed nor precept. Its most pronounced feature was a spirit of intellectual adventurousness."[11] This same spirit still characterizes liberalism. Although liberalism does not have a large number of advocates now, its supporters are fiercely loyal. It offers its adherents a way of life that enables them to follow their religion *and* be fully immersed in their culture. It presents religious truth in a way that people can accept without playing down the importance of human reason.

6. **The vast majority of people in the United States identify themselves as Christian.** Protestants account for about 60 percent of the people in the country. Roman Catholics are the next largest group, with about 26 percent of the population. There are also people who are Christian, but neither Protestant nor Catholic, such as members of the Eastern Orthodox faith and members of the alternative communities of faith. This means that approximately 90 percent of Americans claim some form of Christianity as their religious preference. Those with no religious preference, Jews, and those with any one of a large number of other preferences each claim less than 10 percent of the population. Seeing these figures in graphic form (Figure 2–3) may help you to understand the relative sizes of the groups.

7. Within that framework, however, people in the United States do not necessarily stay with the religion in which they were raised. **Roughly one-third report having changed religious affiliation.** Of those, two-thirds have changed once, and one-fourth have changed twice.

8. **We are a nation of people who believe in God.** Survey data uniformly show that very few people doubt the existence of God, a Higher Power, or a Universal Spirit. For most, this is a personal being who has a continuing interest in human beings and who can be counted on to hear and respond to prayers. Although the great majority of people in the United States do believe in such a being, there are those who do not. About 5 percent of the population either does

---

[11]William McGuire King, "Liberalism," in *Encyclopedia of the American Religious Experience*, ed. Lippy and Williams, p. 1129.

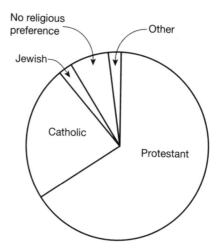

No religious preference

Jewish

Other

Catholic

Protestant

Figure 2–3   Approximately 60 percent of the population of the United States are Protestant. About one-fourth are Roman Catholic. Approximately 2 percent claim Jewish as their religious preference, while approximately 4 percent say they have some other religious preference. About 9 percent claim no religious preference.

not believe, or does not believe that we can know whether or not God exists. Approximately two-thirds also believe that a devil exists.[12]

We are a nation of believers, but we are not a nation without doubt about those beliefs. While about two-thirds of believers say they have no doubts, the rest do have at least a little doubt mingled with their faith.

9.   **Americans attend public worship in large numbers, although the number is less than one might suspect from what was said above.** Although almost half attend less than twelve times annually, nearly one-third report attending worship at least weekly. About 17 percent attend at least monthly. For over two decades, about 40 percent of the population has reported attending worship in any given week.[13] It is clear from these figures that being religious and believing in God do not necessarily mean that people attend church or synagogue. In part, this may have to do with a lack of confidence in organized religion. About one-fourth of the population say they have a great deal of confidence in organized religion, and half say they have only moderate confidence. The remaining fourth have no confidence in it at all.

The above figure that about 40 percent of the population attends worship in any given week has remained remarkably stable in survey research using self-reporting. Recent research based on actual field studies suggests that the percentage may in fact be lower than reported. Although further count-based stud-

---

[12] *The Gallup Poll Monthly*, no. 352 (January 1995), 14.
[13] Robert Bezilla, ed., *Religion in America, 1990* (Princeton, NJ: Princeton Religious Research Center, 1991), p. 45.

ies would be needed to confirm it, this research suggests that attendance may be about half what it has been reported as being.[14]

Research indicates that a person's stage in the life cycle is the factor that most strongly influences attendance. Young adults, for example, may temporarily leave the church when they go off to school or leave home, but later in life, marriage, children, and family formation, reinforced by a need for fellowship and community, give strong impetus to many to return to the church. Some who are older find that handicaps, infirmities, and lack of transportation make it more difficult to get to church as often as they like. Others find that retirement has given them more time to enjoy the offerings of religious services, and still others associate advanced age with the wisdom and maturity that leads to increased religious participation.[15]

Some people also participate in informal home worship, or "house churches," with others of their faith. Most of these people remain active in their church or synagogue as well, but appreciate the increased intimacy of a smaller, less formal experience. As one Catholic woman says of her small worship meetings,

> They're very participatory, held in a circle, which implies a certain equality. . . . Our liturgy leaders come from our community, our friends, not someone who is thrust upon us. Whatever you have is drawn from your own experience and not somebody lecturing at you. There's time for shared reflections, time for silence, we sing together, we pass bread and grape juice in Eucharistic commemoration of our faith.[16]

10.   **The majority of Americans believe that their lives will not end with their earthly deaths.** This belief is linked with belief in eternal reward or punishment. Recent data indicate that about 90 percent of Americans believe in heaven, while nearly three-fourths believe in hell.[17]

11.   We have already discussed the importance of the Constitutional guarantee of civil liberties, such as the right to speak freely. The overwhelming majority of people in the United States does believe in God. **How do we, as a nation, feel about those who do not believe?** About one-fourth of the population favors preventing such a person from giving a public speech against churches and religion. Slightly under half would not allow such a person to teach in a college or university. Nearly 30 percent would not permit a book by such a person to be in a public library. In other words, between one-half and one-fourth of the population believe that the civil liberties of a person who is against churches and religion should be curtailed. The majority of the population supports freedom of

---

[14]C. Kirk Hadaway, Penny Long Marler, and Mark Chaves, "What the Polls Don't Show: A Closer Look at U.S. Church Attendance," *American Sociological Review*, 58 (December 1992), 741–52.

[15]*Emerging Trends* (Princeton Religious Research Center, Princeton, NJ), 13, no. 6 (June 1991), 1.

[16]Quoted in Jane Redmont, *Generous Lives: American Catholic Women Today* (Liguori, MO: Triumph Books, 1992), p. 92.

[17]*The Gallup Poll Monthly*, no. 352 (January 1995), 14.

religious belief and the freedom to speak openly about that belief, but a significant minority does not support freedom to speak openly about one's *lack* of belief.

12.   Religious organizations support a vast array of social service agencies in the United States. These include hospitals and clinics, homes for the aged and for children, camps, counseling centers, food pantries, and housing projects. Some religious organizations support such programs through their national offices. Local congregations often engage in more local projects that provide assistance within their own communities. Countless numbers of individuals involve themselves, both personally and financially, in charitable projects as a way of applying their faith in the world. A National Council of Churches survey indicated that over half of congregations in the United States have programs that address health needs such as nutrition, substance abuse, mental health, and prenatal care.[18]

At the same time, **there is continued interest in evangelism among members of Christian churches.** Slightly under half of the adult population has actively encouraged someone else to accept Jesus as his or her savior. Humanitarian assistance and evangelism work together in most of America's Christian churches. People of Jewish faith are actively involved in a wide variety of humanitarian concerns but usually do not actively try to bring other people into their faith.

13.   Interfaith cooperation among people of different religions is another feature of religion in the United States. Christians and Jews cooperate locally, setting aside theological differences to work toward common goals. The National Council of Christians and Jews promotes dialogue and understanding between America's two major faiths. As the number of Asian immigrants to the United States has increased, so has the Buddhist population, and there is increasing interest in dialogue between Buddhists and Christians. The East-West Religion Project, sponsored by the University of Hawaii, was founded specifically to encourage dialogue and understanding between followers of Western religions and those of Eastern religions, especially Christians and Buddhists.

Ecumenical cooperation between Christian groups is also strong. The National Council of Churches of Christ in the USA (NCC) includes most of America's consensus Christian churches. The National Association of Evangelicals is composed of more conservative Christians who want cooperation among themselves but find the NCC too liberal in its approach to religious and social questions.

Among Protestant Christians, a study by four denominations in the Reformation tradition recommends "full communion." While the institutional structures of the churches would remain separate, the plan would mean "recog-

---

[18] *Religion Watch: A Newsletter Monitoring Trends in Contemporary Religion,* 7, no. 4 (February 1992), 6.

Figure 2–4   The Baha'i House of Worship, located just north of Chicago on the shore of Lake Michigan at Wilmette, Illinois. The nine-sided building symbolizes the unity of all religions. It is listed in the National Register of Historic Places. (*Photo courtesy of Baha'i Publishing Trust.*)

nizing each other's ministry and members, withdrawing past condemnations, sharing in the Lord's Supper, and providing for exchange of ministers and for channels of joint consultation and decision-making."[19]

Two major denominational mergers highlight the interest in cooperation and reunion among Christians. The United Presbyterian Church in the United States of America and the Presbyterian Church in the United States, separated since before the Civil War, merged in 1983 to form the Presbyterian Church (USA). Three major Lutheran churches—the American Lutheran Church, the Lutheran Church in America, and the Association of Evangelical Lutheran Churches—joined together in 1988 to become the Evangelical Lutheran Church in America.

The historical interplay of establishment and pluralism and the constitutional guarantees of religious liberty that emerged out of that interplay provide the context for the unique development of religious pluralism in the United States. That diversity is manifest in both institutional and popular religion.

[19] *Muncie Star* (Muncie, IN), March 23, 1992, p. 10A.

THE 1990S: RELIGIOUS CHANGE
IN THE UNITED STATES

Religion in the United States has always been marked by change and variation. The "centers of energy" shift and regroup, with old centers not so much disappearing as taking second place to newly ascendant centers. Several significant changes of this type are occurring in the 1990s. The list below summarizes them, from a report by historian of American religion Martin E. Marty.[20]

Religion in the 1990s is more focused on the personal than on the communal. While religious institutions in America continue to attract a much higher percentage of adults than elsewhere in the industrialized world, the emphasis is on individualized faith.

As a corollary, religion is more private than public in the 1990s. Increasing specialization in all spheres of life continues to assign religion to the private sphere. Countertrends also exist, however, as some religious groups focus on influencing the public arena.

Similarly, people value religious autonomy over inherited authority. Finding a religious organization that meets one's needs usually takes precedence over staying with one's denomination. It's a "buyers' market" in religion. Authority exercised by religious organizations and authorities must be persuasive rather than coercive if it is to find a hearing.

Religion and group belonging are not as tightly linked as they have been in the past. "In America, . . . most can easily violate the boundaries of their racial or ethnic group, the expectations of class, and even the constraints of family to follow their chosen spiritual trajectories." However, religion itself continues to be an important aspect of self-identification for many persons.

The local is increasingly emphasized over the cosmopolitan or global, seen especially in what congregations choose to do with their money. Money tends to be kept in local congregations, used to support local projects, or given to parachurch organizations over which people have more direct control.

Following a surge of ecumenism in the 1960s, the 1990s are seeing a rise in particularism, the connection of religion with other types of identifications—racial, ethnic, or gender. Ecumenism continues, but a lot of it focuses on working together on particular issues, so that a group or individual may engage in a number of "criss-crossing" ecumenical endeavors as the issues change.

There is a new focus on healing. Congregations become places of healing as they develop twelve-step programs, for example. Healing services have been instituted in congregations that had not had them, in response to member requests. Many of the "alternative healing" therapies are based on the practices and beliefs of Asian religions. Increasing disillusionment with the cost and high-tech quality of standard medicine has led people to look to religion for alternatives (as well as looking elsewhere).

Increasingly, American religion has a practical rather than a mystical focus, although there is a strong undercurrent of mysticism as well, especially in popular religion. American religion is oriented toward doing rather than being.

[20]Martin E. Marty, "Where the Energies Go," in *Religion in the Nineties*, ed. Roof, pp. 11–26.

Religion in the 1990s is primarily affective and experiential rather than intellectual. There are no American theological "giants" on the current scene.

The integration of women and women's issues into American religion continues apace, bringing with it greater recognition and utilization of the intuitive and affective dimensions of religion.

There is less interest in, and less agreement on, a civil religion. "Political candidates have . . . been trying to seize the symbols of such religion, but they have tended to reduce it to partisan claims and justifications and have failed to match the aspirations of the whole of society."[21]

Having noted a wide variety of changes and trends, Marty concludes by making a very important point: Throughout the changes, the "energies remain, to the surprise of those who thought secularity would see the dissipation, not the rechanneling"[22] of religious vitality.

QUESTIONS AND ACTIVITIES FOR REVIEW, DISCUSSION, AND WRITING

1. How would your life be different if it were not for freedom of religion? You might want to discuss this question with friends or with others in your class and compare answers.
2. Relate each of the general characteristics of religion in the United States to your own experience.
3. In the *Yellow Pages* of your telephone directory, find listings for churches, religious organizations, and synagogues. How many different ones are listed? Which groups have the most listings?
4. To get a better idea of the relative numbers of people in the various religious preference groups, divide your class into corresponding groups and have each group stand in a specific area.
5. Do you think that religious liberty in the United States is in danger? Why or why not? Are you personally aware of a person's civil liberties having been limited because of his or her religion?
6. Discuss with others in your class some of the manifestations of popular religion with which you are familiar. Why do you think people who are active in their communities of faith supplement their activities with more popular religious activities?
7. Of the three basic religious attitudes described in this chapter—fundamentalism, conservatism, and liberalism—which seems the most compelling to you, and why?

FOR FURTHER READING

Carter, Stephen L, *The Culture of Disbelief: How American Law and Politics Trivialize Religious Devotion*. New York: Basic Books, 1993. A thoughtful discussion of the role of religious people and the voice of religion in public discourse in light of the assignment of religion to the private sphere of life.

Eastland, Terry, ed., *Religious Liberty in the Supreme Court: The Cases That Define the Debate over*

---

[21]Martin E. Marty, "Where the Energies Go," in *Religion in the Nineties*, ed. Roof, p. 26.
[22]Martin E. Marty, "Where the Energies Go," in *Religion in the Nineties*, ed. Roof, p. 26.

Church and State. Washington, DC: Ethics and Public Policy Center, 1993. Texts of major decisions with brief commentary and a few essays. An excellent resource.

Lippy, Charles H., *Being Religious, American Style: A History of Popular Religiosity in the United States.* Westport, CT: Greenwood Press, 1994. As the subtitle indicates, primarily historical, but also has a good beginning chapter describing popular religion in the United States and a concluding chapter that examines the interplay of popular culture and popular religiosity.

Lippy, Charles H., ed., *Twentieth-Century Shapers of American Popular Religion.* New York: Greenwood Press, 1989. Includes biographical information, appraisals and critiques as well as bibliographic information for over sixty people, from the well known to the little known. Fascinating.

Lippy, Charles H., and Peter W. Williams, eds. *Encyclopedia of the American Religious Experience: Studies of Traditions and Movements.* New York: Charles Scribner's Sons, 1988. A three-volume work that covers both historical and contemporary topics. This book and the Melton book below are basic reference books for religion in the United States.

Melton, J. Gordon, *The Encyclopedia of American Religions*, 4th ed. Detroit, MI: Gale Research, Inc., 1993. A thorough and unbiased presentation of information about both consensus and alternative religions. Carefully indexed.

Religion and American Culture: A Journal of Interpretation. Indianapolis, IN: The Center for the Study of Religion and American Culture. Biannual journal devoted to religion and United States culture.

Robbins, Thomas, and Dick Anthony, eds., *In Gods We Trust: New Patterns of Religious Pluralism in America*, 2nd. ed. New Brunswick, NJ: Transaction Publishers, 1990. A survey of the many pluralisms that characterize American religion, including the traditionalist resurgence, gender issues, mainline religiosity, New Age spirituality, and religion and politics. Collected essays from a variety of social science perspectives.

Roof, Wade Clark, *Religion in the Nineties: The Annals of the American Academy of Political and Social Science*, vol. 527. Newbury Park, CA: Sage Publications, 1993. Collected essays from a wide range of viewpoints concerning major trends in religion in the United States in the 1990s. Scholarly but readable and highly recommended.

Wald, Kenneth D., *Religion and Politics in the United States*, 2nd ed. Washington, DC: CQ Press, a division of Congressional Quarterly, Inc., 1992. A thorough and closely reasoned study of the impact of religion on politics that covers both positive and negative aspects of this trend.

3

Consensus Religion

WHAT THE CONSENSUS IS AND MEANS

Think for a moment about how you would answer these questions: What is "ordinary" religion in the United States? Are people who follow it very different from other people in the culture? What religious groups would you include in the category of "ordinary" religion? One way of beginning to understand what **consensus religion** is and means is to think in terms of "ordinary" religion, of the religions followed by the vast majority of people in the United States. These communities of faith are located at the center of the culture. They are strongly influenced by the culture of which they are a part, and, in turn, exercise a lot of influence on it. Consensus religion on the institutional level accounts for approximately 90 percent of the population of the United States.

In the early days of statehood, at least four religious groups could be distinguished. Most people simply were not interested in organized religion. There were also a few antireligious radicals. There were some who were passionately religious and for whom religion was the center of life. And, there was a significant minority of churchgoers to whom religion was important but who wanted a style of religion that would neither embarrass nor inconvenience themselves or others.[1] The passionately religious welcomed being set apart from the society around them by the intensity or distinctiveness of their religious beliefs and practices. The moderate churchgoing minority wanted exactly the opposite. For them, religion was a part of the culture and one among many aspects of life with a legitimate claim on their time and attention. It was these people who made up consensus religion at that time. To a large extent, they still do. Consensus religion, then, represents the religious sensibilities of the majority of people in the culture and fits into the culture well. It participates in the larger society of which it is a

---

[1]Martin E. Marty, *Protestantism in the United States: Righteous Empire*, 2nd ed. (New York: Charles Scribner's Sons, 1986), p. 41.

part, rather than withdrawing from it. It is strongly **culture-affirming** religion. It is willing to make at least some degree of compromise and accommodation with the secular world, and it does not see such accommodation as destructive of religion. Those who follow one of the consensus religions **usually do not make sharp distinctions between the sacred and secular worlds.** As in the beginning decades of statehood, consensus religion is at home in the larger culture, and the larger culture is comfortable with it.

What sociologist Robert Bellah writes about "mainline" Protestantism in the United States applies equally to consensus religion generally: These communities of faith

> have tried to develop a larger picture of what it might mean to live a biblical life in America. They have sought to be communities of memory, to keep in touch with biblical sources and historical traditions not with literalist obedience but through an intelligent reappropriation illuminated by historical and theological reflection.[2]

Consensus religion has **relatively open membership requirements.** To begin with, there are few conditions for joining. Usually, one must simply affirm one's acceptance of the group's principal teachings and practices, its scriptures, and its form of government. There are few restrictions, if any, placed on members' personal lives, apart from the publicly accepted morality that prevails in the culture. Consensus religion recognizes that its members have multiple loyalties and commitments, many of which are legitimate and valuable. It does not expect to be the whole life of its members.

Consensus religion is also **inclusive** of many races, ethnicities, and nationalities. Especially among consensus Protestants and Catholics, membership and, to a somewhat lesser extent, leadership, reflects this inclusiveness.

Religion in this mode **works with other religious groups** and with secular groups whose goals mesh with theirs. For example, these communities of faith cooperate with and support the work of secular social agencies that provide for the needs of people in areas such as food, shelter, medical care, and the care of children and the frail elderly. They do not think it necessary or helpful to draw sharp boundaries between themselves and the world in providing for peoples' needs.

This openness and tolerance leads these religious groups to form **voluntary associations** to carry out programs that single groups by themselves could not manage as well. Examples are numerous: The American Sunday School Union (1824) and the American Tract Society (1825) were two of the early ones. The American Bible Society (1816) was formed when several Christian churches

---

[2]Robert N. Bellah, Richard Madsen, William M. Sullivan, Ann Swidler, and Steven M. Tipton, *Habits of the Heart: Individualism and Commitment in American Life* (New York: Harper & Row, Publishers, 1985), p. 237.

joined together for the purpose of distributing the Christian Bible throughout the inhabited world. Its continuing goal is to provide copies of the Bible worldwide, without comment or doctrinal notes, in whatever language and format the reader can use. Between 1801 and 1852, the Presbyterians and the Congregationalists in the Northeast cooperated for Western mission work through the Plan of Union. This was one of the first long-term efforts of churches working together for a common purpose.

The **National Council of Churches of Christ in the USA** came into being in 1950 when a group of churches agreed to try to demonstrate in their organization the unity they believed the Christian Church should have. It was the successor to the Federal Council of Churches, which had begun in 1908. It has become known as an organization of liberal Protestant denominations and includes many Eastern Orthodox and other Christian churches as well. Its position statements characteristically have affirmed social action and justice while downplaying evangelism and doctrinal precision. The inclusiveness of consensus Protestantism is reflected in the election of Syngman Rhee, a Korean Presbyterian minister who came to the United States as a refugee in 1950, as President of the National Council for 1992–93. The magazine *Christian Century* is an important national voice for this perspective. *Sojourners* focuses on social issues, while the *National Catholic Reporter* embodies this perspective in Catholicism.

The **National Association of Evangelicals** was formed in 1942 in response to the liberal theological and social positions and perceived doctrinal looseness of the Federal Council of Churches. Its aim is to promote and uphold conservative Christianity while at the same time overcoming the separatist and isolationist tendencies present in much of the evangelical and fundamentalist movement. It is a cooperative association of denominations, independent churches, Christian schools, and some individuals who affirm a creedal statement that begins with the affirmation of the Christian Bible as "the inspired, the only infallible, authoritative Word of God." The creed also requires belief in the doctrine of the Trinity, the virgin birth of Jesus, the substitutionary theory of the atonement, and the unity of all true believers in Christ. *Christianity Today* has long been a significant national journalistic expression of this viewpoint in the United States.

Perhaps the most dramatic ecumenical effort came in December 1960. The Reverend Eugene Carson Blake, at the time Stated Clerk[3] of the United Presbyterian Church in the United States of America, preaching in the Episcopal Grace Cathedral in San Francisco, proposed an actual merger of the Presbyterian, Methodist, Protestant Episcopal, and United Church of Christ churches. The first meeting of representatives from the four churches took place in 1962. In 1970, the **Consultation on Church Union**, with nine member churches in full support, drafted *A Plan of Union for the Church of Christ Uniting*. The organization is still alive, although no major organizational realign-

---

[3]The *Stated Clerk* is the "chief executive officer" of this denomination.

ments have come out of that historic effort. However, the impact of the COCU documents on the thinking of consensus religious groups in America remains. An example of this influence is the suggestion by some of the member denominations that ordination in any of them be accepted as valid by all. People ordained in one of these denominations could become ministers in another without being ordained again.

In addition to being open to other groups, consensus religion **tolerates** and even embraces within itself no small **diversity of opinion.** Furthermore, diversity is not simply tolerated, but is accepted, celebrated, and seen as a resource for the ongoing process of growth, renewal, and revision that must always occur. Methodism and Presbyterianism, for example, are far from being homogeneous movements. Each has within itself diverse opinions on both belief and practice. Lutheran congregations vary widely from each other. Individual local congregations, likewise, are home to people with widely varying views. There may well be more difference between a Methodist church in the South or in a rural area and a Methodist church in the North or in an urban area than there is between Methodist, Presbyterian, and Episcopal churches in the same community. Baptist churches, especially, tend to vary in style according to geographic and demographic[4] factors.

Consensus religion **draws its members from a wide range of socioeconomic classes and includes among its members many leaders** in all fields and walks of life. We see here the operation of both cause and effect on the position that consensus religion occupies in American culture. Because it fits in well with the prevailing culture, it appeals to the cultural leaders. Because it has this appeal, it is in a position to exercise decisive influence on the culture.

These communities of faith usually **employ highly educated and trained full-time religious leaders** such as ministers, priests, and rabbis. For most positions, a clergyperson must have completed an undergraduate college degree and a seminary[5] degree, now usually called a Master of Divinity degree. Many religious groups of this nature expect and are willing to support their clergy's advanced training. Several seminaries have responded by developing Doctor of Ministry programs that offer advanced education in professional ministry. Through their national offices, these groups also provide advanced training, and seminaries frequently offer workshops and other in-service educational opportunities. The major Protestant denominations and some branches of Judaism ordain both women and men. The Roman Catholic Church does not. Because of this emphasis on education and on fairly formal, structured worship, many of these organizations also employ full-time directors for their religious education programs and persons such as ministers of music, choir directors, and organists.

---

[4]*Demographic characteristics* are those pertaining to the characteristics of a population, such as age, gender, race, education, and income.
[5]A *seminary* is a school for educating people for professional ministry.

COMMONALITY IN POPULAR RELIGION?
AMERICAN CIVIL RELIGION

Neither the idea of a **civil religion** nor the use of the concept in the United States began with sociologist Robert Bellah, but his work brought it to scholarly attention and ultimately to the American popular mind. In a 1967 essay, Bellah wrote that in the United States

> There actually exists alongside of and rather clearly differentiated from the churches an elaborate and well-institutionalized civil religion in America. . . . This public religious dimension is expressed in a set of beliefs, symbols, and rituals that I am calling the American civil religion.[6]

Bellah cited founding documents such as the Declaration of Independence and the Constitution, as well as the inaugural speeches of several presidents, along with holiday observances, in support of his thesis. He included belief in God, belief in America's role in God's plans for the world, commonly accepted standards of morality and civic virtue, and routinely observed holidays among the verities of civil religion.

Bellah's seminal essay gave religious studies scholars a new way of analyzing the roles that religion plays in the public life of the United States. It moved the study of religion beyond the study of ecclesiastical institutions and laid the groundwork for recognition of the importance of popular religion. It also provided great insight into the ways in which civic ideals and the legitimating principles of a culture are expressed powerfully in symbols which link them to divine realities.

Changes in how we view the culture of the United States have made Bellah's assertion that there is a common set of religious and civic convictions that underlies American life increasingly problematic. As one scholar describes the current situation, the sense of national consensus that is required by Bellah's civil religion theses "flies in the face of observed reality. . . . Instead of a single civil religion harmoniously uniting all Americans, an alternative hypothesis rooted in the pervasive sense of cultural conflict that characterizes much of America's past seems,. . . far more persuasive."[7]

Rather than a single voice, the vision of what the United States is and ought to be has become a chorus of many voices, each vying for a hearing. Any attempt to describe a single American voice inevitably seems sectarian and exclusive. Increasing cultural pluralism has made the broadly liberal Protestant outlines of Bellah's civil religion misleading when they are used to describe an agreed-upon set of civic standards and virtues. It seems necessary at this point in our history

---

[6]Robert N. Bellah, "Civil Religion in America," *Daedalus*, 117, no. 3 (Winter 1967).
[7]Phillip E. Hammond, Amanda Porterfield, James G. Moseley, and Jonathan D. Sarna, "Forum: American Civil Religion Revisited," *Religion and American Culture: A Journal of Interpretation*, 4, no. 1 (Winter 1994).

to focus on the variety of religions and cultures that are present in the United States, rather than looking for a unity which many have come to doubt.

COMMONALITIES: PROTESTANT AND CATHOLIC CHRISTIANS

The religious life of Christians—Protestant, Catholic, Eastern Orthodox, and others as well—centers on the person, life, death, and resurrection of Jesus. Christians are those people who are defined by their faith in Jesus as their Lord and Savior.

Two classical **creeds**[8] of the early Christian church form the basis for our discussion of the beliefs and practices that are shared by most Christians. There are certainly variations in interpretation, but, with a few exceptions, most members of this largest community of faith in the United States could affirm what is contained in the Apostles and Nicene creeds.

The **Apostles Creed** (Figure 3–1) is so named because it is a summary of essential Christian beliefs as held by the Church at the time of the Apostles. It was not written by the Apostles, as legend has it, but goes back to the very old Roman Creed. In its current form, it probably dates from the seventh century, C.E.

The **Nicene Creed** (Figure 3–2) was written at the Council of Nicaea in 325 C.E. and revised at the Council of Constantinople in 381 C.E. It is somewhat longer than the Apostles Creed. Both, however, contain much the same material.

Both the Apostles and the Nicene creeds cover four basic topics: God the Father, Jesus Christ, the Holy Spirit, and a paragraph of miscellaneous affirmations. God is said to be the Father. Christians, following Jesus' example, believe that God is a loving parent who cares deeply for humankind and for the rest of creation, as well. God is also the creator who brings everything "seen and unseen" into being. Nothing, in other words, came or comes into being except by God's will and power.

Of Jesus Christ, it is stated that he is the only Son of God who came into being through the power of the Holy Spirit and was born to a virgin. Whether these affirmations are taken literally or not, the intent is clear. Jesus was not simply a human being, although Christians believe that he was fully human. He is somehow special, related to God in a way that makes him unique. According to most Christians, Jesus was God incarnate. The church's belief about the most relevant points of Jesus' career is summarized: his birth, his suffering and death, his resurrection, and his future return to Earth. According to the Nicene Creed, all of this was for the salvation of humanity. One of the most striking elements of Christian belief is the affirmation that the one God became fully human in or-

---

[8]A *creed* is an official, written statement of the beliefs of a particular religious group.

Figure 3–1

THE APOSTLES CREED

We believe in God, the Father Almighty
Creator of heaven and earth.

And in Jesus Christ, his only son, our Lord,
Who was conceived of the Holy Ghost,
And born of the Virgin Mary.
He suffered under Pontius Pilate,
Was crucified, dead, and buried.
He descended into Hell.
[Alt: "He descended to the dead." Some omit completely.]
On the third day he rose again from the dead.
He ascended into heaven
And sits at the right hand of God the Father almighty,
From whence he will come
To judge the living and the dead.

We believe in the Holy Spirit, the holy catholic church,
The communion of saints, the forgiveness of sins,
The resurrection of the body, and the life everlasting.

---

der to save human beings from the results of sin. It is stated also that Jesus will return to earth to judge both the living and the dead. When he returns, Christians believe, those who have put their faith and trust in him will live eternally with him.

These and other classic creeds of Christianity reflect the teachings that are found in the Christian Bible. Although Protestant and Catholic versions of the Bible are very similar, the Catholic Church had not until recently given its approval to any of the translations of the Bible commonly used by Protestant Christians. In late 1991, the National Council of Catholic Bishops gave their Church's official approval to the *New Revised Standard Version* of the Christian Bible. This means that Catholic and Protestant Christians (as well as Eastern Orthodox Christians, whose leadership had approved the new translation earlier) now have a translation of the Christian Bible that all can use.

These beliefs have led to the Christian practice of Communion, also known as the Last Supper or the Eucharist ("thanksgiving"). Bread in some form and wine or unfermented grape juice are shared among believers with appropriate and often very solemn ritual. It is a ritual that brings the faithful into intimate contact with the central truths of their faith. Interpretations of the exact meaning of Communion vary among Christians. Some believe that the bread and wine ac-

Figure 3–2

THE NICENE CREED

We believe in one God, the Father, the Almighty, maker of heaven and earth, of all that is, seen and unseen.

We believe in one Lord, Jesus Christ, the only Son of God, eternally begotten of the Father, God from God, Light from Light, true God from true God, begotten, not made, of one Being with the Father. Through him all things were made. For us and for our salvation he came down from heaven: by the power of the Holy Spirit he became incarnate from the Virgin Mary, and was made man. For our sake he was crucified under Pontius Pilate; he suffered death and was buried. On the third day he rose again according to the Scriptures; he ascended into heaven and is seated at the right hand of the Father. He will come again in glory to judge the living and the dead, and his kingdom will have no end.

We believe in the Holy Spirit, the Lord, the giver of life, who proceeds from the Father [some add, "and the Son"]. With the Father and the Son he is worshipped and glorified. He has spoken through the prophets.

We believe in one holy catholic and apostolic Church. We acknowledge one baptism for the forgiveness of sins. We look for the resurrection of the dead, and the life of the world to come.

tually become the body and blood of Christ. Others teach that Jesus is present symbolically in the elements, while some understand Communion simply as a way of remembering Jesus' death and resurrection.

Along with the Father and the Son, Christians believe in the Holy Spirit or Holy Ghost as the third person of the **Trinity**. To say that God is a trinity means that most, though not all, Christians believe that God is best understood as three persons who are one and yet distinguishable. This doctrine itself is not directly biblical (although it is supported by certain passages in the New Testament such as Matthew 28:19 and 2 Corinthians 13:14), but it was defined very early in the history of the Christian church, especially in these two creeds. Most Christians believe that this is something about God that people could not have figured out for themselves but that can be known because God revealed it.

When the creeds refer to "one holy catholic church," the word **catholic** is being used to mean "universal," rather than "Roman Catholic." In spite of the many divisions within Christianity, it is understood to be but one Church, having one Lord, and continuing back to the time of the twelve apostles whom the Christian New Testament says that Jesus gathered around himself during his earthly life. The followers of Jesus the Christ are called into a community, the church.

The ritual of baptism is the rite of incorporation into the Christian community of faith. It is also a public witness of commitment to Christ. Some Christians believe that it is necessary for the forgiveness of sin, as well. Water is nearly always used. Specific practices vary from full immersion into water to a sprinkle of water on the head of the person being baptized. Some churches baptize people of all ages, including infants. Others believe that people who are being baptized must be old enough to understand its meaning. Most Christians are baptized in the name of the Father, Son, and Holy Spirit, although some churches baptize in Jesus' name only.

Finally, Christians do not believe that earthly death is the end of life. The faithful will be resurrected at the end of time and will live eternally with God. Some Christians believe that Heaven is an actual place. Others believe that eternal life is simply life with God.

The worship of God is the principal **ritual act** of Christian believers, who worship in patterns that may be described as either liturgical or nonliturgical. In **liturgical** churches, worship is central to the life of the congregation. If you were to worship with a liturgical community of faith, you would find the service much the same whether you were in North or South, East or West, in a large city or a small country town. It might well be very similar overseas. The form of worship is usually handed down from its earliest beginnings, and much importance is placed on and pride taken in keeping the tradition alive. The congregation's part in liturgical worship follows complex patterns of response, most of which are printed in a book; it is formal, structured worship. In addition to regular Sunday morning services, there are orders of worship for morning and evening prayer, perhaps noon prayer, and other special services throughout the day and week. The Lutheran and Episcopalian Protestant churches fit this pattern. So do Catholicism and Eastern Orthodoxy.

Nonliturgical communities of faith, such as Baptist, Methodist, and Presbyterian Protestants, have a great deal more variety in their worship. The style of worship is decided upon by the local congregation and changes as circumstances warrant. Many of the same elements are included in every service, and certain things may well be considered essential. Some churches, such as the Methodist and Presbyterian, have a suggested order for public worship, but individual churches can and do modify it. Worship itself is not quite as central to the life and work of these churches, because social service activities, mission work, and fellowship opportunities are also very much in the forefront. There may not be as much importance placed on attending worship regularly, although this remains important.

There are differences, too, in how Christian communities of faith organize themselves. There are three principal patterns of **institutional organization**. These three types are reflected both in how local congregations relate to the denomination as a whole and in how decisions are made within the local congregation. The **congregational** pattern places the majority of the power in the hands of the local congregation. Although these congregations may be part of larger associations or confederations, those bodies have no authority over the local group. Further, all important decisions are made, at least in theory, by vote of the entire congregation, with each adult member having a vote. Clergy, for example, are employed and replaced at the local level, by direct vote of the membership.

The **connectional** form is a type of representative government that is common in many Protestant denominations. Local congregations have considerable power to make their own decisions, but most major decisions, such as the ordination and employment of clergy, are made by higher governing bodies to which local congregations send delegates. Statements of belief and policy may be written through these higher boards, and the denomination's major involvement with other denominations and groups is at that level. Usually there are several such levels, often based on geography, with both nonordained and ordained representatives, culminating in a national decision-making body. In the local congregation, members elect representatives to the official governing board or boards, which, along with the clergyperson or people, make decisions on behalf of those who elected them.

The **hierarchical** form of government centers on bishops, who are officers appointed by those higher up the organizational ladder than themselves, rather than elected by the membership at large. Local congregations are guided by the bishops above them, and power flows downward from the top. Theoretically, local decision making is very strongly influenced by the clergy, who are usually called priests in these churches.

It must be noted that these three are *types* only. A community of faith is often a mixture of types. Baptists, especially Southern Baptists, embody the congregational form quite well, and Presbyterian Christians illustrate the connectional system almost perfectly, which is why this form of government is sometimes referred to as presbyterian. Lutherans, on the other hand, blend elements of congregationalism and connectionalism, and Methodists, although they use the terminology associated with a hierarchical system, have become quite connectional. The Episcopalians, the most hierarchical of U.S. Protestants, have also become more connectional. The most hierarchical among the Christian churches in the United States are the Catholics and the Eastern Orthodox, both of which are also somewhat less hierarchical here than elsewhere in the world.

In the United States, emphasis on a democratic way of doing things spills over from government to life as a whole, including religion. Gradually, this has led to a greater emphasis on local congregations rather than on large national organizations. It has also led to the increased involvement of **laypeople**, the nonordained members of a community of faith, in the decisions of those local congregations, even in churches of the hierarchical type. Thus, the democratizing influence of the American cultural style has affected denominational religion to a large extent.

COMMONALITIES: PROTESTANTS

As you will learn in Chapter 4, Protestant belief and practice vary somewhat among denominations, and even among congregations within a denomination. There are features of Protestantism that make it distinct, however, and that transcend denominational differences. Despite the diversity, there were, and still are, certain beliefs and practices that, although with modifications, have been a part of Protestantism since Reformation times. We will use the now-familiar four elements of religion to organize our thinking about what most Protestants hold in common.

Belief

We can identify a core of **beliefs** that most Protestants share. We have already touched on some of these as we discussed the beliefs that most Christians have in common. First, **the Bible plays an absolutely central role for Protestants.** Protestants, along with other Christians, Jews, and Muslims are a "people of the Book," and this theme is highly developed in Protestantism. Martin Luther's classic phrase was *Sola Scriptura*, the authority of the Bible only. With this, he pointed out the sharp contrast between the new faith and Catholicism.[9] Catholics recognize two sources of religious authority: the Bible and the long record of the Church's teaching and interpretation. The Church is, in effect, the guardian and official interpreter of the Bible. Protestants, on the other hand, go directly to the Bible, using the churches' interpretations of its meaning only in an advisory capacity. John Calvin, for example, emphasized the need to check one's own private interpretation against that of the community of faith in the interest of preserving good order.

It was this need for some statement of the church's belief to counterbalance a too-individualistic view that led some of the Reformation churches to formulate creeds. For Protestants, the authority of any creed or confession of faith is subordinate to that of the Bible, and any such document is valid only insofar as it is an accurate representation of what the Bible teaches. Creedal groups use written creeds or statements of faith to express the essence of their beliefs. The Presbyterians developed the Westminster Confession of Faith and the Episcopalians retained much of the Church of England's theology in their Thirty-Nine Articles

---

[9]The Catholicism of Luther and Calvin's time was vastly different from Catholicism in the United States now. Significant changes came about with the Second Vatican Council in the early 1960s. In particular, the differences between the two types of Christianity were much larger than they now are. Chapter 5 provides more information on contemporary American Catholicism.

of Religion. Lutherans use the Augsburg Confession as one standard statement of faith. There are also more recent statements such as the Presbyterian Confession developed following the 1985 merger and the Barmen Declaration. Some groups require that candidates for membership affirm that a particular creed or confession of faith embodies biblical teaching. Congregational repetition of a creed is usually a regular feature of worship, and the study of the creed is an important part of religious education.

Other communities of faith do not have a formal creed as such, although some of them may make occasional use of creeds, especially of the early ones. Adherence to a creed is not a prerequisite to membership in these groups. Communities of faith that do not have a formal creed take this position for a variety of reasons. Some believe that formal creeds are too restrictive and violate the right of individual conscience in religious matters. Others fear that acceptance of a creed can too easily become a substitute for faith in Jesus.

What is important for Protestants is not the Bible itself, but the Word of God contained in it. This has two meanings. First, the Bible is the direct access to the Word made flesh in Jesus: "In the beginning," writes the author of the Gospel according to John, the Word that was with God, that was in fact God, became flesh and came to live on the earth, where people could see God's glory made visible (John 1:1–2). The only mediator between God and humankind, according to Protestants, is revealed to be the eternal Word made flesh, and this all-important story is told in the pages of the Bible. The term "Word of God" also has a second layer of meaning in Protestant thought. Through the action and influence of the Holy Spirit, the words of the Bible become the Word of God for the believer, God's direct and personal communication to each and every individual.

It was the prominence given to the Word contained in the Bible that led to the Protestant enthusiasm for translating the Bible into the language of the people. Having only Latin Bibles had very effectively reinforced the Church's position as the only interpreter and official custodian of biblical truth, since only the priests and higher officials of the Church could read and understand Latin. Even though illiteracy was high—few people could read even in their own language—having Bibles available in the common language of a people meant that people could hear the Scriptures read in the language they understood and could come to their own interpretation. It is perhaps difficult to imagine the thrill some of these people must have felt upon hearing the Bible read in their own language for the first time. It was as if God were speaking directly to them, rather than addressing them through a translator or interpreter.

Protestants believe that **salvation is a gift from God**, an effect of grace and grace alone. There is nothing that people can do to earn salvation. All are equally guilty, equally subject to death due to sin. People cannot possibly make themselves worthy before God. At the same time, there is nothing that people need to do to earn salvation, because God has made it a gift of his grace in and through Jesus, who for this reason is known by Christians as Savior (Ephesians 2:8–9).

The Protestant reformers taught that salvation is a free gift from God that need only be accepted in trusting faith.

Protestants believe that **the church is the gathered fellowship of believers**. It is the people meeting together to hear the Word preached, to participate in the sacraments of baptism and communion, and to encourage and help each other. It is the people, rather than the institution or the hierarchy. In a very real sense for Protestants, the church is not a "something" that "is" as much as it is an event that happens each time and place that believers gather.

In contrast, Catholics view the church as a complex system of two-way mediation between God and people. Through the Church's teaching (including but not limited to the Bible), hierarchy, and sacraments, God's will and grace are communicated to people. People are helped to reach God by following those teachings and participating in the means of grace the Church makes available. The reformers simplified this structure of mediation, teaching instead that God relates to people through their trust and faith, on a model analogous to human relationships. This relationship then calls people into the church, the community of the faithful.

This gathered fellowship, Protestants say, is a **priesthood of all believers**. Protestants find support for this belief in the New Testament and in the writings of the Reformers. In the first letter to Peter, the faithful are called a "chosen people, a royal priesthood" (1 Peter 2:9).

The priesthood of all believers means shared responsibility, shared worship, and shared authority. Each Christian has the same responsibility to pray for, teach, and encourage every other Christian and to tell God's story to nonbelievers. The responsibility for a shared ministry belongs to all equally; it is not reserved for those who are ordained as priests or ministers. Each person offers his or her own worship to God and is a priest in that sense also. Worship is the collectivity of the worship of each and every individual, not a common act of the church's worship in which individual worshippers are overshadowed. And, each Christian shares with all others the same authority. No one has an inside track and no one is relegated to outsider status in matters of religious authority. All are equal, because all have equal access to the Word.

Protestants, in other words, distinguish between priesthood and ministry. Baptism makes all Christians priests, some of whom are then called out of the congregations to preach, administer the sacraments, and govern as ministers. The minister is one who is chosen to serve a congregation, rather than one given special powers by God or special honor by the institution.

Lifestyle

What of **Protestant lifestyle**? This is not as easy to identify as are the specific beliefs, and we must make some distinctions. For those Protestants who believe that the world is a wicked and evil place, the only reasonable lifestyle is to separate themselves from it insofar as possible. Contact with the world brings with it the danger of spiritual contamination and should be avoided. This attitude remains today in some of the holiness churches. For consensus Protestants, their faith directs them squarely into the middle of the world. Martin Luther entered a monastery early in his life, believing that to be the surest way to salvation. He later left the monastery. Christian faith, say most followers of its Protestant branch, must be lived out in the midst of the world, not in retreat from it. God provides all the various arenas of human activity, such as marriage and family, vocation and work, civil government and politics, leisure and play. Each in its place is equally good, equally capable of being transformed by grace. One is not to turn one's back on the world, but to live in it, glorifying and obeying God in all things.

For Luther and his followers and for those who were a part of the English reformation, enjoying life and one another and the good things the earth had to offer was a way of praising God, although moderation was important. The Calvinists, on the other hand, were more strict. Restraint and sobriety were the hallmarks of their way of life. Too much enjoyment might lead one away from the proper path, and a certain sternness pervaded all they did.

For all Protestants, living decently, charity toward others, upholding the law, and being faithful in one's commitment to God and to the community of God's people are recognizable virtues. Freed from its role in bringing about salvation, morality became a central feature of Protestants' lifestyle, as a joyful (Luther and the English reformers) and obedient (Calvin) response to God's freely given gift of salvation.

Ritual

Two things stand out when we look at the **specific religious acts** of Protestants. Whereas the Catholic Church practices seven sacraments, most Protestants have only two. **Baptism and the Lord's Supper or Communion** are the only two acts that Jesus specifically commanded his followers to carry on after his death, according to the Protestant reading of the New Testament. The age for baptism varies; many Protestants baptize babies, but not all do. Immersion, pouring, and sprinkling each have their advocates within the Protestant community. Likewise, the exact understanding of the Lord's Supper varies, but Protestants are united in their denial of its sacrificial character. Architecturally, its context is that of a table that echoes the one around which Jesus and the disciples are said to have gathered, rather than the altar of sacrifice. Some congregations pass the elements through the pews and some come to the front of the church. The roles played by the minister and laypeople vary somewhat. All use bread, leavened or unleavened; some use wine, and some use unfermented grape juice.

Here again, we must note both Protestantism's uniformity and its diversity. On the one hand, the Episcopal Church celebrates all seven of the traditional Roman Catholic sacramental rituals. On the other, Baptists, although they observe the Lord's Supper and baptize believers, do not consider these acts to be sacraments. They are ordinances, important rites of the church with no sacramental character.

The second thing that stands out is the **importance of preaching**. The pulpit occupies a prominent place in Protestant churches, and the sermon is considered the focal point of worship. Ministers usually receive extensive training in biblical preaching, and a potential minister's skill as a preacher plays a large role in the selection process when it is time to call a new pastor. Because of the centrality of the Word made flesh, words become very significant in Protestantism.

Organization

Finally, what can we say about Protestant **organization**, or structure, its institutional arrangements? In the first place, there is no papal authority. The Pope may well be respected as the leader of the world's many Catholic Christians, but he has no authority for Protestants. Each Protestant denomination is self-governing. There is no worldwide organization. Individual denominations have various organizational patterns, as we have seen. We have also seen that all, in one way or another, allow for and encourage active participation of the laity in the life of the church.

Another institutional feature is that most ministers are married rather than celibate. The rejection of monasticism goes together with a rejection of celibacy as the proper lifestyle for ministers. Some denominations, although not all, ordain women as well as men to the ministry.

A summary in brief outline form (Figure 3–3) will help to fix these points about Protestantism in your mind.

COMMONALITIES: CHRISTIANS AND JEWS

As many of you know already, Christianity began as a small sect in Judaism, as a variation on the teaching and practice of that ancient religion. The two share a common history, up to a point, and a common geography. The cultural conditions out of which Christianity was born were those of the Judaism of its time. It is not surprising, therefore, that the two have many things in common.

To begin with, they have some of the Scriptures in common. The Jewish Bible[10] and the Christian Old Testament are nearly the same in content. The history that is recounted and the religious teachings that are contained in both are quite similar. In most Christian churches today, the Christian Old Testament is used for one of the regular Bible readings during worship.

These common scriptures tell of one God who commands that people worship no other gods. Judaism originated in an area in which it was most common

---

[10]The preferred name among Jews themselves for the Jewish scriptures is **Tanakh**, an acronym for the Hebrew names of its three major divisions: the Law (*Torah*), the Prophets (*Nevi'im*), and the Writings (*Ketubim*).

Figure 3–3

SUMMARY OF PROTESTANT BELIEFS AND PRACTICES

Beliefs
1. The centrality and sole authority of the Bible
2. Salvation by grace through faith
3. The church as the gathering of believers
4. The priesthood of all believers

Lifestyle
1. For most, religion lived out in the midst of world
2. For some, separation from the world
3. Morality is of central importance

Religious Acts
1. Two sacraments: Baptism and the Lord's Supper/Holy Communion
2. Preaching important aspect of worship

Organization
1. No papal authority
2. Clergy usually marry; women ordained in some denominations
3. Variety of organizational styles

for people to worship many gods and goddesses. The Jewish, and, later, the Christian, view held that there was but one God. This God is believed to be the creator of all that was, is, or ever will be. God is righteous and holy and acts in a just, upright, moral manner. God is personal; it is appropriate to talk of God's will, wrath, love, mercy, and judgment. God hears and responds to peoples' prayers, according to both Judaism and Christianity. Above all, God's character and will for people are shown to them by God's self-revelation.

History is important, because it is believed to be the record of God's continuing involvement with people. God is intimately involved in history, primarily through **covenants** with people. There are covenants with Noah and with Abraham, for example, described in the Hebrew Bible, and Jesus is referred to in the Christian New Testament as the bearer of a new covenant. These covenants define a people by their relationship with God. Judaism teaches that Israel was called into being as a people by God. Christianity teaches that the entire church is the Body of Christ, called into being by God.

Because the God whose story is told in the Bible is righteous and holy, the people who live in covenant with God are to live holy and righteous lives themselves. Their special relationship with God is to be embodied in all that they do. The well-known Ten Commandments are revered in both Judaism and Christianity. Some of these commandments deal with people's actions with respect to God: having no other gods, keeping the Sabbath day holy, and not taking God's name in vain. Others have to do with relations between persons and groups of people: not murdering or stealing, not lying, and not wanting what is not one's own, for example. In both Judaism and Christianity, the way people relate with God and the way they relate with each other cannot be separated. For both, a lifestyle defined by the proper worship and attitude toward God as well as by loving and morally upright relations with other persons is basic.

Although this is what is called for, both faiths teach that people will fall short of the goal. They will, in a word common to both, *sin*. If they are truly sorry and committed to doing better and wholeheartedly seek God's forgiveness, then God will forgive.

Worship in each community of faith is both individual and corporate. Individual worship usually takes the form of prayer and devotional reading. Corporate worship provides time for the entire community of faith to focus on God. Prayers are said and praises given. Instruction is given to the faithful in a sermon. It is usually based on one or more readings from the Bible. The importance placed on history creates many holidays and festivals that recall and celebrate God's actions. For example, the Christian holidays of Christmas and Easter keep the stories of the birth and resurrection of Jesus alive in that community of faith. The Jewish Passover celebrates the rescue of the Hebrews from slavery in Egypt, and the giving of the Ten Commandments is recalled in the Festival of Weeks. Corporate worship also includes rites of passage. These are religious ceremonies that mark transitions from one stage of human life to another. Both faiths mark birth, coming of age, marriage and death, for example.

We have seen that there are a variety of organizational styles to be found in consensus religion in the United States. In both Judaism and Christianity, the fundamental point is that the people of God are not to exist in isolation, but are gathered together by God into communities for mutual support and instruction and to carry out God's will. In both instances, the group—the people of Israel or the Church—is not thought to be simply a human invention, but something brought into being and guided by God.

There are many smaller points of agreement that could be discussed. These major points, however, clearly demonstrate that the two major religions found in the United States—Judaism and Christianity—have a great deal in common. Their common heritage and devotion to the same God means that they are neighbors and not strangers.

WOMEN IN THE RELIGIOUS CONSENSUS

Before you begin reading this section, take a moment to reflect on your own experience. Have you thought about the role and status of women in religious organizations? What is your impression? If you attend or have attended worship services, what roles did women play? Have you heard a female minister or pastor preach? If so, how did you feel about that? Imagine that you had a personal problem that you wanted to discuss with a religious counselor; would it matter to you if that person were a woman or a man? Why or why not? How much do you think your answers to these questions are influenced by your own gender?

Recently, a lot of attention has been paid to the role and status of women in American religious organizations. Religion has often limited women to traditional female roles. It has often supported and encouraged the belief that women's proper roles were those of wives and mothers. The home was often thought to be women's only proper sphere of action. Until recently, women have been unable to be ministers, pastors, rabbis, or priests in most of America's communities of faith. Nor have they been able to be deacons, elders, or other lay officers of their congregations. Religion has also offered encouragement and comfort to those women who themselves support traditional female roles in the face of cultural demands for change.

However, religion has also been a catalyst for change. Women have found encouragement in the scriptures of both Judaism and Christianity to work toward full equality and rights. Churches and synagogues have supported movements for women's rights. Although many communities of faith denied official roles to women, in others, men and women functioned as equals. It is very important to evaluate the role that religion has played in the context of its own time. If we approach history from the viewpoint of the twentieth century, religion's tendency to support traditional roles will loom larger than it actually was, and we will be in danger of missing the extent to which religion has encouraged change.[11]

Changing religious beliefs and practices in ways that make them more favorable to women has understandably been of greater interest to women than to men. However, it should be pointed out that men are also involved in the search for women's equality in communities of faith.

Whether women search the past to come up with a usable present and future, seek to revise the present, or create new ways of being religious, all four dimensions of religion are affected. A challenge to gender-based bias or exclusivity in any one area leads to challenges in other areas. In what follows, we will look at some of the changes that are taking place in each of the four main dimensions of organized religion today. This is not an all-inclusive list, but the major issues are represented.

Belief

One of the first things that feminists questioned was the Jewish and Christian habit of thinking and speaking of God as if God were male. The sentence above provides a quick example. Traditionally, the last phrase would have been written, "of God as if He were male." The Lord's Prayer, or "Our Father," prayed by Chris-

---

[11]Rosemary Radford Ruether and Rosemary Skinner Keller, eds., *Women and Religion in America, Volume I: The Nineteenth Century* (San Francisco: Harper & Row Publishers, 1989), p. x.

tians is another example. Jews and Christians have always believed that theirs is a personal God, not an impersonal divine force. This makes it difficult to think and speak about God without introducing gender distinctions. The work of many feminist theologians shows that it can be done.

The Bible was written by men who lived in a very male-oriented culture. Its language describes God in masculine words. There are a few passages, however, that modify this image. God is spoken of in images related to bearing and suckling children. Examples include Deuteronomy 32:18, Isaiah 46:3, Isaiah 49:14–15, and Psalms 2:7 in the Jewish Bible, and Matthew 23:37 and Luke 13:34 in the Christian New Testament. Several words used to describe God in the Hebrew language of the Jewish Scriptures and the Christian Old Testament are in the feminine gender. For example, the Hebrew word for "spirit" is the feminine *ruach*, which becomes *pneuma*, a gender-neutral word, when translated into the Greek of the Christian New Testament.

Feminists also point out that, since the Jewish and Christian scriptures were written in a patriarchal culture, it was probably unavoidable that God be described in words like *father, lord*, and *king*. They hold that this is neither necessary nor desirable in our own culture. God can better be thought of as mother, father and mother, lover, spouse, or friend. To do so adds richness to the picture of God presented in the scriptures. Because both communities of faith teach that the Bible is revealed by God, making changes like these is threatening to some people. Those who support change claim that these images bring the Bible's language closer to what its writers actually intended.

A critical point for feminist scholars in the Christian community of faith is the references to the Christ as male. There is no doubt that the person Jesus was male. But feminists point out that "Christ" refers to a role, that of savior, that does not have to be male identified. When Christ is referred to as the wisdom of God (1 Corinthians 1:24–30), the word used is the feminine *sophia*.

The *Inclusive Language Lectionary* was written by a committee of scholars for the National Council of Churches. A *lectionary* is a cycle of Bible readings to be followed throughout the church year. The committee based its work on the Revised Standard Version of the Christian Bible, paraphrasing it to eliminate gender-exclusive language as well as other language deemed exclusive. The easiest way to begin to understand its impact is to compare a well-known passage. In the Revised Standard Version, John 1:1–5, 14, 18 reads as follows:

> In the beginning was the Word, and the Word was with God, and the Word was God. He was in the beginning with God; all things were made through him, and without him was not anything made that was made. In him was life, and that life was the light of men. The light shines in the darkness, and the darkness had not overcome it. . . . And the Word became flesh and dwelt among us, full of grace and truth; we have beheld his glory, glory as of the only Son from the Father. . . . No one has ever seen God; the only Son, who is in the bosom of the Father, he has made him known.

The *Inclusive Language Lectionary* paraphrase eliminates masculine references:

In the beginning was the Word, and the Word was with God, and the Word was God. The Word was in the beginning with God; all things were made through the Word, and without the Word was not anything made that was made. In the Word was life, and the life was the light of all. The light shines in the deepest night, and the night has not overcome it. . . . And the Word became flesh and dwelt among us, full of grace and truth; we have beheld the Word's glory, glory as of the only Child from God the Father and Mother. . . . No one has ever seen God; the only Child, who is in the bosom of God the Mother and Father, that one has made God known.[12]

The committee's revision also attempts to eliminate other biased uses of language. In John 1:5, references to opposition to the light of Christ as "darkness" have been replaced by "night." The use of "dark" and "darkness" in this way offends some people of color.

Two issues, authority and the source for God-concepts, are uppermost in deciding how we will think and speak about God. Judaism and Christianity have used their scriptures and the tradition of the community of faith as both source and authority. As we have seen, these scriptures were written in a very patriarchal culture, and they reflect this in how they name God. For the most part, the communities of faith have been shaped by male leadership. Women have found in their own experience as women another source and authority to offset the male dominance in the received tradition. It is experience that has led women to name the God of the Jewish and Christian religions "Mother and Father." Experience supplements, and from a feminist viewpoint, corrects, the tradition.

Biblical authority is also involved when people use the Bible to justify the traditional role and status of women. Often, specific passages are taken out of context and cited as the Word of God. But feminist scholars believe that the message of the Bible as a whole is one of liberation, and that specific passages must be read in this larger context. In the account of creation in Genesis 2, for example, woman is created second to man, and out of his rib. Adam and God already have a history in the Garden of Eden before woman is created. And, it is man into whom God breathed the breath of life directly. This passage is often used to support the idea that women are subordinate to men. But in Genesis 1, woman and man are created simultaneously, each in God's image.

Several passages in the Christian New Testament are used to justify the subordination of women. Feminist scholars have shown that many have been taken out of context. Although 1 Corinthians 11:9 says that the woman was created for the man, and not the reverse, 1 Corinthians 11:11 says that neither is complete without the other. An often-quoted verse in Ephesians 5 says that the husband is head of the wife. In context, that verse is seen to be part of a discussion of both husbands and wives being mutually submissive, after the model of Christ and the church. A similar verse, Colossians 3:18, tells wives to be submissive to their husbands. In the next verse, husbands are told to love their wives.

---

[12] *The Inclusive Language Lectionary: Readings for the Year A*, rev. ed. (New York: National Council of Churches of Christ in the USA, 1986), pp. 35–36.

People who favor traditional women's roles in the church often rely on the fact that all of Jesus' disciples were men to substantiate their case. Women who want to counter this argument point out that, in the culture of that time and place, it could hardly have been otherwise. On the other hand, Jesus often affirmed the worthiness of women. According to John 4:25–26, one of the earliest times that Jesus revealed himself to be the Messiah was to a woman. According to Luke's gospel, Jesus appeared first to Mary Magdalene and other women after the resurrection (Luke 24). These are some of the ways that women who look to the Christian Bible to support women's rights attempt to show that the message of the Bible as a whole, and Jesus' own life especially, supports their cause.

Lifestyle

The lifestyle issues that are of concern to religious feminists are the same ones that concern their secular counterparts. They work side by side on issues such as the Equal Rights Amendment, day care, and shelters for battered or homeless women and children. Some churches and synagogues have opened day care centers for children. Lack of affordable day care for elderly dependents also prevents some women from working outside the home, and both religious and secular feminists have campaigned for the provision of such care. Centers for elderly day care have been opened by some churches and synagogues. Although some women in churches and synagogues work for the repeal of the 1973 Supreme Court decision that gave women the right to legal abortions, other religious women work to prevent that repeal.

Ritual

There are three ways in which ritual has become an important issue for women: (1) the leadership of corporate worship, (2) the language used in liturgy, and (3) the creation of new rituals for women.

1.   Significant changes have occurred in the **leadership of corporate worship.** As was noted, consensus communities of faith ordain women to the ministry in increasing numbers. Many Christian churches provide equal opportunities for women to serve as lay leaders in worship, as eucharistic ministers,[13] and as readers of the scriptures. Reform, Reconstructionist, and some Conservative Jewish temples and synagogues likewise make leadership in worship independent of gender.

2.   The **language used in hymns and prayers** has been as much influenced by male dominance as the language of scripture. Think back over the titles of hymns you may know: "God of Our Fathers," "O Brother Man," "Good Chris-

---

[13] *Eucharistic ministers* are laypeople who are specially trained to assist with the serving of communion in liturgical churches.

tian Men, Rejoice," "Turn Back, O Man," "Rise Up, O Men of God," "God Rest Ye Merry, Gentlemen," and "Once to Every Man and Nation," are examples. You may be able to add others. The language of prayers that are repeated by the congregation or by the leader of worship often use words like *man* for "humankind" and *brothers* when "the entire community" is meant. This is added to the use of exclusively male imagery in the Bible itself as it is read in worship.

In one way, it is easier to change the language of liturgy than it is to change the language of the Bible, because liturgy is not believed to be revelation. On the other hand, many of the prayers and hymns are very familiar and beloved. To change them is threatening and disturbing to many people. Ingrained habit is also hard to break. One Christmas season, a woman gently suggested that the word *folk* be substituted for *men* in "Good Christian Men Rejoice." *Friends* would have been another possible substitution. The congregation readily agreed to her request. That evening, as the congregation gathered around the piano in the fellowship room to sing carols, it was this same woman's strong soprano voice that was heard to sing "good Christian men, rejoice!"

3. For many women, these changes are not enough. They long for **alternative rituals** that reflect their own experience. Christian women have written Communion liturgies that celebrate women's bonds in the church and link the Bread of Life (a way that Christians refer to the Christ) with common, ordinary bread that they themselves have baked. New hymns have been written that highlight the femaleness of God. Sharon Neufer Emswiler and Tom Neufer Emswiler have suggested several of what they call "liberated services" in their study of sexism in worship. These services include one that concentrates on acceptance and self-worth (sometimes hard for women to find in traditional services in which their femaleness is devalued), many new hymns, and a communion service in which men and women confess their complicity in stereotyping each other.[14]

Jewish women have written new rituals for the traditional retelling of the Passover story that emphasize the role that the foremothers played in Jewish history.[15] Others have rewritten the Sabbath prayers so that they invoke God as Mother and focus on the bearing and nurturing qualities that are a part of Judaism's understanding of God.[16] Other Jewish women have developed rituals that provide a meaningful way to welcome the birth of a baby girl. In one part of this ritual, the father of the baby says that it "is not only our sons who are our guarantors, but also our daughters, for the laughter of Sarah is part of the history of our people" and a friend reads the story of Sarah and her laughter at the prospect of bearing a child in her old age (Genesis 18). The stories of Miriam (Exodus 15), Deborah (Judges 4), and Huldah (2 Kings 22) are also read.[17]

---

[14]Sharon Neufer Emswiler and Tom Neufer Emswiler, *Women and Worship: A Guide to Non-Sexist Hymns, Prayers, and Liturgies* (New York: Harper & Row, Publishers, 1974).

[15]Aviva Cantor, "A Jewish Woman's Haggadah," in *Womanspirit Rising: A Feminist Reader in Religion,* ed. Carol P. Christ and Judith Plaskow (San Francisco: Harper & Row, Publishers, 1979), pp. 185–92.

[16]Naomi Janowitz and Maggie Wenig, "Sabbath Prayers for Women," in *Womanspirit Rising,* ed. Christ and Plaskow, pp. 174–78.

[17]Judith Plaskow, "Bringing a Daughter into the Covenant," in *Womanspirit Rising,* ed. Christ and Plaskow, pp. 179–84.

Organization

The organizational or institutional issue that concerns women most is **ordina-tion.** Many women will continue to feel a sharp sense of exclusion from the lives of their religious groups until women are ordained as priests, ministers, or rab-bis. This is true no matter how many lay offices and responsibilities open up for women and no matter how careful a community of faith may be to balance rep-resentation on boards and in lay leadership in worship. Full ordination represents full participation and full inclusion, and for women who seek that goal, anything less is not enough.

Those who favor the ordination of women give several reasons: (1) Women have sensed God calling them to preach, just as men have. (2) Women are as ef-fective in these roles as are men. (3) Women already preach, as Christian mis-sionaries, for example. (4) The scripture passages that speak against the ordina-tion of women can be balanced with others that support it, and with the liberating message of both the Hebrew and Christian scriptures as a whole. (5) Women were involved in the ministry of the early church, and were active in early Judaism as well.

On the other hand, arguments against women's ordination include the fol-lowing: (1) Women's calls from God are not valid because only men are called to the ordained ministry. (2) Divine calling must be confirmed by the community of faith, so if that confirmation is not given, the call is invalid. (3) Eve, not Adam, was the first to sin, according to Genesis. (4) The place for women's testimony and preaching is in women's prayer and Bible study groups, not in churches and synagogues. (5) Women's roles have been those of wives and mothers, and there is no reason to change that. (6) It violates tradition.[18]

A related area is **service on boards of trustees, boards of elders or sessions, boards of deacons, and vestries.** These lay groups assist the minister with the leadership of the church. Their duties and influence vary widely from group to group. Until recently, the pattern has been to have men as officers. The one ex-ception was boards of deacons. In many congregations, their work centers on providing practical help to those who cannot help themselves. They visit the sick, take food baskets to the hungry, and collect clothing for poor children. Since their activities are a logical extension of women's accepted care-giving function, they often were made up partly or solely of women. Decisions about how to govern the organization, employing a new minister or rabbi, and financial decisions were left to the men. In some Christian churches, and in Orthodox synagogues, women do not yet have the right to vote in congregational meetings, and some won that right only recently. This is especially ironic, since women make up the majority of most congregations.

One way that Christian women have organized themselves is through Church Women United. **Church Women United** is an ecumenical group of

---

[18]Adapted from Barbara Brown Zikmund, "The Struggle for the Right to Preach," in *Women and Religion in America, Volume I: The Nineteenth Century,* ed. Ruether and Keller, pp. 193–205.

Protestant, Catholic, Eastern Orthodox, and other Christian women involved in church, civic, and national affairs. It has been a valuable way for consensus Christian women, especially, to take an active role in their religion. Today, at a half-century old, the organization includes over 1,500 local organizations. A key issue facing CWU is that the pressure of combined job and family responsibilities gives its younger members less flexibility and less time than earlier generations of women had.[19]

Religious organizations function both as agents of change in a culture and as forces that hold back change. Religion sometimes leads people to cling tightly to the status quo, whereas it encourages others to work tirelessly to change it. Nowhere in American culture has this been more true than in the changing role and status of women throughout American history. Laypeople and religious leaders have been in the forefront of both movements.

A Brief Note about Women and Popular Religion

Historically, while women have been denied official and institutional leadership in religion, they have been encouraged in the development of personal piety. This pattern began with the Puritans and continued until the mid-twentieth century in the consensus religions. It still continues in many communities of faith outside the consensus. Exclusion from official roles within ecclesial or institutional religion led women to increased participation in the kind of private religious activity that is characteristic of popular religion. Even within the religious consensus, women engage in more personal religious activity than do men. For example, among consensus Protestants, women pray and read the Bible more frequently than do men, and they identify themselves more frequently as being strongly religious. Among Catholic women, the same pattern applies for self-identification and prayer, but there is no significant difference in Bible reading. The Jewish subsample in the General Social Survey data is too small to permit this type of analysis.

QUESTIONS AND ACTIVITIES FOR REVIEW, DISCUSSION, AND WRITING

1. Write a brief essay in which you reflect on the advantages and disadvantages of consensus religion's culture-affirming stance.
2. Define both liturgical and nonliturgical worship as clearly as you can. Then write a brief essay in which you reflect on the advantages and disadvantages of each. Which is more attractive to you, and why?
3. Attend a worship service at both a liturgical church and a nonliturgical one and write an essay in which you compare and contrast them.
4. What seem to you to be the advantages and disadvantages of having a formal creed?
5. What roles do you think women should be able to play in their communities of faith?

[19] *EcuLink* (New York: National Council of Churches of Christ in the USA), 34 (October–December 1991).

Why do you feel as you do? You might want to organize a discussion of this issue as a class project.

6. If you had a problem that you wanted to discuss with a pastor, minister, priest or rabbi, would it make a difference to you if this person were female or male? Why?

7. With your professor, invite a female minister, priest, or rabbi to discuss with your class how she perceives the situation of women in consensus religion. Or, organize a panel discussion on this topic.

FOR FURTHER READING

Bradshaw, Paul F., and Lawrence A. Hoffman, eds., *The Changing Face of Jewish and Christian Worship in North America*. South Bend, IN: University of Notre Dame Press, 1992. A careful examination of recent changes in Jewish and Christian worship. Includes critiques of these developments from a feminist perspective.

Engel, Edith S., and Henry W. Engel, *One God: Peoples of the Book*. Cleveland, OH: Pilgrim Press, 1990. A well-written book that combines factual information about Judaism, Catholicism, and Protestantism (as well as Islam) with narration of personal stories of faith.

LaCugna, Catherine Mowry. *Freeing Theology: The Essentials of Theology in Feminist Perspective*. San Francisco: HarperSanFrancisco, 1994. Includes essays by many notable and respected feminist theologians, writing from a variety of viewpoints and traditions.

Mollenkott, Virginia Ramey, ed., *Women of Faith in Dialogue*. New York: Crossroad, 1990. Essays by eighteen women—Protestants, Catholics, and Jews (as well as Muslims)—who have chosen to stand firmly within their own communities of faith and work for change. Each discusses both positive and negative aspects of her tradition and discusses the challenges that it presents to women and men working together for equality. Includes a suggested outline for an interreligious service and guidelines for founding local chapters of Women of Faith.

Newsom, Carol A., and Sharon H. Ringe, eds., *The Women's Bible Commentary*. Louisville, KY: Westminster/John Knox Press, 1992. Essays representing a wide range of views, offering distillations of gender-sensitive scholarship that are readable by a nonspecialist audience. Provides general introductions to each biblical book and discussions of gender-specific issues.

4

*C*onsensus Protestantism

The United States is a thoroughly Protestant country. About 60 percent of the population is Protestant (Figure 4–1). The consensus Protestant denominations are all around us in the United States—so much so, in fact, that you may not have given them much thought. Many of you probably attend worship in one of these churches. Using the *Yellow Pages* directory for your town, city, or rural area, count the number of churches listed for each of the following denominations: Baptist, Methodist, Lutheran, Presbyterian, Episcopalian, United Church of Christ, Disciples of Christ, and Friends (Quaker). Count the total number of churches and synagogues listed. What percentage of the whole are the consensus Protestants, and what is the proportionate distribution of individual Protestant denominations in your area? Compare these figures with the figures shown in Figure 4–2.

INTRODUCTION

The five churches with the largest percentage of that membership make a convenient and natural grouping for beginning our study of Protestantism as it is found in the consensus denominations. We will then look at three other churches that belong in this category.

Protestantism is not a homogeneous faith, but one composed of many variations. It is appropriate to speak of it as a group, however, because of the many important beliefs and practices that most or all Protestants have in common. In Figure 4–2, you can see what percentage of Protestants belongs to each of the five largest denominational families in the United States. Slightly over one-third of Protestants in the United States are Baptists. Another 16 percent are Methodists. Eleven percent are Lutherans. Presbyterians and Episcopalians each have fewer than 10 percent. Other Protestants account for the remaining quarter of the

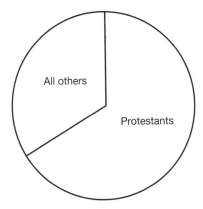

Figure 4–1 About 60 percent of the people in the United States are Protestant.

Protestant population, with about 7 percent identifying as "nondenominational" Protestants.

Because Protestants are a majority of the population, the basic demographic data about Protestants reflects the national figures very closely. In categories such as marital status, age, income, and education, Protestants differ little from people in the nation as a whole. However, the historical dominance of Protestantism has led to its having an influence that is greater than its numbers alone would suggest. Thus, not only demographic factors, but values and ideals in the United States often have a Protestant look to them.

Figure 4–2 Proportionate distribution of Protestants

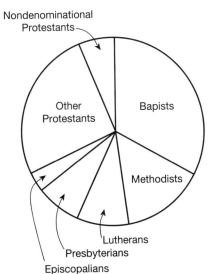

There are certain observations that can be made concerning Protestantism as a whole. In terms of religious attitude, Protestants are the most likely of all the religious preference groups (Protestant, Catholic, Jewish, none, and other) to be fundamentalist. This is reflected in several other figures. Of all the religious preference groups, Protestants are the most likely to curtail freedom of expression for those with whom they disagree. Nearly one-third would not allow a speech against churches and religion in a public forum; half would not permit such a person who was against all churches and religion to teach any subject at the college level; and about one-third would favor removing a book against churches and religion from the shelves of the public library. Of all the religious preference groups, Protestants are the most likely to regard premarital sex, extramarital sex, and homosexual sex as always wrong.

While there is no significant correlation between gender and religious preference, there is a clear-cut relationship between race and religious preference. Nearly 90 percent of the nation's blacks are Protestant. Most of them are either Baptists or Methodists. This is largely a result of the work that both of these denominations carried out with the slaves and later with free blacks after the Civil War.

We turn now to an investigation of each of the five major Protestant denominations, taking them in order beginning with the largest. For each, a brief history will be given first. Then the four elements of religion will be used to organize our discussion of the beliefs and practices of each. You may wish to go back to Chapter 3 and review the sections dealing with what most Christians have in common and what most Protestants have in common. In this chapter, we will concentrate on those things that make each denomination unique, different, and distinctive from the others. This presupposes the shared heritage reviewed in Chapter 3, for, in many ways, the consensus Protestants are as alike as they are different.

THE BAPTISTS

The Baptist churches are a part of what is known as the *free church movement*. They believe that the church should be a free or voluntary association of adult believers. They are the largest Protestant denominational family in the United States, and second only to the Roman Catholic population in size.

Baptists first came to the colonies as part of an influx of nonconforming Puritans fleeing persecution in England during the reign of King Charles I (1625–1649). The historical accounts of the early Baptists are not in complete agreement, but the best-supported view is that the first Baptist church in America was founded by Roger Williams in Rhode Island in 1639 at Providence. In 1648, John Clarke founded a church in Newport. Though not a Baptist for very long, Williams (1599–1683) had a profound influence on Baptist thought in America. He was an ardent defender of freedom of conscience and full religious liberty, and he authored a classic statement on religious liberty in 1644. It is fitting that the first Baptist church in the colonies was founded in the colony Williams had founded earlier as a haven for people persecuted for their beliefs.

People who believed religion should be voluntary and that baptism should be limited to believers old enough to understand its meaning for themselves had appeared in large numbers in Europe in the 1500s. English Baptists arrived in America soon after. When they did, they faced severe and sometimes deadly opposition; Williams himself had fled England to the Massachusetts Bay Colony, and from there had been forced to flee again, thus leading him to found Rhode Island. As we have seen, the American Revolution and the adoption of the Constitution, especially the Bill of Rights, brought about a climate in which the Baptists, as well as other groups, could flourish.

Substantial growth occurred between 1700 and 1750, and, by the 1800s, the Baptists were the largest denomination in the young nation. The church became more institutionally structured, with a publishing house, missions, and a college being developed. There were several distinct Baptist groups, and cooperation among them was common. As with several of the Protestant churches, controversy and conflict over the slavery issue immediately before the Civil War split the Baptists into two opposing camps. The northern Baptists (who became the American Baptist Churches in the USA) held that slavery was a sin. The southern Baptists (the Southern Baptist Convention) maintained that, although slavery was a gross evil and a serious misfortune, there was nothing in the Bible that would declare it a sin. These two branches of the Baptist denomination are still kept apart by differences in theology and practice.

Belief

Baptists in the United States are distinguished by their belief in a regenerate church membership, their emphasis on the New Testament as interpreted to each individual through the Holy Spirit, the absence of an official creed, and their passionate interest in the separation of religion and government. Baptists believe that the church should be made up of only those who are spiritually reborn and fully sincere in their pursuit of the Christian life. This is what is meant by the concept of a *regenerate church membership*, which is a basic Baptist teaching. Church members are people who have been baptized upon their profession of faith in Jesus Christ as Lord and Savior. It is sometimes said that people are "not Baptist by birth, but by rebirth."

According to Baptist teaching, the New Testament is the divinely inspired, authoritative, fully trustworthy, and all-sufficient rule of both faith and practice. Furthermore, Baptists believe that the Holy Spirit guides each individual person to the correct interpretation of the Scriptures. This has led to considerable diversity of interpretation among different Baptist churches and among individual Baptists as well. This diversity has often been accompanied by remarkable tolerance.

Baptists have no official creed. Although some local congregations and certain associations of congregations have written creeds or statements of faith, no convention of Baptists has ever set forth a binding creed. This reflects their belief in the guidance of the Holy Spirit as each person reads the Bible. Baptists support the right of private judgment and freedom of conscience in belief. They regard all creeds as inadequate because they believe that no creed can adequately express the fullness of the Christian gospel, and the full significance of vital, living faith cannot be bound by any statement. Some early Baptists experienced persecution at the hands of those who would make and enforce creeds, and some died in defense of their faith.

Baptists are passionate supporters of religious liberty. Freedom of religion is an inherent right of the human soul, say the Baptists, because human beings are created to be both free and responsible. For freedom of religion to be a reality, religion and the civil government must be kept strictly apart. Because of this belief, early Baptists encountered persecution. They also played a decisive role in the achievement of civil and religious liberty for all persons, especially in colonial New England and Virginia. Baptists certainly are not alone in their support of religious liberty and the official separation of church and state. However, these concepts play an especially significant role in both Baptist history and present-day concern.

Other Baptist beliefs, such as baptism by full immersion and the centrality of the local congregation, will be treated in the discussions of worship and organization.

Lifestyle

As was mentioned earlier, the lifestyles of most denominational Protestants are very similar to those of others in the culture. Baptists are the most likely of any of the Protestants to be fundamentalist in their religious outlook. Some, though certainly not all, are somewhat more strict in their morality than is the custom prevailing in the culture. Individual congregations can and sometimes do set standards for their members, and these standards may include opposition to drinking alcohol, theater-going, and dancing, as well as a code of modesty and moderation in women's dress. There is, however, a wide range, and these standards do not apply to all Baptists. Those in the North are inclined to be more liberal both theologically and morally than those in the South, and rural Baptists are likely to be more strict than those in cities.

Socioeconomically, measured in terms of educational level and family income, Baptists rank somewhat lower than do other Protestants. At least part of this has to do with location; Baptists are most numerous in the Southeast, where Baptist missionaries worked during the colonial and early statehood eras. Although the economic and educational picture in this part of the country is changing rapidly, the average income and educational level remains lower than that of the rest of the nation.

Believing that what is taught in the schools should reflect and reinforce what is taught in church and home, many Baptists have been quite active in the Christian school movement. The Christian school movement as a whole supports the establishment of independent Christian schools, sometimes free of the requirements that apply to public schools (such as those for teacher licensing and the inclusion of certain materials within the curriculum). They may advocate tax breaks to help compensate parents who pay tuition to these schools rather than sending their children to the free public schools.

Ritual

There is a free church element in Baptist worship also. That is to say, many Baptists emphasize openness to the leading of the Holy Spirit over the use of set format and ceremony. Their worship tends to be somewhat more emotional and evangelistic than that of the other consensus Protestants, although this is not always the case. Each congregation develops its own patterns of ritual activity, blending repeated common elements with innovation (Figure 4–3).

Figure 4–3

TYPICAL BAPTIST ORDER OF WORSHIP

Each Baptist church is free to determine its own order of worship. Thus, there is considerable variation from one church to another. This is a typical example of how those in the Baptist community of faith order their worship.

The Church Gathers

Invocation and Call to Worship
Responsive Reading
Special Music

To Present Tithes and Offerings

Worship Through Giving
Doxology

To Hear the Word of God

Scripture Readings
    Old Testament
    New Testament Epistle
    New Testament Gospel
Pastoral Prayer and Choral Response
Anthem
Sermon

To Respond in Faith

Hymn of Invitation
Prayer at the Altar

The Church Scatters

Benediction and Choral Response
Postlude

Baptists practice two ordinances: Baptism and the Lord's Supper. By calling these two rites of the church ordinances rather than sacraments, Baptists describe their belief that these are acts that Jesus told his followers to continue after his death, but they have no sacramental significance.

Baptism as it is practiced in most Baptist churches has two distinctive features. Most important, those receiving baptism must be old enough to know what it means for themselves and to make their own declaration of faith in Jesus and intent to live by his standards. Thus, in contrast with those Protestant churches that grew out of the Lutheran, Calvinist, and English reformations, Baptists do not baptize infants or young children. It is a rite of incorporation into the church community, and this must be a free and knowledgeable act of the one participating in it, not something done on behalf of a child too young to understand. Second, baptism in the Baptist tradition is also by full immersion of the person into water. It may be performed in an indoor tank built into the church for that purpose, or in an outdoor lake or stream if one is available. Immersion is believed to be the only truly scriptural mode of baptism. Immersion also is regarded as an enacted parable of spiritual regeneration, a symbolic burial of the former life and resurrection to the new life in Christ, as well as echoing Jesus' burial and resurrection. Baptists differ in their willingness to accept baptism by modes other than immersion as valid. Nearly all agree, however, that, whatever the form, it must be performed with the full consent of the baptized person.

The Lord's Supper is believed to be a remembrance of Jesus' last supper with the disciples and a memorial of his sacrificial death. Like baptism, it is not a sacrament, and the elements of bread and unfermented grape juice remain simply what they are. Baptists do not believe that Jesus is present spiritually or symbolically in the elements. Some Baptist congregations restrict participation in this ordinance to those who are members of that specific church. Others, most notably the large American Baptist Churches in the USA convention, practice open communion.

Organization

Each local Baptist congregation sets its own standards and regulations, calls and removes its own pastors, and so on. The church, as it is understood by free church Christians, is the local congregation. Denominational organizations, made up of representatives from local congregations, plus professional and support staff, act in an advisory capacity only. They have no authority over the local congregations. Although Baptists cherish their congregational independence, they are also interdependent, and these larger denominational organizations (frequently called conventions) are important for the whole fellowship of Baptists. The conventions also perform activities that cannot be maintained efficiently by local congregations alone, such as higher educational, missionary and social service work, and retirement programs for church employees. Some local congregations, however, do refuse to join any larger group, maintaining a strict independence.

The two major Baptist churches that are a part of consensus religion are the American Baptist Churches in the USA (or "northern Baptists") and the Southern Baptist Convention ("southern Baptists"). The Southern Baptist Convention is the larger, with nearly half of all Baptists in the United States in its ranks. The Baptist family of churches also encompasses many other churches that are outside the religious consensus because they are smaller, more fundamental in belief, restrictive in lifestyle, ethnically oriented, or regional in location.

To summarize the Baptists' place in the religious culture of the United States:

> A key to Baptist identity, then, is a certain passion for spiritual freedom, not only in faith and order but also in piety and worship. The ideal of a congregation thriving in spiritual fellowship of "newly born" regenerate believers, each one personally experiencing divine grace through Jesus Christ, is a recurring theme in Baptist history. Preaching, praying, and singing freely without uniform directive or constraint, balancing ordered formality with spirit-moved spontaneity, have framed most kinds of Baptist worship. The ordinances . . . of baptism and the Lord's Supper . . . likewise are practiced with a minimum of liturgical formality. At the center of worship is the Bible, which through the guidance of the spirit is expected to provide sufficient resource for understanding and practicing the faith.[1]

THE METHODISTS

The denominational family that we know today as the Methodists came to America from England. It began with John Wesley (1703–1791), a devout priest in the Church of England. He was strongly influenced by late seventeenth-century Pietism, a movement whose followers emphasized religious experience and expression over doctrinal rigidity. Wesley organized small groups within the church, intending to give more substance to people's practice of religion. The members of these groups were to pray and study the Bible together and watch over and encourage one another to live the best Christian life of which they were capable. The name *Methodist* was originally a term of contempt with which those who disagreed with Wesley's techniques labeled his methodical approach to the religious life. The movement was given additional strength by John Wesley's brother, Charles, a prolific hymn writer who wrote more than 6,000 hymns. Many of Wesley's hymns are still sung in American churches, both Protestant and Catholic, to this day.

The Wesley brothers came to the colonies for the first time in 1736, to Georgia. A somewhat unsuccessful trip, it lasted less than two years. Later in the 1700s, Methodism was able to spread rapidly because of the circuit-riding horse-

---

[1]Eldon G. Ernst, "The Baptists," in *Encyclopedia of the American Religious Experience: Studies of Traditions and Movements*, vol. 1, ed. Charles H. Lippy and Peter W. Williams (New York City: Charles Scribner's Sons, 1988), p. 576.

back preachers, for which the denomination was known for many decades. The circuit riders went from place to place, taking their Bibles and their engaging preaching style to many more people than could be reached by preachers who remained in one place. Eventually, Methodists outnumbered Anglicans (Church of England), Presbyterians, and Baptists alike.

The first Methodist society in the United States was organized by Philip Embury, an Irish lay leader, in about 1766. The first official conference of the church was held in Philadelphia in 1773. The well-known Christmas Conference of 1784 organized the Methodist Episcopal Church as a fully functioning religious group and elected Francis Asbury and Thomas Coke as its leaders. The first general conference of the new church was held in 1792.

Various divisions over religious differences and racial issues plagued the growing church. Methodism split into the Methodist Episcopal Church, South, and the Methodist Episcopal Church, North, in 1844, over the question of slavery and whether the owning of slaves by bishops and ministers was proper. The two were not reunited until 1939.

Belief

In their beliefs, Methodists are distinguished by a great latitude and variety in what is acceptable. They affirm the central beliefs of Western Christianity while continuing Wesley's emphasis on experience over the details of doctrine. Their focus has always been more on how life is lived than on what is believed. Wesley taught that religion should be "of the heart," and that believers should trust in God's love, and accept Christ's redemption in faith. It should be "of the will," manifested in personal piety and devotion and steadfast love and concern for one's neighbor. Belief in the inner experience of religion and its social application in love and charity toward other people are still hallmarks of Methodism.

Methodist interpretation of the Bible, as might be supposed from what has been said above, ranges widely from literalism to more liberal, figurative styles of interpreting its message. The overall tendency is toward flexibility. Most Methodists believe that the main message of the Bible is the love and mercy of God toward all of creation.

Methodists cite four sources of religious truth. It is unique in its spelling out of these four, although other denominations also use similar sources. The first and primary source is the Bible, primarily—but not exclusively—the New Testament. Second, Methodists recognize their roots in the tradition of the theology and worship of the Church of England. The third is experience, a pragmatic taking into account of what works for people in particular circumstances. The last is reason; faith must be in accord with what the mind says is rational and true.

Methodists teach a threefold order of salvation that is based very closely on Wesley's teaching. *Justification* is the individual's acceptance of salvation as the free gift of God's grace. *Conversion* is regeneration and cleansing through the action of God. Finally, *sanctification* is the ongoing and increasing expression of holiness through a life of prayer and works that attempts to do something positive in the face of the ethical and social problems that prevail in one's time and place.

Although there are doctrinal standards set out by the denomination as a whole, each congregation and each individual is free to use them as they see fit. There is thus no precise answer to the question: What do Methodists believe? Their use of the four guidelines and the threefold order of salvation to interpret the basic Christian teachings, with the accent on the love and mercy of God, are emphases that have been carried forward from John Wesley himself.

Lifestyle

Most churches in the Methodist family fit easily into the culture of which they are a part. Their members' lifestyles differ little from those of others in their communities. Some, such as those in the Wesleyan tradition, are somewhat stricter than the prevailing culture. They often disallow dancing, going to movies, and the use of alcohol or tobacco, and they often require modest dress and long hair for female members.

A prohibition against the use of alcoholic beverages was a key point of the Methodist lifestyle for decades. For many Methodists, it still is. Others regard it as a matter of personal choice. Officially, abstinence from alcohol is no longer required of either clergy or laity.

John Wesley formulated three simple but far-reaching rules for members of his religious societies:

Do no harm and avoid evil of all sorts.
Do good of every possible sort, and insofar as possible to all people.
Observe the ordinances of God, including public worship, the ministry of the Word both read from Scripture and explained in preaching, participation in the Lord's Supper, family and private prayer and Bible reading, and fasting and abstinence.

With the exception of fasting and, in some instances, abstinence from alcohol, many Methodists' lives today can be described in the same way.

Many Methodists are deeply involved in social causes. Most believe that their participation in such socially oriented activities is every bit as much a part of their religion as is prayer and worship.

Like all of the communities of faith that make up consensus religion, the United Methodist Church includes a wide diversity of racial, ethnic, and other special groups and provides specific means through which their concerns can be heard. There are groups such as Black Methodists for Church Renewal, The National Federation of Asian American United Methodists, the Native American International Caucus, and Methodists Associated Representing the Cause of the

Hispanic Americans, as well as a Commission on Religion and Race and a Commission on the Status and Role of Women.[2]

Ritual

Like their beliefs, Methodists' patterns of worship vary widely. There is no required form of worship, although the *Book of Worship* gives suggested forms for Sunday services (Figure 4–4) as well as for several special services, including those for the special occasions of the church year, the significant passages of human life, and a new service of healing. Local congregations make use of it and modify it as they adapt it to their particular needs.

Methodists baptize people of all ages. Water is usually sprinkled on the head of the person being baptized. It is a rite of incorporation into the community of faith. As is always the case, people baptized as infants or young children are expected to make their own profession of faith and declaration of intent to live a Christian life within the church when they are capable of understanding what it means to do so. At that point the person becomes a full church member. This confirmation of the promises made on one's behalf at baptism usually occurs at twelve or thirteen years of age and is preceded by a period of instruction.

Most Methodists believe that Christ is symbolically present to the faithful in the elements of bread and grape juice in the communion service in a "heavenly and spiritual manner." It is a solemn yet joyful service, taken with great seriousness by most members of this diverse group of Protestants.

Organization

Like the Baptists, though to a somewhat lesser extent, Methodist organization is marked by its being a large family of related church groups. There are more than twenty separate religious bodies that claim the Methodist heritage. Those Methodists who are a part of the religious consensus in the United States make up the United Methodist Church. The United Methodist Church came into being in 1968 with the merger of the Methodist Church and the Evangelical United Brethren, both of which were themselves products of earlier mergers. The United Methodist Church has approximately 80 percent of the Methodist population.

Besides the United Methodist Church, there are three large, predominantly black churches in the Methodist group: the African Methodist Episcopal Church, the African Methodist Episcopal Zion Church, and the Christian Methodist Episcopal Church. These churches have begun discussions with the United Methodists concerning an eventual merger.[3] In addition, there are several smaller groups, the names of which often point to either their geographic region or a particular point of view, such as the Free Methodist Church of North

---

[2]Charles Yrigoyen, Jr., "United Methodism," in *Encyclopedia of the American Religious Experience*, vol. 1, ed. Lippy and Williams, p. 539.

[3]"Methodist Bodies Take First Steps toward Possible Merger," *Eculink*, no. 33 (May–September 1991), 3.

Figure 4–4

TYPICAL UNITED METHODIST ORDER OF WORSHIP

Announcements
Call to Worship
Hymn
Old Testament Lesson
New Testament Lesson
Responsive Reading
Affirmation of Faith
Gloria Patri
The Prayers of the People
Silent Prayer
Pastoral Prayer
The Lord's Prayer
The Children's Sermon
Hymn
Gospel Reading
Sermon
Presentation of Tithes and Offerings
Doxology
Prayer of Dedication
Hymn
Benediction

America, the Southern Methodist Church, and the Evangelical Methodist Church. Others use the name *Wesleyan* to refer to their link with John Wesley and his teachings.

Two long-standing elements are distinctive in the organization of the Methodist Church. One is the conference system, so named for Wesley's practice of conferring with his preachers before making decisions on important issues. There are local, regional, district, and national conferences. The local charge conference (Methodist congregations are technically called charges) is a yearly business meeting of the local congregation. The larger conferences connect local congregations with the whole church. Each of these conferences includes both clergy and laity. The form of government of most Methodist churches blends elements of the hierarchical (bishops) and the connectional (conferences) styles of organization.

The other characteristically Methodist organizational feature is the itineracy. Methodist ministers travel to various congregations in their regions as they are assigned by the annual conference, rather than the congregation beginning the process by calling a person as their minister. The traditional length of time that a minister could expect to stay in a particular charge was one year; now, that term has lengthened considerably and may be five years or more.

Methodists have a long history of ecumenical cooperation. They were early members of the National Council of Churches and one of the founding members of COCU. Their tolerance in matters of religious thought enables them to work easily with those whose views are different from their own. They were among the first to ordain women to the ministry. At the present time, more than half the student body at some Methodist seminaries is female. Methodists' involvement in social concerns does not stop at the individual or congregational level. They support many institutions for long-term health care and infant care, and many colleges.

The Methodists are a religiously diverse people noted for their tolerance and their involvement in social action, who strongly believe with their founder that religion is a matter for both heart and will, as well as for the intellect.

THE LUTHERANS

The followers of Martin Luther's reformation in Germany were first called "Lutherans" in the decree from the Roman Catholic Pope who condemned Luther. The name was also used by their opponents in Germany and elsewhere as a term of derision, a claim that they were followers of Luther rather than of Christ. The name stuck and became the name of a respected denomination, in spite of Luther's plea that the people who gathered around his message be called Evangelicals, or "bearers of good news."

A group of Lutherans from Denmark arrived in the Hudson's Bay area in 1619. They tried, without success, to found a colony. The first permanent settlement of Lutherans in what is now the United States began in 1638, when a group of Swedish colonists built a church on the shore of Delaware Bay. Later, in 1649, Dutch Lutherans organized in New Amsterdam (New York). Lutheran growth in the colonies was hampered because each European group held tightly to its own national background. Being Swedish or Finnish or Dutch was every bit as important to these immigrants as was being Lutheran.

Growth did occur, although slowly at times. Henry M. Muhlenberg arrived in the New World in 1742. He founded the first regional organization of Lutheran churches in 1748 and led in the writing of a constitution for American Lutheranism in 1792. Large waves of central European and, later, Scandinavian immigrants swelled the Lutheran population in the 1800s.

Belief

Lutherans take pride in remaining as close as possible to the beliefs Luther himself set forth at the time of the German reformation. They are distinguished from other Reformation churches by their highly liturgical style of worship and by their understanding of the Eucharist or Holy Communion. Lutherans believe that right Christian living follows from right believing. For Lutherans, the Bible is the inspired Word of God, containing God's full revelation to humankind. It is the only source of true Christian teaching and the only rule and norm of Christian faith and life. When Lutherans use the phrase "Word of God," they mean not only the Bible itself, but the living Word, transmitted in the Bible, through Christ, the sacraments, preaching, and the life of the church. They insist on strict adherence to the Bible and reject practices and beliefs that are not in accord with it.

Lutheran churches are creedal churches. Alongside the Bible, certain creeds and confessions of faith are said to express correct belief. The three **ecumenical creeds** of the whole church are among them: the Apostles, Nicene, and Athanasian creeds. The creeds have no authority in themselves but are of value only as they reveal the true Word of God. The **Augsburg Confession**, written in 1530, is the central statement of Lutheran essentials. It was written as a statement that set forth Luther's position on points wherein he differed from the Roman Catholic Church. In addition to the Augsburg Confession, Lutherans hold that the Apology[4] for the Augsburg Confession, the Smalcald Articles, the Formula of Concord, and Luther's Large and Small Catechisms contain true Christian teaching. Luther wrote the two catechisms as a way to teach new believers the most important Christian truths in a way that made them easy to learn. The Catechisms outline basic Lutheran teaching in a question-and-answer format. Many of the important creeds of Lutheranism are drawn together in the *Book of Concord*, first published in 1580.

Lutherans emphasize the importance of lifelong education in the faith. Sunday School classes for all ages are a central part of the Lutheran way of doing things. Sermons are often highly instructional in nature, explaining the Bible readings for the day and relating them to the life of the congregation. Confirmation is usually preceded by two to three years of study and preparation. Lutherans believe that each individual Christian must continually turn from sin to righteousness, and they emphasize the importance of proper guidance and instruction. Sudden and highly emotional conversions are often thought to be shallow and short-lived. Growth in faith is seen as a lifelong process, and instruction of children from an early age is encouraged.

The Small Catechism is the core of the instruction that takes place in preparation for confirmation. Luther's explanations of the various articles of the creeds are regarded highly, and these and his other writings are often referred to as Lutherans seek guidance in making decisions about contemporary issues. It should be said again that all such writings are to be measured against Scripture and are of value only as they accurately reflect Biblical teaching. Many of Luther's writings came out of controversy and are stated very strongly, as such controversial writings often are. Therefore, contemporary Lutherans feel free to modify and tone down the sharp edges of Luther's statements.

---

[4]Here, *apology* means a defense.

Lutherans emphasize the Second Article of the Apostles Creed, which deals with God's work of redemption through Christ, more than the First (God the Creator) or the Third (the Holy Spirit) Articles. This means that much importance is placed on Lent.[5] There are frequent references to Christ's suffering and death in Lutheran hymns, and the cross itself is a prominent symbol in Lutheran churches. This emphasis echoes Luther's focus on what God had done for humanity in Christ. Lutherans teach that both the law and the gospel are necessary. The law is necessary to awaken sinners to their sinful condition and to arouse them to repentance and a longing for redemption. The gospel assures the repentant sinner of God's forgiveness in Christ. Thus, both must be held together. Like so much in Lutheranism, this belief follows Luther's own teaching closely.

Lifestyle

Lutherans' lifestyles are usually culture affirming. Some smaller and more conservative groups impose restrictions on their members that go beyond the prevailing standards of the culture, but usually, Lutherans are very much like their neighbors. They emphasize temperance in all things, observance of the Lord's Day, and decent living. Their way of life is understood as the free and willing response of a grateful heart to God's grace. With Lutherans, the accent is always on free and grateful response more than on obedience. Good works are not thought to assist in any way in a person's salvation, but they are expected as an outward sign of inward faith. True faith inevitably leads to works of love and charity toward one's neighbor.

There are no enforced fasts, abstinence from worldly activities, or obligatory attendance at worship. However, Lutherans are expected to worship regularly, support the work of the church, receive holy communion regularly, and bear witness to their faith by the life they lead.

One of the more conservative branches of the Lutheran family, the Missouri Synod Lutheran Church sponsors a church-related school system in the United States that is second in size only to the Roman Catholic school system. Like the Baptists, who are involved in the Christian school movement, these Lutherans want the education their children receive at school to reinforce and complement that which they receive at home and at church.

Ritual

Worship is very important to Lutherans. Lutheran worship follows a precise liturgical format (Figure 4–5). Worship is orderly, using an adaptation of the worship of the early church as interpreted through Luther's modifications. Lutherans be-

---

[5] *Lent* is a six-week period of preparation before Easter during which Christians focus on Christ's suffering and sacrificial death for humankind.

Figure 4–5

TYPICAL LUTHERAN ORDER OF WORSHIP

Prelude
Welcome and Announcements
Confession of Sin and Declaration of Forgiveness

Liturgy of the Word

Opening Hymn
Greeting
Kyrie
Hymn of Praise
Salutation
The Collect (Prayer) of the Day
First Lesson (Old Testament)
Psalm
Second Lesson (New Testament Epistle)
The Gospel Response
The Gospel Lesson
Hymn
Sermon
The Creed (Apostles or Nicene)
The Prayers
Sharing the Peace
The Offering, with Music
Offertory Prayer

The Liturgy of the Sacrament

The Great Thanksgiving
    The Preface (seasonal prayer)
    Words of Institution
    The Lord's Prayer
    Lamb of God
The Communion
The Post-Communion Canticle
Closing Prayer
Benediction and Amen
Dismissal

lieve that weekly worship is central to the life of faith, and many churches hold services during the week so that those who cannot worship on Sunday may do so at another time. Many hymns are used. Prominence is given to hymns written by Luther, who is often regarded as one of the greatest hymn writers the Christian church has ever known. He is probably best known for "A Mighty

Fortress Is Our God," which became the key hymn of the Reformation. Worship follows the cycle of the church year built around the recollection of the major festivals such as Easter, Pentecost, and Christmas. Different special liturgical colors help the congregation call to mind the meaning of the various seasons.

Preaching and the sacrament of communion are both very important elements in Lutheran worship. The altar, a symbol of Christ's presence in the sacrament, and the pulpit, symbolizing God's presence through the Word, are equally important in their church architecture. This contrasts with many Protestant churches, in which the pulpit (perhaps along with a lectern from which the Bible is read) vastly overshadows the altar, which is frequently a simple table.

Lutherans recognize only holy communion and baptism as true sacraments, although great importance is attached to other rites of the church, especially confirmation. Sacraments are what they are, according to Lutheran belief and practice, because they were commanded by Jesus. They use symbolic earthly materials (water or bread and wine) to convey spiritual truth, and carry with them the promise of forgiveness, deliverance from evil, and life eternal.

Baptism is usually performed by sprinkling water on the forehead of the person being baptized. Other methods, such as pouring and immersion, are acceptable as long as baptism is done in the name of the trinitarian God. What is crucial is that the Word of God be spoken, for it is here that the power to make baptism effectual is to be found. Infants are baptized as well as adults, because Lutherans hold that the Bible clearly shows that the children of believers are included with them in the covenant of God's grace.

Communion is an important part of Lutheran worship. Lutheran congregations are encouraged to include communion as a part of each Sunday's worship. While some churches include it weekly, most celebrate the Eucharist either monthly or biweekly. Usually, people come to the front of the sanctuary and kneel at the altar to receive the elements. Many Lutherans also receive communion privately in times of personal difficulty or emergency. The Lutheran view of what takes place in the communion incorporates images of remembrance, fellowship, thanksgiving, confession and forgiveness, and celebration. The distinctive Lutheran view differs from both the Catholic belief in transubstantiation and from those who hold that there is no presence of Christ in the elements. They believe that the risen Christ is truly present in the bread and wine. The bread and wine continue to exist as bread and wine, but along with this, Christ is actually present. This teaching is sometimes referred to as the "Real Presence." This, Lutherans believe, is what Christ promised at the Last Supper.

Organization

The Lutheran churches make up the third-largest body of Protestants in the United States. They are especially strong in the Upper Midwest because of the presence of descendants of early German and Scandinavian immigrants. Lutheranism is the established church in many European countries, such as Iceland, Sweden, Norway, Finland, and Denmark, and immigrants from these countries brought their religion with them when they came to America.

Lutheran church government is connectional. The basic unit is the local congregation. It joins with other local churches of similar belief and practice in regional, national, and international organizations. Groups of like-minded congregations joined together are referred to as a synod. The synods are responsible for matters that concern the denomination as a whole. When Lutherans came to America from their various countries, they clung tightly to their national identity. From the late 1800s to the present time, many mergers of these nationally based groups have occurred and have blurred national boundaries and increased the size of Lutheran churches and synods. Mergers in 1959 and 1962 brought approximately 95 percent of American Lutherans into one of three groups: the Lutheran Church in America (LCA), the American Lutheran Church (ALC), and the Lutheran Church–Missouri Synod. In May 1987, the LCA and the ALC, along with the Association of Evangelical Lutheran Churches, voted to merge to form the Evangelical Lutheran Church in America. Differences of national background, and the fine points of doctrine and practice, still keep other Lutheran churches apart. Their strong conservatism and desire to remain separate places them outside the consensus.

As the religious consensus in the United States has become more conservative, religious groups that would have been outside the consensus a decade or two ago are now within it. The Missouri Synod Lutheran Church is one of two major evangelical and conservative Protestant groups in the United States that is now a part of the broad consensus, along with the Southern Baptist Convention. Neither completely fits the description of consensus Protestant churches. For example, both have remained outside the National Council of Churches. However, their size and the increased conservatism of the consensus warrants their inclusion here.

Lutherans usually refer to their clergy as pastors, a word that connotes one who is the shepherd of a flock. Church members are usually quite close to one another and to their pastor, to whom they turn frequently in times of both joy and sorrow.

In sum, Lutherans are a group of Protestant Christians whose understanding of basic Christian teachings and practices is guided by the interpretations given them by Martin Luther at the time of the German reformation. They place great importance on worship and believe in a life of faith lived in grateful response to God's grace.

THE PRESBYTERIANS

John Knox founded the Presbyterian Church, based on the teaching and organizational pattern developed by the Genevan reformer John Calvin. Presbyterianism became the established church in Scotland. Presbyterian churches are distinguished by their theology, which is usually called "reformed," and their form of church government, which is strongly connectional, so much so that this type of church organization is sometimes called *presbyterian* (lowercase *p* to distinguish it from the denomination). The Presbyterian Church (USA) is the largest embodiment of Reformed theology among churches in the United States. Another consensus denomination in the Reformed theological tradition is the United Church of Christ, discussed later in this chapter.

Early Presbyterian immigrants to America faced many problems. They were widely scattered. They also lacked ministers and houses of worship. Early growth was slow at best, and reverses were not uncommon. A large immigration of English and Scotch-Irish Presbyterians who fled persecution in their home countries in the first half of the 1700s made up the backbone of colonial Presbyterianism. These immigrants settled especially in the middle colonies.

The Reverend Francis Makemie, known as the "father of American Presbyterianism," came to the colonies in the late 1600s. There were Presbyterians in several of the colonies (Virginia, Massachusetts, Connecticut, and New York, for example) in the 1600s. Their numbers were small, and they were widely scattered. Makemie was responsible for the founding of the first American Presbytery, in Philadelphia in 1705.[6] In 1717, the Synod of Philadelphia was organized with 19 ministers, 40 churches, and about 3,000 members.

These early Presbyterians, most of whom were highly educated for their time and well acquainted with culture, soon assumed positions of influence, so that their importance outweighed their numbers quite considerably. They were the most influential religious group in the rebellion of the colonies, which led the English House of Commons to call the uprising the "Presbyterian rebellion." At least fourteen signers of the Declaration of Independence were Presbyterians.

Belief

Early Presbyterianism was strongly Calvinistic. Later, especially in the United States, Presbyterianism dropped most of the harsher teachings of Calvinism. Doctrines such as predestination and limited atonement[7] no longer have any role in the teaching of most Presbyterian churches.

Like Lutheranism, Presbyterianism is a creedal faith. A group of religious leaders gathered at Westminster Abbey from 1643 to 1648 to write the Westminster Confession of Faith, as well as the Larger and Shorter Catechisms that are based on it. A later *Book of Confessions* (1967) contains the creeds and confessions. Following the merger in 1983, a new statement of faith was written for the newly formed Presbyterian Church (USA). It is not intended to stand apart from the other confessions of faith included in the *Book of Confessions*, but to

---

[6]Historians do not agree completely on the date, but 1705 is widely supported.

[7]*Predestination* is the belief that God elects only some people to be saved and that nothing whatever can change whether someone is elected or not. *Limited atonement* is the belief that Christ died only for the elect.

continue them. The Preface is a good statement of the Presbyterian and Reformed vision of what it means to be a creedal church:

> The new Statement of Faith celebrates our rediscovery that for all our undoubted diversity, we are bound together by a common faith and a common task. The faith we confess unites us with the one, universal church. The most important beliefs of Presbyterians are those we share with other Christians, and especially with other evangelical Christians who look to the Protestant Reformation as a renewal of the gospel of Jesus Christ. . . . We are convinced that to the Reformed churches a distinctive idea of the catholic faith has been entrusted for the good of the whole church.[8]

The creeds important to Presbyterianism state essential Christian teachings, understood to be based on the Bible as the "only infallible rule of faith and practice." A distinctive Presbyterian emphasis that influences the interpretation of most points of doctrine is the sovereignty of God and God's Word. This includes the sovereignty of God over all aspects of the created world, the absolute sovereignty of Christ in human salvation, and the sovereignty of the Bible for faith and practice.

The Presbyterian definition of the church does not refer to bishops or apostolic succession as do the definitions common in liturgical churches, such as the Lutheran and Episcopal churches. Rather, the church is defined as that place where the pure Gospel is preached (that is, by ordained ministers according to reformed understandings) and the sacraments rightly administered (that is, the two sacraments of baptism and communion). With other Protestants, Presbyterians believe that salvation comes by grace alone. They do, however, make a distinctive interpretation of it in saying that justification occurs only in the church. By this, they mean that reconciliation with God and reconciliation with one's fellow human beings are inseparable. They are two sides of one and the same event. The church is a community of those who are being reconciled to God and to each other.

In general, biblical and theological interpretation among Presbyterians ranges from fairly conservative and literal to more liberal and figurative. The larger churches within the denomination tend toward the liberal, while the smaller ones, many of which grew out of doctrinal disputes, tend to be more conservative.

Lifestyle

Presbyterians can be found everywhere and in all walks of life, living very much like others in their culture. Little is distinctive about their lifestyle. The belief that God is sovereign over all of life propels Presbyterians directly into the world as they find it, with the mandate to make it better.

---

[8]Preface to A Brief Statement of Faith—Presbyterian Church (USA).

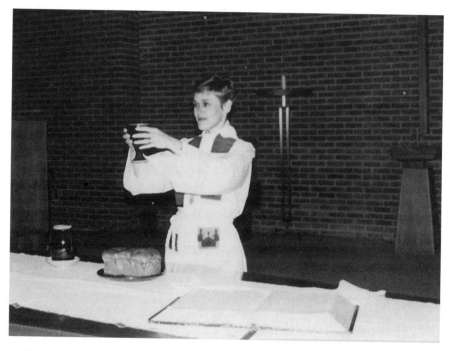

Figure 4–6   Presbyterians, like most consensus Protestants, ordain women to the ministry. (*Courtesy of Pastor Jean Holmes, Nauraushaun Presbyterian Church, Pearl River, NY.*)

Calvinistic teachings about the value of hard work and frugality made Calvinism a useful element in the life of the colonies and the new nation. Presbyterians are to this day found in the ranks of the more highly educated and the economically better off. They count among their members a disproportionate number of society's leaders, whether in government, business and industry, or education.

Ritual

Presbyterian worship is usually carried out with great dignity and order. It is stately, as befits the worship of a sovereign God (Figure 4–7). It is centered on the sermon, including the exposition of the Scriptures and the ordered presentation of the great truths of the Christian faith as Presbyterians understand them. The sermon has mainly a teaching function. Presbyterian ministers are formally called "teaching elders," to distinguish them from the "ruling elders," whose function is church governance.

Hymns and prayers center on the main beliefs of the faith, such as confession and forgiveness and praise to the sovereign God. Presbyterian worship is usually more intellectual than emotional and gives the worshipper an experience of logical thoughts, ordered behavior, and a restrained atmosphere. According to

Figure 4–7

TYPICAL PRESBYTERIAN ORDER OF WORSHIP

Prelude
Call to Worship
Opening Hymn
Congregational Confession of Sin
Declaration of Pardon
Choral Response
Concerns of the Church (Announcements)
Choral Anthem
Old Testament Lesson
Offering
Offertory Anthem
Doxology
New Testament Lesson
Sermon
Closing Hymn
Benediction
Postlude

Presbyterians, worship is not something done for God, who does not need to be worshiped, nor is it something done for the people themselves. It is preeminently a part of God's work in the world, one of the means whereby God interacts with the created order.

Presbyterians believe very strongly that children, along with their parents, are members of the "household of faith," and they baptize people of all ages. Parents are encouraged to have their children baptized. While baptism is not thought to be necessary for salvation, it is considered a sacrament and is important as the rite of incorporation into the church. It is usually performed by sprinkling.

Presbyterians reject, as did Calvin and Knox, Luther's view of the real presence of Christ in the elements of communion. They also reject the view of some of the reformers that the communion is only a memorial. In the elements of bread and (usually) unfermented grape juice, Christ is spiritually present and is known by faith. Being in a proper frame of mind and spirit to receive communion is important to Presbyterians, for whom this is a very solemn service of worship.

Organization

The name *Presbyterian* derives from the specific form of connectional church government used in these churches. The organizational arrangement of this church is made up of four levels, each of which includes both ministers and laypeople.

The session, made up of people elected by the congregation, is the policy-making body of the local congregation. The General Assembly is the national policy-making body.

There have been various Presbyterian groups in the country at different times in the church's history. A major division occurred between North and South before the Civil War, a split that was not resolved until 1983. The Presbyterian Church in the United States of America (PC,USA) was formed when the Presbyterian Church in the United States (PCUS, the southern branch) and the United Presbyterian Church in the USA (the northern branch) met in a simultaneous General Assembly in Atlanta, Georgia, in 1983 and voted to merge the two organizations. This merger was the end point of at least ten different mergers in the last two and one-half centuries. Besides the newly formed PC (USA) there are several smaller groups that are part of this denominational family, such as the Cumberland Presbyterian Church, the Orthodox Presbyterian Church, and the Reformed Presbyterian Church. Most of these smaller branches are more conservative to fundamentalist in their thinking and often adhere more closely to Calvin's original teaching than does the PC (USA).

The Presbyterian Church (USA) includes congregations that are predominantly black or racially integrated as well as those that are largely white. Outreach to immigrants, especially to Koreans, has led to the establishment of Korean congregations served by Korean-speaking ministers. Other congregations have been established among Native Americans.

Presbyterians, then, are the fourth-largest group of Protestant Christians in the nation. They interpret the basic Christian teachings according to the reformed tradition of John Calvin and John Knox. They emphasize the sovereignty of God and worship in a dignified and stately manner.

THE EPISCOPALIANS

The first Episcopal worship in the New World probably took place in 1578, when Sir Francis Drake landed on the shore of what is now California. His Church of England chaplain, the Reverend Francis Fletcher, raised a cross and read a prayer of thanksgiving.

The Church of England came to America with some of the very first explorers. The first settlement was at Jamestown, Virginia, in 1607. Soon, several of the southeastern coastal colonies, such as Georgia, Virginia, and the Carolinas were predominantly Anglican. In the Southeast, Anglicanism frequently received the support of the colonial government. The Anglican Church in the colonies remained firmly attached to the Church of England for quite some time.

The church suffered greatly and was nearly destroyed at the time of the Revolutionary War. Although most Anglicans, clergy and laity alike, supported the Revolution, or at least did not support the Loyalists, it was branded the Tory Church, and many of its clergy had to flee back to England or to Canada. A reorganized church came out of the chaos. At its General Conference in Annapolis in 1783, it took the name Protestant Episcopal Church to indicate its separation from the English monarch. It is called Protestant because it is not Roman Catholic, although it strongly resembles the Catholic Church. It is Episcopal because its form of government is hierarchical rather than connectional or congregational. In 1789, a constitution was adopted for the new American church, the *Book of Common Prayer* was revised for American use, and the Protestant Episcopal Church became independent and self-governing.

Belief

In belief as in many other ways, the Episcopal Church is regarded as a bridge between Protestant and Catholic. It is sometimes said to be Protestant in belief while being Catholic in worship. Some interpreters consider it to be "a different way of being Christian than Protestantism, Roman Catholicism, or Eastern Orthodoxy."[9] It accepts the Apostles and Nicene creeds as accurate reflections of the teachings of the Bible. "The Thirty-Nine Articles of Religion" is a distinctive statement of Anglican belief in the United States. The Episcopal Church encourages any honest human attempt to study and investigate religious matters, and it accepts a wide range of opinion in matters of theology and doctrine. It stresses the importance of "loyalty in essentials and liberty in nonessentials," and the smaller points of theological difference fall into the nonessential category. Episcopalians believe that the Bible contains all doctrine necessary for salvation and that therefore nothing that cannot be read in or proven by the Bible should be required of anyone.

The *Book of Common Prayer* is the product of the service books used in the church throughout the centuries and contains orders for Sunday worship and for many other services of worship. A contemporary American revision that was approved in 1980 was the first major revision since 1928.

The Episcopal Church honors the saints of the church in ways similar to what is done in the Catholic church. Churches are frequently named for saints, and saints' festival days are celebrated in worship. Oftentimes, Episcopalians name their children for saints.

Most Episcopal priests are married, and whether to marry or not is left up to the individual. The Episcopal Church does have a few groups of nuns and monks who take the traditional three vows of poverty, chastity, and obedience.

Lifestyle

Episcopalians are culture affirming. Historically, the Episcopal Church has been the church of the upper classes, and, to some extent, it still is. Along with the Presbyterians, Episcopalians rank at the top of such socioeconomic status indi-

---

[9]David L. Holmes, "The Anglican Tradition and the Episcopal Church," in *Encyclopedia of the American Religious Experience*, vol. 1, ed. Lippy and Williams, p. 392.

cators as education and income. They are often leaders in their communities. They are among the most liberal of Protestants both theologically and morally, and they are among the strongest advocates of civil liberties for all people.

Ritual

The sacraments are at the center of Episcopal worship. Episcopalians believe that the sacraments are "visible signs and effectual means" of God's acting in people. The understanding of the sacraments as "effectual means," having power in and of themselves to convey God's grace, sets Episcopalians apart from other Protestants.

The principal act of Christian worship on Sundays and on other significant church festivals is the Holy Eucharist, which is very similar to the Catholic Mass (Figure 4–8). The Eucharistic service is frequently called a Mass. The Eucharist is the most frequently used term for holy communion among Episcopalians; it comes from a Greek word meaning *thanksgiving*. Episcopalians believe that Christ is actually present within the elements of bread and wine, although they refrain from trying to express or explain what they consider to be a holy mystery.

Infants, as well as children and adults, are baptized, usually by sprinkling. Baptism is believed to cleanse from sin, unite the person with Christ in Christ's

Figure 4–8

TYPICAL EPISCOPALIAN ORDER OF WORSHIP

The Holy Eucharist: Rite One
The Word of God

Preparation
Collect for the Day
Lessons
Sermon
Nicene Creed
Prayers of the People
Confession of Sin and Absolution
The Peace

The Holy Communion

The Offertory
The Great Thanksgiving
The Communion
The Dismissal

death and resurrection, bring about rebirth by the action of the Holy Spirit, and make people adopted children of God the Divine Parent. These two sacraments are understood to have been instituted by Jesus as the chief sacraments of the church.

Episcopalians also believe that other traditionally important rites, such as confirmation, reconciliation of a penitent (also called confession and forgiveness), marriage, ordination to the priesthood, and the anointing of the sick, have sacramental significance. The importance placed on the sacraments is distinctive for this group of Christians.

This is a liturgical church, the most so of any of these five. Episcopalians use music, stately buildings, elaborate symbolism, and special clothing worn by the priests to enrich their worship. Incense may be used to remind people that their prayers rise to God as the smoke from burning incense rises to the ceiling of the sanctuary.

The services for morning and evening prayer are frequently used, often being said daily in large churches. There are also services for special times in the church year, such as saints' days and other holy days such as Christmas and Easter, and for special times in peoples' lives.

Episcopal worship is more dramatic than is worship in most other Protestant churches. The teaching, the prayer, and the praise that characterize all Protestant worship are present there, but they are set in the context of a sweeping drama that unfolds as priest and congregation together interact in a set pattern of responses from the *Book of Common Prayer*.

Organization

The Episcopal Church is both hierarchical and connectional in its organization. There are bishops, and they do have quite a lot of authority. Usually, the clergyperson is called a priest. Episcopalians believe that the bishops' authority has been handed down across the centuries in an unbroken line of succession. They trace this back to an account in Matthew 16, in which Jesus is said to have given Saint Peter the keys to the kingdom of heaven. In recent years, the Episcopal church has involved laypeople more at all levels. Each congregation elects a vestry to govern the local church. In consultation with the bishop, the vestry is responsible for calling a priest to the congregation. The spiritual head of the Episcopal church worldwide is the Archbishop of Canterbury, England. Although the American church is self-governing, its members give spiritual allegiance to the head of the whole Church of England.

In 1979, the Episcopal Church voted to ordain women to the priesthood and also revised the *Book of Common Prayer*. These two actions gave rise to the Anglican Church of North America (or Anglican Catholic Church; both names are used), dedicated to upholding traditional Episcopalianism. There are also several other small Episcopal denominations. In spite of this, the Episcopal Church in the United States is remarkably unified. Latitude in belief is complemented by uniformity in worship, and this shared worship has made for the greatest amount of cohesion in this Protestant community. There are differences of emphasis. High church congregations emphasize liturgical worship, whereas low church ones have a simpler service with greater emphasis on the Bible (in a sense, a more Protestant service). Broad church Episcopalians may be in favor of either way of worship but emphasize a liberal approach to theology and place a great deal of importance on social ethics. In England, these differences have led to a divided church, but in the United States they have remained differences of style.

The Episcopal Church is the Church of England in the United States. Although it has spiritual ties to England, it is independent. Its churches combine wide latitude and tolerance in matters of belief, with uniformity in stately, liturgical worship that is centered on the seven sacraments.

OTHER CONSENSUS PROTESTANTS

We now turn to a consideration of three more Protestant denominations that are not as large as the major five but which clearly fit into the category of consensus Protestantism. These include the United Church of Christ, the Christian Church (Disciples of Christ), and the Friends Yearly Meeting, also known as the Quakers.

The United Church of Christ

The United Church of Christ, like the Presbyterian Church, has its roots in Reformed theology and connectional church government. Its earliest roots go back to Congregationalism, the major form that the Puritan tradition took in the Massachusetts Bay Colony. The United Church of Christ itself came into being with a merger of the Congregational Christian Churches and the Evangelical and Reformed Church in 1957. However, both of these churches were themselves products of earlier mergers.

The beliefs and practices of the United Church of Christ are very similar to those of other consensus Protestants. Its statement of faith, adopted in 1959, loosely follows the format of the Apostles Creed, with sections on God the Father, Jesus Christ the Son, and the Holy Spirit. Concluding paragraphs discuss the nature of the church and the role of Christians and affirm the two Protestant sacraments and eternal life in the Kingdom of God. The statement of faith is not binding on any local congregation, nor is it used as a test of faith for individual members. Its beliefs bring together the various emphases of the churches that make up its heritage. Concerning belief, the UCC affirms, "in essentials, unity; in nonessentials, liberty; in all things, charity."

Its patterns of worship, decided on by local congregations, vary considerably. They are similar to those we have seen previously. Sermons frequently address social problems and crises, seeking to apply the historic beliefs of Christianity in the modern world. There are educational activities for all ages, and, especially in larger churches, a variety of specialized ministries and outreach efforts.

Organizationally, the United Church of Christ blends a local government that is congregational with a connectional regional and national organization. Local congregations have autonomy in making most decisions that affect them. This denomination is a strong supporter of ecumenism, and, with other consensus Protestants, is a member of both the World and National Councils of Churches. Geographically, its greatest strength is in the northeastern United States.

The United Church of Christ is one of the most socially liberal and activist churches in the United States. Nationally, its Council for Racial and Ethnic Ministries is responsible for coordinating the efforts of councils and boards that focus on the church's ministry to Asian American and Pacific Islands immigrants, Hispanics, Native Americans, and blacks, as well as for overseeing its Ministers for Social and Racial Justice.

The Christian Church (Disciples of Christ)

The Christian Church (Disciples of Christ) is one of the communities of faith that grew out of what we now call the **Restoration Movement** in American Christianity. It is the only one of the denominations in this chapter that began in America.

Prior to the Civil War, religious thinkers in many parts of the country found themselves dismayed over the divisions within the Christian churches. They believed that the Bible taught that there was to be but one Christianity, yet there were many churches. As often as not, the relationships between these churches were not friendly, marred by arguments over creeds and church structures. In Virginia and North Carolina, James O'Kelly reacted against what he thought were authoritarian structures and practices in Methodism. In Vermont, Elias Smith and Abner Jones led a movement they called Eastern Christians, rejecting all other churches then a part of American religion. In Kentucky, following the famous Cane Ridge revival, Barton Stone rejected both the doctrine of the Trinity and predestination, on the grounds that neither was to be found in the New Testament. Thomas and Alexander Campbell, father and son, spoke out in favor of creedless, autonomous local congregations made up of believers who were baptized by immersion after accepting Jesus Christ as their Lord and Savior, and for the weekly celebration of the Lord's Supper as a memorial of Jesus' death. In Ohio, Walter Scott put his main emphasis on the baptism of believers only. These themes characterized what eventually came to be called the Restoration Movement.

A passionate desire for Christian unity lay behind the Restoration Movement. Everyone in the movement believed that the multitude of divisions in the Christian Church was offensive to Jesus' intentions for his followers. They believed that the unity that they sought could be achieved by a return to the New

Testament as the only guide to faith and practice, down to the smallest detail of church government. The Restorationists said that division had come about through creeds and organizations invented by human beings, rather than given by God. Thus, the way to peace and purity was a radical return to the past and to the church as it had been in New Testament times. An early slogan, "No creed but Christ," highlights their belief in the importance of avoiding humanly invented creeds.

The Restorationists believed that each local congregation should be autonomous or self-governing. They held that each local gathering of believers was, in fact, the church. There should be no structures that took over things that were properly the responsibility of the local church (such as mission boards), nor any that limited the authority of each local fellowship of believers (such as presbyteries). The Restorationists had other beliefs in common, including the following: All people have the capacity and the responsibility either to accept or to reject God's offer of salvation in Jesus the Christ; there is no predestination. While God is properly thought of as Father, Son, and Holy Spirit, the actual term *Trinity* is not biblical and therefore ought not to be used. Communion, for which they preferred the term *Lord's Supper*, was understood to be a memorial only. Some advocated weekly celebration, and others spoke in favor of less frequent administration.

The Restoration Movement—occasionally called the Campbellite movement after Alexander and Thomas Campbell—was a true, indigenous American religious movement. Besides the Christian Church (Disciples of Christ), it gave birth to two other groups of churches that continue to claim the allegiance of significant numbers of Americans. These two, the Christian Churches/Churches of Christ and the Churches of Christ, are discussed in Chapter 9. It also produced many smaller, independent churches.

The Christian Church (Disciples of Christ) includes both religious conservatives and liberals among its members, giving it a wider range of religious attitudes than is true of the other two. As with all of the Restoration churches, there is no creed, and complete freedom of personal interpretation is the rule. Although the Disciples believe that all persons are sinful and in need of redemption through Jesus, they do not believe in original sin that is inherited in some way from Adam and Eve. Church membership is based on a simple affirmation of the Lordship of Christ. Congregational worship is dignified and rather formal, with both instrumental and vocal music. The Lord's Supper is celebrated every Sunday. The Disciples support a network of schools and colleges as well as other institutions for the betterment of society. They maintain residence halls on many university and college campuses, called Disciples Divinity Houses. They are members of both the National and World Councils of Churches and support ecumenical efforts of many types. On several campuses they are involved in ecumenical campus ministries. A strong national structure was developed, beginning in 1968, but the local congregation remains the basic unit. Most of the Disciples of Christ churches are located in the lower Midwest and the Southwest.

The Friends

The Religious Society of Friends, also known as the **Quakers**, is the last community of faith we will consider in this chapter. The name "Friends" comes from John 15:15 in the Christian New Testament, in which Jesus says to his followers, "I have called you friends." The Friends began in England in the 1600s. The co-founders, George Fox and his wife, Margaret Fell, were sincere seekers who had failed to find religious peace in any of the churches of their time. They did find it in a quiet, personal relationship with God, and this trait has been a part of the Quaker heritage ever since. Fox, Fell, and their followers came to believe in the presence of an Inner Voice or an Inner Light in every person. They thought of this as each individual's capacity to know and respond to God and to truth.

Many members of the Society of Friends came to the colonies because they were persecuted in England. Their religious beliefs led to actions that were offenses to the norms and procedures of civil duty (required by law): refusal to enter the army or navy, to swear oaths, to attend liturgical worship services [i.e., those of the established Church of England], to pay *tithes* [required, a sort of religious tax] to the state church, to take off hats to honor an official, and to use titles.[10]

The belief in the Inner Light has two very important consequences. It means that the individual's conscience is absolutely sacred and cannot be violated. The unusual religious liberty in William Penn's colony of Pennsylvania was a direct result of Penn's conviction that every person had an absolute right to worship God according to the leading of the Inner Light. It also meant that all persons were, without exception, equal.

These beliefs led to some of the distinctive attributes of the Society. The sanctity of individual conscience means, for example, that people cannot be drafted into the military against their will. The Society of Friends is among the best known of the historic peace churches. They advocate conscientious objection from military service and the pursuit of peace in all of life. A colleague of mine, for example, whose outlook is strongly influenced by Quaker teachings, has helped make us all more aware of the violence implied in certain expressions that are very common in our language, such as "I could have killed him!" or even "That was a killer exam!" The Friends' commitment to the sanctity of individual conscience, however, leaves room for participation in the military for those to whom it seems right, and there are Quaker chaplains in military service.

The emphasis on the equality of all people has made the Friends leaders in the movement for racial justice. It also relativizes such social customs as the use of titles. Letter salutations often read "Dear Jane Smith" or "Dear John Jones" rather than "Dear Dr. Smith" or "Dear Professor Jones." Among strict Quakers, even titles such as Mr. and Mrs. are not used.

[10]William B. Williamson, *An Encyclopedia of Religion in the United States: One Hundred Religious Groups Speak for Themselves* (New York: Crossroad, 1991), p. 281.

Another result of this same conviction was traditional Quaker worship, in which there was no programmed worship and no worship leader. People sat in quiet meditation, speaking as they felt moved by the Holy Spirit to do so. Today, the Friends United Meeting (the largest church in the Quaker family in the United States) usually has ministers and programmed worship. Other churches retain the unprogrammed style, at least in some services. In any case, all members are considered ministers. Those who are "recorded ministers" are set apart for specific service to a congregation, or "meeting." Communion and baptism are taught to be spiritual ordinances and no outward elements are used.

A hallmark of Quaker practice is that they do not vote in meetings for business in local congregations or larger assemblies. They seek spiritual consensus among themselves, based on the will of God as they perceive it. Not just a meeting of the minds or even of the hearts, this consensus grows out of the Inner Light within each person present.

The American Friends Service Committee (often known by its initials, AFSC) has an outstanding record of relief work in both wartime and peace. Wherever there is a disaster, at home or abroad, AFSC volunteers can usually be found helping people pick up the pieces and begin to put shattered lives back together again. This Committee was awarded the Nobel Peace Prize in 1947.

The Friends have never actively sought converts. They are content to be a quiet presence in the culture, seeking to worship and live in their own way, free from interference, and granting the same privileges to others. Although the "thee" and "thou" of plain speech and the simplicity of traditional Quaker dress have largely disappeared, the Friends remain distinctive in their emphasis on the Inner Light and their witness to peace.

WOMEN IN CONSENSUS PROTESTANTISM

Along with the Anglicans in the Southeast coastal colonies, the New England Puritans were the backbone of American religion for many decades. They shared a positive, although limited, view of women's roles. Women were to be helpers for their husbands and coauthorities with them over children and servants. Their proper sphere of activity was their home and family. In this accepted sphere, women exercised considerable power and autonomy.[11]

Revivalism in the 1700s and 1800s helped to expand women's roles. Most revivalists preached that women were superior to men in moral and spiritual goodness and more naturally religious than their male counterparts. Women were therefore responsible for evangelizing their children and for leading their husbands away from worldly influences. This led naturally into women taking an increasing role in the evangelization of their extended families and their

---

[11]Rosemary Radford Ruether and Rosemary Skinner Keller, *Women and Religion in America, Volume II: The Colonial and Revolutionary Periods* (San Francisco: Harper & Row, Publishers, 1983), p. xvii.

friends. Beyond this, it led to opportunities for women to lead women's prayer groups during revivals. This paved the way for the increasing involvement of women in Protestantism in the years to come.

The debate over the ordination of women to the ministry began in the nineteenth century. It still continues in some Protestant churches and is a key issue in Roman Catholicism. Ordination was denied to most women in the nineteenth century. Because they were denied ordination, women created separate organizations that were largely self-governing. These organizations were active mainly in social reform, missionary work, and education. In other words, they, too, grew out of the traditional view of what roles were proper for women. They were extensions of caregiving and nurturing. In the context of their time, however, they provided ways for women to fit into to organized religion. The view that women's nature is different from that of men has been discredited by some feminists. In the context of its time, the idea that women's nature is distinctive led to a cluster of opportunities that might have been unavailable otherwise.

Many religious groups organized home missions boards to guide the work of evangelization at home and overseas missionary boards to supervise similar work in other countries. Relief societies were organized to provide care for the ill, the impoverished, the homeless, and orphans. Anna Kugler and Ida Scudder are two outstanding examples of what women could achieve. Kugler was a Lutheran medical missionary to India, as well as an evangelist. Scudder founded the Vellore Medical School in 1918. Vellore was the first school in India to train Indian doctors. Orders of deacons, women set apart for this care-giving work, provided other women with opportunities to enact the biblical mandate to care for those unable to care for themselves.

Many women became religious teachers. Opportunities for women in Christian education came earlier than similar opportunities in other fields. The first woman to hold the rank of professor in a U.S. seminary was Edna Baxter, an Episcopal deacon and professor of Christian education at Hartford Seminary. Belle Harris Bennett founded Scarritt Bible and Training School in Nashville, Tennessee, in 1887. The position of Professor of Applied Theology at the Garrett Biblical Institute (now Garrett-Evangelical Theological Seminary) was created for Dr. Georgia Harkness in 1939. Harkness was the first woman to teach in a field other than education in a major U.S. seminary.

What do we find when we turn to our own time? Consensus Protestantism has been very receptive to the cultural and social changes that have brought about new opportunities for women. Most consensus Protestant churches ordain women to the ministry. Examples include many Baptist congregations, the United Methodists, the Presbyterian Church, USA, many of the Lutheran churches, the Episcopal Church, the United Church of Christ, the Disciples, and the Friends. Women are entering the ministry in increasing numbers. By and large, the opportunities have never been better for women who want to enter the professional ministry. "Women in the late twentieth century are experiencing their day in the sun in many areas of institutional church work. More positions of greater responsibility and authority are being opened to them than ever before. For the first time in history, a woman often receives preferential treatment for posts of leadership in volunteer and professional capacities."[12]

Women are also successful in gaining placements in churches, although a disproportionate number are employed in smaller churches that pay less than their larger counterparts. Most of the churches that have called a woman as minister or pastor are well satisfied with that choice. Women have also moved into the ranks of church officials in larger numbers than before.[13]

Lay positions that historically had been closed to women, such as usher, communion server, and membership on the board of trustees or board of elders, usually are open to both sexes equally. Some local churches have made it a policy to have equal numbers of women and men in such capacities.

The communities of faith described in this chapter attempt to use gender-inclusive language in worship and in publications. They have supported publication of revisions of the biblical books of Psalms, the Gospels, and the Pauline Letters in which inclusive language is used. They have also supported publication of inclusive language lectionaries.

The following examples are representative of the ways in which these churches address the need for gender-inclusive language. In United Church of Christ publications, it is no longer permissible to use language that refers to God as "Father, Son and Holy Spirit." An acceptable alternative is God as "Creator, Redeemer, and Sanctifier." A new *Book of Worship* endorsed by the United Methodist General Conference includes prayers addressed to God as "Mother and Father." A 1976 revision of the United Church of Christ statement of faith eliminates the gender-specific language of the earlier version. The language of the new Presbyterian statement is inclusive as well.

Consensus Protestant churches have been instrumental in supporting women's rights in general. For example, most of them do not discourage women who want to work outside the home or who want to remain single. Many also help sponsor day care centers. The National Council of Churches of Christ in the USA formally supported the passage of the Equal Rights Amendment to the U.S. Constitution, unanimously passing a resolution urging its passage.

CONSENSUS PROTESTANTISM SUMMARIZED

In many ways, the consensus Protestant denominations in the United States are remarkably similar. Yet, they are also quite different in some respects. These differences are important to their members, who, whether from upbringing, belief,

[12]Rosemary Skinner Keller, "Patterns of Laywomen's Leadership in Twentieth-Century Protestantism," in *Women and Religion in America, Volume III: 1900–1968*, ed. Rosemary Radford Ruether and Rosemary Skinner Keller (San Francisco: Harper & Row, Publishers, 1986), p. 276.

[13]Edward C. Lehman, Jr., *Women Clergy: Breaking Through Gender Barriers* (New Brunswick, NJ: Transaction Books, 1985).

or preferred style of worship (or, for some, simple habit and custom) find one denomination more satisfactory than others. The similarities and differences taken together have enabled consensus Protestantism to become a major religious force in the nation. It is unified by its similarities, while its differences enable it to attract a wide variety of people. It appeals to a range of people and both reflects and helps to determine the culture of the United States as a whole.

QUESTIONS AND ACTIVITIES FOR REVIEW, DISCUSSION, AND WRITING

1. Describe what is unique about each of these communities of faith.
2. In what ways does the phrase "neighbors, not strangers" apply to the Protestant denominations discussed in this chapter?
3. Try to get together a group of students that has one or two people from each of these denominations. Discuss similarities and differences in belief, worship, lifestyle, and church organization.
4. If possible, attend services at a Baptist church and at an Episcopal church. How are the services alike? How are they different? You might also attend a one of the other churches described in the chapter and make a similar comparison.
5. If you have not had this experience already, try to visit a church that has a female minister. Write a paragraph in which you reflect on your feelings about that experience.
6. Write a paragraph in which you reflect on your feelings about the use of gender-inclusive language in worship.

FOR FURTHER READING

Chapman, Audrey R., *Faith, Power, and Politics: Political Ministry in Mainline Churches.* Cleveland, OH: Pilgrim Press, 1991. Discusses the role of consensus religion in promoting peace, justice, and human rights.

Dillenberger, John, and Claude Welch, *Protestant Christianity Interpreted Through Its Development.* New York: Macmillan Publishing Company, 1988. A combination of thematic and historical approaches that does a good job of showing how various movements fit together.

5

Catholics in the United States

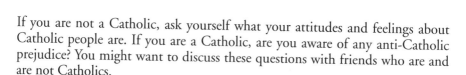

If you are not a Catholic, ask yourself what your attitudes and feelings about Catholic people are. If you are a Catholic, are you aware of any anti-Catholic prejudice? You might want to discuss these questions with friends who are and are not Catholics.

Roman Catholics make up approximately one-fourth of the population of the United States, making this group the largest single community of faith in the nation. It is these people's story, or rather, stories, to which we now turn in our exploration of consensus religion. We will look first at the history of Catholics in America, then at basic beliefs and practices, and, finally, we will investigate the issues that have occupied the Church's thinking as it became and continues to become a notable part of the American religious scene. Before we begin, it would be a good idea for you to review those religious beliefs and practices that all Christians—Catholics and Protestants—share. As we did when discussing Protestants in the United States, we will be concentrating on what is unique about Catholics, and, in doing so, we must remember that there is a great deal that they share with other Christians, and, indeed, with members of the Jewish faith as well.

FROM IMMIGRANT CHURCH TO CONSENSUS RELIGION: THE HISTORY OF THE CATHOLIC CHURCH IN THE UNITED STATES

In one sense, every European religion in the United States is an immigrant faith, since the only indigenous religions were those of the various Native American tribes that lived on the North American continent long before the arrival of the first European explorers. Because the union that eventually became the United States included most of the Spanish territories, the oldest non-native religion in the United States is Catholicism, not the Puritanism of the Pilgrims. It is particularly true of Catholics that their history has been, and in many ways continues to be, influenced by their being an immigrant Church.

Catholics were among the first, if not the first, Europeans to set foot upon the shores of America. Christopher Columbus (the name Christopher means "Christbearer") sailed from Catholic Spain, with the backing and blessing of a Catholic monarch. Later missionaries came seeking to convert Native Americans and to provide for the religious needs of the soldiers and others who came to conquer territory for Spain. It is likely that the first Catholic Mass[1] in what is now the United States was celebrated by one of those early Spanish Catholic missionary priests.

Spanish Catholic missionaries had the greatest impact in the American Southwest, although the first Spanish settlement began in 1565 at what is now Saint Augustine, Florida. The Spanish missions fared best in what is now California.

Early missionaries came not only from Spain but also from France. French missionaries, most of whom were Franciscans or Jesuits, had already settled in what is now Canada. From there, French explorers traveled throughout what we know as New York, Maine, Pennsylvania, Wisconsin, Michigan, and Illinois, as well as down the Mississippi River to Alabama and Louisiana. The imprint of its French heritage remains on American Catholicism to this day, and the French influence was particularly strong in the early nineteenth century.

There is still evidence of these early missions and the people who built them. In California and elsewhere in the Southwest, old and restored missions can be visited. Cities named after saints abound. San Francisco and San Diego are named after Saint Francis and Saint James, respectively. *Los Angeles* means "the angels." The areas in the Southwest and Florida where the missionaries worked remain centers of Catholic population today. In Louisiana, what are called counties elsewhere are still referred to as parishes, the smallest unit of Roman Catholic Church organization. Marquette and Duquesne universities are named after two of the well-known missionaries, and a huge statue of Father Junipero Serra stands in San Francisco.

The Spanish and French Catholic explorers came to the New World with two goals: territorial conquest and evangelization of the native peoples. Catholics from England arrived here for a different reason.

English Catholics were the next Catholics to colonize in the New World. There was an important difference between them and the Spanish and French. The English came as settlers and not as missionaries and territorial conquerors. The English came to the eastern seaboard area after the persecution of Catholics in England launched by King Henry VIII forced many to flee for their lives. The English disliked the Native Americans, whose lands they took over whenever possible. Nor did they get on well with the French or Spanish, bringing Old World hostilities with them into their New World.

---

[1]The *Mass* is the central act of Catholic worship.

The most influential of the English settlements was in Maryland. Maryland was chartered expressly to provide a place of refuge for persecuted Catholics. George and Cecil Calvert, the First and Second Lords Baltimore, both endorsed the principle of religious toleration. The Maryland Assembly passed an Act of Toleration in 1649 that extended religious toleration to all Christians who believed in God as Father, Son, and Holy Spirit. Baltimore, the first center of American Catholicism, was also the home of the illustrious Carroll family. Charles Carroll was the only Catholic signer of the Declaration of Independence. John Carroll became a Jesuit priest while studying in Europe and was later elected by his colleagues to be the first bishop in the United States (in November 1789). Daniel Carroll, John's brother and Charles's cousin, was one of two Catholics who helped draft the Constitution for the new United States.

Outside Maryland, the only places where Catholicism flourished during this period were Rhode Island and Pennsylvania. Chartered by Quaker (Society of Friends) William Penn, "Penn's Woods" was a haven from persecution for some Catholic faithful. Honoring the Friends' belief in an Inner Light of conscience within each person, Penn was not inclined to legislate religion for other Christians. The breadth of tolerance in Rhode Island was even greater; the charter negotiated by Roger Williams granted freedom of conscience to believers of whatever persuasion and nonbelievers alike.

Throughout the colonial period, as before, the number of Catholics remained small, less than one percent of the population. Most were English or Irish, but this was soon to change. Land acquired in the South and West added numbers of Spanish Catholics, and European immigrants would soon arrive in great waves.

About 8,000 immigrants arrived in 1820. A quarter of a century later, by 1846, that number had risen to a total of 90,000. The following year, famines and political upheaval that lasted for decades began in Europe. In all, between 1830 and the close of the nineteenth century, nearly 19 million immigrants arrived. During the next thirty years, almost that many more joined them. Between 1820 and 1850, the majority were Irish, followed by Germans and a few Russians (including immigrants from European Russia, Latvia, Finland, Estonia, and Lithuania) and Italians. In the decade of the 1850s, Germans and Irish came in roughly equal numbers, with fewer Italians and Russians. Then from 1861 to 1900, the German immigration greatly exceeded that of the Irish, and the numbers of Italians and Russians grew steadily. Between 1891 and 1900, the numbers of German, Russian, and Italian Catholic immigrants were roughly equal, and each outstripped the Irish 5 to 3.[2]

The growing presence of Irish and German clergy and laypeople increased diversity in a Church that had been dominated by the English and French. The Irish priests, especially, were different from their French counterparts. They ac-

---

[2]Compiled from data in Don Brophy and Edythe Westenhaver, *The Story of Catholics in America* (New York: Paulist Press, 1978), pp. 59, 64.

tively raised funds for and supervised the construction of new churches and schools to meet the needs of the growing Catholic population. As well, the Irish combined their religion with a degree of political involvement that enabled them to be a strong influence culturally as well as religiously.

The 1924 Immigration Act sharply reduced immigration until Congress removed the restrictive quota system in 1965. After 1965, a great influx of immigrants from Asian countries that were devastated by war, from the Philippine Islands, from Haiti, and from Mexico again swelled the ranks of immigrant American Catholics. Again the Catholic Church in America was faced with the two monumental tasks that have occupied it during much of its history: caring for the spiritual and oftentimes the physical, educational, and social needs of a vast immigrant membership, and integrating within itself the varying styles of religiousness brought to it by these immigrants. It is estimated, for example, that by the year 2000, 50 percent of all Catholics in the United States will be Hispanic Catholics.[3]

The influx of Spanish-speaking or Hispanic Catholics brings the story of Catholic immigration full circle, in at least two senses. The first Catholics to set foot on the shores of what would become the United States were Spanish Catholics. And, the growing number of Hispanic Catholics is changing the face of the Catholic Church in the United States and is reopening many questions that were a part of the picture of Catholicism in its early days in the nation.

Hispanic Catholics bring with them a warm and pietistic style of Catholicism, ways of being religious that are very much influenced by their Latin American roots. They have contributed greatly to the growth of the charismatic movement within Catholicism. Their sheer numbers have helped force the Church to deal with the charismatics in its midst. Their presence has raised other questions as well. Nationalistic tensions among the early Catholic immigrants—Italians, Germans, French, and Irish—were resolved. Many Hispanic Catholics want Spanish-language masses and Spanish-speaking priests to better serve their religious needs. Questions of Church leadership have arisen again as Hispanics move up the organizational ladder. The unemployment, poverty, lack of education, and discrimination faced by many of the Catholic Church's Hispanic members challenges their Church to help provide for the pressing needs of immigrants in a new land.

Along the way, and despite tremendous obstacles, the Church has grown, prospered, and become a central element in American life. The parish, or parochial, school system (described below) was developed and grew, providing quality education consistent with Catholic values for a multitude of children, most of whom were Catholic. Colleges and universities were established, many of which have attained national recognition as among the best in the nation. Seminaries for the training of an American priesthood were built. Hospitals, orphanages, and shelters for unwed mothers and abused women and children have

---

[3]"God Is Not Elected!" *NBC News Special Report*, September 1987.

been an outgrowth of the Catholic concern for the plight of the unfortunate in society. Social service agencies have contributed to the assistance of Catholic and non-Catholic alike, especially in urban areas. The American Church has met the needs of a growing number of Catholic people on a day-to-day basis. It provides centers for worship and community life, counsel in times of trouble and crisis, and celebrations for important life passages such as birth, marriage, and death.

American Catholics have had an impact on American culture, and they have been influenced by it. While the Catholic Church in America has been shaped by the environment in which it grew up, it has also shaped that environment. In the first place, Catholics have often led the rest of the culture in tolerance, in two ways. By their very presence, as a minority faith made up of many ethnic groups, American Catholics have kept the matter of tolerance before the American people and have made tolerance a necessity. Second, Catholics have consistently led the Protestant majority in religious, racial, and ethnic tolerance. Catholics have traditionally favored a strong role for government in meeting peoples' needs, from support for the New Deal and the Great Society to their lack of support for Reagan-Bush economics. They have supported the labor movement with leadership, money, and membership. A strong sense of the communal dimensions of society among Catholics has helped to shape this sense of things in the United States. Finally, Catholics in America have supported and continue to support the growing peace movement. More promilitary than Protestants before Vietnam, Catholics became more peace-oriented than their Protestant counterparts at that time and have remained so, a position highlighted by the U.S. Bishops' Pastoral Letter on Peace.[4]

The majority of people in the United States consider Catholics to be a part of consensus religion. Catholicism is not viewed as "out-of-the-ordinary" religion. This has not always been the case. The history of Catholics in America is in part a history of prejudice and discrimination. In some of the original thirteen colonies, Catholicism was illegal. In all of the colonies, there were times in which Catholics could neither vote nor hold public office.

Unorganized and informal anti-Catholic sentiment has existed in the United States for as long as Catholics have been here. An attitude of "America for Americans" has all too often meant America for *Protestant* Americans.[5] Non-Catholic Americans have often feared that, should Catholicism ever become dominant, religious liberty would be lost. This fear overlooks the constant and outspoken support that America's Catholic people, both lay and clergy, have given to the separation of church and state. Some people have also thought of Catholics as subjects of a foreign ruler (the Pope) and hence as less than fully loyal to the United States. This, too, overlooks the historical record. Protestant Americans, accustomed as they are to a style of worship that values words above

[4]George Gallup, Jr., and Jim Castelli, *The American Catholic People: Their Beliefs, Practices, and Values* (Garden City, NY: Doubleday and Company, 1987), pp. 188–91.
[5]Catholics have not been the only ones to encounter this attitude. It has also affected how Jews, Muslims, black Americans, Asian Americans, and other ethnic groups have been and are treated.

ceremony and ritual, have looked with suspicion, born of a lack of understanding, upon Catholicism's ornate ritual and have often regarded beliefs such as transubstantiation (to be discussed later) as "superstitious mumbo jumbo." Vigorous anti-Protestant sentiment on the part of some Catholic people, including leaders, at times, has compounded the problem of relationships between the two faiths.

This informal anti-Catholic sentiment has become organized into specific groups at various times throughout American history. The American Party, also known as the Know-Nothing Party, actively opposed Catholics in the 1800s. The American Protective Association formed in 1887. Although its stated goals were political rather than religious, its aim was said to be to change the minds and hearts of those who were in "the shackles and chains of blind obedience to the Roman Catholic Church." There was another outburst of organized activity in the first half of the 1900s. A resurgent Ku Klux Klan directed its energies as much against Catholics as against blacks and Jews.

It might seem as if anti-Catholic sentiment ended in the 1960s. John Fitzgerald Kennedy was elected President, albeit by a narrow margin. His conduct while in office and his charming ways greatly increased his popular support, and his tragic death by an assassin's bullet made him a national martyr. Meanwhile, Pope John XXIII, a man of presence and tact, with an openness that won the respect of many, had been elected to the highest office in the Church. Furthermore, he called together the Second Vatican Council and set about modernizing the Church, making changes that were seen as positive by those who were disturbed by Catholic "differentness."

Much of the prejudice against Catholic Americans today originates with Protestants who do not recognize Catholics as fellow members of the Christian community of faith. While not all fundamentalists hold this view, some do. Most bitter, perhaps, is the work of Tony and Susan Alamo's Christian Foundation, whose widespread circulation of anti-Catholic pamphlets in the 1980s drew national attention to the group. Television evangelist Jimmy Swaggart has offended many, non-Catholic and Catholic alike, by his outspoken attempts to convert Catholics from "superstition and manmade religion" to Christianity.

Many Americans are also critical of the Catholic Church's stand on issues such as abortion, the use of artificial birth control, and the role of women in the Church. It must be pointed out here that this criticism comes not only from non-Catholics but from within the ranks of Catholic Americans as well.

BELIEFS AND PRACTICES OF CATHOLIC PEOPLE

Any discussion of contemporary Catholic belief and practice must begin with the Second Vatican Council (Vatican II) that was convened by Pope John XXIII between 1962 and 1965. Pope John called the council together to review policy and practice for the Catholic Church worldwide. His specific aim, as he described it, was to update the Church. Vatican II made sweeping changes in all areas of Church life. Bishops were given a greater role in Church government, and laypeople were given greater responsibility for parish life and worship. The primary importance of the Bible was affirmed. The Church pledged its support for ecumenism and explicitly recognized Protestants as true Christians. It also recognized the presence of limited truth in non-Christian faiths. It permitted the celebration of the Mass in the common language of the people, with the priest facing the congregation more of the time and the role of laypeople increased and expanded. It changed the understanding of some of the sacraments. It affirmed the right of conscience and freedom from civil coercion in religious matters. The *Index*, an official list of books that Catholics were forbidden to read, was done away with. The changes that Vatican II brought about have made many once-sharp differences between Catholics and other Christians into differences of emphasis only. However, there are still aspects of the faith that are uniquely Catholic, and it is these that will occupy us in this section.

Beliefs

There are unique beliefs and emphases within Catholicism that set it apart from other forms of Christianity. One of these is the **teaching authority of the Church**. Catholics, although they regard the Bible as the original revelation, also teach that the tradition of the Church is equal with it in authority. They believe that the Church is the official interpreter of the Bible. Tradition and Scripture together are accorded the same respect and veneration. The writings of the Church Fathers, the decisions of Church councils, and the pronouncements of the Popes from Peter onward are all regarded as genuine sources of religious truth and as a part of the whole revelation of God to the Church. The Second Vatican Council placed greater emphasis on the Bible. For example, it said that the Liturgy of the Word, in which the Bible is read, is not just preparation for the Liturgy of the Eucharist in the Mass but is an integral part of a single act of worship. It also urged people to seek renewed spiritual vitality through increasing attention to the Word of God in the Bible, as well as through continued participation in the Eucharist. The sharing of authority between the Bible and the Church and the Church's role as the official interpreter of the Bible are unique to Catholic belief.

The doctrine of **papal infallibility** is unique to the Catholic Church. Many non-Catholic people misunderstand this teaching of the Church. It does not mean that the Pope never makes a mistake or never sins. In reality, this doctrine applies in only a very few circumstances. When the Pope speaks officially on matters of faith and morals to which Catholics are required to give their assent, it is believed that God prevents him from making errors. The principal biblical support for this belief comes from a passage in the Gospel of Saint Matthew. In these verses, Jesus is speaking to one of the apostles:

You are Peter, and on this rock I will build my church, and the powers of death shall not prevail against it. I will give you the keys of the kingdom of Heaven; and whatever you bind on earth shall be bound in heaven, and whatever you loose on earth shall be loosed in heaven (Matthew 16:17–19).

Catholics also believe that authority in the Church has come down in a direct line from Peter, and hence from Christ himself. This view is called **apostolic succession**.

According to Catholic teaching, **the Catholic Church is the one true Church**. Although Vatican II opened up the Church's attitude toward non-Catholic Christians, Catholics still believe that people find the fullness of religious truth and salvation only within Catholicism. The Catholic Church teaches that its leaders are the only ones whose authority comes in an unbroken line from Jesus himself and that it is the only Church that teaches everything taught by Jesus. Catholics believe that their Church is a community of the faithful (as do Protestants), but they place more emphasis on the Church as a visible institution with a hierarchical leadership.

The Catholic Church shares with Protestants the belief that **salvation comes to people by the grace of God**. However, a great deal more emphasis is placed on the role of the Church as the official agent and mediator of God's grace. The Church mediates by its official teaching and interpretation of the Bible, and it mediates through its administration of the sacraments. The sacraments as administered by the Church are believed to be channels through which the grace of God flows to people.

There are other mediators as well. Any discussion of Catholic belief and practice would be incomplete if the Catholic **devotion to Mary**, the mother of Jesus, **and to the other saints** were not mentioned. Unlike Jesus, who, the Church teaches, was both divine and human, the saints and Mary were fully human and no more while alive on Earth. A good deal of Catholic private devotion centers on these figures, who are in a sense "closer" to the believer because of having shared their human condition without benefit of simultaneous divinity. Catholics teach that Mary and the other saints pray to God on the believers' behalf and watch over the needs and concerns of the faithful. As the author of a recent study of Catholic women stated,

> For Catholics, . . . Mary the mother of Jesus has been the feminine face of God. To be sure, Mary is not God, according to orthodox Christian theology. . . . Nevertheless, people pray to Mary. She may not be God in their spoken creed, but in the language of the heart, she functions as God.[6]

Catholics believe with other Christians that the faithful will have life after physical death. Catholics also believe in **purgatory**, which is believed to be **a place**

---

[6]Jane Redmont, *Generous Lives: American Catholic Women Today* (Liguori, MO: Triumph Books, 1992), p. 102.

or condition of further purification after death in which some must exist before they attain the beatific vision of God. This doctrine, rejected by Protestant and Eastern Orthodox Christians, is unique to Catholicism. Upon death, individuals without any taint of sin may enter Heaven directly. However, few people are this pure. In purgatory, people make amends for less serious sins that were not forgiven or for more serious sins that had been forgiven prior to death. Freed from guilt and punishment, the soul can enter into heaven, not only beholding God directly but being of the same mind and heart with God. The justice of God that requires that sin be punished, and the mercy of God that seeks the salvation of all, are thus reconciled. The doctrine of purgatory also provides a means by which the living may assist the souls of the dead through prayers and good works, since it is taught that such prayers and works may shorten the length of time a soul spends in purgatory. In this way, the belief in purgatory can help those who grieve for a loved one to work out their grief. It is important to note here that Catholics believe that God is an infinitely loving parent who will not reject anyone who does not reject God. God creates people with free will and the freedom to sin or to obey, and God goes to great lengths to see to it that disobedience does not result in condemnation unless there are no other alternatives.

Lifestyle

What differences does being Catholic make in peoples' everyday lifestyles? In the two small midwestern towns in which I grew up, it was very clear—or at least, most people thought it was very clear—who the Catholics were. They were the ones with the big families, the blue-collar workers who kept the mills and factories running. They went to church a lot and ate fish on Fridays. They were mostly immigrants, or the children or grandchildren of immigrants, and they were inclined to be clannish, sticking together in a way that made the non-Catholic outsiders feel uncomfortable. Whatever truth there might have been in that portrait of Catholics has long since become a stereotype. **In most ways, Catholics are very much like other Americans.** We have seen that they are somewhat more inclined to be tolerant of racial, ethnic, and religious differences. They are somewhat less likely than their Protestant neighbors to condemn people whose moral standards differ from theirs. They are also more likely to uphold the civil liberties of atheists. In part because Catholics have been persecuted, they are less likely to inflict the same burden on other people.

Catholics are at least as well educated as other Americans are, and there are no significant differences in family income between Catholics and non-Catholics. They are married, separated, divorced, and widowed in approximately the same proportions as the population in general. No longer overrepresented in blue-collar jobs, they make significant contributions in every occupational field. They attend worship at about the same rate as do their Protestant neighbors. Members of the consensus religions usually do not stand out from their friends and neighbors, and most Catholics fit this description.

A key feature of life for some Catholic youngsters is that they attend **parochial schools** sponsored by their Church. Parochial schools provide education within the context of Catholic values. Education about their faith and regular participation in Mass are included in their school experience. So is learning about religions other than Catholicism. They may be taught by nuns or brothers or by lay teachers. A flourishing parochial school is a focal point of the parish and a center for its social life.

Fewer Catholic youngsters attend parochial schools now than in the past, a part of the loss of distinctiveness of Catholic life in the United States. Slightly over one-fourth of Catholic elementary and middle school children and under one-fifth of Catholic high school students attend parochial schools. Among Catholic college students, only 10 percent attend colleges sponsored by their Church.[7]

The Catholic Church supports many colleges and universities in the United States. These schools provide Catholic and non-Catholic students alike a quality education in the setting of Catholic moral and religious values. The Church also supports Newman Centers on other college and university campuses. Newman Centers provide a religious and social meeting place for Catholic students.

The Catholic Church has always been strong in its support for charity, and that support continues, benefiting Catholic and non-Catholic, Christian and non-Christian alike, through hospitals, social service agencies, and other channels by means of which help reaches the entire community.

Religion is important to most Catholics, and even though they may disagree with their Church on certain issues, they remain very loyal to it. While picking and choosing which of the Church's teachings they will follow, they still consider themselves "good Catholics," and for most, their fundamental commitments do not waiver.

Worship

Catholic worship in the United States is more distinctive than Catholic lifestyle. The central act of Catholic worship is called the **Mass**. The Mass is an integrated experience of worship that is made up of two parts that work together (Figure 5–1). The **Liturgy of the Word** includes those parts of the Mass that focus on verbal communication, such as Bible readings, prayers, responsive readings, and a sermon, often called a *homily* by Catholics. The Bible readings always include a reading from one of the four Gospels and another reading from either the New Testament or the Old Testament. The **Liturgy of the Eucharist** reenacts, in words and actions, Jesus' sharing bread and wine with the disciples at the Last Supper. Catholic worship is highly liturgical, with ornate symbolism; the use of incense

---

[7]Dean R. Hoge, "Catholics in the U.S.: The Next Generation," in *The Public Perspective: A Roper Center Review of Public Opinion and Polling*, 2, no.1 (November/December 1990), p. 11.

and chanting, symbolic colors, and vestments worn by the priest; and an air of high solemnity. Since the Second Vatican Council, many Catholic Churches have experimented with more casual Masses that often include folk songs and liturgical dance, but the twin elements of the Liturgy of the Word and the Liturgy of the Eucharist are always present.

Figure 5–1

THE ORDER OF THE MASS*

Introductory Rite

Entrance Song
Greeting
Rite of Blessing and Sprinkling of Holy Water
Penitential Rite
Acclamations, including Kyrie
Gloria
Opening Prayer

Liturgy of the Word

Initial Songs and Responses
Old Testament Reading
Responsorial Psalm
New Testament Reading
Gospel Acclamation
The Reading of the Gospel
Homily
Profession of Faith

Liturgy of the Eucharist

Preparation of the Gifts
Eucharistic Prayer
Preface Acclamation
Memorial Acclamation
Communion Rite
Lord's Prayer
Rite of Peace
Breaking of Bread
Communion Song
Prayer after Communion

Concluding Rite

Blessing
Dismissal

*There are some variations, but this is a typical order of service for the Mass.

The Catholic Church has **seven sacraments.** Catholics believe that participation in the sacraments changes people inwardly, as a result of the special grace conveyed by the sacraments. The first sacrament that Catholics participate in is **baptism.** Catholics believe that baptism is necessary for the removal of the inborn sin that is a part of all persons simply because they are human. Most Catholics are baptized when they are babies. When the sacrament is performed for an adult, it is often called the Rite of Christian Initiation, a name that points to its other function as the ritual of incorporation into the Church. The sacrament of **confirmation** completes what is begun in baptism. It signifies that the person has become an adult in the eyes of the Church and confirms the promises made by others at baptism. The one who is being confirmed is touched on the forehead with oil that has been blessed to signify the seal of the Holy Spirit. This sacrament is believed to give the grace necessary to live a mature Christian life in the Church.

Catholics believe that in the sacrament of the **Eucharist**, the bread and wine actually become the body and blood of Jesus Christ when the priest speaks the words of consecration ("This is my body. . . . This is my blood"—words that the Gospel records Jesus as saying to his disciples at the Last Supper). This belief in **transubstantiation** is based on a philosophical distinction between what something actually is (its substance) and what it appears to be. In transubstantiation, the substance of the bread and wine become the body and blood of Christ, who is fully present under the appearances of bread and wine. This sacrament, received often throughout a Catholic's life, is ordinarily received at Mass, but it may also be received privately when circumstances such as illness call for doing so.

Another sacrament that nourishes Catholics spiritually throughout their lives is the sacrament of **reconciliation, or confession.** Formerly, confession was made with the person seeking forgiveness kneeling in one side of a small cubicle, with the priest in the other side, and a screened window in between so that priest and penitent did not see each other. Since Vatican II, various other forms of reconciliation are also used, including congregational confessions of sin and priest and parishioner talking together face to face. Penitents confess their sins to God through the priest who, in the name of God and with the authority of the Church, pronounces forgiveness. Special prayers or other activities may be assigned to assist people in recovering from the effects of their sins. Catholics are expected to confess through a priest at least annually, but many find that the practice helps them be aware of God's forgiving grace, and confess more frequently. Non-Catholics often stereotype Catholics by saying that Catholics can confess to a priest and then go out and sin all over again. It needs to be noted here that the rite of reconciliation must be accompanied by genuine sorrow for having sinned and by true intention to avoid it in the future. The Second Vatican Council revised the Church's understanding of this sacrament somewhat, lessening the emphasis given to the penance performed and emphasizing the rite as one of *recon-*

ciliation, which is the spiritual reuniting of the penitent with God, other persons, and the Church.

A fifth sacrament is now commonly known as the sacrament of **anointing the sick;** formerly, it was called extreme unction or, simply, the last rites. This sacrament, in which a priest uses oil to anoint a person who is ill or in danger of dying from accident or old age, is a way of mediating the concern of Christ and the Church for the suffering person. Catholics believe that the sacrament gives grace for healing, if that is God's will, or to assist a person in the passage from life to death and beyond if that is to be the final outcome. The understanding of this rite was broadened by Vatican II to include its use for those who are seriously ill but not in immediate danger of death.

The sacrament of **marriage** is one to which most Catholics look forward. The majority of Catholics, as well as the majority of all Americans, marry at some time in their lives. Although the stereotype of Catholics having larger-than-average families no longer holds true, marriage and family continue to be very important, and this is reflected in marriage being a sacrament. Blessed by a priest, authorized by the Church, and entered into only after a period of required counseling, Catholics believe that the sacrament of marriage gives the couple the special grace necessary to carry out the promises they make to each other. Because marriage is a sacrament, in which two people are believed to be joined by God, the Catholic Church teaches that it is a lifelong commitment. The Church does not recognize divorce and teaches that persons who divorce and remarry are living in sin and are barred from receiving the sacraments. There is a process through which a couple can obtain an annulment of their marriage. If an annulment is granted, it is as if the marriage had never happened. People whose marriages have been annulled can remarry in the Church. Because the marriage bond is sacred, however, such annulments are difficult to obtain. Statistical data indicate that, in actual practice, American Catholics divorce and remarry in about the same proportions as do non-Catholics. In this matter, American Catholics are influenced more by the culture of which they are a part than they are by the teachings of their Church.

The sacrament of orders, or **ordination to the priesthood,** sets a man apart for the official sacramental ministry of the Church. Catholics believe that it gives the priest the grace required to carry out the demands of his priesthood. Only men are ordained to the priesthood.

In addition to these seven sacraments, the Church celebrates many days such as Easter and Christmas with special liturgies. Lent and Advent[8] have their own observances. There are days dedicated to specific saints. There are days that commemorate the Immaculate Conception of Mary, Jesus' Mother (the Church teaches that Mary was conceived without sin), and the Assumption (the Church teaches that Mary's body was taken up into Heaven immediately upon her death). Many Catholic people also take part in a variety of private devotional ac-

---

[8]*Advent* is a time of anticipation prior to Christmas.

Figure 5–2 The Pope is the leader of worldwide Catholicism. (*Bettmann*)

tivities, such as praying the rosary, other prayers, reading the Bible, and praying and lighting candles on behalf of those who are ill or have some other need.

Organization

The Catholic Church is hierarchical in its organization. The **Pope** is the worldwide leader and is revered by Catholics as the **Vicar**[9] **of Christ on Earth**. He is also **Bishop of Rome** (Figure 5–2). The Pope is assisted by the College of Cardinals and by the Roman Curia. The College of Cardinals advises the Pope and is responsible for electing a new Pope upon the death of the previous one. The Curia has a more administrative function. Archbishops and bishops are appointed by the Pope, taking into account the recommendations of local leaders. Archbishops are in charge of large geographical or population units and bishops have authority over smaller areas. Local priests have jurisdiction to the extent that it is delegated to them by their bishops. In the Catholic Church in America, local councils of priests and bishops meet in an advisory capacity, and lay parish councils in the local church advise the priest and serve as a link between the ordained leadership and the laypeople who make up the broad base of the organizational pyramid.

The Catholic Church has many male monastic orders and many orders of nuns for women. Nuns and monks serve as full-time religious workers in parochial schools, in Church-sponsored hospitals and other agencies, as teachers

[9] *Vicar* means "official representative."

in Catholic colleges and universities, and in a variety of other tasks. Much of the outreach work of the Church is done by these dedicated men and women who, while not priests,[10] have a ministry that is of equal importance in the life of the Church. Like priests, nuns and monks take vows of poverty, celibacy, and obedience to Christ in the Church. The requirement that priests remain unmarried is an important part of Catholic practice. Although this practice has not always been a part of the Church's teaching, and its historical development is somewhat confusing, its present-day practice seems to have two main functions: The priest is understood to be in the likeness of Christ, and, as far as we can know from the biblical accounts, Jesus never married. Not having the responsibility for a family also frees the priest to devote his full attention to his priesthood.

There are many laymen and laywomen who work professionally in Catholic churches, as well. They often have seminary training, as do the ordained. They serve as chaplains in hospitals, schools, and prisons; as parish outreach workers; as counselors; as teachers of theology in colleges and seminaries; and as leaders of retreat centers and other organizations.

THE CATHOLIC CHURCH IN THE UNITED STATES: TRADITION AND ADAPTATION

The situation in which the American Church found itself—pluralism, disestablishment, and freedom of religion in a democratic state—differed greatly from that which had prevailed throughout most of its worldwide history. This led directly to a process that has been called *inculturation*. Inculturation, according to one Catholic author, is "the process of deep, sympathetic adaptation and appropriation of a local cultural setting in which the Church finds itself in a way that does not compromise its basic faith in Christ."[11] Inculturation, then, is something the Catholic Church has done worldwide. In the United States, it has taken place almost from the beginning of the Church's presence here. However, in the United states, this process has more often than not brought the American Catholic Church into conflict with Rome.

The early conflict between the those who favored inculturation—also called *Americanization*—and those who did not had to do with how the Catholic Church was to operate as one voluntary society among others in a pluralistic state. There was a group of thoughtful clergy and laity who believed that America afforded the Church the greatest opportunity to make the transition into the modern world. Others saw the Church's American experience as a threat to its very being. This issue still vexes the Catholic Church in America in the closing decade of the twentieth century.

Nor is it simply a conflict between the "American Church" and "Rome."

---

[10]Some monks are also priests.

[11]William Reiser, "Inculturation and Doctrinal Development," *Heythrop Journal*, no. 22 (1981), p. 135.

Although the Catholic Church in the United States is predominantly under the influence and control of those who favor Americanization, there is a contingent of people, both lay and clerical, who disagree. They believe that the route taken by the Church in the United States has in fact "compromised its basic faith in Christ." Catholic sociologist Joseph A. Varacalli describes it this way: the Americanizers are "attempting (quite successfully) to incorporate secularism into the Church with contemporary anti-Americanizers trying to uphold the autonomy of the Catholic tradition and the unchanging foundational principles of the Faith. . . . The vast majority of American Catholics . . . are a scattered flock presently being highjacked by various secular ideologies and commitments."[12]

The differences between the American Church and the hierarchy in Rome (as well as within the American Church) were drawn sharply in 1994 with the publication of Pope John Paul II's encyclical, "Evangelium Vitae," or "Gospel of Life." In it, the Pope calls on the full teaching authority of the Church, making its teachings binding on all Catholics, without declaring them infallible. He deplores a growing "culture of death," marked by support for abortion rights, euthanasia, capital punishment, and the use of human embryos for medical research. The encyclical also restates the Church's opposition to the use of artificial birth control. Over half of the nearly 200-page document addresses an alternative "culture of life," in which human life is affirmed from conception through death.

Current controversies in the Church center on three sets of issues: one having to do with family life, one concerning the priesthood, and the last having to do with the Church's authority over its members. We shall consider each in turn.

Regarding **family life issues**, most American Catholics differ little or not at all from their non-Catholic counterparts. They are, in other words, at least as American as they are Catholic. Abortion and the use of artificial birth control are both against the teachings of the Church. The ban on the use of artificial birth control is, according to one study, the "subject on which there is the greatest disagreement" between the people and the Church. Among American Catholics under fifty years of age, about 80 percent favor the use of artificial birth control for family planning. Many Catholic couples quietly use it, and many parish priests support their doing so, either explicitly or by encouraging them to follow their own conscience.[13] Nor is there a significant difference between the extent to which Catholic and non-Catholic Americans favor making birth control available to teens aged fourteen to sixteen even if their parents disapprove.

The Catholic Church has consistently upheld its ban on abortion for any reason. There is, however, little difference between the attitudes of Catholics and non-Catholics in the United States on the abortion question. A substantial majority of Catholics and non-Catholics alike support legal abortion when there is a strong chance of a serious fetal defect, when the mother's health is in danger,

---

[12]Joseph A. Varacalli, *The Catholic and Politics in Post–World War II America: A Sociological Analysis* (Garden City, NY: Society of Catholic Social Scientists, 1995), pp. 9–10 and 45–46.

[13]Gallup and Castelli, *The American Catholic People*, pp. 50–51.

or if the pregnancy resulted from rape or incest. While fewer support legal abortion for any reason that a woman wants it, there is no significant difference in degree of support between Catholics and non-Catholics.

The Church also teaches that sex outside marriage is wrong. Again, analysis clearly demonstrates that there is not much difference between Catholics and their non-Catholic counterparts on this issue. Catholic and non-Catholic attitudes toward premarital sex (most approve) and extramarital sex (a strong majority disapproves) are very similar.

Homosexual activity is also against the teaching of the Catholic Church. However, survey results indicate that no significant differences exist between Catholics and non-Catholics regarding homosexual activity. Gay and lesbian Catholics and their supporters founded "Dignity," an organization that acts as a support group and advocate for them in the Church. Its existence is not officially recognized, although some parish priests permit members to meet in the parish hall.

Attitudes about the proper approach to AIDS education for young people are an instructive and specific example of sexual morality attitudes. Despite their Church's teaching of sexual abstinence outside of marriage and for all homosexual people, Catholics are more likely than Protestants to favor teaching "safe sex" over "abstinence."[14]

Overall, there are only slight differences between Protestant and Catholic people in the United States concerning matters of sexual morality. The differences that do exist indicate that Catholics are somewhat more in favor of individual freedom in sexual matters than are Protestants. Catholics in the United States also want their Church to adopt a more flexible stance on matters of sexual morality.[15]

Another area of widespread disagreement is the Church's treatment of its separated and divorced members. Official Church annulments are time-consuming, expensive, and difficult to obtain. Divorce and remarriage are against the official teaching of the Church. However, an increasing percentage of American Catholics say they believe that a divorced Catholic should be permitted to remarry in the Church and continue to receive the sacraments. Meanwhile, amid all the disagreement, priests quietly give the Eucharist to divorced and remarried people and calmly overlook premarital and homosexual sex in their congregations, believing that decisions about such matters are not subject to official Church control.

Catholics are not satisfied with how their Church deals with single people and with its divorced, separated, and remarried members. Fully two-thirds of

[14] *The Gallup Poll Monthly*, no. 314 (November 1991), p.4. The figures are 49 percent of Protestants favoring safe sex and 46 percent favoring abstinence, whereas 60 percent of Catholics favor safe sex and 37 percent favor abstinence.

[15] George Gallup, Jr., and Sarah Jones, *100 Questions and Answers: Religion in America* (Princeton, NJ: Princeton Religious Research Center, 1989), pp. 126–27.

Catholics disapprove of how the Church deals with these members. Three-fifths believe that the Church system of marriage annulment needs to be reworked.[16]

A second category of issues concerns the **priesthood**. There are two major questions here: whether or not priests should be permitted to marry and whether or not women ought to be ordained to the priesthood. The Church's official position on both issues has been stated strongly many times: There will be no married priests, and there will be no female priests. There has been a steady increase in support for permitting priests to marry. Support for female priests, while not as strong, has increased steadily also. Between one-half and three-fourths of Catholics favor the ordination of both women and married people. The strongest support comes from Catholic men, and those who are younger, more highly educated, and have higher incomes.[17]

The third issue concerns the **authority** the Church has, or does not have, over the lives and beliefs of its members. It is clear that Catholics see their Church as an institution having legitimate authority on matters of faith and morals in a way that Protestants do not. It is equally clear that Catholics would like to see the Church come closer to the realities of American life in many instances. Its authority is relative in a way that it was not even a quarter of a century ago. There is a strong commitment to the Pope and to his teachings, but on terms that are much more individualized and flexible. Over 90 percent of American Catholics say they can disagree with the Pope and still consider themselves good Catholics, and nearly half feel that the Pope is out of touch with American Catholics. Over three-fourths feel free to make their own decisions about moral issues. Only slightly over one-third believe that the Pope is infallible in his moral teachings. Slightly over half believe that he is infallible on matters of faith.[18] In other words, American Catholics respect the Pope and his teachings. But they accept these teachings only when they make sense in terms of their own lives and are in accord with their own consciences. If they must choose between one and the other, they will probably follow their own consciences.

Catholics want to see the leadership of their Church remain in the hands of the ordained hierarchy—bishops, priests, and permanent deacons. They also support strong lay involvement. Over 70 percent believe there should be greater lay input in parish decision making and would like for their parishes to employ lay marriage and personal counselors. Nearly that number supports the hiring of full-time lay religious educators and liturgists. Over half believe that parishes should play a larger role in selecting their own priests and that full-time lay parish administrators are a good idea. In other words, American Catholics want more lay leadership and more input into their churches, but they do not want their churches to become Protestant.[19]

---

[16]Gallup and Jones, *100 Questions and Answers*, p. 88.
[17]Gallup and Jones, *100 Questions and Answers*, pp. 90–91.
[18]"John Paul's Feisty Flock," *Time*, September 7, 1987, pp. 46–48.
[19]Gallup and Castelli, *The American Catholic People*, pp. 56–57.

There is a severe shortage of priests in U.S. Catholic churches. This shortage is forcing churches to rely on laypeople to perform functions formerly reserved for priests only. Many believe that even if the shortage of priests were resolved, there can be no going back. The practical problem of providing for parishes without priests has opened up a vision of lay involvement in Catholicism.

The traditionalists worried early on that Catholic University might become a center of advocacy for change in the Church. In some measure, that early fear came true in the 1980s. American teachers of theology have been critical of the Church's views. Father Charles Curran, a theologian at Catholic University, was relieved of his teaching duties for not teaching a strict interpretation of the Church's position on certain issues. The Church claims it has a right to expect doctrinal allegiance from those who teach. The Board of the Catholic Theological Society of America says that silencing doctrinal dissent destroys the academic legitimacy of theology, which has to be able to function in the rough-and-tumble of free inquiry if it is to be viable.

Teachers are concerned that such limitations violate the standards of academic freedom common in the United States. The Vatican response to this American test case was to issue tighter restrictions, giving bishops added power to watch over the orthodoxy of theologians at the more than 200 Catholic colleges and universities in the United States.[20]

What is ahead for the Catholic Church in the United States? Sociologist Dean R. Hoge sums it up well:

> The future will see pressure on the institutional Church from an educated laity who have come to think for themselves. They will ask for more lay participation, more open debate about moral teachings on sexual topics, and more accountability of leaders to followers. The overall result will be a gradual movement in the direction of convergence with Protestant-permeated middle-class culture.[21]

Sociologist and Catholic priest Andrew M. Greeley's analysis of survey data tends to support a similar conclusion. Greeley looked at demographic characteristics of Catholics whose answers indicate that they support the official teachings of their Church, as defined by the hierarchy. He found that these people are considerably older and less educated than the majority of Catholics in the United States. Thus, their influence can reasonably be expected to wane as time goes by. He concludes,

> The "conservatives" are not winning. They have been reduced in the Catholic population . . . to a segment that is both aging and fundamentally at odds with mainstream America and mainstream Catholic America. . . . [They have] little impact on the life of the typical U.S. Catholic.[22]

[20]"John Paul's Feisty Flock," p. 51.
[21]Hoge, "Catholics in the U.S.," p. 12.
[22]Andrew M. Greeley, "Who Are the Catholic 'Conservatives'?" *America*, 165, no. 7 (September 21, 1991), p. 161.

WOMEN AND THE CATHOLIC CHURCH

The Catholic Church's attitude toward women has always been complex. Mary, as the mother of Jesus, has been given great respect and honor and is looked upon as the first among women. Her status comes from her motherhood. She fulfilled in a very special way the role traditionally held up as the most important one for women. Traditional Catholic teaching also emphasizes Eve, the temptress, as the key figure in the drama of original sin and the human fall from grace, partially offsetting the effect of the veneration of Mary.

Catholic orders of nuns are another example of this complexity. These orders were the first institutional opportunity for the involvement of women in religion in America. They provided a setting in which women could carry out specific duties within the context of a close-knit community of women. Especially for those who did not have the desire or the opportunity to marry, these orders were a means to security and respectability. Negatively, the female orders were closely governed by male superiors in the Church and had little, if any, autonomy in their early years.

In the nineteenth century, many nuns taught in public and private schools, as well as in parochial schools. Others worked as nurses in hospitals and other institutions, and in private homes. They served heroically as nurses during the Civil and Spanish-American Wars. They played a major role in overcoming American suspicion and hostility toward Catholicism and Catholic people because of their dedicated work in these areas.[23]

During the nineteenth century, nuns in America sought ways to adapt to democracy. They often broke with their European motherhouses (the American nuns were branches of European orders and responsible to them) in order to adopt regulations that were better suited to their new environment.[24] They also founded American orders. **Mother Elizabeth Bayley Seton** was the first American to be officially declared a saint by the Roman Catholic Church. Seton established the **Sisters of Charity**, the first religious order founded in the United States, in 1809. She is also remembered as the founder of the Catholic parochial school system.

In the twentieth century, nuns have demonstrated continued commitment and service in the areas of nursing, education, and social work. They have also broadened their participation in the cause of international peace and in addressing the plight of the Third World nations. They are in the forefront of a more general Catholic concern for personal spiritual formation, developing and practicing new ways of personal and community devotion that are compatible with life in the modern era.

The twentieth century will be remembered in the Catholic Church as a

[23]Mary Ewens, "The Leadership of Nuns in Immigrant Catholicism," in *Women and Religion in America, Volume I: The Nineteenth Century*, ed Rosemary Radford Ruether and Rosemary Skinner Keller, (San Francisco: Harper & Row, Publishers, 1981), pp. 101–102.

[24]Ewens, "The Leadership of Nuns," p. 105.

time of confrontation between the age-old traditions of the Church and American Catholics. Many of these conflicts have to do with issues of special concern to women. Both Catholic female religious and laywomen have challenged the Church leaders and the Church's historic views on women. For many women who are both Catholics and feminists, the response from the Catholic Church has been too little and too slow.

The Second Vatican Council brought about new opportunities for nuns. It permitted greater self-government in religious orders. It allowed nuns to increase their contact with the world outside their convents. They no longer had to live in communities with groups of nuns, but could live much more on their own in the society. They could find employment in agencies that were not related to the Church. They began attending graduate schools in significant numbers and went on to teach in colleges, universities, and seminaries. In many orders, being a nun no longer meant wearing the distinctive clothing that set them apart from other women in the population.

There are other issues of concern to American Catholic women. In general, many Catholic feminists see their Church as unresponsive to their complaints that its teachings limit women to the roles of wives and mothers or nuns. The Catholic Church has been a strong source of support for women remaining at home with their children. One example of this was Pope John Paul II's recommendation of a family wage. He defined this as "a single salary given to the head of the family for his work, sufficient for the needs of the family without the spouse having to take up gainful employment outside the home."[25] Although the gender-neutral word *spouse* is used to refer to the person who remains at home, the use of the pronoun *his* angered feminists. They heard in it the implication that the head of the household was the husband and that working outside the home was expected only of him.

A cluster of reproductive issues has been at the forefront of much of the discussion about the Catholic Church's attitude toward women. The U.S. Catholic Conference (USCC), the official Washington lobby of U.S. Catholic bishops, has consistently worked to have abortion and abortion funding banned. It has voted to work to eliminate clinics that make contraceptive information available in public high schools. The Church continues to restate its well-known teaching that the use of artificial birth control is sinful. The Church teaches that the natural result of sexual intercourse is the procreation of children, and that any method of contraception that interferes with this end is against the laws of God and the Church. The Church also teaches that the fetus has a soul and is a human being from the moment of conception. Therefore, abortion is murder. Feminists see the Church's position on all these issues as a violation of women's rights to control over their own bodies.

Many women view traditional Catholic teaching about marriage and divorce as yet another unwarranted intrusion of the Church into areas that are best

---

[25]Mary Jean Collins, "A Public Policy Analysis of the Pastoral," *Conscience*, IX, no. 3 (May/June 1988), p. 11.

left up to individual morality. The Church's teachings limit women's (and men's) options to lifelong marriage or celibacy. The presence and at least partial acceptance of other options in the larger culture has caused many Catholics to question and sometimes openly challenge their Church's official teachings.

Another set of particularly troublesome issues centers on the priesthood. As it is now, only men can be ordained priests. Many women are particularly distressed that full priesthood is denied to them. The Second Vatican Council did not prohibit women from engaging in many important lay ministries such as assisting with the Eucharist and reading the Bible during Mass. As a result, many, if not most, Catholic churches in the United States permit this. Girls as well as boys can now be altar servers. In most instances, any lay position available to men is now also available to women. Progress? Yes, say the women who want full ordination as priests in the Church. But not enough. For many, the only way for their Church to make good on its pronouncements about the equality and full personhood of all people is to grant women full ordination to the priesthood and accept women as equals for ordination to the higher ranks of bishop, archbishop, and cardinal. According to these women, the necessary changes will not have been made until it is possible for a woman to be elected Pope.

Many Catholic women also think that the ordination of women would help to solve the severe shortage of priests that the Church faces. Fewer and fewer men have entered the priesthood in recent years, leading to shortages that are nearing crisis proportions. These women claim that the Church can ill afford not to use the additional resource that their ordination would make available. Often, people who urge the ordination of women also urge that priests be allowed to marry, another move that many feel would help to increase the number of candidates for ordination.

For some Catholic women, the quest for ordination has transformed into a quest for an entirely new approach to worship and liturgy, one that does away with the need for priests altogether. The *Woman-Church* movement understands all Christians to be engaged in equal ministry to each other, with no hierarchy. While it is difficult to say exactly how many women are involved, such communities are being formed nationwide, and national Woman-Church conferences draw thousands of attenders.[26]

Current official Catholic teaching can be summarized this way: The Church clearly approves of efforts to assure the equal rights of all persons. Many Vatican documents emphasize this and repeatedly recognize the importance of the changes that are occurring in women's roles. However, this must be qualified by these same documents' repeated references to women's nature. This nature is clearly different from that of men, since it is defined by "the woman's childbearing function in procreation which in turn dictates her primary and indispensable role in nurturing children."[27]

[26]Rose Solari, "In Her Own Image," *Common Boundary*, July/August 1995, pp. 18–27.
[27]Nadine Foley, "Women in Vatican Documents 1960–Present," in *Sexism and Church Law: Equal Rights and Affirmative Action*, ed. James A. Coriden (New York: Paulist Press, 1977), pp. 83–98.

A Catholic nun writes poignantly of her disillusionment, and that of other Catholic women, at the time of Pope John Paul II's historic visit to the United States. After remarking on the still-strong symbolic role of the Pope, she says:

> We saw this ground-kissing, baby-hugging pope, surrounded by a retinue of men, singing and joking with students, bantering with seminarians, meeting farmers in Iowa, but not once engaged in serious conversation with Catholic women. We learned that the Leadership Conference of Women Religious had tried to arrange an audience with the pope and had failed, and that it was the pope's own wish that none of the eucharistic ministers who served communion at the papal masses be women. . . . The problem was not that this pope said anything different from the popes before him; it was just that we expected more.[28]

The Church's position on these issues is not likely to change in the foreseeable future. Someone once remarked that people would know that the Catholic Church had made progress when bishops were permitted to bring their wives to Church conferences. They would know that even more progress had occurred when bishops brought their husbands to these conferences.

All in all, it would seem that the Pope's stated goals of "discipline, order, commitment, and obedience" for the Catholic Church will not meet with easy acceptance in the United States. On the other hand, it must be noted that American Catholics, as they have always been, are loyal to their Church. They are a people of two clear loyalties: to their nation and to their Church. Neither has wavered over the course of Catholic presence in America.

We have seen that American Catholics share a great deal with Catholics around the world, as members of the one Catholic Church. They are also unique, and, in many ways, this uniqueness has come about as a direct result of the conditions under which American Catholicism has developed.

QUESTIONS AND ACTIVITIES FOR REVIEW, DISCUSSION, AND WRITING

1. If you are not Roman Catholic, try to attend a Catholic Mass. If you are Catholic, try to attend a Protestant service. Notice both the similarities and the differences.
2. If you are not Catholic, talk with friends who are about what being Catholic means to them. If you are Catholic, talk with someone about what being a Protestant Christian means.
3. Look at a good road atlas of the United States. Note the prevalence of place names that reflect the Spanish and French Catholic influence in the Southwest, Florida, Louisiana, and the upper Midwest.
4. Are you aware of any anti-Catholic prejudice in your community? Elsewhere? Among other students? What forms does it take? Is it organized or informal? What might be done to end it?

---

[28]Anne Patrick Ware, "Change and Confrontation Within the Roman Catholic Church," in *Women of Faith in Dialogue*, ed Virginia Ramey Mollenkott, (New York: Crossroad, 1990), pp. 31–32.

5. Think about the issue of how much authority a community of faith ought to have over the lives of its members. Should it have a little or a lot? Are there things that you believe should be left up to the individual? What are the advantages and the disadvantages of a community of faith having great authority? Little authority? You might also discuss this issue with other people in your class.
6. In your opinion, should women be able to be ordained as priests in the Catholic Church? Why do you think the way you do on this issue?

FOR FURTHER READING

Allsopp, Michael, and John J. O'Keefe, *Veritas Splendor: American Responses*. Kansas City, MO: Sheed and Ward, 1995. Pope John Paul II's encyclical, *Veritas Splendor*, is an extensive analysis of Catholic morality. In this book, Allsopp and O'Keefe collect a series of essays dealing with the response of American Catholics to this controversial document.

Butler, Francis J., *American Catholic Identity: Essays in an Age of Change*. Kansas City, MO: Sheed and Ward, 1994. Contains twenty-two addresses concerning what it means to be Catholic in postmodern America. Provides a good overview of late twentieth-century American Catholicism.

Chittiser, Joan, *Womanstrength: Modern Church, Modern Women*. Kansas City, MO: Sheed and Ward, 1990. A collection of essays on the role of women in today's Catholic Church. Wide-ranging and provocative.

Cunningham, Lawrence, *The Catholic Faith: An Introduction*. Mahwah, NJ: Paulist Press, 1987. A lively introduction to contemporary Catholic Christianity, written for college students.

Hurley, Bishop Mark J., *The Unholy Ghost: Anti-Catholicism in the American Experience*. Huntington, IN: Our Sunday Visitor, 1992. Carefully documented study of prejudice against Catholics in the United States throughout history and in the present. Three sections: (1) 1776 to Vatican II; (2) post-Vatican II; and (3) focused specifically on the abortion issue and support for parochial schools.

Redmont, Jane, *Generous Lives: American Catholic Women Today*. Liguori, MO: Triumph Books, 1992. Excellent study of American Catholic women. Discursive chapters alternate with first-person accounts by women of all ages, nationalities, and economic backgrounds, both lay and ordained.

Sweeney, Terrance, *A Church Divided: The Vatican versus American Catholics*. Buffalo, NY: Prometheus Press, 1992. A study of two divisive issues in the American Catholic church, papal authority and priesthood. Sweeney examines these questions from sociological, theological, ethical, and historical perspectives.

Weaver, Mary Jo, and R. Scott Appleby, *Being Right: Conservative Catholics in America*. Bloomington, IN: Indiana University Press, 1995. Looks at conservative Catholics in the United States both from their own self-perception and that of religious studies scholars. Describes how Catholic conservatives are addressing the problems they see arising from Vatican II, as well as their basic worldview and goals.

6

Consensus Religion in the Jewish Framework

Do you know any people of Jewish faith? If you live in a city, they may be your neighbors. If you live in a small town, you may never have met a Jew. Are you aware of any stereotypes about Jewish people? Many of us grow up with these stereotypes. Have you seen or perhaps been inside a synagogue or temple?

There are many similarities between Jews and Christians. Some of these were discussed in Chapter 3. The Jewish and Christian Bibles have a lot of material in common. They tell of one God who is personal, just, loving, and holy, and whose self-revelation occurs within the process of history. In response to this God, people are called to worship and to a life of moral action within the human community.

FROM IMMIGRANT RELIGION TO CONSENSUS RELIGION: SECTORS OF JUDAISM IN THE UNITED STATES

From Immigrant Religion to Consensus Religion

Jews were the smallest religious minority in the Colonies prior to the Revolution, and their numbers did not increase significantly until the 1800s. The majority of Jews in colonial America were Sephardic Jews of Spanish origin who were thoroughly traditional in their religious belief. They had distinctive ritual practices and a distinctive language that blended medieval Spanish with Hebrew and Ara-

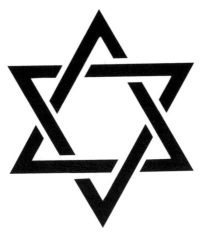

Figure 6–1   The *Magen David* (Star of David): The origin of the Star of David is lost in the mists of early history. It appears on synagogues as early as the second or third century C.E. In the early fourteenth century, it was used as a protective amulet or magical symbol. Apparently, it came into widespread usage as a symbol of Judaism (in the nineteenth century) because there was a desire to have a sign that would symbolize Judaism in the same way that the cross symbolizes Christianity.

bic. They were localized along the eastern seaboard. A congregation was formed at New Amsterdam (New York), and a synagogue was dedicated in 1730. An early Jewish community in Newport, Rhode Island, virtually disappeared, but was revived in 1750. The classic Touro Synagogue was dedicated in Newport in 1763. It is an outstanding example of synagogue architecture. Synagogues were also dedicated at Savannah, Georgia, in 1733, at Philadelphia in 1747, and at Charleston, South Carolina, in 1749. The Sephardic Jews mainly kept to themselves, insulated by their language and the strictness of their orthodoxy from their non-Jewish neighbors. This, along with their small numbers, prevented their making much impact, if any, on the surrounding culture.

Beginning in the early 1800s, two large waves of Jewish immigration broke over the shores of America. The first, which occurred during the half-century from 1820 to 1870, brought the arrival of many Jews of German origin, numbering about a quarter of a million. By and large, they were middle-class and relatively well educated, with a strong interest in fitting into their adopted homeland. They had been influenced by a very liberal current in German Judaism which came to be known as Reform, and they immigrated to the United States because they believed that its freedom of religion and democratic government offered an ideal situation for Reform Judaism. They spread out over the entire country, having no desire to remain in sheltered enclaves as had their Sephardic predecessors. By the mid-nineteenth century, they had become the largest group of American Jews.

An even larger immigration occurred from 1880 to 1914. It was of a very different character. These were Jews from Eastern Europe, primarily from Russia, Rumania, Poland, and Austria. They had fled their home countries in response to harsh persecutions and devastating attacks aimed at destroying the entire Jewish population. Many were desperately poor, uneducated, and, for the most part, unskilled and illiterate in English. They stayed on and near the eastern seaboard where they had entered the country. They had reacted in two ways to the attacks made upon them in Europe. The majority had retreated into a rigid and somewhat strident orthodoxy, whereas some had renounced religious Judaism altogether in favor of radically secular movements of social reform. They brought these attitudes with them to the United States. By 1914, the number of Jews in the United States had risen by more than tenfold, from a quarter of a million in 1870 to about 3 million.

Picture, then, the complex situation of American Judaism in 1914. The German Jews who had made up the first great immigration were well on their way to accomplishing their dual goals of fitting in to the life and culture of their adopted land and developing a distinctively modernized style of Judaism. These two elements were intimately linked. Suddenly, they were confronted by a new and larger group of Jews who were ill prepared to make any adjustments to American life; they had neither interest in fitting in nor skills that would facilitate doing so. In addition, their radicalism and stridency was an embarrassment to their more urbane predecessors. At the same time, the newer immigrants, especially the majority who were very traditional in their Judaism, questioned the validity of the modernized form of Jewishness practiced by the German Jews. Yet, and this must be borne in mind, both groups were Jewish, and they were linked by very strong ties. American Judaism was fragmented into a mosaic of languages and patterns of belief and practice, overlaid by glaring cultural differences. This fragmentation challenged the strong Jewish sense of peoplehood and unity and set the stage for the development of the varied styles of Judaism that have remained important into the present. A rather clear-cut pattern has emerged in the development of Judaism in the United States. The first generation, the immigrants themselves, largely remained close together, seeking comfort and protection among those most like themselves. At the same time, and somewhat ironically, they did not take many steps to preserve their heritage, taking it for granted that their children in the next generation would become more American and thereby less Jewish.

The urge toward integration and assimilation was greatest among the second generation, the largest segment of adult Jews during the period 1935 through about 1970. Many were willing to pay a high price for assimilation, feeling that their acceptance was based on an unspoken demand: they would not be treated as if they were Jewish, providing that they would cease acting as if they were. It is difficult to determine to what extent this attitude actually existed in the gentile culture, although it certainly did. Some of it was undoubtedly in the minds of the Jews themselves.

This situation left the third- and fourth-generations with the task of re-covering what had been lost in the struggle for acceptance. By about 1960, the majority of Jews in America had achieved the acceptance they sought. Today, they continue to lead the nation in education, professionalization, and income and are a noteworthy presence in politics and culture. Tolerance has increased also, at least to some extent. With acceptance has come the realization that the price has been high and that it is necessary to recover what has been lost if Judaism is to remain a vital faith and culture.[1] There is a saying, "What the son wishes to forget, the grandson wishes to remember," and this has been very much the case with third- and fourth-generation American Jews. Among all sectors of Judaism in this country, there is renewed interest in Jewish life and culture. Religious ob-servance is increasing, even among liberal Reform Jews. Attention to the dietary laws and to holiday observances is growing. The Hebrew language is being taught more, learned more, and used more in the synagogues. There is a lively interest in Orthodoxy among younger Jews, as well as in the Jewish mystical tradition of Hasidism.

The foregoing discussion of assimilation and acceptance raises the question of **anti-Semitism**[2] in the United States. While the situation of most Jews in the United States was vastly better than it had been in the countries from which they came, it was not perfect. Along with the fragmentation of American Judaism that resulted from the great immigrations, the dramatic increase in the number of Jews in the United States gave rise to discrimination and prejudice.

One of the factors that led, and still leads, to anti-Semitism is the erroneous belief held by some Christians that Jews were responsible for Jesus' death. It is quite clear that Jesus was put to death by the Romans, not the Jews. Nonethe-less, this idea persists. Many Christians also find it very difficult to understand why Jews do not accept Jesus as the savior of humankind. This leads to both anti-Semitism and efforts to convert Jews to Christianity.

A second historical facet of Jewish-Christian relations is that the Christian church in medieval times did not allow charging interest on money loaned. Eu-ropean Jews thus became associated with money and banking, and many people came to feel that the Jews were prospering at the expense of the Christians. This historical fact gave rise to a distrust of Jews in financial matters and to the stereo-types that "all Jews are rich" and "all Jews are stingy."

The Sephardic Jews who settled in what was to become New York found in Peter Stuyvesant a governor who referred to them as a "deceitful race" who would "infest and trouble" his colony. Civil liberties and the vote were denied to any except Christians in many of the colonies and in some states for a time after the Revolution. In 1861, when Congress established a chaplain corps for the Union army, it was restricted to ministers of any Christian denomination.

---

[1]Stephen M. Cohen and Leonard J. Fein, "From Integration to Survival: American Jewish Anxieties in Tran-sition," *Annals, The American Academy of Political and Social Science*, no. 480 (July 1985), pp. 75–88; and Jacob Neusner, *Israel in America: A Too-Comfortable Exile?* (Boston: Beacon Press, 1985).

[2]This word refers to discrimination against Jews.

President Lincoln succeeded in securing an amendment to that action that allowed for Jewish chaplains, but some damage had been done, nonetheless. The immigration bill adopted by Congress in 1924 was shamefully xenophobic, and that attitude was not eliminated until this measure was replaced by Lyndon Johnson's Immigration Measure. The Ku Klux Klan has been quite active throughout American history in anti-Semitic activities and diatribes. Henry Ford supported the publication of *The Protocols of Zion.* This classic piece of hate literature embodied an idea that also had currency elsewhere—that the Jews were engaged in a conspiracy to take over the world by overthrowing Christianity.

More general patterns of discrimination also occurred, such as quota systems that barred all but a few Jews from prestigious Eastern colleges and restricted Jews to a handful of the professions. There are still private clubs that either restrict the number of Jewish members or do not admit them at all. Discrimination in housing has also been fairly commonplace. Synagogues have been defaced, frequently being spray-painted with Nazi swastikas, and crosses have been burned in the yards of synagogues and Jewish homes. Often, the attacks are verbal in nature, but there is also a pattern of physical attacks on Jewish property and Jewish people.

The Identity Movement (see Chapter 12) is staunchly anti-Semitic in its thinking, as well as advocating prejudice against Catholics, blacks, homosexuals, and various other people. People in the movement often describe the current situation as one in which a battle for the world is being fought under the direction of God, a battle between the whites whom God intends to inherit the earth and the Jews (and others) from whom they must wrest control of it. The close identification of some groups within this movement with the neo-Nazi movement is especially troublesome to Jews, as well as to other people.

That there is less anti-Semitism now than at some other times in our history must not lull us into indifference. Remaining anti-Semitism, as well as other forms of discrimination, prejudice, and bigotry, whether religious or otherwise, must be blotted out.

Acceptance must not and cannot be contingent on differences being reduced to some sort of lowest common denominator or to minorities conforming to the majority opinion of how the minority ought to be. To do so dehumanizes the individuals in the minority and impoverishes the entire community, which is denied the richness of variety that healthy, culturally conscious minorities provide.

Community is in large part a dialogue, and for a lively dialogue to occur, there must be lively differences. To insist upon conformity as a condition of acceptance and as a criterion of membership in the community, will ultimately destroy the dialogue upon which genuine community is based and which is its lifeblood. It will create strangers where there might have been neighbors, because they will have nothing to discuss.

Judaism in the United States: One Religion, Several Sectors

Judaism in America is a single religious tradition that is spread across a wide range of practices, and to a lesser extent, beliefs. It remains, however, a "unified and unitary structure," and its varieties are "sectors of one tradition."[3] Due regard must be given to both the differences and the commonalities. We will examine some of the commonalities in the next two sections. We will look at the differences in this section.

The very small percentage of Jews in the United States population as a whole makes obtaining accurate statistics difficult. Less than 10 percent of American Jews are Orthodox. Between 20 and 40 percent each are Conservative or Reform. Fewer than 5 percent are Reconstructionists. Approximately 20 percent claim they are "just Jewish."[4]

Orthodoxy.   We will begin with Jewish **Orthodoxy.** Orthodox Jews believe that their way of being Jewish embodies the authentic Jewish tradition that had existed since Judaism began. They emphasize submission to the Law; the revealed will of God is absolute and is not to be tampered with under any circumstances. Orthodoxy, despite what the name and basic outlook might suggest, is not a monolith. There are a vast number of variations in what Orthodox Jews actually believe and do. There are, however, factors that we can identify as clearly distinctive. The Bible is regarded as divinely revealed and altogether accurate, at least in the Books of Moses. It has absolute divine authority. The ceremonial law is as binding as the ethical commandments, since both come from the same source and it is not for human beings to make divisions among them. They are to be observed simply because they are commandments and because they were given to the people of Israel by God with the directive, "Do this." **Halakhah**[5] is as authoritative as Torah itself, having sprung from the same source and having divine authority behind it.

For most non-Jews, the two most distinctive things about Orthodoxy are the strict Sabbath observance and the keeping of the kosher dietary laws. Work of any kind is strictly forbidden on the Sabbath. The **kosher dietary laws** are a collection of instructions regarding food, its preparation, and consumption. Some of the major ones are as follows: Pork is not to be eaten at all. If an animal is to be used for food, it must have a cloven or split foot and also must be a cud-chewing animal. Pigs are not cud-chewers, though they do have a split foot. Rabbits, on the other hand, chew the cud but do not have a split foot. Cattle meet

---

[3]Jacob Neusner, ed., *Understanding American Judaism: Toward a Description of a Modern Religion, Volume II, Sectors of American Judaism: Reform, Orthodoxy, Conservatism, and Reconstructionism* (New York: KTAV Publishing House, Inc., 1975), p. xiii.
[4]I. A. Lewis, "American Jews and Israel," *Public Opinion*, 11/2 (July/August 1988), p. 53.
[5]*Halakhah* is the rabbinic record of the application of Torah law to specific circumstances through history.

both criteria, so beef may be eaten. Fish must have both fins and scales. In practice, this eliminates all shellfish as well as such things as eels and octopus. Some foods that may be eaten are restricted in certain ways. Chief among these is the prohibition on mixing meat and milk dishes in the same meal. This goes back to three different places in the Torah in which it is forbidden to cook a baby goat in its mother's milk (Exodus 23:19 and 34:25 and Deuteronomy 14:2). For example, cheeseburgers may not be eaten, and milk may not be drunk at a meal containing meat. In a fully kosher kitchen, the same set of cookware, utensils, and dishes would not be used for meat and milk. Furthermore, a separate set of dishes is kept for Passover, necessitating a total of four completely different sets of dishes. Meat must be slaughtered in a special way under the approval of a rabbi and must be treated to remove as much of the blood as possible before cooking, or in the cooking process. Foods that are kosher have been prepared under close rabbinic supervision throughout. Foods so certified are marked, often with a "U" (for the Union of Orthodox Rabbis) or a "K" (for Kosher) on the container.

The overall effect of the kosher commandments, of which I have named only a few, is to keep the following of God's commandments uppermost in the minds of faithful Jews in matters as common as cooking and eating. In Judaism, the body is as holy as the soul and must be treated as such; keeping kosher is one way of doing so. The other outstanding effect is to reinforce community among observant Jews and insulate them from outsiders. Much of the time, they live close together because it is necessary to have ready access to a kosher butcher shop, bakery, and grocery. They socialize together, because full observance prohibits eating at the table of one who does not keep kosher.

Other features also are common among Orthodox Jews. In synagogue, women and men sit separately, and, in some communities, it is not common for the women to attend. The separation varies from simply being seated on separate sides of a center aisle to a partition that cannot be seen over. All of the service is in Hebrew, and the holidays and festivals are observed to their fullest. Men wear the **kippah**, or skullcap, at all times, out of respect for their always being under the watchful eye of God. They wear prayer shawls and **tefillin**[6] for formal daily prayer. Marriage to a non-Orthodox Jew is regarded as invalid even if performed by a rabbi. Orthodox rabbis do not perform interfaith marriages.

Reform Judaism. At the opposite extreme is **Reform** Judaism, which, you recall, began with German immigrants to this country who fervently wanted to fit into their new land. Reform is the most modernized and liberal of the main three Jewish groups. According to Reform teaching, Judaism is a fully modern religion that must change to keep pace with changes in the rest of culture. Monotheism and the moral law are constant. Everything else is conditioned by circumstances and therefore changes as circumstances change.

---

[6] *Tefillin* are small leather boxes containing Bible verses. Orthodox Jewish men wear them on their foreheads and left arms during prayer.

Isaac Mayer Wise, one of the main founders of Reform in the United States, began Hebrew Union College–Jewish Institute of Religion in Cincinnati, Ohio, which became the intellectual center of Reform. The Pittsburgh Platform of 1885 and the less radical Columbus Platform of 1937 spelled out the basic premises of Reform. In keeping with Judaism's affirmation of the freedom of the individual, neither had the status of an official creed. Both affirmed Judaism an ever-adaptable faith, constantly changing yet with a core that held constant amid the changes.

Reform began by discarding everything "not adapted to the views and habits of modern civilization" (Pittsburgh Platform) and taught that only the moral law is binding. There has been increasing interest in recent years in reappropriating the tradition and affirming the importance of continuity with Judaism throughout the ages. As with Orthodoxy, there are features that distinguish Reform. Families sit together in services, and the house of worship is most often called a temple rather than a synagogue. English is often used for at least a part of the service, although certain prayers are most often in Hebrew. Although some people wear the kippah, prayer shawl, and tefillin, many do not. Dietary and Sabbath laws are kept less rigorously, and festival observance may be simpler and shorter in duration. Reform Jews are strong supporters of women's rights and were the first major group within Judaism to ordain women to the rabbinate, as well as being the group that developed coming-of-age rituals for girls.

Conservatism. Conservative Judaism is an attempt to follow a middle road between Orthodoxy and Reform Judaism. Like Reform, Conservatism believes that Judaism changes with time, but it changes because it is a living religion, and change is a part of that aliveness. American Conservatism is dedicated to preserving the knowledge and practice of historic Judaism without utter refusal to accommodate. The truth of the tradition is maintained through the interpretation of living rabbis, so that the focus is not exclusively on the past (as is the tendency in Orthodoxy) nor on the present (as Reform tends to do). Its main founder in the United States was Solomon Schechter, who came to America from England in 1902 to revitalize the Jewish Theological Seminary in America, which became the intellectual center of Conservatism.

The dietary laws illustrate the types of accommodation that Conservative Jews may make. Most do keep kosher at home. However, when eating with friends or in restaurants, they do not insist on full observance. Thus, they can dine at the homes of nonkosher friends, and any Jew, even the most observant, can dine at their table.

In addition, there are other practices and beliefs that distinguish Conservatives from others. Family seating is the rule in worship. Men usually wear skullcaps for worship, but not at other times. Much of the service is in Hebrew, and there is intensive emphasis on Hebrew education. A distinction is made between avoidable and unavoidable types of work, with that which cannot be avoided being permitted on the Sabbath. For example, it is permissible to drive to the synagogue on the Sabbath, if distance requires it.

Conservatism emerged in the United States in response to the fragmentation and division brought about by the two large immigrant groups and their differing styles of being Jewish. It was more a reaction to the perceived excesses of accommodation in Reform than to the traditionalism of Orthodoxy. Its goal was to be both fully Jewish (in which its adherents felt Reform had failed miserably) and fully American (which it felt Orthodoxy's strictness prevented happening in a meaningful way). This remains its goal today.

Reconstructionism.   Conservatism did not unify American Judaism as much as its proponents had hoped. The **Reconstructionist** movement was another attempt at unification. Reconstructionism's founder, Rabbi Mordecai Kaplan, was a teacher at the Jewish Theological Seminary. When he looked out over the whole of American Judaism, he saw two things. As we have indicated earlier, it was still rather fragmented. More seriously, by 1920, those Jews not affiliated with any synagogue at all far outnumbered the total of Orthodox, Conservative, and Reform Jews combined. In 1934, Kaplan wrote a book entitled *Judaism as a Civilization*. In it, he said that Judaism should be thought of as an evolving religious civilization. It is a civilization that has evolved through the ages, based not so much on belief or practice as on the continuous life of the Jewish people themselves. It has come about as the Jewish people have expressed their values through the patterns of behavior, religious and otherwise, that they have developed. Its focus, then, was not religion but Jewishness in all of its forms, and Kaplan sought to bring about an organic community centered in school and synagogue, one that would meet all the needs of its members. In other words, it was to express in organizational form the unity of the Jewish people.

Reconstructionism is the only expression of Judaism that has been produced solely in America. It was a response to the situation of Jewish people in this country. Its influence on American Judaism has been large, although its numbers have remained small.

Zionism.   The last sector of American Judaism we will consider here is **Zionism**. Zionism is based upon the importance of Judaism as a nation. Theodor Herzl was a Viennese reporter who wrote an emotional pamphlet titled *The Jewish State* (1896), in which he said that the only hope for the Jews was the establishment of a national homeland, preferably in Palestine itself. In 1897, the First World Zionist Congress met in Basel, Switzerland.

Although the leadership of the Zionist movement tended to be mainly nonreligious, Orthodox Jews supported it because it correlated with the Orthodox belief in the eventual restoration and rebuilding of Israel and the Holy City of Jerusalem. The Conservatives also were in favor of most points in the Zionist program. Reform Jews at first found little in it that was attractive, because it conflicted with their desire to be at home in whatever culture they found themselves and with their teaching that Judaism was a religion that could be at home anywhere.

After the Holocaust,[7] virtually all American Jews supported Zionism wholeheartedly. When the State of Israel was founded in 1948, American Jews raised huge sums of money via United Jewish Appeal to help resettle refugees. This focus on the State of Israel remains a powerful unifying force for American Judaism.

PRINCIPAL BELIEFS AND PRACTICES OF JEWISH PEOPLE

As you have seen, Judaism in the United States has many variations in belief and practice. However, there are certain features that nearly all Jews share, in one way or another. Interpretations vary, but the basics are the same. Lists of what these basics are will be different from one author to another; what is included here is a minimal listing of very fundamental points.

Beliefs

Jews define themselves in part by their special relationship to the Torah and the Talmud. In a broad sense, **Torah** refers to a guide for life, instruction in living as a Jew, the whole of what it means to live a proper Jewish life. In a more specific sense, it refers to the first five books of the Bible—Genesis, Exodus, Leviticus, Numbers, and Deuteronomy (Figure 6–2). These five books, which for Jews are the core of God's revelation, are believed to have been revealed to Moses and are known as the **Five Books of Moses**. They are also known as the *Pentateuch*, a Greek word that means "five books."

The Hebrew Bible is very similar to the Old Testament in the Christian Bible, containing the same books. However, it is inappropriate to refer to the Hebrew Bible as the "Old Testament." That collection of writings is called the Old Testament by Christians because, for them, the New Testament is a part of the Bible. The Christian New Testament is not a part of the Jewish Bible. It has no authority and does not contain the revelation of the God of Abraham, Isaac, and Jacob. To refer to the Torah as the "Old Testament" is offensive to persons of Jewish faith, for whom the revelation of God recorded in the Hebrew Bible can never be superseded by another revelation such as Christians believe is contained in their New Testament. The word **Tanakh** is often used for the Hebrew Bible. *Tanakh* is an acronym taken from the Hebrew first letters of its three divisions.

After the five Books of Moses are the Books of the Prophets. Some of these

---

[7] *Holocaust* refers to the extermination of 6 million Jews, as well as other people deemed "undesirable," under the Hitler regime in Germany from 1933 through 1945.

Figure 6–2   A Torah scroll is an important part of any synagogue or temple. (*Bill Aron/Photo Researchers, Inc.*)

books are primarily historical, covering the time between the Hebrews' entry into the promised land and the exile in Babylon. Others are composed of a variety of prophetic utterances and stories. The rest of Tanakh is made up of the Writings and includes such well-known books as Psalms, Proverbs, Job, and Ecclesiastes, along with several others. In addition to the Tanakh itself, there is the **Talmud**, which is the written record of several centuries of discussion, interpretation, and commentary on Torah by the earliest rabbis, who were primarily scholars and teachers of Torah. In spite of differences in interpretation and varied understandings of exactly what authority the Talmud has, Jews are united in their self-understanding as the people of the history and way of life described therein.

The cornerstone of the Torah is the **commandments** that Jews believe God gave to Moses at Mount Sinai. They are found in the Book of the Exodus, chapter 20 (paraphrased in Figure 6–3). The core commandments can be divided into two groups: The first four deal with how one ought to relate to God, and the latter six with how one is to relate with other persons. These commandments are the heart of the Torah and the heart of Jewish life and living.

Most Jews agree on the basic understanding of God. **In Torah, God reveals God to the Jewish people.** It is not a matter of people discovering God through a process of human searching; rather, God chooses to reveal God to people. People of Jewish faith believe that there is but one God. The Jews are a people of uncompromising **monotheism.** This central point is learned by Jewish children early in life and repeated many times a day by most Jews as the **Shema:** "Hear, O Israel! The Lord our God, the Lord is One," (found in Deuteronomy 6:4). The passage goes on to prescribe that this God is to be loved with one's entire

Figure 6–3

THE TEN COMMANDMENTS

1. You shall not worship any other gods.
2. Do not make images of God.
3. Do not take God's holy name in vain.
4. Remember to keep the Sabbath holy; in particular, you are not to work on this day.
5. Honor your parents.
6. Do not murder.
7. Do not commit adultery.
8. Do not steal.
9. Do not bear false witness against anyone.
10. Do not covet [i.e., be envious of] that which is your neighbor's.

self, holding nothing back. Monotheism was a part of Judaism from its earliest beginnings. In the area in which Judaism began, it was customary for a tribe to worship many deities. The biblical accounts of the founding of Israel describe how Abraham turned from the worship of many deities to the worship of only one, who is described as *the* God.

The God revealed to Moses is a God who acts within history. God did not bring the world into being and then abandon it to its fate, but continues to be actively involved with people, as demonstrated primarily in the Exodus from Egyptian bondage. The creator of the world is also the Lord of history. God is called Father, King, Judge, and Redeemer.

Because the Jews are ever watchful to guard the uniqueness of God, they will not represent God in any material form; to do so would be to make an idol. Nor is there any way, in the Jewish understanding of God, that any human being could ever be God. This is one reason that **people of Jewish faith do not accept the Christian teaching that Jesus is the Messiah whose coming is foretold in Isaiah.** The idea of a person who is at once divine and human is utterly repugnant to Jewish sensibility. We must remember that the link between the verses in Isaiah that speak of the coming of the Messiah and the person Jesus are found in the Christian New Testament and are not a part of Hebrew scripture. The Messiah as understood by those of Jewish faith will be a leader who will bring freedom and restoration to the entire people of Israel in more political than individual terms. Jesus as described by the early Christian church—the savior of individual persons from sin and separation from God—is a different sort of savior than that expected in Judaism. According to most Jews, Jesus was a religious leader and teacher, perhaps a prophet, but not God.

The character of God has definite implications for how people treat each other. God is a just, loving, holy, and righteous God, according to the Hebrew Bible, and God's people must reflect these qualities in their lives and in their dealings with others. **Peoples' actions with other people must be characterized by an attitude reflective of God's own nature.**

Under the terms of the covenant, people are responsible to and for one another. One's fellow human being is God's son or daughter and hence is one's brother or sister. Righteousness, love, and tolerance must be the rule, not only among Jews but with all persons. It extends to strangers, servants, and animals. Special concern is to be given to the less fortunate, such as widows, orphans, the poor, and the ill. Fair treatment is to be given even to one's enemies. The rabbis told a story that makes the point that we are all interconnected. It goes this way:

> Along with other people, a man was traveling by boat. He took a drill and began to drill a hole under his seat. Understandably alarmed, the other passengers asked what he was doing. "It's my business, not yours!" he retorted. "I'm drilling the hole under my own seat!"[8]

Jews are united in their understanding of themselves as a people. In spite of being scattered around the world, and, in spite of speaking many languages and following different practices and beliefs, **the people of Israel are one people.** They are linked by the love they have for each other, by their common tradition and history, and by their shared past and present experience. The Jews understand themselves to be the people of the covenant. They came into being as a people because a covenant was forged between them and God. In Exodus 19, it is recorded that God said to the people of Israel that if they would keep the commandments of God, then God would be their God and they would be the people of God. This brings up the frequently misunderstood concept of the Jews as God's **chosen people.** The language of Exodus speaks clearly of this chosenness. The normative Jewish understanding of chosenness is that the Jews are a people with a special mission in the history of humankind. They have specific responsibilities and obligations under the covenant, even when following these obligations means suffering and death. It means living under the watchful eye of God. It does not indicate that the Jews see themselves as somehow better or more important to God than are gentiles.[9]

The Jewish belief in peoplehood takes on concrete form in widespread support for the state of Israel. Since the destruction of the Temple in Jerusalem in 70 C.E., the Jews have been a wandering people. But they have maintained the conviction of belonging to the land into which the Bible records they wandered under God's leading. For centuries, Jews have prayed for the restoration and rebuilding of Jerusalem. "Next year in Jerusalem!" is spoken at the end of the Seder meal every Passover. Land and covenant are linked; the people of the covenant are the people of the land. This linking of land and people took political form in

---

[8]Samuel T. Lachs and Saul P. Wachs, *Judaism* (Niles, IL: Argus Communications, 1979), p. 50.
[9]As used in this context, a *gentile* is anyone who is not Jewish.

the Zionist movement. The founding of the State of Israel in 1948 is numbered among the most significant events of Jewish history.

Practices

What can we say about Jewish **lifestyles**? Especially in the United States, Jews live as many different lifestyles as do their neighbors. Overall, survey data tell us two factors that are important in understanding what it means to be a person of Jewish faith in modern day America. Of all the religious preference groups, Jews lead the nation in both education and income. Education has long been seen as a way to acceptance, and the Jewish community has made use of it. The second outstanding feature of the American Jewish population is that, across the board, Jews are more tolerant and broad-minded about moral issues, civil liberties, and non-believers than are their Christian neighbors. Yet another general feature than can be mentioned is the heavy involvement of Jews in social reform and assistance programs and in occupations such as social work and professional psychology and psychiatry. The terms of the covenant and responsibility for one's neighbor translate into vocational terms, for both religious and nonreligious Jews.

Judaism in its traditional form has a very rich **ritual life**. A set of rituals pace individual Jews through their lifetimes, and another set paces the community through its collective life. Differences in observance abound, but Judaism is united by these individual and collective religious practices. They are the people whose life, both corporate and private, is demarcated by these ritual observances. Here we will note the principal ones.

We will first turn to those rituals that pace the individual through the life cycle. Although these events mark important transitions in an individual's life, they are also ways in which the community shares in the life of the individual member. As is the case with every religion, birth is the first step of the life cycle to be ritually marked. After the birth of a girl, it is the father's responsibility and honor to read the Torah at the next synagogue service. He recites the usual benedictions before and after reading and officially announces the child's name. For a boy, it is more complicated; **circumcision** is a major Jewish ceremony. Although other peoples circumcise infant boys, Judaism understands this as a visible sign of the covenant between Abraham and God, made again in each generation (Genesis 17:9–14). It takes place on the eighth day after birth. The ceremony involves both religious and surgical elements and may be performed by a physician or by a specially trained **Mohel** who has both the necessary surgical and religious knowledge. A festive meal follows. A second birth-related ceremony follows on the thirty-first day following birth. In the Book of Exodus, chapter 13, it is stated that every first-born male must be redeemed. No explanation of the reason is given. In practice, the father goes to a stand-in for the priest (the priesthood having been discontinued after the destruction of the Temple) and pays $5, which is then given to charity. Again, a festive meal completes the celebration.

The next life cycle rite in the life of a Jewish youngster is the **Bar Mitzvah**.

Some Jews, although not all, celebrate the **Bat Mitzvah** for girls also. The words mean "son or daughter of the commandment" and mark the coming of age of the child. The child is then considered to be an adult, responsible for observing the commandments and able to fill adult roles in the congregation, although the ceremony traditionally occurs on the Sabbath following the child's thirteenth birthday. The highlight of Jewish life for many, it is preceded by intensive study. The young person is called up to read Torah before the congregation for the first time. This is a great honor. The young person may also make a speech in which parents and teachers are thanked. Especially in the United States, this ceremony has grown in importance and is frequently the occasion for a lavish party with family and friends to recognize the person's new status. In some congregations that practice the Bat Mitzvah, the ceremony parallels that for boys, while other congregations have developed distinctive practices for it.

Some Reform Jewish congregations have an additional ceremony of **Confirmation** at about age fifteen or sixteen. Although originally intended as a replacement for the Bar or Bat Mitzvah, it is now a separate ceremony for Reform and Conservative Jews, in which the now somewhat older youths reaffirm their intention to live as Jews in the household of Israel.

Marriage is the next life cycle ritual in the lives of most Jewish women and men. Judaism places a very high value on marriage and family, and celebrating the beginning of a new family unit in marriage is very important. The **Ketubah**, or marriage contract, which spells out the responsibilities of both spouses, is signed during the ceremony. It is a legally valid document as well as a religious one. The wedding ceremony itself is complex and reflects the sacred nature of marriage and family life. A celebration with family and friends follows. Although divorce is permitted by Jewish law, it is strongly discouraged. In practice, actual divorce statistics among Reform Jews differ little from those among their gentile neighbors; for Conservative and, especially, Orthodox Jews, the rate is somewhat lower. To be recognized as valid among traditional Jews, there must be a religious divorce as well as a legal one.

The final passage from life into death is the occasion for the last life cycle rite. The Jew who fears death is approaching recites a prayer that contains a plea for help in recovering and a confession of sin. The Shema is also said. Burial takes place as soon as possible after death, preferably on the day of death or the day following. Interment is chosen over cremation of the body, and embalming is not practiced unless required by law. The funeral is a simple service that emphasizes the goodness of God and offers comfort to the bereaved. Mourning customs are paced so as to allow time for the expression of grief while gradually returning the mourners to the life of the community.

As well as marking the stages in the individual's life with celebration and consolation, Judaism hallows time through a yearly cycle. This cycle lifts time out of the realm of a merely mechanical tracking of days and hours and uses it to keep history and tradition alive in the present.

The **Sabbath** is a high point in every week. In line with the accounts of creation in Genesis, the Jewish Sabbath is observed from sundown on Friday until nightfall on Saturday. The Sabbath is considered one sign of the covenant between God and Israel. God is said to have rested after the creation, and people, too, are to devote one day per week to rest. The Sabbath meal is prepared in advance. The Sabbath begins when the mother lights special Sabbath candles and recites the appointed blessings. There may be a synagogue service to welcome the Sabbath (Figure 6–4). The following morning, the family may attend the synagogue together, although, in some congregations, it is customary for the women to remain at home with the children. A quiet day follows. Perhaps the best-known feature of the Jewish Sabbath is that any kind of work is strictly forbidden. To understand what it means to "keep the Sabbath," however, we must see beyond the prohibition of work. The Sabbath is intended as a way of separating

Figure 6–4

SABBATH WORSHIP*

There is a lot of variation along the spectrum from Orthodox through Conservative and Reform Jewish worship, as well as within each of them. However, these four elements can usually be found, sometimes in a longer and sometimes in a more abbreviated form.

1. *Birkhot ha-Shahar*, or "Morning Blessings." An introductory part of the service that contains blessings that express gratitude and praise to God for a variety of things. They have the form "Blessed art Thou, O Lord our God, King of the Universe" at the beginning, and end with "Blessed are You, Lord."
2. *Shema* and its blessings. At one time, this was the entire service. The congregation recites the Shema, prays accompanying blessings of praise and gratitude to God, and recites passages from the Tanakh (Deuteronomy 6:5–9 and 11:13–21).
3. *Amidah* and *Kedushah.* Additional prayers.
4. *Torah Service.* The Torah scroll is removed from its place in the Ark, readings are read from the Torah and the Prophets, and the Torah is returned to the Ark. The removal and return may take place with great ceremony, in which the highly decorated Torah scrolls are carried through the congregation. This is followed by additional prayers and benedictions.
5. In Reform services, the Rabbi gives a sermon that relates to the Torah readings for the day.
6. *Kiddush.* Not technically a part of the service, but most congregations have a time of gathering together with refreshments and wine.

---

*Based on material in *The Second Jewish Catalog: Sources and Resources,* ed. Sharon Strassfeld and Michael Strassfeld (Philadelphia: Jewish Publication Society of America, 1976), pp. 270–91.

oneself from the cares and toils of everyday living to make time for what is truly important. It is a time to be with one's God, with one's family, and with oneself, and, for that to be possible in our busy world, a special effort must be made to make it so. Torah study is an important part of what may be done on the Sabbath. Prayer and meditation are encouraged. Taking moderate walks with the family, doing quiet family things together, and visiting friends who live close by are often done.

Like the individual life, the year is marked throughout with festivals and days of great significance. Although each of the festivals leads naturally into the one that follows it, the most reasonable place to begin is where the Jewish religious calendar (which differs from the one we use to follow secular time) itself begins, with the Jewish New Year.

Rosh Hashanah (literally, the "head of the year") takes place in early autumn (September-October). Preparation for it begins the month before, which is used as a time of contemplation and spiritual self-searching. The Jewish New Year is not a time of partying and rowdiness, as the secular New Year often is. Rather, it is a time for looking back over the past year, for reflecting on deeds done and left undone. Judaism emphasizes human beings' free choice in whether we will do good or evil, and our responsibility for that choice. With responsibility comes accountability, and God is known as the judge of human actions. It is this sense of judgment that pervades the Jewish New Year and the period that follows it. The oldest and probably best known of the rituals connected with this festival is the sounding of the **shofar**, an instrument made from the horn of a ram, which makes a sound some have likened to the wailing of the heart of the human race.

Rosh Hashanah is the beginning of a time of intense reflection. Taking stock of one's life and behavior over the preceding year is accompanied by the resolve to do better. Two types of sin must be dealt with: those against God and those against other people. People can be forgiven for those against God by the rituals of **Yom Kippur**, the Day of Atonement, which follows the days of penitence. For those sins in which one has wronged another person as well, forgiveness must be sought not only from God but from the person wronged, and one must seek to make amends if at all possible. There is no savior in Judaism except God, and no mediator between God and people. Jews stand before God as individuals and as members of the household of Israel with their prayers for forgiveness and their resolve to live a better life. Given these factors, Judaism teaches, God will forgive the sincere penitent. The entire day of Yom Kippur is spent in fasting, prayer, and contemplation. Thus cleansed of previous sin and strengthened to live the Torah more fully, the Jew begins another year.

The next holiday is one that has come to be celebrated much more in the United States than it is elsewhere: **Hanukkah**, the Festival of Lights. It comes in November or December, and the increased emphasis it has received in the United States has come about in part because it is close to the time that the Christian majority and the culture in general celebrates Christmas. The word *Hanukkah*

Figure 6–5   The Menorah

means "rededication" and refers to the rededication of the Temple after the Maccabean revolutionaries successfully recaptured it from the Greco-Syrians in approximately 160 B.C.E. Legend has it that only enough oil could be found to keep the Temple lamp burning for one day. Miraculously, the oil lasted for eight days, the time required to prepare and consecrate new oil. Thus, the Hanukkah candle holder, or **menorah**, has eight branches plus a ninth which holds the lighting candle, whereas the regular menorah holds seven candles (Figure 6–5). Another candle is lit every night of the eight-day celebration. There is another very beautiful Hanukkah story that the rabbis tell. When the Maccabees entered the Temple, they found that the menorah was not usable, having been destroyed by the raiding pagans. The Maccabees took their spears and used them to make a new menorah, turning the weapons of war into a symbol of peace.[10]

The Jewish holiday that gentiles probably know best is **Passover**, which comes in the spring. It has both associations remaining from the early times when the Israelites were an agricultural people and the historical significance that was given to it later. It exemplifies the way that religious rituals keep the important stories of the faith alive and assist in transmitting them to each new generation. As an agricultural festival, it recalls the spring harvest. Its primary significance is now the historical one, however, in that it commemorates the exodus of the Hebrews out of slavery in Egypt. This is one of the two foundational events of Jewish history. It is sometimes called the Feast of Unleavened Bread, and **matzah**, a crackerlike bread, is eaten. Unleavened bread is eaten because the hurried flight

[10]Leo Trepp, *Judaism: Development and Life*, 3rd ed. (Belmont, CA: Wadsworth Publishing Company, 1982), p. 303.

of the Hebrews left no time for bread to rise (Exodus 12:37–39, 13:3,6–8, Deuteronomy 16:1–4). The name Passover comes from the biblical promise that the angel of death would pass over those houses marked on the doorpost with the blood of a sacrificial lamb (Exodus 12:12–14). The central ritual of Passover is the **Seder** meal in which the story of the Exodus is retold. Special foods are eaten that help to bring the story alive. This ritual involves everyone present and uses virtually all the human senses, mixing food, fun, and serious intention to serve as an outstanding educational and community-reinforcing tool. Jews who must be away from home at this special time may count on being taken into the home of another Jewish family wherever they may be for the Seder.

Following Passover is another ritual calling to mind a founding event. The **Feast of Weeks (Shavuot)** has roots as a harvest festival, but its contemporary meaning is as a celebration of the giving of the Ten Commandments to Moses on Mount Sinai. Thus, the two interwoven themes of Jewish life, God-given freedom from slavery and the giving of the Torah, are celebrated and remembered. Either one without the other is incomplete and does not do justice to the fullness of Jewish understanding.

The final festival to be described also has its roots in the agricultural experience of the early Israelites and in the later historical interpretation given it by the rabbis. **Sukkot, or the Feast of Booths,** comes in September or October. As a harvest festival, it is the fulfillment of the agricultural year. Historically, it refers to the Israelites wandering for forty years from Egypt to the Promised Land, without having any permanent homes (Leviticus 23:42–43). The booth, constructed of natural materials, symbolizes the protection of God during this perilous period in Jewish history. Jewish families may build such a structure at their homes, or they may visit one built outside the synagogue.

Yom Ha Shoah is a Jewish observance of more recent origin. It is also called Holocaust Remembrance Day and takes place in the spring. The activities on this solemn day have two foci: It is a time to remember those people—both Jewish and gentile—who died in the Holocaust. It is also a time for rededication to the principle that such a thing can never be allowed to happen again. In many communities, Jews and Christians sponsor joint Yom Ha Shoah observances.

Whether in the individual's life or the life of the community as a whole, Jewish festivals and ritual practices pace life, marking off transitions and recalling significant events. They keep the founding events alive, offer opportunities for education and celebration, integrate the individual into the community of Jews past and present, and, most important, offer ways for each person and the community to relate to the God of Abraham, Isaac, and Jacob.

Organization

Judaism in the United States is a mosaic of different groups, as you have seen. Although each congregation is self-governing and thus free to determine its own policies, there are various associations of rabbis and several seminaries that function as policy-making bodies whose decisions are taken with utmost seriousness by their constituent congregations.

JEWISH RELIGIOUSNESS: PRIVATE AND PUBLIC SPHERES

In a recent book on American Judaism, Jacob Neusner notes that there are two different spheres of Jewish religiousness, both accorded equal legitimacy. There is, in the first place, the Judaism of home and family. This aspect of Jewish religious practice focuses on rites of passage—birth rituals, the Bar and Bat Mitzvah, marriage and death rituals. It also centers on the celebration of the Days of Awe (Rosh Hashanah and Yom Kippur), Passover, and Hanukkah. These two sets of ritual observance mark the religious life of a majority of Jews in the United States.

Alongside the religion of home and family there is the second aspect of Jewish religiousness, the public and political sphere, which Neusner calls the "Judaism of Holocaust and Redemption":

> "The Holocaust" of the Judaism of Holocaust and Redemption refers to the murder of six million Jewish children, women, and men in Europe between 1933 and 1945 by the Germans. "The Redemption" is the creation of the state of Israel. . . . The Holocaust then corresponds in the here and now to anti-Semitism, exclusion, alienation, which Jews experience solely by reason of being Jewish.

The creation of the state of Israel is also given transcendent meaning. It provides the answer to the existential question raised by the Holocaust:

> [N]early all American Jews identify with the state of Israel and regard its welfare not only as a secular good, but a metaphysical necessity. Nearly all American Jews are supporters of the state of Israel. But they also regard their own "being Jewish" as inextricably bound up with the meaning they impute to the Jewish state.[11]

It is this second, public manifestation of Jewishness that leads the majority of American Jews to contribute to the United Jewish Appeal and other Jewish charities. Many also contribute to the American-Israel Political Action Committee (AIPAC) and engage in other political action supportive of the state of Israel. Like participation in life-cycle rites and certain widely celebrated holidays, it helps to hold the community together and define it as a community, at the same time relating it to values perceived to be ultimate.

---

[11]Jacob Neusner, *Introduction to American Judaism: What the Books Say, What the People Do* (Minneapolis, MN: Fortress Press, 1994), pp. 115–17.

WOMEN IN JUDAISM IN THE UNITED STATES

There were few Jews in America during the Colonial period. The roles of those Jewish women who were here were similar to those of their gentile counterparts, with one notable exception. Judaism made the observance of religious ritual and the study of Torah the responsibility of men. Jewish women frequently carried on a family business so that their husbands were free to study Torah and to fulfill their religious duties. This pattern continued into the nineteenth century.[12]

Throughout Jewish history, the "vital participation of women of all degrees of orthodoxy" has played a key role.[13] The roles of American Jewish women were transformed in the late 1800s and the 1900s. The growth of Reform Judaism and the pressures of Americanization combined to encourage new and different roles for Jewish women. A Congress of Jewish Women met during the World Parliament of Religions in Chicago in 1893. The National Council of Jewish Women grew out of that conference and became a permanent organization. Jewish women have also been very active in the Zionist Movement. Hadassah, the Women's Zionist Organization of America, was founded in 1911 by Henrietta Szold. It is the oldest and still the largest American Zionist organization. Zionism teaches the equality of men and women, and the women of Hadassah have held the movement to that belief in practice.[14]

The current status of women in Judaism, like women's status in Catholicism and Protestantism, is complex. Women's roles and status have changed dramatically in the twentieth century. Jewish women have responded to these changes in the same ways that Christian women have. Some have left Judaism as they have come to feel that the changes did not occur fast enough or go far enough. Some have remained within their synagogues to work for change. And, some have chosen to fight against changes that threaten to make their familiar traditions less meaningful to them.[15]

As you might expect, the overarching support for traditional Judaism among **Orthodox** Jews means that women's status has changed little, even in America. Religion remains the responsibility of men, to a large extent. Women often do not attend the synagogue. Although the Bar Mitzvah is a very important ceremony marking a boy's religious maturity, there is no comparable ceremony for girls, as in Reform, Conservative, and Reconstructionist Judaism. The **minyan**, or group of ten adult Jews required to hold services or conduct synagogue business, must be ten male adult Jews.

[12]Rosemary Radford Ruether and Rosemary Skinner Keller, eds., *Women and Religion in America, Volume I: The Nineteenth Century* (San Francisco: Harper & Row, Publishers, 1981), p. xi.
[13]Ann D. Braude, "The Jewish Woman's Encounter with American Culture," in *Women and Religion in America, Volume I*, ed. Ruether and Keller, pp. 150–59.
[14]Ann D. Braude, "Jewish Women in the Twentieth Century: Building a Life in America," in *Women and Religion in America, Volume III: 1900–1968*, ed. Ruether and Keller, (San Francisco: Harper & Row, Publishers, 1986), p. 141.
[15]Braude, "Jewish Women in the Twentieth Century," in *Women and Religion in America, Volume I*, ed. Ruether and Keller, p. 143.

Women are not ordained to the rabbinate in Orthodoxy. There are several reasons for this. In ancient Israel, there were no female rabbis, and, traditionally, this has continued to be so. For Orthodoxy, this is reason enough to forbid the practice now. Women are considered ritually unclean during menstruation and for a week thereafter, as well as for a time following childbirth. This would make it impossible for a woman to perform many of the duties of a rabbi during this time. The period of ritual uncleanness following the birth of a baby girl is twice as long as that following the birth of a boy. Ritual uncleanness has little to do with cleanliness and hygiene as we usually think of them. It concerns whether or not a person is ritually pure enough to approach God. Nevertheless, many women experience ritual uncleanness as a painful rejection of themselves and their femaleness, since men are ritually unclean for fewer reasons, and their uncleanness does not last as long.

On a more positive note, the role of wife and mother is highly respected. Women are required to perform three religious duties. One is to visit the ritual bath after her menstrual period. The other two, baking the Sabbath bread, or **challah**, and lighting the candles that officially begin the Sabbath observance are among the most important rituals in Judaism. Children are very important in Judaism, and especially so in Orthodoxy. Women's role as the bearer and nurturer of children earns her great honor.

Women also play the central role in maintaining a kosher home. As we have seen, following all the kosher observances is complicated and time consuming. It is also considered one of the most important Orthodox observances because it serves to set the Orthodox apart from other people and reminds them on a daily basis of their life as the covenant people. The contribution of the wife and mother in the family is indispensable.

Recent research points to the emphasis on family and the clear definition of gender roles as the primary reasons that young Jewish professional women are attracted to Orthodoxy. For women who have come of age in a culture in which the norms of family life are in flux, clearly defined gender roles and norms for family life come as a relief. As one recent study found, for women who had become Orthodox Jews as adults, "the women's attraction to Orthodox Judaism is fundamentally based on a desire for family and clear definitions of femininity and masculinity."[16]

The attitude toward women in **Reform** and **Reconstructionist** Judaism is much more liberal by present-day standards. The first woman to be ordained as a rabbi was Sally J. Preisand, daughter of Reconstruction founder Mordecai Kaplan. A significant number of women have been ordained as rabbis and as cantors.[17] Reform and Reconstructionism have eliminated the distinctions between

[16]Lynn Davidman, "Women's Search for Family and Roots: A Jewish Religious Solution to a Modern Dilemma," in *In Gods We Trust: New Patterns of Religious Pluralism in America*, ed. Thomas Robbins and Dick Anthony (New Brunswick, NJ: Transaction Publishers, 1990) p. 395.

[17] *Cantors* are people who assist the rabbi by chanting some of the prayers.

men and women in synagogue seating and in the performance of religious ritual. Women are encouraged to study Torah alongside their husbands and in women's groups as well. Reform and Reconstructionist women have led in developing new forms of traditional rituals, such as the Passover ritual. The newer rituals include women's contributions to the story of Judaism in explicit ways. These branches of Judaism also pioneered the development and celebration of the Bat Mitzvah to mark a young girl's attainment of religious responsibility. The old ideas and practices concerning ritual impurity have been discarded. Women in these two branches of Judaism have been among the leaders of the women's rights movement in the United States. While motherhood remains important in the more modernized forms of Judaism, there is no bias against women holding jobs outside their homes.

Conservative Judaism has tried to maintain a middle-of-the-road position where women are concerned. Actual observance varies a good bit from family to family and from woman to woman. Men and women sit together in worship. Although the Conservative rabbis voted officially some time ago to ordain women to the rabbinate and as cantors, the actual practice varies from congregation to congregation, and the degree of acceptance of female rabbis is uneven. While many Conservative Jews welcomed the ordination of women as a needed step forward, a significant number refuse to recognize those women who have been ordained.

Observance of the kosher laws and the laws concerning ritual uncleanness varies considerably. While not required, it is strongly supported by many Conservative congregations. Freedom from compulsion makes it possible for some women to observe the tradition without experiencing it as an oppressive burden. For many, Conservatism has been a way to uphold aspects of the tradition that are meaningful while moving toward greater male-female equality.

Like Christianity, Judaism has strong elements of support for women's equality. It also has comparably strong elements that reinforce traditional roles for men and women. It has both encouraged and held back the changes sought by feminists. In either case, it helps to provide the structure within which women can lead meaningful lives.

THE FUTURE OF JUDAISM IN THE UNITED STATES

The situation of Judaism in the United States has been a unique one, unlike the situation in which Jews have found themselves in most of the world. Elsewhere, Jewishness has been largely an involuntary matter, meaning "involuntary association with the local Jewish community, uncritical acceptance of its religious authority and general acquiescence to the demands of classical Judaism." In the United States, Jewishness is voluntary, offering Jews a situation of "virtually unrestricted freedom." It offers every Jew "the opportunity to involve himself or herself in whatever aspects of Judaism or Jewish life appeal, or in none."[18] One result has been the development of Jewish "denominationalism", discussed above. Results also include large numbers of unaffiliated Jews in the United States, high rates of intermarriage, and uncertainty about the future of Judaism as a religion in this setting.

One way of looking at what may be Judaism's future in the United States is to look at the characteristics of *younger* Jews now. A number of features distinguish younger from older Jews in the United States:

More intermarriage
Lower birth rate
Increasing geographic dispersal
Less attachment to the State of Israel
Less enthusiasm for Jewish civil religion and its attendant fund-raising drives
New vitality and commitment among the Orthodox and Conservative branches and greater attention to Jewish tradition among Reform Jews
Greater interest in and expanded opportunities for Jewish education from day care through college levels
Greater attention to ritual observance.[19]

The increasing importance of the private sphere of life highlights the question of Jewish intermarriage. There is concern among some Jews that intermarriage threatens Jewish survival in the United States, since the children of such marriages often do not affiliate with a temple or synagogue. The coming decades will see especially Reform, Reconstructionist, and Conservative congregations challenged to find ways of accepting and integrating gentile spouses who choose not to convert to Judaism.

Another indicator of what may be the future of Judaism is to look at Jewish college students now. What we find by doing so seems to support the increasing impact of an essentially private Judaism. Declining numbers of college students are participating in Hillel, the Jewish student organization. For example, of 6,000 Jewish students at the University of Maryland, only about 125 are in touch with Hillel regularly. Of 3,600 University of Wisconsin students, only about 10 percent participate. According to one former Hillel director, the change can at least in part be attributed to assimilation, in that at the time Hillel began, Jewish students were not comfortable mingling with gentile students, whereas now, they interact freely.[20]

In addition, after decades of emphasis on Judaism as cultural and ethnic identification, there are signs of renewed interest in Judaism as a distinctive *religious* option among American Jews. The rabbinical schools of all three major

---

[18]Richard J. Margolis, "The Jewish Experience in America—A Religious Perspective," *Chicago Studies*, 30, no. 2 (August 1991), pp. 128–29.

[19]Steven M. Cohen, "Jews in the U.S.: The Next Generation," *The Public Perspective: A Roper Center Review of Public Opinion and Polling*, 2, no. 1 (November/December, 1990), pp. 9–10.

[20]*Jewish Currents*, March 1994.

branches report increased enrollments, and new temples and synagogues are forming at a record rate. Small groups of adults form to study Jewish texts and enjoy fellowship. Rabbinical training is putting more emphasis on specifically theological questions than has been the case in the recent past.[21]

QUESTIONS AND ACTIVITIES FOR REVIEW, DISCUSSION, AND WRITING

1. Write an essay on the topic "How my life would be different if I were an Orthodox Jew."
2. If possible, attend a service at a temple or synagogue. This might be done by the entire class together. Write an essay in which you describe what you observed.
3. If possible, arrange to interview an Orthodox Jew about Sabbath and kosher practices. Do the same with a Reform or a Conservative Jew.
4. If there is a kosher deli nearby, arrange a visit there. Talk with the owner(s)/employees about kosher dietary practices and what they mean to Jews in the United States.
5. Of the several sectors of American Judaism, which seems the most attractive to you, and why?
6. If possible, interview a Jewish woman about what being Jewish and female means to her.

FOR FURTHER READING

Kaufman, Debra R., *Rachel's Daughters: Newly Orthodox Jewish Women.* New Brunswick, NJ: Rutgers University Press, 1991. A very interesting study of several young Jewish women who have turned to Orthodox Judaism for spiritual fulfillment. Many interview excerpts.

Neusner, Jacob, *Introduction to American Judaism: What the Books Say, What the People Do.* Minneapolis, MN: Fortress Press, 1994. Comparison of "book" Judaism in the United States with how Judaism is actually lived by its adherents. Neusner uses this analysis to discuss the importance of both the private sphere and civil religion in the United States more generally.

Wertheimer, Jack, *A People Divided: Judaism in Contemporary America.* New York: Basic Books, 1993. Discusses American Jewish behavior in terms of how *American* it is and how *Jewish* it is, analyzing the impact of events in the culture at large on how Judaism is practiced.

---

[21]"A Rekindling of Faith," *U.S. News and World Report,* October 21, 1991, pp. 78–79.

7
$\mathcal{H}$umanism and the Unitarian Universalists

LIBERAL RELIGION IN POPULAR
AND ECCLESIAL MODES

As you have already learned, most people in the United States who are religious are either conservative (moderate) or fundamentalist in their religious attitude. However, in both ecclesial and popular modes, we find those who identify themselves as religious **liberals**.

Those who are religiously liberal tend to be more socially and politically liberal, as well. More men than women and more whites than blacks identify themselves as religious liberals. The two coastal areas have more religious liberals than do other parts of the country. Liberalism is somewhat more common among those who live in more urban areas than among those whose residence is rural or small town. Those who identify themselves as religious liberals are better educated, on the whole, than those who do not. They are somewhat less likely to be affiliated with specific religious organizations than are conservatives and fundamentalists.

Liberal religion outside of religious organizations tends to become identified with ethics. Belief in the supernatural is largely replaced by commitment to the human community and to doing good for the entire planet. In other words, the line between popular liberal religion and humanism is somewhat blurry.

In its popular mode, liberal religion emphasizes the equality of all religions. The various religions are many approaches to the same goal. The similarities between them are thus more important than their historical differences. The comparative study of religion is important because it provides a variety of perspectives that can enrich and complement each other. Huston Smith is one of the leading spokespersons of this point of view, and the title and subtitle of his recent book summarize the perspective in one phrase: *Forgotten Truth: The Common Vision of the World's Religions.*[1]

Popular liberal religion appeals more to those with higher levels of education, and two of its modern embodiments reflect this intellectual emphasis. One is the search for transcendent meaning through a recovery of the mythic dimension of life and experience. Undoubtedly the best known spokesperson of this viewpoint is Joseph Campbell, whose book, *The Power of Myth*, and the public television series of the same name received widespread acclaim.

The second is reflected in public interest in the work of the Jesus Seminar, a group of seventy scholars from universities and seminaries throughout the world that was founded in 1985. The work of the seminar focuses on the question, "What did Jesus *really* say?" Some of you may remember "red-letter" King James Bibles, in which Jesus' words were printed in red. The aim of the Jesus Seminar is to take the words attributed to Jesus in the Christian New Testament and determine which can be guaranteed authentic, which are questionable, and which Jesus did not speak. The seminar participants concluded that less than 20 percent of the words attributed to Jesus can be said to have been spoken by Jesus. While those to whom a literal reading of the Bible is important deplore the work of the Seminar, intellectual religious liberals have been stimulated by the dialogue that it has generated.

HUMANISM IN THE UNITED STATES

Before we go any further, stop for a moment and reflect on what associations, if any, the word *humanism* brings to your mind. Does it have positive or negative connotations? What do you think about people who say that they are humanists? Do you think humanism necessarily excludes belief in God? Is it possible to have a religion without belief in God or in anything supernatural? Does your school have a college or department of humanities? Do you think these two words are related? How?

Humanism can be defined briefly as a worldview or philosophy that derives its values from the experience of human life in this world, without reference to God as Jews and Christians understand God, or to anything else supernatural. This definition will now be expanded, and you will learn about some of the themes that are a part of most humanists' understanding of what humanism is and means.

The brief definition of humanism just cited is useful in that it states the

[1]Huston Smith, *Forgotten Truth: The Common Vision of the World's Religions* (San Francisco: HarperSanFrancisco, 1992).

view that is at the core of much modern secular humanism. There are several themes that recur in virtually all descriptions of secular humanism. Taken together, these themes provide a working description that fills out the brief definition and enables us to understand what is important to secular humanists and why. Other humanists interpret these basic principles in ways that are compatible with Jewish or Christian monotheism. Religious humanism will be discussed more fully in the following paragraphs.

Humanism begins with human beings, people like ourselves. Humanists believe that people have evolved over a long period of time and will continue to do so. People are basically good, although we certainly have the capacity for evil as well. In other words, although humanists recognize that people do things that are dreadfully wrong, they do not believe in the idea of original sin or in an inherited or inherent tendency toward evil. Their conviction about the basic goodness of human nature gives them tremendous confidence in the possibilities of human beings. Human beings have genuinely free will. This is one of our most important characteristics, according to humanists. We are, in other words, both "response-able" and responsible beings. Humanists oppose all views of human nature that include determinism or predestination because each compromises our free will.

Body, mind, and emotions are linked together in a unity that cannot be broken without severely damaging the organism. Because we are embodied (rather than simply having a body as a sort of appendage), we are a part of the natural world, kin to everything else that lives and to nonliving things as well. For most humanists, embeddedness in the natural world means that there is no human survival after earthly death.

But, in our freedom, we transcend the natural world, at least in part. Although we can never move beyond it, we can think and envision beyond it. Other living beings are limited by their embodiment in ways that we are not. We can manipulate the world for our own purposes. And we have a responsibility for it. Our capacity to transcend the natural world also gives rise to another very important human capacity, that of giving meaning. As far as we know, we are the only beings who give meaning to our existence. We are not content simply to be; we seek meaning as well. To give meaning to life, or to find meaning in it, is a distinctively human act. It is for this reason, too, that people may be religious, whereas animals are not.

Humanists also say that we are most fully ourselves only in the context of the entire community of humankind and in those smaller communities of which we are a part. Human beings do not exist in isolation. We were born because two people came together in sexual union. At our death, other people will mourn our dying. There is convincing evidence that babies who do not have sufficient contact with other human beings do not thrive as well as those who do, and, in extreme cases, may even die. All people are linked together. For the humanist, all humanity is one large community. Our lives are lived more immediately in the context of those smaller communities of which we are a part, such as immediate and extended families, workplaces, neighborhoods, and our various social groups. The important point here is that our relationships with other people are a part of us; they are not simply added on. It is no accident that when someone close to us dies, we sometimes say "I feel as if a part of me has died, too." It did. According to humanists, a human being is a complex of physical, intellectual, and emotional elements, embedded in both the natural world and the world of human relationships.

Another important humanist belief is that **this world, this universe, is complete in and of itself.** Like ourselves, it is the product of a long evolutionary process that still continues. It is the totality of existence. There is nothing else. Specifically, the universe needed no God to create it or to set it in motion, nor does it need God to keep it going. It came into being as a result of natural forces and operates according to natural laws. It is meaningful in and of itself and needs no reference to a God outside the world to make it meaningful. While it is an appropriate place for human beings, it is neither hostile nor positive toward human existence; it is neutral.

The **morality and ethics of humanism** are based on humanism's assessment of human nature and its understanding of the world. It is a morality based on human responsibility. It is up to each of us to figure out the most responsible course of action in any given situation, using the best of our ability to reason and weigh alternatives. There is no divine source of moral guidance, no divine authority whose ethical pronouncements can simply be accepted. Reason, experience, and the guidance of other people are all helpful, but the ultimate responsibility rests with the individual.

Humanism advocates an ethic of the good rather than an ethic of the right. There is not one absolute right that holds for all times and all people. Morality is contextual in that it takes account of the situation or context in which moral decisions are made. Moral decisions must be made on the basis of both principles and the demands of particular situations. For example, humanists regard human life as having a very high value. Each of us has inherent dignity and supreme worth simply because we *are*. Thus, in general, human life is to be preserved. In situations in which the preservation of biological life conflicts with the quality of life, humanists may well give the preservation of biological life second place and thus support euthanasia or death with dignity for persons who are terminally ill. Similarly, respect for human life prevents humanists from supporting the casual use of abortion as a means of birth control. However, most humanists do support women's right to safe and legal abortions when the circumstances warrant them.

Within these basic guidelines, there are certain principles that most, if not all, humanists affirm. They oppose all types of prejudice, whether on the basis of race, gender, age, nationality, religion, or anything else. Prejudice violates the fundamental equality and worth of all persons. Humanists advocate the establishment of international peace, and believe that all persons are entitled to a reasonable standard of living. Most are in favor of strict nuclear weapons regulation or elimination and believe that much of the money spent on the military could be better spent in providing for the needs of people. Respect and responsibility for the natural world of which we are a part have come to be increasingly emphasized as it has become clear that the lack of such respect has jeopardized the very planet on which we live.

Humanists **oppose authoritarianism in all its forms.** Humanism is built upon the belief in personal freedom and individual responsibility, and authoritarianism is seen as a violation of that freedom and that responsibility. Note that authoritarian*ism* is not the same thing as the exercise of legitimate authority. Because of their commitment to individual freedom and responsibility, most humanists assert that some form of political democracy is the best style of government.

Reason and the use of the scientific method is the central humanist approach to knowledge and verification. That is, all phenomena are susceptible and accessible to human investigation and understanding. Specifically, religion is to be investigated and evaluated according to the same criteria that we would use to analyze anything else. Nothing is exempt, and nothing is so removed from the ordinary world that it cannot be understood by using reason and careful investigation. As a corollary to this, most humanists emphasize the **importance of educating all people** to the fullest of their abilities. Education is necessary to enable people to fulfill their potential to the greatest extent possible and to provide the necessary tools for rational problem solving. The type of education favored by humanists teaches children to reach and support their own conclusions by reasoning, rather than teaching them to follow authorities without questioning.

Humanism, in other words, is based on the faith that people can live truly good lives in the here and now, that we have the capacity to cooperate to build a good society that balances out the needs of the individual and the larger group, and that we can find meaning and fulfillment without recourse to anything supernatural. Or, as one humanist puts it, humanism is "the use of reason in human affairs, applied in the service of compassion."[2]

Not all humanists are secularists, although many are. Jewish and Christian humanism also have a significant place in the story of American humanism. The humanist belief in the dignity and worth of every person, the emphasis on ethical conduct and human responsibility, and compassion in the context of human community are all shared by most religions. Liberal religion shares with humanism a belief in the basic goodness of human nature, its insistence that the context must be taken into account in making moral decisions, and its support for the use of reason and opposition to authoritarianism. Much of liberal religion agrees with humanism that supernaturalism in religion is outdated and that scientific inquiry can and should be used to evaluate claims to religious truth. Humanism and liberal religion also share the belief that the sacred and secular worlds

---

[2]H. J. Eysenck, "Reason with Compassion," in *The Humanist Alternative*, ed. Paul Kurtz (Buffalo, NY: Prometheus Books, 1973), p. 91.

cannot, in the final analysis, be separated. Social justice, opposition to prejudice in all forms, and an interest in peacemaking also characterize both.

"The adventure of religion," writes one advocate of religious humanism, "is not in the discovery of Eternal Truth or Absolute Meaning—arenas in which human beings do not and cannot deal—but in our individual and communal search for and creation of meanings and values that dignify and enhance life."[3] Another explains how humanism seeks to modify religion: "Humanism attempts to rid religious institutions, myths, creeds, prayers, and sacraments of superstitious beliefs, while enhancing their significance as expressions of human needs, hopes and values."[4]

As you will see, the first of three significant statements of the humanist perspective was written as an expression of religious humanism. Two later statements, although they reflect increasing skepticism about the viability of religion, also echo the understanding of it expressed by Pfifer and Schneider.

The recent history of humanism in the United States is built on the foundation of centuries of earlier history, both in the United States and throughout the world. Rather than tracing this early history, however, this discussion will focus on the more recent course of humanism in the United States. Humanism as a self-conscious movement began in the United States in 1933, when *Humanist Manifesto I* was written. There had been humanists and humanist philosophers in America as far back as the Declaration of Independence and even farther. Conscious attempts to articulate the principles of American humanism date from the first manifesto, however. We will look at three relatively recent documents in which people committed to the humanist point of view attempt to spell out what humanism is and means to those who follow it.

THREE HUMANIST STATEMENTS

The first of these three statements is the *Humanist Manifesto I*, written in 1933 by a group of humanists in the United States who set out to draft what they understood to be the basic principles of the movement. It is an optimistic and upbeat document that expresses great confidence in humanism as the wave of the future. "In every field of human activity," they wrote, "the vital movement is now in the direction of a candid and explicit humanism." The humanism of this document is explicitly religious humanism. Its authors wanted to separate religion from doctrines and from methods that they believed were "outmoded" and not workable in the twentieth century. They intended it to be a "new statement of the means and purposes of religion." It is written in the form of a series of fifteen brief statements with an introduction and conclusion. It deals with those themes that we have already seen in connection with humanism.[5]

[3]Kenneth W. Pfifer, *The Faith of a Humanist* (Boston, MA: Unitarian Universalist Association, n.d.).
[4]Herbert W. Schneider, "Religious Humanism," in *The Humanist Alternative*, ed. Paul Kurtz, p. 65.
[5]Paul J. Kurtz, *Humanist Manifesto I* (Buffalo, NY: Prometheus Books, 1973).

The authors of the first major humanist statement *were* critical of the religious institutions of their day and regarded many religious beliefs and practices as unsuitable for life in the twentieth century. It is equally clear that they were not, on the whole, hostile to religion. Religion, while in need of dramatic transformation, would, once transformed, continue to serve many of the same functions it had served in the past. Their confidence in the capacity of human nature to accomplish what was needed was high. As a whole, the document carries its reader along on a tide of goodwill and optimism.

By 1973, when *Humanist Manifesto II* was drafted, the events of the intervening forty years had made the first program seem far too optimistic. Still, its authors expressed great confidence in people's ability to solve the problems that existed. It calls for people to "fuse reason with compassion in order to build constructive moral values."

It groups its seventeen propositions together under five categories. The first deals with religion. A major change from the first document is that this manifesto states that religion cannot be reinterpreted sufficiently to be made viable; something radically new is needed. Promises of eternal salvation and threats of eternal hellfire are especially harmful. They distract people from their proper focus on life in this world. A closely related section deals with ethics. Ethics are derived from human experience in this world, and moral decision making must take the situation into account. Reason and intelligence are the best tools we have for making moral decisions, coupled with the cultivation of appropriate emotional attitudes of love and compassion.

The authors then affirm the dignity and worth of every person as a central humanist value. A section on the democratic society affirms the importance of a full range of civil liberties for all people. Participatory democracy is to be extended into all human affairs in all nations. Government and religion or ideology are to be kept strictly separate. Economics must be responsive to human needs. All discrimination must be eliminated, and the right to universal education is affirmed.

The next section encourages the building of a true world community with a system of world law and government. Violence and force must be eliminated. A call for ecological responsibility on a worldwide scale is included. The developed and developing nations are called upon to assist the underdeveloped ones in all possible ways. Technological development is to be supported, but it must be judged by the effects it has on humanity. Travel restrictions must be lifted and open, worldwide communication is encouraged.[6]

The second manifesto was originally signed by 114 people and was later endorsed by many more. It is a statement sobered by a world war and by economic chaos in several places throughout the world. It has a much more clearly political tone than did its predecessor. Political and economic arrangements between nations are given more explicit attention. And, as previously noted, its at-

---

[6]Paul J. Kurtz, *Humanist Manifesto II* (Buffalo, NY: Prometheus Books, 1973).

titude toward religion has changed. The changes between the two manifestos reflect the changes in the thinking of the humanist community in the United States and abroad. (The list of signers includes people from Great Britain, Canada, West Germany, the former USSR, India, France, and Sweden, as well as the United States.)

A Secular Humanist Declaration, written in 1980, is a very different sort of document. It outlines an explicitly secular humanism that clearly believes itself to be under attack and on the defensive. It attacks by name a variety of points of view and groups such as Christian fundamentalism, the Catholic papal hierarchy, Moslem clericalism, nationalistic Judaism, and many New Age beliefs and practices. It accuses these groups of promoting unthinking reliance on authority, restricting human freedom, and bypassing the use of reason and the scientific method to solve problems. It then moves on to a series of positive affirmations and calls for action that reflects the humanist values we have seen before.[7]

As these three documents reflect the evolution of humanist thought in the United States, we can see that the situation has become more and more polarized into two opposing sides. As Christian fundamentalism has named secular humanism as the main focus of its attack, religious fundamentalism has become the focus of secular humanism's attack. There can be no doubt that the views of fundamentalists and humanists are sharply different at almost every point. Fundamentalists tend to oppose both secular and religious humanism, believing that both are examples of human rebellion against God's authority. The kind of society envisioned by the one would have no room for the other. Each provides a framework within which significant numbers of Americans live and attempt to construct a meaningful life. If we really are to become neighbors and not strangers, there must be room in the neighborhood for both points of view. The tendency of each to view the other as an obnoxious enemy must give way to an appreciation of what each provides for those who live their lives by it.

Humanist Organizations in the United States

Humanist organizations are not nearly as well known as more traditional religious organizations, but there are several such groups in the United States. They are more common in major urban areas than in smaller communities and along the coasts more than in the heartland. In 1857, the Free Religious Association was formed by a group of young Unitarians who had come to believe that all religion, even Unitarianism, worked against freedom and progress. They supported empiricism and scientific naturalism, and the organization took an antireligious, rather than simply a nonreligious, approach.

Felix Adler founded the **Ethical Culture Society** in 1876. He had been trained as a rabbi but left Judaism in favor of ethical humanism based on the dignity and worth of every individual. The member societies of the Ethical Culture

---

[7]Paul J. Kurtz, "A Secular Humanist Declaration," *Free Inquiry*, 1, no. 1 (Winter 1980).

Society hold Sunday meetings that are of an educational and morally uplifting nature. The group is also characterized by intense social activism in the areas of education, war and peace, and racism, among others.

The **American Humanist Association** was formed in 1941 as an effort to link the various humanist interests in the United States. Like the Ethical Culture Society, it supports an active program of social involvement that is based on the principles in the *Humanist Manifestos*. It publishes a periodical, *The Humanist*, and supports Prometheus Books, the largest American publisher of humanist literature. There is a **Fellowship of Religious Humanists**, headquartered in Yellow Springs, Ohio, that publishes a journal, *Religious Humanism*.

The **Society for Humanistic Judaism** is the major Jewish humanist organization. It was founded by Rabbi Sherwin T. Wine in 1968. According to the Society, a Jew "is someone who identifies with the history, culture, struggles, triumphs, and future of the Jewish people." Moral decisions are to be based on the circumstances of the particular situation, with evaluation based on the consequences of the action. Humanistic Judaism emphasizes the human value of life cycle and holiday celebrations.[8]

These and other smaller groups provide some organizational cohesiveness to the humanist movement in America and provide a means by which people in agreement with this point of view can find fellowship and engage in social action. They serve at least some of the same functions that churches and synagogues do for those who are more traditionally religious. They also provide a means by which humanists can voice their concerns. The humanist organizations work to get legislation passed that reflects their viewpoint, just as do other political interest groups.

Let's look again at the definition of religion with which we began and examine humanism from that angle. Religion is an integrated system of beliefs, lifestyle, specific ritual acts, and organization by means of which people give meaning to their lives (or find meaning in them), by relating their lives to what is taken to be holy, sacred, or of highest value. We have seen that humanism certainly offers its adherents a coherent set of beliefs. Many humanists do in fact live a lifestyle that is closely based on those beliefs. There are also, as we have seen, several organizations that give an institutional dimension to humanism. Things do get more complicated when we look at specific ritual acts. Many humanists believe that religious ritual is unnecessary. A substantial number of humanists feel that ritual is superstitious and supernaturalistic. Humanism certainly gives meaning to its followers (or is a way that they find meaning in their lives). That meaning comes in part at least from relating their lives to humankind, which humanists take as the highest value. On balance, then, it seems that humanism qualifies as a religion on the basis of our definition. We do need to be sensitive to the fact that the majority of humanists themselves do not think of it as a religion.

---

[8]William B. Williamson, ed., *An Encyclopedia of Religions in the United States: One Hundred Religious Groups Speak for Themselves* (New York: Crossroad, 1992), pp. 194–96.

They are more likely to describe it as a philosophy of life or a worldview. And, the courts have held that humanism is not a religion in the legal sense.

There can be no doubt that humanism serves many of the same functions for its adherents that traditional religions do for theirs. It has many of the same emotional dynamics. Like the religions, humanism deserves a place among the myriad ways that Americans organize their lives in a meaningful fashion. It is a continuing element in the American landscape, one that will interact with religion for a long time to come.

UNITARIAN UNIVERSALISM

Unitarian Universalism is an ecclesial embodiment of the very liberal religious tradition in the United States. The present **Unitarian Universalist Association** is the result of a merger between the Universalists and the Unitarians. We will first consider the two separately and then look at the Unitarian Universalist Association today.

The Universalists

Simply put, **universalism** is the belief that all persons will eventually be saved by God; in other words, salvation is universal, not limited to an elect number. This belief is suggested by certain biblical passages. For example, Acts 3:21 speaks of a time of restoration or restitution of all things. John 1:29 refers to Jesus as the Lamb of God who takes away the sins of the [whole] world, and Romans 5:18 speaks of the righteousness of Jesus being imparted to all people. In the twenty-first chapter of Revelation, God is said to say, "I make all things new" (verse 5). Clearly, traditional Christian teaching has not taken these and other similar passages in this light, but this interpretation was seized upon by those who could not reconcile the concept of a God of love with the idea that such a God would condemn anyone to everlasting punishment. Nonetheless, universalism usually has been regarded as a heresy throughout Christian history.

By the time of the American colonies, universalism was already present on the American religious scene and would remain there. Englishman John Murray (1741–1815) is sometimes considered the father of American Universalism. In 1770, he preached what may well have been the first Universalist sermon in America, in New England. The first covenant for a Universalist church was drawn up in Murray's church in Gloucester, Massachusetts, in 1779, and, in 1780, he met with a group in Philadelphia to help draft a Universalist declaration of faith.

Elhanan Winchester (1751–1797) was another early leader, an intellectual and a writer whose writing ability helped to spread the Universalist message and give it credibility. Both Murray and Winchester remained within the framework of trinitarian Christianity.

Hosea Ballou (1771–1852) was not a trinitarian, however, but a unitarian, who believed that God was one—instead of three—persons. Ballou's universalism was blended with his unitarianism in ways that prefigured the eventual merger of the two groups. Ballou's *Treatise on the Atonement* was the first American attempt to develop a coherent theology along Universalist lines. He became the pastor of the Second Universalist Church in Boston and held that post for over thirty years, becoming the chief spokesperson for Universalism in the new world. He also founded the *Universalist Magazine* and the *Universalist Expositor*, both of which helped to spread the universalist theology. During part of his pastorate in Boston, he worked closely with William Ellery Channing, who would become known as the father of American Unitarianism.

The denomination spread slowly in the nineteenth and twentieth centuries. It was especially successful in the rural and frontier areas, while the Unitarians were more concentrated in urban areas. By the mid-1900s, Universalism had become known as a liberalized and universalized form of Christianity, which it remained until its union with Unitarianism.

The Unitarians

While the universalists were teaching universal salvation as a clearer expression of the will of an all-loving God, the Unitarians reacted to other elements in traditional Christian teaching. First among these was the doctrine that God is a trinity, formalized at Nicaea in 325 C.E. This doctrine, you will recall from the discussion of basic Christian beliefs, holds that God is three distinct persons with but one substance. The **Unitarians** taught the oneness of God, against the trinitarians. Although their name derives from this one teaching, there were other Christian doctrines to which they objected. Among these were the infallibility of the Bible, human depravity and the inheritance of original sin, and the doctrine that some will be damned eternally. This last point aligned them with the Universalists. The Unitarians also encouraged the use of reason as a way of determining religious truth, a theme that we saw in our discussion of humanism and one that remains a hallmark of modern-day Unitarianism.

The first church in the United States that took an explicitly Unitarian view of God did so in the late 1700s. In 1785, the Episcopal King's Chapel in Boston appointed a young minister with Unitarian views, James Freeman. Freeman led his congregation in changing the Anglican Prayer Book to eliminate all references to the Trinity. The Episcopal Church refused to recognize the church as Episcopalian, and, in 1787, Freeman became the first American-ordained Unitarian minister. What had been the first Episcopal Church in Boston became the first Unitarian Church.

William Ellery Channing (1780–1842) is often said to be father of American Unitarianism. American religious historian Sydney Ahlstrom compares Channing's role in the Unitarian reformation in America to that of Martin Luther in the German reformation.[9] In 1819, Channing preached his famous

[9]Sydney E. Ahlstrom, *A Religious History of the American People* (New Haven, CT: Yale University Press, 1973), p. 398.

sermon "Unitarian Christianity" in which he defined the new movement. Channing's Unitarianism remained firmly Christian. In his interpretation, God the Father sent the Son and gives the Holy Spirit to those who seek it. These three are not to be considered three persons in one God, however. Six years later, Channing founded the American Unitarian Association. **Transcendentalism** played a large role in the early Unitarian movement. An American adaptation of English romanticism and German idealism, transcendentalism sought to refine Unitarianism and bring in into conformity with what it believed was the common substance of all the world's religions. Ralph Waldo Emerson (1803–1882) was the best-known leader of the Transcendentalist movement. Emerson preferred to be called a theist rather than a Christian, because the term was more general.

Harvard Divinity School and College (later, Harvard University) became the intellectual stronghold of Unitarianism. Most faculty and students were consciously Unitarian in their outlook, and especially in the decade between 1811 and 1820, Harvard became the leading Unitarian training center in the United States. Unitarianism remained strongest in New England and in the more urban areas of the growing nation. In rural areas and along the frontier, where Universalism was stronger, Unitarianism was looked upon as an elitist religion. It was that aspect of Unitarianism that led someone to remark that Unitarians believed in "the fatherhood of God, the brotherhood of man and the neighborhood of Boston."

Unitarianism gradually transformed itself from the distinctly Christian Unitarianism of Channing's sermon into an ethically oriented, pragmatic, humanistic, and sometimes theistic, religion. Along the way, and indicative of the changes that were taking place, American Unitarianism played a dominant role in organizing and supporting the Parliament of Religions in Chicago in 1893. It was this transformed Unitarianism that carried over into the present-day Unitarian Universalist Association.

The Unitarian Universalist Association

As we have seen, the Universalists and the Unitarians shared both a dissatisfaction with the prevailing religious orthodoxies of their times and a substantial body of common beliefs and religious sensibilities. Nonetheless, despite Hosea Ballou's repeated calls for unity, there was almost no interest in cooperation on the part of either group in the early years. They came from different social backgrounds, and, while many of their quarrels with traditional Christianity were similar, they arrived at their positions by different routes. The Universalists began with the conflict between the doctrine of God's love and the idea of eternal damnation. This gave their protest a different emotional quality than that of the more rational and intellectual Unitarian objection to what they saw as the illogic of the trinitarian viewpoint.

However, as both groups changed, in many ways moving even closer together, interest in cooperative efforts grew, spurred by the fact that neither group was large. Their size meant that they needed each other. Finally, in 1947, a commission was set up to determine what kind of cooperation was actually possible. By 1951, this commission had drawn up a plan, which was accepted by both its constituencies, for cooperative work in several key areas such as religious education, public relations, and publications. They also recommended moving gradually toward a full merger. The merger was completed in the spring of 1961, bringing into being the Unitarian Universalist Association, the national organization for the church today.

Unitarian Universalism Today

Many of us, when we encounter a community of faith with which we are unfamiliar, want to know, "What, exactly, do you believe?" Unitarian Universalism has no specific creed. There is no official statement of beliefs to which members must give assent. There is no confession of faith that is repeated regularly in Sunday services. Rather than having a set of firm beliefs worked out and handed to people, the Unitarian Universalists support a set of very broad operating principles that serve as guidelines for individual and community decision making.

Individual freedom of religious belief is perhaps the most fundamental of all these guidelines. All people, following the guidance of their own best understanding and informed by the community of faith as a whole, are responsible for working out their own beliefs. There is no outside authority. Each person lives "by a thought-out covenant with himself [or herself] and with life as a whole," and people understand that their "beliefs may change as insights deepen and experiences broaden."[10] Unitarian Universalists believe that people are capable of doing this without divine revelation. This understanding of how religious beliefs come about leads Unitarian Universalists to a large measure of tolerance for differences within their ranks, as well as appreciation for religious views other than Unitarian Universalism. The emphasis, in other words, is not on having a correct set of beliefs handed down from church authorities or from a sacred book, but on responsibly working out one's own beliefs, subject to change as one's understanding grows.

Unitarian Universalists believe that religious beliefs should change as people change throughout the course of their lives, rather than saying that there are beliefs that should be clung to throughout life. The process of arriving at religious beliefs is of central importance. For most, if not all, ethical action in the world, with and on behalf of other people, is of greater importance than belief.

The set of principles currently in use was approved by the member congregations in 1985. Many of these are humanist principles with which we are now familiar, such as the dignity and worth of every person, the importance of justice and compassion, freedom in the search for truth and meaning, the use of the democratic process in decision making at all levels, the goal of world com-

---

[10]Jack Mendelsohn, *Meet the Unitarian Universalists* (Boston: Unitarian Universalist Association, 1979), p. 6.

munity, and the affirmation of the interconnectedness of all life. Other principles highlight a variety of resources from which the church draws inspiration and guidance. A sense of wonder at the natural world and the people who inhabit it is the first such resource. The words and deeds of prophets, which, in a very wide sense of the term, includes all those people who have challenged injustice wherever they found it, are also important. The wisdom of all the world's religions is affirmed, with specific mention given to "Jewish and Christian teachings which call us to respond to God's love by loving our neighbors as ourselves." This item aroused considerable controversy among the congregations as they discussed the new statement. While some welcomed it, others believed strongly that setting Judaism and Christianity apart in this way implied an unacceptable ranking of them above the other world religions. Finally, the importance of humanist teachings is cited.

These principles of belief lead most Unitarian Universalists to a lifestyle that includes engagement in social action. One notable characteristic of the members of this church is that they are, compared with their relatively small numbers in most areas, vastly overrepresented in those organizations that are identified with liberal social concerns. Organizations that work to make life better for all citizens can usually count on support from Unitarian Universalists. Groups that work on increasing civil liberties also attract Unitarian Universalists' interest. For most, political involvement, in the widest sense of that term, is a central way of working out their religious commitments in day-to-day life.

The freedom to work out one's own religious beliefs without pressure from any external authorities attracts the highly educated into Unitarian Universalism. They are the most highly educated, on the average, of any American church. This also means that this church includes many professional people among its members, both men and women. The freedom of religious belief that characterizes Unitarian Universalist churches also draws couples of mixed religious faith, because they can attend services at the same place without either of them compromising their own faith. People may also become part of a Unitarian Universalist congregation if they live too far from their own community of faith to participate in its activities.

Unitarian Universalists are also among the most culture-affirming people. They raise hard questions about the culture in which they live, especially when that culture seems less humane than it might be. Nonetheless, Unitarian Universalists believe in full participation in the life of the society of which they are a part. Restrictions on individual decision making about things like drinking alcohol, dress, and sexual arrangements between consenting adults are simply not a part of the Unitarian Universalist philosophy.

Unitarian Universalist congregations provide corporate ritual activity, but describing a "typical" service is difficult. The freedom that we have noted in belief translates into freedom in deciding what format religious meetings will take. Regular services usually occur on Sunday morning (Figure 7–1). It is not unheard of, however, for a church to hold services at some other time that suits the needs

Figure 7–1 Unitarian Universalist services attract people seeking freedom of religious thought. (*Joe Traver/Gamma-Liaison.*)

of the congregation better. In some churches, the service may be hard to distinguish from any other very liberal Protestant service. In others, greater experimentation and innovation are the rule. There is a *hymnal,* or hymn book, that includes traditional hymns that are modified to eliminate gender-exclusive language. Other hymns specifically reflect the church's own teachings. Readings in a typical service might be taken from many sources. The Jewish and Christian scriptures, the sacred writings of other world religions, contemporary poetry, and novels are only a few illustrations. It is not unusual to find a reading from the Christian New Testament and a reading from a John Updike novel side by side. The minister or a guest speaker gives a sermon, talk, meditation, or commentary (some churches do not use the more distinctly religious word *sermon*). It may concern a matter of ethical importance, social involvement, self-development, or human relationships, to name but a few examples. An offering is usually received. A person expecting prayers might be surprised; Unitarian Universalist church services sometimes do not include them.

I have avoided using the word *worship* to describe the church services. Worship carries with it the idea that there is a god or supreme being that is being worshipped, an idea upon which not all Unitarian Universalists agree. There are no sacraments. Children are welcomed into the congregation and dedicated, at which time their parents and the congregation affirm their commitment to the child and celebrate the new life that has come into being. Other ceremonies such as marriages and funerals echo the liberal and humanistic perspective that is so much a part of the life of these communities of faith. Nearly all services include time for fellowship and refreshments before or after.

Fellowship is important for the members of Unitarian Universalist congregations. One Unitarian Universalist church in the Midwest, where midweek worship services are the order of the day for the Christian majority, sponsors a weekly Wednesday Revival Hour at which those who want to do so can get together for discussion and fellowship. The group meets at various local restaurants or cocktail lounges or may have a carry-in dinner at someone's home. Larger churches support a full range of activities from which members and friends can choose. Discussion, education, and debate characterize the life of these communities of faith. Education for adults, young people, and children is built into the Sunday morning activities, and other activities may occur during the week.

Organizationally, each local church is fully autonomous. The Unitarian Universalist Association, with headquarters in Boston, takes care of many operational details and serves as the central offices for the group. Its statements have only an advisory function where local congregations are concerned. There is a national annual conference. Beacon Press is the church's publishing house. The Association also supports a unique outreach program. Called the **Church of the Larger Fellowship**, this program was designed especially for religious liberals who live too far from a Unitarian Universalist church to attend. It makes available a news bulletin that contains sermons and inspirational writings, as well as reports on activities. A *Handbook of Services* for the major celebrations of life is provided for each member. A minister is available by mail or telephone. A religious education director provides parents with assistance in developing a religious education program for the home. A lending library is also maintained.

Humanism and liberal religion provide meaningful alternatives to traditional religion for significant numbers of Americans. They have influenced more traditional religion in the direction of increased social concern. Humanism and humanitarianism have been and continue to be very closely linked in the United States, and the presence of humanism has made the society more humanitarian. Like their sparring partners, the fundamentalists, humanists deserve a place in the community of neighbors, not strangers.

QUESTIONS AND ACTIVITIES FOR REVIEW, DISCUSSION, AND WRITING

1. Take a current ethical or moral problem of which you are aware. Think it through (1) beginning with the assumptions of Judaism or Christianity and (2) again from a humanistic viewpoint. What differences in the process and in the conclusions do you notice? You might want to organize this as a debate with a friend, each of you taking one point of view.
2. Humanism opposes all forms of authoritarianism. Do you agree, or do you feel that authoritarianism has a place in certain situations? Is it important to distinguish between authority and authoritarianism? For what reasons and in what circumstances might one person or group exercise authority over others?
3. In your opinion, is humanism a religion? Why or why not?
4. Visit a Unitarian Universalist Church or Fellowship if there is one in your community or close by. In what ways is the Sunday service similar to others with which you may be familiar? How is it different? Many members of these churches became Unitarian Universalists after having been part of other religious groups. If possible, make

arrangements to speak with the minister about how some of the people in the congregation came to their present religious outlook.

5. What might be the advantages and disadvantages of being a part of a community of faith that expects that religious beliefs will change throughout people's lives, rather than offering a set of beliefs that are expected to remain constant?

FOR FURTHER READING

Allen, Norm R., Jr., *African-American Humanism: An Anthology*. Buffalo, NY: Prometheus Books, 1991. Humanism has played a strong role in the development of the African-American intellectual tradition. Allen's book has biographies of noted black humanists, essays, and interviews. A thorough documentation of an aspect of humanism of which few are aware.

Funk, Robert W., Roy W. Hoover, and the Jesus Seminar, *The Five Gospels: The Search for the Authentic Words of Jesus*, a new translation and commentary. New York: Macmillan Publishing Company, 1993. "Five" in the title refers to the mystical Gospel of Thomas, included with the four canonical gospels in the sources from which the Seminar drew. Not an "easy read," by any means, but if you are interested in this issue and the work of the Jesus Seminar, worth the effort.

Knight, Margaret, ed., *Humanist Anthology: From Confucius to Attenborough*, rev. by James Herrick. Buffalo, NY: Prometheus Books, 1995. The full range of humanist thought, from the ancient world to the twentieth century.

Kurtz, Paul, *Eupraxophy: Living Without Religion*. Buffao, NY: Prometheus Books, 1989. Kurtz' unusual word derives from the Greek words for good, practice, and wisdom. *Eupraxophy* thus means "good conduct and wisdom in living." He deals with both ethics and the view of the universe that underlies his position.

————, *The Humanist Alternative: Some Definitions of Humanism*. Buffalo, NY: Prometheus Books, 1973. Collection of brief essays from a variety of humanistic viewpoints, defining humanism and setting out its main principles. An accessible introduction. As relevant and engaging now as it was in 1973.

Mendelsohn, Jack, *Being Liberal in an Illiberal Age: Why I Am a Unitarian Universalist*. Boston: Beacon Press, 1985. A personal statement from one of the country's most articulate Unitarian Universalists.

Wine, Sherwin T., *Humanistic Judaism*. Buffalo, NY: Prometheus Books, 1978. A collection of essays defining the approach to Judaism advocated by the Society for Humanistic Judaism. Judaism as practiced by many Jews in the United States focuses on the humanistic elements in Judaism and plays down its religious dimensions.

Christianities that Began in the United States

The religious groups that are the spiritual home of the majority of America's population came to the United States from Europe. By contrast, the four religious groups discussed in this chapter began in the United States, and the nature of each bears the marks of that beginning. The four communities of faith described below account for somewhat less than 5 percent of Christians in the United States.

America was the "New World," a time and a place of new beginnings, of a sense that anything was possible and that experimentation was desirable. In this climate, it is not surprising that new religious groups came into being. As historians of American religion Winthrop Hudson and John Corrigan point out, the entire area east of the Mississippi River had seen many religious revivals. Revival preaching contributed to the formation of new religious groups in at least three ways: The revival preachers demanded a direct confrontation with God, a demand that often led to visionary or mystical experience that people took as a new revelation. They also preached the necessity of perfect holiness and a sinless life. Last, they also stressed the belief in a new age to come. As Hudson indicates, the new religious groups that formed during this time "stemmed from at least one of these emphases, and most represented a blending of all three."[1]

The communities of faith to which you were introduced in the first part of this book fit in with the culture of which they are a part, so much so that they have tended to disappear into that culture. More important, their way of seeing

[1]Winthrop S. Hudson and John Corrigan, *Religion in America: An Historical Account of the Development of American Religious Life*, 5th ed. (New York: Macmillan Publishing Company, 1992), p. 181.

the world has come to be regarded as the normal view in the culture. It is necessary to distinguish **majority view** from **normal view**, even though the two often coincide. The *majority view* is simply the opinions held by the majority of those in a given population. It takes on a different status when it comes to be thought of as the *normal,* correct, proper, or appropriate view. Then, it is the only one given full respect in a society. When this happens, it becomes a handicap for those whose views do not happen to be those of the majority. The indigenous American Christianities have much in common with traditional Christianity. In this, they are aligned with the majority culture. However, they interpret the tradition differently than do most Christians. The ways in which indigenous Christianities depart from more traditional teachings and practices usually result from the views of the founder of each group. They are the result of Christianity being passed through the lens of the unique vision of one person or a small group of people. It is changed in the process, although it retains clear and obvious links with more traditional groups. In the community of neighbors, these are neighbors whose lives are centered in a faith that is different yet similar, clearly other and yet alike. The uniqueness of their insights and practices adds to the richness of religion in the United States. All of them, without exception, have been persecuted and looked down upon as a result of their nonconformity. Sometimes, they still are. They are living proof that the community of neighbors and not strangers has not been fully realized among us, because they are still looked upon as outsiders.

Have young Latter-day Saint (Mormon) missionaries ever come by your home asking to speak with you about their church? Have you perhaps seen them on your college campus? Have you seen a building in your community that is identified as a Kingdom Hall? It is the gathering place of Jehovah's Witnesses. Are you aware that Seventh-day Adventists worship on Saturday, or that followers of Christian Science do not rely on doctors and hospitals for medical care? All these people are representatives of the religions that you will learn about in this chapter. Ask yourself how you feel about people whose religion makes them stand out from the rest of the culture. Are you curious about why they behave the way they do?

These communities of faith contrast with consensus religion in several respects. Their members often have a sense of separation from the world. Although they may work very hard at making converts, their expectations for their members are high. The Mormons and the Jehovah's Witnesses are good examples of this. Members must be willing to accept more stringent rules and standards than those that apply outside the group. It is in this sense that they are somewhat exclusive. Their standards lead to a sense of separateness from the rest of the world, and members usually believe that they are following the one true way in religion while the rest of the world goes astray.

In addition to the Bible, other writings are often considered authoritative. They may be thought of as part of a group's scriptures, or as interpretations of the Bible. These additional writings, usually those of the founder, may be regarded as new revelations or as interpretations inspired by God.

The material contained in the founder's writings gives rise to beliefs or practices—and usually both—that are distinctively different than those of more traditional Christianity. New revelations or new interpretations give rise to these new beliefs, rituals, and lifestyles and at the same time provide support for them.

A corollary of the sense of being set apart from the larger society is that these groups tend to be very close-knit. Separation from those outside is complemented by closeness and community among those on the inside. They socialize together much more than they do with outsiders, and members of the group can count on strong support from other members in time of need. They often provide their members with a complete lifestyle and a full round of activities, not necessarily all of a religious nature. This reinforces the closeness of the community and limits contacts with outsiders.

Their lifestyles are frequently distinctive, making their separation from the culture somewhat obvious. There may be restrictions on dancing, gambling, and the use of alcohol and tobacco. There may be food regulations, and sometimes there are dress codes, especially for female members.

Authority in these religions is usually strictly enforced from the top down, with little room for innovation at the local or individual level. It would, however, be incorrect to conclude that members of these religious groups are blindly following their leader. For most, the acceptance of a strong religious authority and submission to that authority is in itself an important belief, one that has been consented to and taken as one's own.

THE LATTER-DAY SAINTS

When most of us think of the Mormons, we probably think of neatly dressed, clean-cut young men, most likely on bicycles or walking, going from house to house talking about their faith with all who will listen, and hoping to make converts. Some may think of well-known U.S. citizens who are Mormon. Examples include the Osmonds; Ezra Taft Benson, former Secretary of Agriculture; and George Romney, former Governor of Michigan. Others might well think of the world-famous Mormon Tabernacle Choir or Brigham Young University. The Mormons have grown from a group whose numbers could be counted on the fingers of one's two hands to one of the larger and better-known communities of faith in this country. Yet, many people still feel that the Mormons are not a part of mainstream America. In some ways, they *are* different and choose to stand outside the mainstream. In other ways, such as their involvement in public life, they have moved into the center. In this section, some of the misconceptions that still surround this religious group will be dispelled. At the same time, some of the differences between their understanding of Christianity and that of their neighbors will be described. Some important ways in which their lives are different because of their faith will also be discussed.

The word **Mormon** itself is not the official name of the group. It is a nickname for members of **The Church of Jesus Christ of Latter-day Saints.** Mormon is believed by the church to have been a prophet in the area that would become the United States. In the concluding years of the fourth century C.E., Mormon compiled a book containing the records of the people of Lehi, a Hebrew who had led a colony of people from Jerusalem to America in about 600 B.C.E. Mormon's son Moroni added some information of his own, including a brief account of the people called Jaredites who had come to North America at the time that the Tower of Babel was built. This record is preserved as the *Book of Mormon.*

The official name, Church of Jesus Christ of Latter-day Saints, tells us how this community of faith understands itself. They consider themselves to be Christians, members of the one true church that follows all the teachings of Jesus Christ. Although some more traditional Christian groups do not consider the Mormons to be fellow Christians, there is no doubt about their self-identification as Christians. They are neither Protestant nor Catholic nor Orthodox, however. The word **saints** is used in the Christian New Testament to mean "church members." Latter-day distinguishes this church from the church in the former days, which, according to Mormon teaching, fell away from the truth of Jesus Christ shortly after it was founded. About 2 percent of the population of the United States is Mormon.

The Latter-day Saints began in the first half of the nineteenth century in an area of New York State that scholars call the burned-over district. It has been given this colorful name because a large number of revivals swept the area with great fires of religious enthusiasm. **Joseph Smith** (1805–1844), who would become the group's founder, grew up in this climate of religious tumult. Confused, he earnestly tried to discover which of the many religious groups in the area was correct, so that he might join it. One day in his reading of the Bible, he read, "If any of you lacks wisdom, let him ask God, who gives to all men generously and without reproaching, and it will be given to him" (James 1:5, Revised Standard Version). Taking these instructions to heart, the young man went and knelt in an isolated grove of trees to seek God's guidance. God spoke to Joseph Smith, according to Mormon belief, telling him that none of the available religious groups was the true church, and that all had fallen away from the truth. Smith was to join none of them. Then, in 1823, the angelic messenger Moroni appeared to him and told him that he would be God's chosen servant to restore the church to the fullness of the Gospel.

Moroni appeared to Joseph Smith again in 1827 and revealed to him the location of golden plates upon which was written what would eventually become the *Book of Mormon.* Since they were written in an unknown script, Smith was also provided with something to assist in the translation (identified as the Urim and Thummim mentioned in Exodus 28:30). The *Book of Mormon* was subsequently published in 1830. According to Mormon history, the golden plates were taken up into heaven after Smith had completed the translation. The Latter-day Saints believe that their church is founded, not upon the human words and work of Joseph Smith, but on the direct revelation of God, as surely as the earlier Christian Church had been founded upon God's revelation in Jesus Christ.

The church was established in the spring of 1830, shortly after the publication of the *Book of Mormon*. It began with only five people. They were persecuted almost immediately. Persecution led to the long westward trek that would eventually take them to Salt Lake City. They first moved from New York to Kirtland, Ohio, and then to a place near Independence, Missouri. From there, their travels took them to Nauvoo, Illinois. Trouble again broke out, and several of their number were jailed at Carthage, Illinois. Among those imprisoned were Joseph Smith and his brother Hyrum, both of whom were murdered by a local mob while in jail. Some of Smith's followers, led by Brigham Young, then began the trek to what would become Salt Lake City, in the Utah Territory. Salt Lake City became the world headquarters for the Church of Jesus Christ of Latter-day Saints in 1847. Some, including Smith's widow and young son, disputed Young's leadership and stayed in Illinois, forming the nucleus of what would become the second-largest Mormon group, the **Reorganized Church of Jesus Christ of Latter Day Saints**.[2] The headquarters of this group is in Independence, Missouri.

One of the best-known and least-understood chapters of Latter-day Saints history is their practice of polygamy. Actually, it was polygyny, in which a man is permitted to have more than one wife. Some of the church's leaders believed that they had received a revelation from God in which God commanded this practice, which they began in 1843. It became public knowledge in 1852. It was met with public outrage, and the U.S. government moved quickly to undercut the power of the church in Utah and made the abandonment of multiple marriage a condition of statehood. In 1890, Mormon leaders announced that the practice was no longer approved. At any given time, probably less than 20 percent of the Church's leaders were actually involved in plural marriage. The only remaining polygynists are isolated in very small groups that are not recognized by the church. The era of plural marriage ended almost as quickly as it had begun.

Belief

Modern-day Mormons have beliefs that are similar to those of other Christians yet are in many ways distinctive. **The *Book of Mormon* is considered to be scripture, alongside the Bible.** In addition, new revelations were received at various times for specific purposes, and these were collected as the *Doctrine and Covenants*. The original edition was published in 1833, with subsequent editions containing additional material. Another book, *The Pearl of Great Price*, also contains revelations believed to have been received by Smith. Based on these writ-

---

[2]The Latter-day Saints use a hyphen and lower-case *d* in the spelling of their name. The Reorganized Church does not hyphenate, and uses an upper-case *D*. When discussing characteristics that pertain to both groups, I will use the *Latter-day Saints* spelling.

ings, there are thirteen Articles of Faith that summarize the Church's beliefs. Some of these are discussed below and others will be included in the discussion of lifestyle and organization.

Mormons **believe in God the Father, Jesus Christ the Son, and the Holy Spirit**, as do most other Christians. They are, however, **three separate individuals**, distinct from each other while being united in purpose. Further, the Father and the Son have physical bodies, "much like our own." The Holy Ghost is a spirit (Article 1). Thus, their understanding of God as Father, Son, and Spirit differs from the traditional Christian view that the trinity is but one God.

Mormons do not hold people accountable for the sin of Adam and Eve, as do some Christians. Being held responsible for a sin in which one had no part is repugnant to Mormon sensibilities. The concept of "**free agency**" is a central aspect of Mormon belief. Human beings have free will and therefore will be punished for their own sins, not those of Adam. People have come to this Earth from a pre-Earth existence, and the "freedom to choose for ourselves between right and wrong is the most important thing we brought to the earth with us" (Article 2). Jesus' sacrificial death makes salvation available to all humankind. **Salvation comes by way of faith and works.** It may be lost from "lack of effort on our part to live the gospel" (Article 3). There are also **degrees of exaltation**. Heaven is divided into various realms or states of being. Mormons teach that the highest of these is available only to those who have followed all the laws and ordinances of the church. Those who attain this exalted status become gods, to whom all other things are subject, even the angels.[3]

A cornerstone of Mormon belief is that God's will is revealed not only in the Bible, but to Joseph Smith, and, following Smith, to the leaders of the church throughout all the years of its existence. God will yet reveal many significant things (Article 9). The concept of **continuous revelation** allows the church's leadership to be flexible in responding to issues and questions that are not dealt with directly in the Bible or the other Mormon scriptures. At the same time, the authority of divine revelation is maintained.

Mormons also believe in the laying on of hands for the receiving of the Holy Spirit, and in the other spiritual gifts such as speaking in tongues, prophecy, visions, healing, and the interpretation of tongues (Article 7).

This is a distinctively American church. The Book of Mormon gives America a scriptural past. Many religious groups in this country have believed fervently that America has a special role to play in God's plans for the world, but none has expressed that belief as concretely as do the Latter-day Saints. They look forward to a literal regathering of Israel, restoration of the Ten Lost Tribes, and the building of the New Jerusalem, to which they refer as Zion, on the North American continent (Article 10).

Mormons believe in freedom of worship as a privilege for themselves and

---

[3] *The Doctrine and Covenants of the Church of Jesus Christ of Latter-day Saints* (Salt Lake City, UT: Church of Jesus Christ of Latter-day Saints, 1982), 132:20.

all other people (Article 11) and in obedience to the laws of the land and its leaders. Unjust laws are to be protested against, but by using only "legal and proper" means (Article 12).

Lifestyle

If you are acquainted with many Latter-day Saints, you probably know them as people with an upbeat and healthful lifestyle. They participate wholeheartedly in the programs of their church. Honesty and truthfulness, chastity, benevolence, and doing good to all are affirmed (Article 13). The body is given by God and is sacred, and taking good care of it is a religious act. This is the reason behind the **Word of Wisdom**, a health code that Mormons teach was revealed to Smith in 1833. The code forbids smoking tobacco, drinking alcohol, drinking beverages with caffeine in them (such as coffee, tea, and many soft drinks), and taking drugs other than those prescribed by a physician for medical reasons. Meat is to be used sparingly, with the emphasis in the diet on grains, fruits, and vegetables. Physical exercise is encouraged, as is good grooming. They teach that following the Word of Wisdom will lead to great wisdom and knowledge, as well as to good health that includes moral, emotional, and spiritual dimensions along with the physical aspects of good health.[4]

As many of you probably know, the **family is absolutely central in Latter-day Saints' thought and practice.** It is the basic unit of church and society and is held to be sacred. Local churches provide many family-oriented activities throughout the week, of both a religious and a nonreligious nature. In addition, families have Family Home Evening once a week, using materials provided by their church. This is a time for families to be together for study and for worship and discussion of religious matters. They also simply enjoy being together and benefit from the interaction of parents and children. Church members called home teachers visit members' homes frequently to bring messages of hope and goodwill. They are the representatives of the church leaders in helping the family to solve problems.

Marriage is valued very highly by the Latter-day Saints. Everyone is enjoined to marry, and requiring anyone to remain celibate is specifically forbidden.[5] Adultery is grounds for dismissal from the Church, and premarital sex calls for severe repentance. Children are valued, and, however great a man's achievements, his highest goal and achievement is fathering children.[6] The husband and father presides over the family. As a male member of the church, he holds a position within the priesthood. The family unit functions as a small church in and of itself. Traditional roles for men, women, and children are encouraged. The husband is the provider and leader for his family. His wife is the primary care-

---

[4]*Doctrine and Covenants*, 89:19–20.
[5]*Doctrine and Covenants*, 49:15.
[6]James E. Talmadge, *A Study of the Articles of Faith* (Salt Lake City, UT: Church of Jesus Christ of Latter-day Saints, 1982), p. 443.

giver in the home and is the emotional heart of the family. Parents expect children to contribute as much as they possibly can by helping with chores and participating in family home evening programs. Through a special sealing ceremony that takes place in temples, husbands and wives, along with their children, may be joined for eternity.

The Mormon emphasis on the family involves the **extended family through many generations**, as well as the nuclear family of those presently living. The Church sponsors one of the largest genealogical libraries in the world and assists millions of people with research into their family backgrounds. Faithful Mormons engage in Temple work on behalf of ancestors who died without being able to follow the ordinances for themselves. This is believed to be a great benefit to those who have died and confers a blessing on the living as well.

Latter-day Saints emphasize **education** for both men and women. Mormon children attend public and private schools but also participate in church educational programs that emphasize religious education. Home study courses are available for those in isolated areas. A basic goal of the church is that every member will be able to read, write, do basic arithmetic, and study the scriptures and other uplifting books.[7] The Church sponsors several institutions of higher education, the best known of which is **Brigham Young University** (BYU) in Provo, Utah. A publicity brochure for BYU describes the university this way:

> The uniqueness of Brigham Young University lies in its special role—education for eternity—which it must carry in addition to the usual tasks of a university. This means concern—curricular and behavioral—not only for the "whole man" but for the "eternal man." Where all universities seek to preserve the heritage of knowledge that history has washed to their feet, this faculty has a double heritage—the preserving of knowledge of men and the revealed truths sent from heaven.[8]

In addition to studying a full range of coursework, students are trained to become the type of people the Mormon tradition expects them to be. It may be of interest to many of you, since you are taking a religious studies class, to know that BYU students take at least one religious studies class every semester, ranging from world religions to Mormon theology.

Self-sufficiency is another trait encouraged by the Latter-day Saints. A detailed program of personal and family preparedness for self-sufficiency is spelled out, including education, career development, financial management, and home production and storage of necessities (sewing, gardening, food preservation, and the manufacture of some household items). These preparations will help individual families through hard times. The emphasis on self-sufficiency is balanced by readiness to help others who cannot help themselves. The church maintains storehouses, administered by local bishops, that are used to help those who have exhausted their own resources. The church also sponsors an employment clear-

---

[7] *Pressbook* (Salt Lake City, UT: Church of Jesus Christ of Latter-day Saints, n.d.), p. 7.
[8] *B.Y.U.: The Mormon University*, (Provo, UT: Brigham Young University, University Relations, n.d.).

inghouse, social services, and other assistance programs that weave together into a comprehensive program of assistance for both members and nonmembers. Mormons who receive assistance through these services are expected to work to help earn what they need and to help others who are in need. "There is," as the *Pressbook* states, "no dole. Instead, independence and freedom from idleness and its attendant evils are encouraged."[9]

As with all religions, Mormons vary widely in their adherence to Mormon beliefs and their practice of the lifestyle that their church advocates. Some take it very seriously and others pay little if any attention to it. Most come somewhere in between the two extremes.

Ritual

When Mormons gather for worship on Sunday morning in local churches or chapels, they do many of the same things that are done in Protestant Christian services. Hymns are sung, prayers are spoken, a sermon is preached, and individuals may have the opportunity to tell how God has been especially active in their lives during the past week. Concerns of the church family are shared. Men and women, boys and girls participate in their own study classes. In the weekly sacrament meeting, communion is observed, using bread and water, since the Mormons do not use alcohol. Other religious services take place during the week, and other activities at the church abound.

The Latter-day Saints distinguish between these local churches and their activities, and Temples (Figure 8–1). The **Temples** and the rituals that take place in them are the most distinctive feature of Mormon ritual life. The first of these special buildings was built in Kirtland, Ohio, and dedicated in 1836. It was built following a pattern said to have been revealed to Smith by God. It was a temporary structure only, without all the features found in modern-day Temples. Temples are reserved for the performance of special ordinances of the church. Many have been open to the public for tours for a time after they were completed, but after they are dedicated they are considered sacred space, and only worthy Mormons may enter.

Before Latter-day Saints can go to the Temple, they must receive a **Temple Recommend** from the bishop. The bishop and the stake president, who is a local officer, conduct interviews to determine worthiness to enter the sacred place and to participate in its ordinances. Among other requirements, people must have "a testimony of the gospel," support the church and follow its programs and teachings, keep the Word of Wisdom, be morally pure, be members in good standing of the church, and be free of legal entanglements. Mormons who are judged worthy and go to the Temple change from street clothing to clean, white clothing provided at the Temple as a sign and symbol of purity. My descriptions of Temple ceremonies are of necessity rather brief and very general. The details

[9] *Pressbook*, p. 10.

Figure 8–1   Salt Lake Temple of the Church of Jesus Christ of Latter-day Saints, Salt Lake City, Utah. Mormon Temples are used only for special Temple ordinances. Because they are regarded as sacred space, they are not open to the public. *Front left:* Tabernacle on Temple Square (egg-shaped building). *Center:* Salt Lake Temple (spired building). *Back center:* LDS Church Office Building (high-rise). (*Photograph copyright Church of Jesus Christ of the Latter-day Saints. Used by permission.*)

are not made available to non-Mormons, and those who participate in the ceremonies promise not to reveal the details of their experience. This reticence to discuss details stems in part from the long history of misunderstanding that has marked the career of the Latter-day Saints. It also reflects the sacredness that Mormons attribute to these special observances.

The first Temple ceremony is the **Endowment**. This is a prerequisite for any of the other ceremonies. The Endowment is said to confer the knowledge necessary for a person to return to God after death. The history of the human race as the Latter-day Saints understand it is retraced, emphasizing the importance of the present time. Covenants or promises are made and obligations conferred, along with their accompanying blessings.

Another very important Temple ceremony is **eternal marriage**. People married according to the laws of the world, even if the wedding is performed in a Mormon church, are bound by the limitation of "until death do us part." Marriages that last a lifetime end with the death of one of the partners. Marriage and family ties can continue into eternity, according to Mormon belief. The relationship of husband and wife, and that of parents and children, can be made permanent by participation in Temple ceremonies. Temple marriage is required for entrance into the highest degree of exaltation following death.[10]

Temple baptism is another Temple ordinance. Temple baptismal fonts rest on the backs of twelve sculptured oxen that represent the twelve tribes of Israel. Mormons are baptized in fonts in their local churches or chapels in a service very similar to that of other Christian churches. Baptism is by immersion and is restricted to those who are old enough to understand its meaning for themselves. Temple baptism is performed by the living on behalf of the dead. Many people die without hearing the teachings that Mormons believe are necessary for exaltation. Mormons believe that the opportunity to do so can be made available to them in the spirit world by a living member of their family who undergoes Temple baptism on their behalf. Only these baptisms on behalf of another are performed in the Temple. Part of the significance of tracing one's genealogy as far back as possible is to find those ancestors for whom Temple work needs to be performed. Sealing ceremonies that join spouses, parents, and children for eternity can also be performed vicariously. In any case, the performance of a vicarious ceremony provides only the opportunity. The soul in the spirit world must give its voluntary consent. The concept of free agency applies even there.

Organization

There are several distinctive things about the institutional or organizational life of the Latter-day Saints. In many ways, the Church is a theocracy believed to be under the direct rule of God, since Mormons believe that the highest leaders of the Church continually receive revelations from God. No officer, however, serves without a sustaining vote from the people he serves, so that there are also democratic elements. There are no professional clergy, and lay members who serve as officers do so without pay. Now, however, both major branches of the church pay a living allowance to those people in the central administration. The Church has a president, considered to be a prophet of God. Former Secretary of Agriculture Ezra Taft Benson became the Mormon president in 1985. He is advised by two counselors who, along with the president, make up the First Presidency. There is a Quorum of Twelve Apostles that advises the First Presidency. The Church is highly organized along geographic lines, with no congregation being so large as to become impersonal.

Priesthood in the Mormon church simply means the authority to act in the name of God. The priesthood is open to all worthy males, twelve years of age or

[10]*Doctrine and Covenants*, 132:15–19 and 131:2–4.

older. There are two divisions. The Melchizedek is the higher order and the Aaronic is the lower. Each is further divided into three subdivisions. Specific responsibilities and privileges come with each designation, and a man moves through the designations in order as he studies and carries out the duties of his present designation. Women are not priests. They have the blessings that Mormons believe are conferred by the priesthood through their husbands. The primary organization for women in the church is the Relief Society. Women are eligible to serve on the governing councils of the Church. Mormons believe that the pattern of organization that they have is the same as that which was found in the primitive church before it fell away from the true Church of Jesus Christ.

Restricting the priesthood to men is only one of the ways in which the Latter-day Saints emphasize the importance of traditional roles for women. Although their general support for education means that women are encouraged to continue their education beyond high school, careers are discouraged and a woman is not expected to work outside the home once she is married. It should be noted, however, that many Mormon women do so, either out of choice or economic necessity. The role of women as wives and mothers is very highly respected. What distresses some Mormon women and angers the more militant among them is that this is the only approved role. Stepping outside it frequently leads to disapproval. Women who do so may be made to feel that they are endangering their eternal life with God. Speaking out publicly on feminist issues has occasionally resulted in dismissal from the church. Mormons have also joined Catholics and conservative Protestants in their support of antiabortion legislation.

Another unique feature of the Latter-day Saints is their **emphasis on missionary work**. The rapid growth of this community of faith can be attributed largely to this energetic program. Thousands of young men and women and retired couples accept missionary assignments for up to two years, normally serving at their own expense, often receiving financial assistance from family and friends. The main work of these missionaries is going from house to house seeking converts to their way of life.

Music is an important part of Latter-day Saints culture. The **Mormon Tabernacle Choir** is a 325-voice group that began in the mid-1800s. Its "Music and the Spoken Word" program has been carried by many radio stations since 1929. The choir's recording of "The Battle Hymn of the Republic" won a Grammy Award. There is also a Mormon youth symphony and chorus, with 100 and 350 members, respectively. They, too, perform regularly.

The two major branches of the Mormon church grew out of a disagreement about who should be Joseph Smith's successor. The **Church of Jesus Christ of Latter-day Saints** (LDS) began with those who thought that Smith's successor should be a member of the Council of Twelve Apostles that advises the President. This group chose Brigham Young as their leader. This branch is now based in Salt Lake City, Utah. The **Reorganized Church of Jesus Christ of Latter Day Saints** (RLDS) was founded by those who believed that Smith's successor should be his biological descendant. After Smith's death they chose his eldest son, Joseph Smith III, as their leader and established their headquarters in Independence,

Missouri. The two groups are bound together by their shared commitment to the *Book of Mormon* as revealed scripture and the prophethood of Smith. They differ on several points. The RLDS churches have a core of salaried local ministers, and they ordain women to the ministry. There are numerous smaller points of difference, as well.

These churches offer their members a stirring vision of how life can be. It provides firm guidelines for life and a set of ritual ordinances that members believe will lead to a greatly enhanced quality of life now and eternal life in the future, with the promise of becoming gods. It offers a strong community and a full program of activities with other like-minded persons. Its emphasis on the family and on traditional morality offers a clear-cut alternative to the problems many people see besetting modern society.

THE CHRISTIAN SCIENTISTS

Christian Scientists (members of the Church of Christ, Scientist) maintain a low public profile. They do not seek converts by missionary activity, but they do maintain **Christian Science Reading Rooms** where people can go and read the Bible as well as Christian Science literature. Christian Science is directly linked to the experiences of **Mary Baker Eddy**, its founder. In 1866, Mrs. Eddy reported a nearly instantaneous cure from a severe back injury after reading the account of one of Jesus' healings (Matthew 9:1–8). Along with the Bible, Eddy's *Science and Health with Key to the Scriptures* (first published in 1875) is the source of Christian Science teaching.

Christian Scientists believe that all that God creates is good, since a good God could not create that which was not good. Therefore, **the only reality that the evils of sin, sickness, and death have is that which we give them, because our erring human thought attributes to them a reality they do not have.** Christian Scientists rely on the power of God for healing rather than on medical treatment, although the church does not pressure those whose lesser faith leads them to see a physician. Such people are not dismissed from the church but are simply encouraged to strengthen their faith in God's healing mercy. Christian Science **practitioners** are specially trained by the church to assist those who seek Christian Science healing through prayer, and Christian Science in-patient facilities can provide supportive care to the seriously ill while treatment is given. Healing by prayer is not thought to be miraculous, but divinely natural, an integral part of the harmonious order of the created world as God means it to be. Christian Science is not limited to physical healing, but extends to psychological and emotional problems, and other types of problems.

Christian Scientists **think of God as divine Principle, Love, Mind, Spirit, Soul, Life, and Truth,** which are the seven synonyms for God.[11] God is under-

---

[11]Mary Baker Eddy, *Science and Health with Key to the Scriptures,* (Boston: The First Church of Christ, Scientist, 1906), p. 465.

stood to be wholly spiritual, and not personalized. God includes qualities associated with both genders, and there is a tradition of gender equality on human terms that is echoed throughout the church's organization. There are no ordained ministers. **Readers elected from the congregation** serve for a period of three years, often without pay. It is preferred that one reader be female, and the other male. Practitioners are more often female than male, and all church organizational offices are open to women.

The words *Christian* and *Science* in this church's name each tell us something important about it. It is a church *focused on Jesus, the Christ.* The tenets of the church include the following:

> We acknowledge Jesus' atonement as the evidence of divine, efficacious Love, unfolding man's unity with God through Christ Jesus the Way-shower; and we acknowledge that man is saved through Christ, through Truth, Life, and Love as demonstrated by the Galilean Prophet in healing the sick and overcoming sin and death.[12]

Christian Scientists distinguish between the human Jesus and his role as the Christ without separating the two:

> Christian Science draws a distinction between the Saviour's divine title of Christ and his human history as Jesus. But it by no means separates the two, for it fully accepts Jesus as the incarnation or embodiment of the Christ.[13]

Christian Scientists also believe that theirs is a **scientific religion.** *Science* is used to describe this religion

> [be]cause it can be demonstrated. We see God as the universal, divine Principle underlying the life and healing work of Christ Jesus. God by His very nature must be unchanging Truth, invariable Love, operating through timeless spiritual laws rather than special miraculous acts. To understand these laws of absolute good is to find that Christianity can be scientifically applied to every human ill.[14]

The church meets for Sunday services that consist largely of readings from the Bible and *Science and Health.* The readings for each Sunday are set by the Mother Church in Boston and are the same in all Christian Science churches. The lesson-sermon is prepared by a committee of the Mother Church and it, too, is the same in all Christian Science churches. There is also music—organ music, hymns, and a solo. Wednesday midweek meetings also include readings from the Bible and from *Science and Health,* but provide an opportunity for members and visitors to give and hear testimonies of healing as well. One writer describes the two services this way:

[12]Eddy, *Science and Health*, p. 497.
[13]*Christian Science: A Sourcebook of Contemporary Materials* (Boston: The Christian Science Publishing Society, 1990), pp. 102–3.
[14]*Questions and Answers on Christian Science* (Boston: The Christian Science Publishing Society, 1974), p. 2.

The Sunday service at a Christian Science church mingles something of the bare simplicity of the New England church services that Mrs. Eddy knew as a girl with a touch of the Quaker quietism and the Unitarian rationalism with which she came in friendly contact later. The midweek meeting. . . , is chiefly known for the spontaneous "testimonies of healing" given by members of the congregation.[15]

There is a Board of Lectureship authorized to give public lectures explaining Christian Science and inviting further inquiry, but this is the extent of this group's missionary activity.

The Church of Christ, Scientist, has faced a number of challenges to its practices over the years. Currently, Christian Science healing is an accepted alternative to traditional medical treatment. Major insurance companies will usually reimburse those who receive Christian Science treatment. The Internal Revenue Service recognizes the cost of treatment as an income tax deduction, as it does medical fees. Christian Scientists do not claim that they have found the only way to God. They claim to have found a way that brings them peace and joy as well as physical healing, a way that they can recommend to others on that basis, but that which they do not ever attempt to force upon someone who is not interested.

Christian Science is also known to the public through its publication of the *Christian Science Monitor* newspaper, widely recognized as one of the best in the nation. It is published in about a dozen languages and also in a Braille edition. There are also Monitor radio and television networks.

THE SEVENTH-DAY ADVENTISTS

The Seventh-day Adventists are by far the largest single church within the group of churches that make up the adventist believers, a family that also includes the Latter-day Saints and the Jehovah's Witnesses. **Adventism** emphasizes the Christian teaching, found especially in the biblical books of Daniel and Revelation, that the return of Christ to the world will be a literal, physical event. Most adventists believe that this will happen in the near future. Those who rebel against God will be destroyed, while true believers will be saved. Adventism began early in the nineteenth century. Soon, the United States was the location where its tenets and practices were best defined. Like many other movements that eventually became separate organizations, most adventists had no intention of breaking off from the churches of which they were a part. They set out to be an emphasis within a church, not a separate body. The emphasis created conflict, however, and many did break away. Adventism is sometimes linked with holiness (see Chapter 9), as believers seek to be prepared on a daily basis for the return of Christ.

[15] *Christian Science: A Sourcebook of Contemporary Materials*, p. 51.

Most of the divisions within adventism occurred when people set dates for the second coming. These dates passed, and nothing happened. In the sharp disappointment that followed such events, differences of opinion led to separations. A second major point of disagreement concerned whether the Lord's Day or Sabbath was properly celebrated on Saturday or Sunday. This difference contributed to the formation of the Seventh-day Adventist Church.

Some adventists predicted that Christ would return on October 22, 1844. When this prediction proved incorrect (sometimes known as the Great Disappointment), some of people whose hopes had been dashed began meeting together. Among them were **Ellen G. White** and her husband. Mrs. White began entering into trance states in which she claimed to receive revelations, and she was soon accepted as a prophet by the group. Among the group's keystones was the **celebration of the Sabbath on Saturday rather than Sunday**. Mrs. White also confirmed the correctness of the 1844 date, but redefined what happened on that date. Christ had not returned to the earth on that date, as was originally predicted, but had initiated the cleansing of the true, heavenly sanctuary described in Hebrews 8:1–2 (an interpretation that required a somewhat idiosyncratic reading of the King James version of the text). Accurate or not, the adventist hope was restored and the effects of the Great Disappointment were overcome.

On the basis of the fourth commandment, these adventists began celebrating the Sabbath on Saturday, a practice they have continued to the present time. The "Seventh-day" in the group's name refers to this practice. Sometimes people who keep a Saturday Sabbath are called **Sabbatarians**. Seventh-day Adventists have a strong commitment to witness to their faith to other people, and are conservative in their theology. They believe in the sole authority of the revelation recorded in the Bible. Ellen White's writings are regarded as inspired interpretations of the Bible but are not given equal authority with it.

Seventh-day Adventists are known for their **support of sound health practices**, because they believe that the body is the temple of the Holy Spirit. Good health practices are a religious obligation. They abstain from the use of alcohol and tobacco as well as illicit drugs, and they advocate healthy habits such as exercise and proper nutrition. They encourage a positive mental outlook. Many are vegetarians. For several years, they have sponsored a very successful stop-smoking program that is open to the public. Their emphasis on physical and mental health resembles that of the Latter-day Saints. Their awareness of the religious dimension of physical health has also led the Seventh-day Adventists to concentrate much of their missionary work, both in the United States and overseas, on hospitals and other **medical missions**.

Seventh-day Adventists practice a **conservative lifestyle** as they await **the return of Christ, which they believe is near at hand**, although they do not speculate about the exact date. Men's and women's roles emphasize the traditional over the innovative. Church and church-sponsored activities play a large role in most of their lives. Especially in some areas of the country, Seventh-day Adventist children attend schools sponsored by their church.

THE JEHOVAH'S WITNESSES

Many Americans have become acquainted with the Jehovah's Witnesses through their aggressive program of **door-to-door evangelism.** These Christians **expect that Jesus will return to the earth quite soon.** For them, this means that there is very little time left for missionary work. Doing all one can is therefore very important, since the unconverted will surely perish. Although most of us know them best as Jehovah's Witnesses, their official name is the **Watchtower Bible and Tract Society.** The name Jehovah's Witnesses comes from Isaiah 43:12, which, in some translations, has God saying to the people that he is named Jehovah and they are his witnesses. Jehovah's Witnesses do not consider themselves to be a church, but rather a group of Bible students and publishers of God's Word. *Publishing* here has two meanings. They **concentrate on the translation and publication of Bibles and tracts,** and they publish (in the sense of making public) their understanding of God's message for modern day people by every means at their disposal.

The group was originally organized by Pastor **Charles Taze Russell** (1852–1916), who is thought of as an organizer and not the founder, because God alone is considered to be the founder. Unlike Joseph Smith and Ellen G. White, Russell disclaimed and condemned contemporary revelation, asserting that God's whole revelation was contained in the Bible. The Witnesses believe that theirs is the one true faith mentioned by Paul in Ephesians 4:5 (there is "one Lord, one faith, one baptism").

The group has never wavered from its focus on Bible study, and its teachings are supported by an elaborate system of references to scripture. When they meet, usually more than once per week, in **Kingdom Halls** (their meeting sites are not called churches), most of their time is spent in Bible study and discussion. They believe that the Bible was written by individuals who recorded God's message accurately. However, they hold that modern translations contain errors, and, in 1961, they published their own *New World Translation* of the Bible. Witnesses believe that their translation corrects the errors of earlier translations.

The Witnesses believe that the time is very near at hand when God will severely punish the wicked. God is presently gathering the righteous together, in order to spare them from the disaster that will take place in the universal battle of Armageddon described in the book of Revelation in the Christian New Testament.

Those who are gathered out are called to separate themselves from the world and form a **theocracy,** a community under the rule of God. To maintain this separation insofar as possible, the Witnesses avoid involvement in the political process by neither voting nor running for public office. They do not serve in the military. Technically, they are not pacifists; they claim that they would fight in God's war. They do not salute the flag nor sing the national anthem. They believe that to do so is to worship the nation and make an idol of it. Oaths of any sort are forbidden. In an extension of the Christian Old Testament prohibition against drinking blood, they do not accept blood transfusions. Jehovah's Witness children do not participate in school celebrations of holidays such as Easter and Christmas, nor do their families mark these holidays, believing that non-Christian elements have overwhelmed their biblical message. Nor do they celebrate birthdays. To do so is believed to focus too much honor on the person whose birthday is being celebrated and take honor away from God.

They are particularly critical of what they regard as the three strongest allies of Satan in his plan to destroy the world. These three Satanic allies are the government, big business, and churches that teach false doctrines (i.e., all those except the Witnesses). They must be destroyed in the coming battle before God can recreate the world. After Armageddon, Witnesses believe that the righteous will live on an earth restored to a paradisal state, to do God's will and enjoy communion with God. The 144,000 mentioned in Revelation 7 and 10 will be taken up into heaven to rule over the restored earth with Christ.

Although their aggressive missionary tactics anger and put off many people, Witnesses have earned the reputation of being honest, courteous, and industrious. Their conservative lifestyle stresses traditional roles for men and women. However, women participate fully in the door-to-door evangelism efforts of this group, and many times children are taken along. By the time they are ten years old or so, many children are accomplished Witnesses.

REFLECTION: COMMUNITY AND REASSURANCE

What is it that motivates the members of these communities of faith to live a life that distinguishes them sharply from the culture of which they are a part? To be sure, there are many reasons. Many followers of this way of life live with a keen sense that the world is a wicked and evil place, and that only by separating themselves from it can they have any hope of salvation. They take the idea of God's last judgment literally and seriously. Many believe firmly that the time is near when Christ will return to earth to judge all persons and make a final separation of the saved from the condemned. Therefore, it is necessary to be ready at all times. They believe that they have increasing evidence of the work of the Holy Spirit in their lives and in the lives of their associates, and this helps to assure them that they will indeed be among the saved when that time comes.

Others have other reasons. For many, becoming a Mormon means joy and community in this life and the assurance that important family ties would remain intact on the other side of death. Christian Science offers not only an alternative to traditional medical care, but an alternative way of understanding God and human nature. For many Scientists, their faith simply makes more sense out of their experience than do other alternatives.

These communities of faith offer their followers two very important things. They offer a strong sense of community that can be a refuge for those who are lonely and without other ties to the culture. It is a community of sharing among like-minded people whose goals and values are very similar. More important, many believe that they are called out of the world and into a small select community of faith. They believe that they are people who have heard and follow the message of the one true faith. The guidelines for life in this spiritual elite are clearly spelled out. The moral ambiguity that characterizes so much of contemporary society is absent.

Second, those who keep the faith and follow the guidelines are assured of salvation. Faith in justifying grace came as a great relief to Martin Luther, as it has to millions of other Protestants. It is nonetheless difficult to pin down. How does one know one is justified? How can one be absolutely certain of a place in heaven? The indigenous Christianities emphasize true faith and an upright life. How to live an upright life is described in clear behavioral terms. This leads to a greater sense of security. Thus, these American-born religions offer their followers answers to some of the deepest and most pressing problems of human life, answers with fewer ambiguities and uncertainties than those proposed by the religions of their neighbors in the religious consensus.

QUESTIONS AND ACTIVITIES FOR REVIEW, DISCUSSION, AND WRITING

1. Think about how you would feel if you were a part of a religion that set very different standards for you than those followed by your classmates. Don't make this exercise too simple by concentrating solely on being different. Remember that such religions also offer security and the assurance that one is on the right path.
2. Most Latter-day Saints are very willing to discuss their faith with non-Mormons, and Mormon churches (chapels) welcome visitors eagerly. If possible, arrange to attend a service. You might also want to ask the missionaries to describe their experiences to you.
3. Visit a Christian Science Reading Room and look over their literature. Report on what you find.
4. If you are not a member of one of the religions discussed in this chapter, write an essay about how your life would be different if you were a member. If you are a member, write about how your life would differ if you were not.
5. With a group, construct a chart that outlines the distinctive features of the communities of faith described in this chapter.

FOR FURTHER READING

Barlow, Philip L., *Mormons and the Bible: The Place of the Latter-Day Saints in American Religion.* New York: Oxford University Press, 1991. Reviews the discussion of the Mormons' status in American religion (sect, cult, new religion, form of Protestant Christianity, American subculture). Then analyzes the writings of LDS leaders to understand their approach to the Bible and compares it with that of other American religions.

Kephart, William M., and William W. Zellner, *Extraordinary Groups: The Sociology of Unconventional Lifestyles,* 5th. ed. New York: Saint Martin's Press, 1994. Has chapters on several major alternative communities of faith. Kephart and Zellner's book is written from an objective, sociological point of view, yet it reads almost like a novel. Fascinating and very accessible.

9

Alternative Themes in Christianity

————————···◦⟨∞⟩◦···————————

This chapter brings together a number of themes that have been and continue to be important in Christianity in the United States. These are not specific groups, by and large, but movements and sensibilities that cut across groups.

FUNDAMENTALIST AND VERY CONSERVATIVE CHRISTIANS

You have already been introduced to fundamentalism as a religious attitude. Some Protestant churches whose members have fundamentalist religious attitudes are part of the religious consensus. The increase in religious conservatism in the last several decades has brought many fundamentalists into the consensus. The type of fundamentalism with which this chapter deals is different. It is characterized by a strong desire to remain separate from other groups and individuals who do not believe as they do. Most of these churches are members of the **American Council of Christian Churches**, founded in 1941 by Dr. Carl McIntire. The final item in their doctrinal statement affirms the "necessity of maintaining, according to the Word of God, the purity of the Church in doctrine and life." For the member churches of the ACCC, this means complete separation from those who do not agree with their standards. A periodical called the *Christian Beacon* reflects this organization's perspectives.

Separatist fundamentalists firmly believe that biblical Christianity is completely incompatible with Christian modernism or liberalism, as well as with anything secular. They try to keep the boundaries between themselves and the secular world drawn sharply. Nonfundamentalist Christians are regarded as part of the unsaved world, so fundamentalists remain separate from them, as well.

Fundamentalism, as one recent essay points out, is not just one style of religion, nor is it just a matter of religious belief. It is "a value-oriented, antimodern, dedifferentiating form of collective action—a sociocultural movement aimed at reorganizing all spheres of life in terms of a particular set of absolute values."[1] In the face of expanding pluralism and what fundamentalists and conservatives see as the takeover of society by rampant secularism, the movement seeks to make a single set of values (hence, "dedifferentiating") based on their reading of the Christian Bible dominant in the culture.

The single demographic factor that is most strongly correlated with fundamentalism in religion is education. Of those with less than a high school education, about two-thirds are fundamentalists, whereas fundamentalists constitute only about one-third of those with a high school education and about 20 percent of the college educated. A less striking correlation between fundamentalism and lower-than-average income reflects this educational difference. Perhaps it is also a reflection of relative needs. Those who are secure in this world may feel less need for great assurance about the world to come. Because of its separatist tendencies, fundamentalism does not appeal as much to those who are deeply involved in the social and career concerns that are typical of higher-income people.

Relatively more women than men are fundamentalists, by a ratio of about four to three. Fundamentalism as an outlook reflects the kind of passivity that our culture has traditionally associated with women. The fundamentalist emphasis on God rather than on human potential encourages that passivity and gives it divine support. Fundamentalism encourages women to be submissive to their husbands, remain at home, and accept a limited and traditional (although significant) role in the life of their church.

Separatist fundamentalists have also been among the strongest supporters of the private **Christian school movement**, as well as of the home-schooling movement. Private Christian schools provide a way for parents to shield their children from the secular influence of the public school system. They also offer greater control over the curriculum. In most private Christian schools, children do not learn the Darwinian theory of evolution, nor do they study sex education and other subjects deemed inappropriate by fundamentalists. Their textbooks support traditional values and attitudes. More important, all subjects are taught from a Christian perspective. The school day begins with worship. The teachers are committed Christians, most of whom understand their work as a religious calling.

---

[1] Irving Louis Horowitz, "The Limits of Modernity," in *In Gods We Trust: New Patterns of Religious Pluralism in America*, 2nd. ed., ed. Thomas Robbins and Dick Anthony. (New Brunswick, NJ: Transaction Publishers, 1990), p. 79.

Perhaps most important in understanding why fundamentalist Christians view the Christian school movement as so important; Christian schools are a primary element in the advancement of fundamentalism's sociocultural goals. "By reuniting the three major socializing institutions of family, church, and school, Evangelicals hope to achieve a greater coherence in their own lives, bring their children up in the faith, and bring morality back to the United States."[2]

The private Christian school movement continues to grow, but not as rapidly as the home schooling movement. "**Home schooling**" simply means that parents teach their children at home, often using materials provided by Christian organizations. Individual parents have even more control with home schooling than with private schools. Both methods help to guarantee that children during their younger, most formative years, will be socialized into the values that are central to fundamentalist Christians, and into those values only.

Fundamentalist Christians also support a number of colleges in which higher education is carried out within the framework of their values and concerns. Among the best known of these schools is **Bob Jones University**. Students take required religion classes, and there is a dress code and careful control of dating behavior among students. The University's charter statement expresses very well the spirit that animates these schools:

> The general nature and object of the corporation shall be to conduct an institution of learning for the general education of youth in the essentials of culture and in the arts and sciences, giving special emphasis to the Christian religion and the ethics revealed in the Holy Scriptures; combating all atheistic, agnostic, pagan, and so-called scientific adulterations of the Gospel; unqualifiedly affirming and teaching the inspiration of the Bible (both the Old and New Testaments); the creation of man by the direct act of God; the incarnation and virgin birth of our Lord and Savior, Jesus Christ; His identification as the Son of God; His vicarious atonement for the sins of mankind by the shedding of His blood on the cross; the resurrection of His body from the tomb; His power to save men from sin; the new birth through the regeneration by the Holy Spirit and the gift of eternal life by the grace of God.[3]

The Christian doctrines enumerated in the charter are a summary of the key elements of fundamentalist faith.

Many of the churches that fit this profile are independent, with no ties outside the local congregation. They believe that this most closely resembles the way in which the church was organized in New Testament times. It also affords each congregation the greatest opportunity to set its own standards of correct belief. Two groups of churches, however, do fit in here. In Chapter 4, you read about the Restoration Movement and the Christian Church/Disciples of Christ that is

---

[2]Susan D. Rose, "Gender, Education, and the New Christian Right," *In Gods We Trust*, ed. Robbins and Anthony, p. 100.

[3]*Bulletin*, Bob Jones University, 1995–96 (Undergraduate), n.p.

a part of it. Two other churches whose roots go back to the Restoration Movement embody the approach to Christianity described above.

The **Christian Churches/Churches of Christ** have no organization beyond the local congregation. There is less variation in belief among members of these independent churches than among the Disciples. Most are strongly conservative to fundamentalist. As in the other Restoration churches, the Lord's Supper is served weekly. Like that of the Disciples, their worship includes instrumental music as well as the singing of hymns. The Christian Churches do not participate in ecumenical discussions or organizations, and the network of schools, colleges, and benevolent organizations they sponsor is supported entirely by local churches. They are located primarily in the lower Midwest and in Kentucky.

The **Churches of Christ** is the largest group within the Restoration churches. They are centered in the South and Southwest, although there are congregations throughout the United States. Like the Christian Churches, there is no organizational structure beyond the local church and no participation in ecumenical boards or groups. These churches seek "to speak where the Bible speaks and to be silent where the Bible is silent" in matters of faith and morality. They believe that this is the biblical pathway to Christian unity. As in the other Restoration congregations, the Lord's Supper is a weekly celebration and believers are baptized by full immersion. Unlike the Disciples and the Christian Churches, the Churches of Christ use no instrumental music in their worship. Instrumental music, these Christians believe, is not biblical, but is instead one of the ways the church accommodated itself to the demands of more wealthy members.

EVANGELICAL CHRISTIANS

Evangelicalism is not new in the United States. Both evangelicalism and pentecostalism trace their heritage back to revivals that began in the eighteenth century. By the early 1700s, Puritan religion in the Northeast had experienced a dramatic decline. In the mid-1700s, the northeastern and the mid-Atlantic colonies were the site of the first of a number of religious revivals that swept through America. Scholars have named this first outpouring of revival enthusiasm the **Great Awakening.**

The revivalists' messages were simple and straightforward. They concentrated on the outlines of the Christian message as Puritanism interpreted it: People are lost, trapped in sin, without any hope of saving themselves. God's free offer of salvation through grace and faith in Jesus must be accepted, because there is no other hope. Acceptance of God's gracious offer brings release from the terrible anxiety of the sin-stricken soul. The preaching style of Jonathan Edwards, George Whitefield, and other Great Awakening preachers assured that their hearers would be moved both intellectually and emotionally. Intense, abrupt experiences that people interpreted as conversion from their old lives to new lives in grace became the standard by which people's response was judged.

The **Second Awakening** occurred on the frontier in the 1800s. The basic theology and the simplicity of the message remained the same. The frontier population, however, was less educated and much less stable geographically; these factors brought about a change in revival preaching. The Second Awakening revivalists developed a style that was more emotional and less intellectual than that of their predecessors. A strong appeal to people's emotions, and equally emotional responses, were very common. Preachers pressed their hearers for immediate conversion, since many in the audience might well move on in a matter of hours. Conversion was often accompanied by emotional and physical manifestations, such as running and jumping about, unintelligible vocalizations, and fainting. Some preachers spoke out against these phenomena, believing that they were unseemly and excessive, but others encouraged them as signs of true conversion and the experience of God.

The simple message and the emotional style of the Awakenings continue in modern-day revivals. Testifying to one's faith and the centrality of the conversion experience are still important aspects of the evangelical way of being religious. Unusual physical manifestations attributed to the action of the Holy Spirit are a significant part of the contemporary pentecostal experience.

Consensus religion in the United States has usually been a relatively private matter. Who has not been reminded that it is "not polite" to discuss politics or religion? People's religion, like their political preferences, has been considered too personal to be discussed very much. Whatever may have been the fate of politics in recent years, religion has come front and center for many Americans. It has gone public. The upsurge of interest in evangelical religion, and its very public presence, has been one of the most noticeable features of American religion in the last decade and a half. Survey data indicate that, among Christians, over 80 percent have talked with someone about their faith with the aim of converting the other person to Christianity.

It is very important to evangelicals to share their faith with other people. The word itself comes from the Greek and means "messenger of good news." Telling other people about the joy, peace, and happiness they have found in their relationship with Jesus is a top priority in the lives of most evangelicals. One campus evangelical organization, for example, is called Top Priority Outreach. In many ways, **witnessing**, or talking about their faith with other people with the intention of leading them to put their faith in Jesus also, defines evangelicalism. Evangelicals believe that the responsibility for missionary work rests on each and every Christian. They believe that Jesus' command to go into the whole world and preach (Mark 16:15) is directed to all Christians.

Most evangelical Christians also say they have been born again, and they emphasize the importance of this particular religious event. Being born again refers to a person's being able to point to a very specific event, a time and place in which they accepted Jesus Christ as their personal Lord and Savior. Being born again and asking Jesus to come into their lives establishes a warmly personal relationship with God that far exceeds anything they might have experienced prior to their conversion. Even those who had been active church members say that they became a Christian at that point in time. They distinguish sharply between being a member of a church and being a Christian. Usually, it is understood that virtually all Christians are church members, but not all church members are Christians. The emphasis on a datable, identifiable conversion experience goes back to Puritanism. The Puritans required testimony of such an experience as a condition of full church membership. Among all Christians, about half can identify such an experience in their religious lives.

Evangelicalism is very public in America in other ways as well. On college campuses, evangelical groups like Navigators, Campus Crusade for Christ, and Intervarsity Christian Fellowship draw many students, many of whom have participated in Young Life in high school. Members of these groups often witness to other students in the library or student center. There are evangelical groups within professional fields, such as Christian Nurses and the Society of Christian Philosophers. Christian bookstores can be found in most cities. They offer a wide selection of books, music, videotapes, and jewelry that reflects the evangelical viewpoint. Christian music has become the music of choice for many listeners, and hymns such as "Amazing Grace" and "Morning Has Broken" have become easy-listening standards (Figure 9–1). Christian music has its own awards program, the Dove Awards. Jewelry featuring crosses, fish symbols, and "One Way" and "Jesus First" slogans is a silent witness to all who see it being worn. Many

Figure 9–1   Christian music is an important part of evangelical Christianity. (*Photo by the author.*)

cars have bumper stickers stating the driver's religious position. *Christianity Today*, a major weekly religious periodical, was founded to promote the evangelical viewpoint. Finally, public testimonies by leading figures in the sports, entertainment, and business communities have increased the public visibility of evangelicals.

Billy Graham (b. 1918) is the foremost contemporary exemplar of the evangelical and revivalist tradition in American religion and is the most public symbol of the style of evangelicalism that began in the 1950s and continues today. His radio program, "The Hour of Decision," began in 1950, and he was soon familiar to television viewers as well. The core of Graham's message is traditional: repent and surrender to Jesus as Lord and Savior. However, his preaching also addresses social problems and national sins. He has spoken out strongly against racism and classism in the United States and supports nuclear disarmament. His style of presentation is restrained and theologically informed. He established a close working relationship with the White House in the 1950s during the Eisenhower administration, a relationship that has continued with Eisenhower's successors.

Somewhat more women than men describe themselves as evangelicals. Evangelicalism is most common among those in the eighteen-to-twenty-nine and in the fifty-and-older age brackets. It is most common in the South, where about half describe themselves this way. A lower percentage of whites and Hispanics say they are evangelicals than do blacks and other nonwhites. The percentage of evangelicals is higher in the lower-income and lower-education brackets. Far more Protestants than Catholics claim the evangelical label, by about a two-to-one margin.

Evangelicals usually distinguish themselves from fundamentalists, who are their closest ideological neighbors. Most evangelicals regard fundamentalists as too militant, too exclusive, and as having too low an opinion of modern scholarship. Evangelicals, although certainly conservative in both theology and ethics, do accept some compromise. The new style of evangelicalism is characterized by a cautious acceptance of some of the insights of biblical scholarship, while maintaining that the Bible is inspired by God. Evangelicals affirm the generally agreed-upon doctrines of Christianity in their traditional forms. Historically, evangelicals have emphasized personal morality, and this emphasis remains. There is a new spirit of sociopolitical involvement, too, that replaces the tendency of earlier evangelicals to remain outside the rough-and-tumble of political action.

Evangelicals preach a relatively simple message that emphasizes human sinfulness and the need for rebirth, the need for and joys of a personal relationship with Jesus, and the necessity of making a definite decision for Christ. Evangelicals certainly believe that conversion is a result of the action of God's grace upon a person. They also teach the important role of human free will in the process. Evangelicalism is more concerned with the quality of religious experience than with belief in particular doctrines. It is pietistic, emphasizing personal prayer, devotion, and Bible reading.

Most evangelicals believe in a supernatural God who constantly intervenes in the affairs of the world through miracles. For example, an evangelical who recovered from a serious illness would probably explain that recovery by referring to God's role in the healing process. A religious liberal or humanist would be likely to attribute healing to the skill of medical personnel and the effect of medication.

Most evangelical churches are not members of the National Council of Churches because they believe that the strong desire for cooperation that led to the formation of the National Council also led to a compromise of biblical faith. Many, however, are members of the National Association of Evangelicals.

One contemporary manifestation of the evangelical spirit is "Promise Keepers," a men's organization founded in 1990 by Bill McCartney, former University of Colorado football coach. Seven conferences around the country drew 300,000 men in 1994, and approximately 700,000 in 1995.[4] A Washington, D.C. gathering in 1996 hopes to attract 1 million men. Its "seven promises" are the guiding principles of the evangelical men's movement: A Promise Keeper is committed to

1. Honoring Jesus Christ through worship, prayer, and obedience to His Word, through the power of the Holy Spirit;
2. Pursuing vital relationships with a few other men, understanding that he needs brothers to help him keep his promises;
3. Practicing spiritual, moral, ethical, and sexual purity;
4. Building strong marriages and families through love, protection, and biblical values;
5. Supporting the mission of the church by honoring and praying for his pastor and by actively giving his time and resources;
6. Reaching beyond any racial and denominational barriers to demonstrate the power of biblical unity;
7. Influencing his world, being obedient to the Great Commandment (see Mark 12:30–31) and the Great Commission (see Matthew 28:19–20).[5]

The numbers of men drawn to this movement indicates that it meets a need that many feel keenly.

Evangelicalsm is not limited to any one Christian church or denomination. Evangelical Christians are people who believe that their lives have been decisively changed for the better by a vibrant experience that they attribute to God's love, the saving grace of Jesus, and the working of the Holy Spirit. In their enthusiasm for their experience, they seek to share it with others (Figure 9–2).

---

[4]David Van Biema, "Full of Promise," *Time* (November 6, 1995), p. 62.
[5]"Profile of a Promise Keeper," *New Man* (July/August 1994), pp. 15–26.

Figure 9–2   Evangelicals seek many opportunities to share their faith with other people. On this business sign, PTL stands for "Praise the Lord." (*Photo by the author.*)

A NOTE ON "MEGACHURCHES"

You may not have heard the word **megachurch** before. It refers to churches that have unusually large attendance at worship. Church growth analysts use different numbers to define megachurches, but the minimum seems to be 1,000 people. The largest count over 15,000 people attending all the weekly services. The largest, in terms of physical plant, Crenshaw Christian Center in Los Angeles, has an auditorium that seats 10,400, and even larger ones are under construction. The basis is attendance rather than membership, since this is what these churches themselves emphasize. Most, if not all, these churches are evangelical Protestant. Some are linked with larger denominations, but many are independent. There is no absolute count of the number of churches that fit into this category, but it is over 1,000 and growing. They have been described as "one of the four or five most significant developments in contemporary American church history."[6]

---

[6]Russell Chandler, *Racing Toward 2001: The Forces Shaping America's Religious Future* (Grand Rapids, MI: Zondervan Publishing House, and San Francisco, CA: HarperSanFrancisco, 1992), p. 163. Other information in this section is drawn from Lyle E. Schaller, "Megachurch!" *Christianity Today* (March 5, 1990), pp. 20–24.

There are a number of reasons for the megachurch phenomenon. People are not as loyal to their denominational affiliations as they used to be. The growing number of people who commute a relatively long distance to their jobs is more willing to do so to attend church as well. The size of these churches, along with the income provided by so many members, enables them to offer a very wide range of activities. Many of these activities are, of course, religious, but numerous others are not. One, Second Baptist Church in Houston, Texas, has weight rooms, saunas, and a movie theater. Another has its own roller skating rink, gym, and racquetball courts. At the same time as such churches benefit from their large size, they put a great deal of emphasis on peoples' participation in small groups that provide intimate relationships and face-to-face interaction. Traditional forms of worship are discarded in favor of music more in tune with secular music, and the use of video is standard. Such churches make an all-out effort to discover what people want from a church, both religiously and otherwise, and then provide it. At the same time, the message is usually simple and straightforward, and salvation is portrayed in ways that make it immediately applicable to peoples' lives. Too, there is the sociological fact that current generations have grown up with big institutions of all sorts, are comfortable in them, and desire the range of choices that size can make possible, whether in religion or in a shopping mall.

It is too early to assess the future of this development. It will take at least a couple of decades to tell what will happen as these congregations mature. None has yet experienced the need to replace a founding pastor. These churches have been built to their large size by a leader with a strong and charismatic personality, and such people often prove difficult to replace. It is also too early in the evolution of megachurches to know what will occur with their second generation membership. Will the children born to members want what their parents' church offers? For the present, they are interesting as an example of one way in which religion can respond to the entertainment-oriented and consumer culture of the 1990s.

THE RELIGIOUS-POLITICAL RIGHT

The involvement of evangelical Christians and fundamentalists in American politics is not a new occurrence. Evangelical religion was a strong force in American politics until the second decade of the 1900s. During the period between the end of World War I and the early 1970s, its influence on American government lessened dramatically. The early 1970s brought a renewal of evangelical and fundamentalist involvement in the political life of the nation. This trend has continued into the 1990s.

The **religious-political right** is a loose coalition of groups and individuals who are united by their conviction that the United States is in the midst of a severe spiritual and moral decline, a decline that could well snowball into a landslide that would lead to downfall of the United States and the defeat of democracy in the world. They believe that a return to the traditional values of American life, best safeguarded by fundamentalist Christianity, will prevent this landslide and again make America the strong and righteous nation that they believe existed in an earlier time. They are also united in their desire to use the legislative process to make their goals into the law of the land. One analysis of the movement has called it "a blend of old-time religion and far-right politics coordinated with Madison Avenue sophistication."[7]

Groups move in and out of the coalition depending upon which issue or issues are being dealt with at a given time. There are several groups whose alignment with the goals and concerns of the religious-political right is fairly constant, however. The most reliable support, in terms of both programs and finances, comes from **those whose religious outlook is very conservative or fundamentalist**, some of whom are evangelicals and some of whom are not. Some are pentecostals, while some are not.

Protestants are clearly the backbone of this group. On certain issues, such as the movement to limit legal abortions, **support also comes from Catholics, Eastern Orthodox Christians, and even some Orthodox Jews.** On others, such as the campaign against ratification of the Equal Rights Amendment (ERA), the coalition has included support from the **Latter-day Saints**, who value traditional male and female social roles. **A second major segment of support comes from political conservatives.** They desire to see the balance of government power shifted from the federal to the state government and hope to return the responsibility for welfare programs to the private sector of American life. This leads them to support the religious right on these types of issues. A third group is related to the second. **Social and economic conservatives** share many of the same concerns that motivate the political conservatives' involvement with the religious-political right. Economic conservatives especially favor the modifications in the welfare program it encourages, as well as its support for private business interests. We can also cite a fourth group—those who, without any clearly defined religious motivation, subscribe to the **belief that America has a special role to play in the history of the world.** They describe this role using the biblical metaphors of a light to the nations and a city set on a hill. A final group is more difficult to define, but just as important. We can call them the **social traditionalists**—those whose motivations are not clearly religious, political, or economic, but who believe that a return to older values would be a beneficial course for America to follow. They comprise a loose back-to-the-basics interest.

The goals of the religious-political right are stated in various ways. However they are described, they revolve around the **intention to bring about major changes in American government and American life.** They seek to make the United States a moral and righteous nation, defining morality and righteousness in terms of the authority of the Christian Bible as the only legitimate guide.

---

[7]Peter L. Benson and Dorothy L. Williams, *Religion on Capitol Hill: Myths and Realities* (New York: Oxford University Press, 1986), p. 173.

The religious-political right also describes its goals as an all-out war on an enemy that they have identified as being at the root of America's moral problems: secular humanism. Secular humanism stands for nearly everything that the new right believes is wrong. Most supporters subscribe to an interpretation of recent history that holds that secular humanists in high government positions are conspiring to make secular humanism the official religion of the land. A significant part of this conspiracy centers on what is being taught and what is permissible in the public schools.

Not all the groups involved in this coalition fully agree about what its specific agenda should be. Nor do they agree on the relative importance of the various items. There are, however, certain planks that can be found in nearly all statements of their platform, and it is these that are described below:

1. A **call for a return to traditional values** means, first and foremost, support for traditional family structures. A number of other items, such as opposition to the ERA and to homosexual lifestyles support their basic interest in traditional families.
2. A closely related category includes several issues relevant to the **public schools**, on one hand, and **support for a private Christian school system** on the other hand.
3. Third is their position on **U.S. military superiority**.
4. **Direct political action**, such as lobbying, voter registration, and the election of candidates who are favorable to their views, is a fourth goal.

The religious-political right regards the family as the mainstay of American culture. They approve of only one form of family structure, which they identify as the **traditional form of family organization** in the United States. The traditional family is the family that consists of a man and a woman, married for life, with children. Women are encouraged to devote full time to their roles as wives, mothers, and homemakers, and fathers should be the sole source of financial support for the family. The economic system should support this arrangement. Premarital chastity and marital monogamy are the only acceptable forms of sexuality. Both the Old and New Testaments of the Christian scriptures are cited in support of the position that homosexuality is a heinous sin and a prime contributor to America's spiritual degeneracy. Sex education should be taught only by Christians to ensure that proper values will be taught along with factual information.

Advocacy of the traditional family is reinforced by several other points. Perhaps foremost among these was the campaign of the religious-political right to block the ratification of the Equal Rights Amendment, a task in which they were ultimately successful. The ERA and the "feminist revolution" appear in every list of national errors that are said to threaten America. Opposition to abortion, especially government support for abortion in the form of Medicaid payments and federal funding for abortion clinics, is another important part of their family policy.

They also support a thorough cleanup of commercial television, not only to eliminate violence and the use of sexually suggestive advertising, but also to eliminate the portrayal of alternative lifestyles. They oppose pornography in all its forms and want to have laws enacted that would mandate stiff penalties for those who create and distribute pornographic literature, films, videotapes, and so forth. Another priority is support for programs that will help to solve the problem of illegal drug use.

The concerns of the religious-political right obviously are shared by people who do not identify with it explicitly. Survey data indicate that approximately 90 percent of Americans believe that extramarital sex is always or nearly always wrong. About 80 percent feel that way about active homosexuality. Over half support at least some restrictions on the availability of legal abortion. Over half the population favors laws prohibiting the sale of pornography to people under the age of eighteen, and almost half oppose the sale of pornography to anyone, regardless of age. Many Americans are concerned about illegal drugs, as they are about sex and violence (and the frequent close association of the two) on commercial television.

The large role the federal government has assumed in administering welfare programs is another concern. The religious-political right does recognize that there will always be people who cannot care for themselves because of age or physical or mental infirmity. They want to shift the responsibility for the care of such people from the government to the private sector, including churches, businesses, and, above all, the families of the people themselves. For example, they support tax credits for those families who have a dependent elderly parent living with them. For all except those completely incapable of working, welfare "programs tend to destroy one's initiative, skill, work habits, and productivity."[8]

Government regulation of business and industry is yet another concern. Free enterprise, ambitious management, and competition unfettered by government regulation are held to be biblical values that are a part of God's plan for humanity. Restriction of the freedom of business and industry is often linked to the loss of other freedoms, such as freedom of speech, of the press, and of religion.

The religious-political right wants the nation to return to the values of an earlier, much less complicated period in history, when the population was much smaller. The members of this movement believe that the values that worked in that setting are what America needs now. Although not all Americans agree with them, their vision of a renewed America based on traditional values has captured the hearts and minds of a significant number of people. The religious-political right is one of the most significant religious and political movements of this century.

The **plan of action** that the religious-political right envisions **for educating children** is closely related to their hopes for a return to traditional values in American society.[9] It is the schools, both public and private, that bear the responsibil-

---

[8]Jerry Falwell, *Listen, America!* (Garden City, NY: Doubleday and Company, 1980) p. 78.

[9]The views of the new religious-political right concerning the schools are based loosely on the following two books: Tim LaHaye, *The Battle for the Mind* (Old Tappan, NJ: Fleming H. Revell Company, 1980) and Tim LaHaye, *The Battle for the Public Schools* (Old Tappan, NJ: Fleming H. Revell Company, 1983).

ity, alongside the family and the churches, for rearing children who have a strong sense of and commitment to these values. Their approach to education has two main facets. The first is what they want to see happen within the public school system. The second is their goals concerning the establishment of a system of private Christian schools to supplement the public schools.

We will look at their goals for the *public schools* first. The public schools, according to this analysis, have been taken over by secular humanists and are being used as the main tool for indoctrinating youngsters with the values held dear by humanists. The U.S. Supreme Court decision that made mandated prayer and other school-sponsored devotional exercises in the public schools illegal is of particular concern. They want voluntary prayer and other devotional exercises returned to the public school classroom. They also want any academic study of religion eliminated, because it maintains a position of neutrality concerning the truth of specific religions. This conflicts sharply with their belief that Christianity is the one true faith. To help accomplish these goals, they have increasingly focused on getting supporters elected to local school boards.

A related concern is that the public schools do not teach one absolute truth in any area. For example, in dealing with families in a high school sociology class, a classroom discussion of many styles of relationships between adults and many approaches to parenting takes the place of the promotion of the traditional family as the only acceptable family. Rather than advocating that women remain at home as wives, mothers, and homemakers, the public schools attempt to prepare their students to assess the strengths and weaknesses of various arrangements. Rather than teaching the immorality of premarital sex, health teachers encourage their students to explore their own values and attitudes and introduce the cautions deemed necessary in the face of disease and the possibility of unwanted pregnancy. Government classes, instead of promoting democracy and condemning other forms of government, have students evaluate various forms of government.

Control over the textbook selection process is also an important agenda item for the new right. A few examples of their criticisms of public school books will help make their position clear. Relativism has already been mentioned. Blurring of traditional sex roles, such as elementary school book pictures of boys cooking and cleaning, girls building things and wearing hard hats, has been one of the things most criticized. Teaching about the European Renaissance is suspect because of its high estimate of humanity and human reason. The philosophy of the Enlightenment comes under the same criticism. Religion is not portrayed as a significant aspect of American history and culture; in fact, it is usually left out altogether. *The Wizard of Oz* portrays a witch as good, and *Cinderella* presents magical acts as if they were fact. You might pause a moment here and think back over the textbooks from which you learned as a child. How was religion portrayed, if at all? What messages were being presented in the pictures of boys and girls, men and women? When you took the required (in most school systems, at any rate) government or civics course, were different types of government portrayed equally, or was democracy held up as an ideal?

The teaching of evolution is another focal point for the critique of public school education. Some want the theory of evolution dropped from the curriculum completely in favor of teaching an account of the beginnings of the world and humankind that is compatible with the creation stories in Genesis. Others want to see evolution and creationism or creation science taught alongside each other as theories. Again, think back to your high school (perhaps junior high or middle school) biology, botany, or life science classes. Were you taught about evolution? Were you taught the creation stories in Genesis? Was the entire subject ignored? Some textbook publishers and some schools have taken this last approach to avoid a confrontation over this very explosive issue.

A final point of contention with the public schools has to do with the teaching of sex education. In the first place, many supporters of the religious-political right want all sex education removed from the schools and left in the hands of parents and the churches. If sex education is to be taught in the public schools at all, the values of premarital chastity, marital fidelity, and lifelong monogamy should be the only things taught. Sex education cannot be separated from family life education, and the traditional family style must be upheld in the public schools.

An editorial reflection is in order here. The values of traditional Christianity have been a major influence in American life for many centuries. The Genesis accounts of how the world began have guided the thinking of uncounted millions of people and continue to do so. Sexual morality based on the teachings of the Christian Bible is the framework that has made family life meaningful and good for generations of Americans. These values deserve a place in public school education because they are a significant part of the story of humanity and of the history and present culture of the United States. In a pluralistic culture, they must be presented as one set of values alongside others from which people have chosen. They must not be taught as the only right values, to the exclusion of others. A similar point can be made concerning the omission of religion in descriptions of the history and present culture of the United States. Religion has been and continues to be an important factor in American life. To omit it is to present an inaccurate picture of both past and present. The distinction between teaching religion and teaching about religion must be scrupulously maintained, however, and the approach must always be descriptive rather than normative.

Every bit as important in the religious-political right's approach to public education is its support for a network of *private Christian schools*. You will recall that when we discussed Catholicism, we learned that the Catholic Church sponsors the largest private school system in the United States. It is usually called the parochial school system. Among Protestants, the Lutherans sponsor a number of schools. The network of Christian schools has grown steadily in the United States. Those who support Christian schools do so largely because they believe that home, church, and school should reinforce each other by presenting the same values and truths. Supporters of Christian schools want to see the development of a system that exists apart from the teacher training and licensing requirements enforced by the states. They do not want to be subject to the same curriculum requirements that guide the public schools.

There is more at stake, according to the supporters of private Christian schools, than simply being able to begin and end the school day with prayer and Bible reading, or to say grace before lunch. Christian school advocates are asking for the right to control their children's education with minimal interference from the government. Government regulation is looked upon as harassment and as infringement of freedom of religion. For those whose values and home life are guided by the views and principles of fundamentalist Christianity, public school attendance is a very real threat to their children's spiritual welfare. It threatens both their earthly happiness and their eternal life.

Catholics pressed for and won the right to their own schools because they believed that there was a clear Protestant bias in the public schools. Fundamentalist Christians believe there is a clear humanistic bias in the public schools. They seek the right to take decisive action to protect their youngsters. It is for this reason that education has become such a pressing issue.

The **military strength of the United States** and its position in relation to the other nations of the world are as great a concern to the religious-political right as are domestic issues. They believe that the United States must always be the first and foremost world military and economic power. They believe this is necessary mainly to protect the values of democracy and capitalism both in the United States itself and in the world. In this line of thought, the strongest possible national defense becomes not only a political necessity but a religious obligation. The United States has been chosen by God for a special destiny in the history of God's interaction with the world, and defending that destiny militarily is part of carrying out the divine plan. Any attempt at disarmament or compromise is seen as taking the United States one step farther along the road toward surrender or takeover by the forces of evil.

The religious-political right works through **direct political action** as well as through its efforts to educate people and persuade them to support their point of view. It seeks to elect public officials who are sympathetic to its programs and views. The role of government is described as the provision of "godly leadership." Only by governing according to the Bible can a leader govern rightly. A direct practical implementation of this point of view came from the Christian Voice organization when it developed the Congressional Score Card to track the way that members of Congress voted on certain critical moral issues such as abortion support and the ERA. Voter registration drives have been another important focus, and voter registration has been done after Sunday morning worship in some fundamentalist churches. After having done less well than they had hoped in national politics, their attention has turned more to local politics, where it remains, for the most part.

In addition to registering like minded-voters and electing agreeable government leaders, lobbying has been a central concern. The **National Conservative Political Action Committee** and the **National Christian Action Coalition** are primarily lobbying organizations. *Political action committees* (often referred to as *PACs*) are interest groups that engage in various activities. They often focus their attention on the election of sympathetic leaders. The Christian Voice Moral Government Fund and the Christian Voters' Victory Fund were formed expressly to help finance the political campaigns of people who would support fundamentalist and conservative values and programs.

The **Moral Majority**, founded by Jerry Falwell in 1979, was one of the earliest organizations in the religious-political right. As its interests expanded and it sought to draw in additional groups of people, it was renamed the **Liberty Foundation**. Late in 1987, Falwell turned over the leadership of the Liberty Foundation to Jerry Nims, an Atlanta, Georgia, businessperson and long-time Falwell associate.

The **Christian Voice** is the oldest national organization aligned with the religious-political right. It has concentrated largely on compiling information about candidates (Congressional Score Card) and providing voters with lists of approved and disapproved candidates. It provides financial support to those whom it approves.

Roundtable (formerly, Religious Roundtable), founded by Ed McAteer, is an organization that directs its efforts to and draws its membership from the elites of both religion and government. It does not have the grassroots support that organizations such as the Liberty Foundation do, nor has it sought such support. Two-day meetings four times per year provide the opportunity for about 150 major conservative and fundamentalist Christian leaders—those with large congregations and visible positions—to be briefed on issues on which they then can inform their followers.[10]

At least two of the organizations were founded and are led by women. Best known is Phyllis Schlafly's **Eagle Forum**, which concentrated on the movement to defeat the ratification of the ERA. The lesser known *Library Court* was organized in 1979, headed up by Connaught Marshner. It is named after the street in Washington, D.C., where it first met. Marshner worked very closely with Nevada Senator Paul Laxalt on the Family Protection Act, which he introduced into Congress in 1979. The Family Protection Act, which did not receive the necessary number of votes to pass, incorporated many of the family concerns of the religious-political right. Marshner has exercised a strong leadership role in the Library Court, as has Schlafly in the Eagle Forum. These organizations have also been leaders in the campaign to get an antiabortion amendment to the United States Constitution passed.

Some of those who supported the Moral Majority went on to become in-

---

[10]Richard A. Viguerie, *The New Right: We're Ready to Lead* (Falls Church, VA: The Viguerie Company, 1981), p. 130.

volved in the **Christian Reconstructionism** movement in the late 1980s and 1990s. The term *Christian Reconstructionism* was coined by Gary North, founder of the *Journal of Christian Reconstruction*. The movement has a think tank called the Chalcedon Foundation at Vallecito, California. Organizationally, it is embodied in the Coalition on Revival and its National Coordinating Council. Christian reconstructionists believe that the whole of American society should be "reconstructed" to conform to biblical law. Israel's theocracy, as portrayed in the Christian Old Testament, is regarded as the blueprint for society. Only Christians and Jews should lead the nation, and all individuals and groups must live by "God's law" as understood by the reconstructionists. One analyst of the future of religion in the United States describes some of the goals of the movement this way:

> [Christian Reconstruction] advocates the abolition of public schools, the Internal Revenue Service, and the Federal Reserve by 2000. It also seeks to "Christianize all aspects of life from the arts and sciences to banking and the news media," according to its twenty-four point platform. And it proposes setting up a "kingdom" counterculture that includes a "Christian" court system.[11]

In a pluralistic culture, the determination of the Christian Reconstructionist movement to impose its views on everyone is disturbing. In a 1987 public television documentary, "God and Politics: On Earth as It is in Heaven," Bill Moyers quoted Gary North as follows:

> We must use the doctrine of religious liberty to gain independence for Christian schools until we train up a generation of people who know that there is no religious neutrality, . . . Then they will get busy constructing a Bible-based social, political and religious order which finally denies the religious liberty of the enemies of God.[12]

Although sharing many of the views of the older-style religious-political right, the reconstructionists are distinguished by their strident militancy.

CHRISTIAN TELEVISION

Do you sometimes, or regularly, watch the television programs on any of the major Christian networks, such as PTL or FAM? If you do, why do you enjoy them? If you do not watch them, why not? What kinds of thoughts come to mind when someone uses the phrase, "television preacher" or "television evangelist"?

The religious message that is broadcast on Christian television is not new.

---

[11]Russell Chandler, *Racing Toward 2001: The Forces Shaping America's Religious Future*, p. 143.
[12]Bill Moyers, "God and Politics: On Earth as It is in Heaven," produced by Gregg Pratt and Jan Falstad (Public Affairs Television, Inc., 1987).

Nor is religious broadcasting itself new. It began with radio and continued with commercial television. What *is* new is the medium. High-tech communications technologies, such as cable television and communications satellites, have revolutionized the religious broadcasting industry.

The early television evangelists such as Graham and Oral Roberts still use commercial programming. Some of the programs specifically identified with the religious-political right, such as Falwell's "Old Time Gospel Hour," are aired on commercial networks in some areas. So is Robert Schuller's "Hour of Power." However, Christian television is no longer primarily a matter of time purchased on commercial networks. The Christian networks, satellite connections, super high-tech studios, and computers have revolutionized Christian broadcasting. Three major Christian networks—the Family Network (FAM, formerly the Christian Broadcasting Network), Trinity Broadcasting Network (TBN), and the PTL (for "Praise the Lord" or "People That Love") Network—provide most of the programs that make up Christian television today.

The electronic church, as it is often called, has been hailed by those favorable to it as the greatest tool the church has ever had for telling "the greatest story ever told." It has also been the most harshly criticized method of outreach the church has ever used. Whatever one's opinion of religious television, it now has a firm place in both the overall landscape of the American love affair with television and religion in the United States.

You have already been learning about Christian television, the electronic church, or "televangelism," because most of the programming on Christian television reflects the views of evangelical Christianity, fundamentalism, and the religious-political right. It is primarily an extension of the revivalist and evangelical tradition that has characterized American religion at least since the Awakenings.

This particular form of religious broadcasting has often been referred to as **televangelism**. That word is somewhat inaccurate, because its main audience is composed of those who already share its point of view and religious beliefs. There is also a problem with the phrase **electronic church**, even though it is commonly used. There are some very important differences between *church* as most people think of it and what happens on the *electronic church*. I propose that we call it **Christian television**, using the phrase analogously to the phrase *Christian music*. Christian music is an outgrowth and an integral part of the conservative/evangelical/fundamentalist point of view in American Christianity. It provides an alternative for those who are offended by contemporary secular music or who simply want music that reflects their own worldview. Similarly, Christian television provides alternative television for those who find it difficult to locate acceptable programs on the commercial channels. It reflects the same religious worldview that supports contemporary Christian music. Christian television, then, seems to be a logical choice.

This designation also helps us to understand the importance of the resurgence in evangelical and fundamentalist Christianity in the United States for

Christian television. There is now a group of consumers available that has clearly defined tastes in entertainment. It is this group of consumers that makes up the viewing audience for Christian television.

One of the best-known of the Christian television personalities is Jerry Falwell, founder of the Moral Majority. He is pastor of the 20,000-plus member Thomas Road Baptist Church in Lynchburg, Virginia, the site of the broadcasting empire he built. Thomas Road Church is an independent Baptist church, unaffiliated with any Baptist convention. Liberty Broadcasting Network, Liberty University, and the Lynchburg Christian Academy are all a part of the multifaceted program that Falwell supervises.

Pentecostal-turned-Methodist Oral Roberts has also put together a complex of operations, all of which revolve around his long-standing interest in religious healing. Known early as a television healer, he downplayed this aspect in his later broadcasts. He built the City of Faith Medical Center in Tulsa, Oklahoma, to bring together medical research and treatment in a modern hospital facility and religious healing by prayer and the laying on of hands. Oral Roberts University, also in Tulsa, is one of the best-known of the conservative Christian colleges. Students attend required chapel and religion classes that are cast in the mold of the devotional study of religion rather than its academic study. They must agree to a strict code of personal conduct. Violations result in quick dismissal. Roberts' "Expect a Miracle" television program has been on the air for a quarter-century.

CBN (now FAM) was founded by Marion G. (Pat) Robertson, an early entrant in the field of Christian television who was among the first to offer a distinctively political orientation in his broadcasts. Following an unsuccessful bid for the 1988 Republican presidential nomination, he returned to his broadcasting career. Robertson built FAM into the largest Christian cable network, and his "700 Club" remains one of the most popular of the religious broadcasts.

Robert Schuller is an ordained minister in the Reformed Church in America. His twelve-story Crystal Cathedral in Garden Grove, California, is noteworthy for its architecture. It is a four-pointed star of reflective glass, 415 feet from point to point in one direction, and over 200 feet in the other. One arm of the Crystal Cathedral slides open so that people can worship in their cars. He has focused his attention on the church and its congregation and has not expanded into educational or entertainment ventures. Schuller's sermons set him apart from the others. He freely acknowledges his debt to Norman Vincent Peale, famous for the "power of positive thinking." Schuller's "Hour of Power" makes much less of human sin than of human possibility. Peale's positive thinking has found new life in Schuller's "possibility thinking," which emphasizes that human possibilities are as vast as is our capacity to visualize them.

Christian television makes use of nearly every format for adults' and children's programming that is used by secular television, including talk shows, quiz shows, soap operas, dramas, cartoons and a various children's programs. A Christian music alternative to MTV offers all the video slickness of MTV without its sex and violence. In addition, worship services and revival meetings are broadcast and Bible studies are conducted. Reruns of earlier programs that present acceptable lifestyles, such as "Life with Father," "Leave It to Beaver," and "Lassie" are also shown.

Who watches Christian television? Several studies have been done in the attempt to answer this question, and they all agree on the main points. Holding evangelical and fundamentalist or very conservative religious beliefs is the factor most strongly correlated with watching Christian television. Most viewers live in the South and the Midwest, with a disproportionate number in the South. The majority of viewers are female and viewers are older than the general population. Between two-thirds and three-fourths are age fifty or over. Another important fact that emerges from these studies is that watching religion on television does not substitute for church attendance and participation. Most viewers are regular churchgoers and contribute to the financial support of their local congregation as well. The early predictions that Christian television would be the downfall of many a local congregation have not proven accurate. Christian television is used as a substitute for attendance by only one category of people—those who, for whatever reason, find it difficult to get out to attend church. The frail elderly, young women at home with small children, those fearful of going out, and those whose handicaps make church attendance difficult make up this group. Ratings indicate, finally, that there are fewer viewers by far than the massive audiences claimed by the broadcasters themselves. There are, especially, fewer regular viewers.

The fund-raising techniques used by Christian television have been widely criticized. Several methods are popular. Seeking donations is a common method. In return for a specified donation, donors may be memorialized in some fashion, such as by having their names inscribed in Oral Roberts' Prayer Tower or on chairs in Schuller's Crystal Cathedral. It should be noted here that donors' names have often been inscribed on pews or stained glass windows as local churches sought to raise money, too. Clubs such as the 700 Club or Faith Partners offer privileges and benefits in return for a specified sum per month. Besides a magazine or newsletter, participants gain a sense of being a part of something important, of being related in a personal way to the work being carried out by their favorite Christian television personality. Money is also raised by the sale of pens, bumper stickers, lapel pins, Bibles, records or audiotapes, and books. Frequently these items are not "sold" but offered in return for a donation. Most Christian television personalities are quite skilled at the personal-appeal style of fund-raising, in which they simply ask for donations. The "going off the air" appeal is a variant of this method, in which the personality makes a highly emotional appeal, in which it is said that only contributions over and above the usual will keep the program from having to go off the air. Again, contributors gain a feeling that they have helped to accomplish the work that the preacher set out to do.

The fund-raising method most closely associated with Christian television is direct mail. Many telecasts show a number for viewers to call to request a free gift, to ask for prayer or counseling, or to make a pledge. The names of the callers are added to a data bank that is used for mailed appeals for funds. The more information that the organization has about the person, the more "personalized" the appeals can be. Women at home with small children will be asked to support the Eagle Forum or the Library Court or will be sent advertisements for children's Bibles and other religious books. Singles can be invited to singles weekend retreats and offered books about Christian singlehood and dating. Sophisticated computer technology makes possible the production of thousands of "original" letters personalized with information like the recipient's name and home town mentioned in the body of the letter. Paragraphs are retrieved electronically and added to customize the letter. Words can be underscored, seemingly with the same pen with which the letter is "signed." Even though most people know that these letters are produced electronically, the illusion of intimacy they offer has a powerful appeal.

For most of its founders, the initial goal of Christian television was evangelism. They wanted to bring their version of the gospel message to millions of viewers, and win additional souls for Christ. Clearly, it does not work well as a tool for evangelism, since the great majority of its viewers already count themselves among those who agree with the viewpoint being presented. It does help to reinforce existing beliefs and behaviors. For the largely convinced viewing audience, what they see and hear models the behavior and beliefs they themselves are trying to live. It reinforces and supports, and many come away from its programs with renewed conviction and determination. As one of my students explained simply, "I watch it; I feel good."

There are important differences between Christian television and "church" as most people usually think of it. Christian television does not and cannot provide the personal dimension, the face-to-face contact that is a valuable part of a community of faith. In spite of "personalized" direct mail, clubs, and requests for contributions, Christian television is not a community. Its television personality-preachers are not pastors. They will not be there for their viewers when the viewers have marital problems or discover that a child is on drugs. They will not be there to baptize a new baby or to bury a grandparent or spouse. They are not accessible by telephone when someone wants to say, "Hey . . . I got the job! Thanks for your support." In a similar vein, an audience is not a congregation. Communities of faith provide their members with a group of people that is small enough to facilitate the development of intimacy. Many people find in their religious fellowships the kind of close interpersonal interaction that is necessary for emotional health. In communities of faith, attitudes and values are refined as people rub shoulders with like-minded others in an atmosphere that encourages trust and openness. Christian television cannot provide this vital dimension.

Why, then, Christian television? We can best think of it as viewer-supported alternative television. A significant number of people cannot find many programs on commercial television that do not run afoul of their values and tastes in entertainment. They want something more from television. One segment of the population turns to public television—PBS stations—for what they want. A larger segment turns to Christian television. It is, in other words, a response to a very real need for viewing options other than commercial and cable networks. As the percentage of conservative, fundamentalist, and evangelical Christians in the population has increased, so has the need for and the popularity of Christian television. The increasing conservatism and evangelicalism of American religion indicates that Christian television will continue to be an important element in the entertainment industry and in religion.

The 1980s was a decade of crisis for Christian television. Federal Communications Commission testimony demonstrated that funds collected by the several television ministries had been seriously misused. Accusations of sexual misconduct, actions that go to the very heart of the fundamentalist definition of sin, were hurled in several directions. Stories broke on top of stories.

Although the **National Religious Broadcasters** organization enacted new, tougher standards for its 1,300-plus members, it is too early to tell what the long-term impact of the crisis will be. The problems of the 1980s and 1990s hurt Christian television. It is also clear that the injuries were not fatal.

Jeffrey K. Hadden, a long-time analyst of Christian television, points out that the scandals of the 1980s and 1990s were "more symptom than cause" of the problems that beset the industry. The three underlying problems that caused the symptoms continue. (1) The Christian television industry has a "classic case of competition and market saturation." The number of broadcasters exceeded the market potential, resulting in a scramble for funds. (2) The industry is essentially unregulated by the Federal government, nor has it done a good job of self-regulation. (3) Finally, some religious broadcasters have mingled religion and politics in a way that led to the loss of part of their audience (and financial base) and delegitimized religious broadcasting in the minds of much of the public.

Hadden also sees two main sources of strength that may enable the industry to survive. Broadcast network structures such as TBN and The Family Channel "provide an enormous quantity of air time for religious broadcasting." Although the audience for individual programs is often small, the cumulative audience is not. Second, local religious television stations provide additional air time and programming that is responsive to the desires of local audiences.[13]

The Faith and Values Channel offers a different type of religious television. Its founders describe it as a "full-time national faith and values cable TV network." It is owned and operated by a coalition of over fifty national groups, that represent a variety of Christian (Protestant, Catholic, Eastern Orthodox, and American-born) faiths, Judaism, and the National Council of Churches. There are three programming guidelines that distinguish Faith and Values: no on-air solicitation of funds, no attempt to make converts, and no attacking of other faiths. Although it is not carried as widely as the better-known Christian net-

[13]Jeffrey K. Hadden, "The Rise and Fall of American Televangelism" in *Religion in the Nineties, The Annals of the American Academy of Political and Social Science*, vol. 527, ed. Wade Clark Roof (Newbury Park, CA: Sage Publications, Inc., 1993), pp. 113–30.

works, Faith and Values does offer an alternative in some areas. In 1992, Faith and Values merged with the Southern Baptists' ACTS (American Christian Television System).

HOLINESS AND PENTECOSTAL CHRISTIANS

Holiness is a movement that affects several groups of Christian believers, rather than being a group in and of itself. It is rooted in Jesus' admonition that his followers be perfect, even as God is perfect (Matthew 5:48). To follow this directive means to work toward ever-increasing holiness and perfection of life in this world. Sin and the evidences of sin are to be progressively rooted out. The search for perfection usually has been accompanied by a sense of separation from those who are not engaged in a similar search. Holiness is a matter of both belief and lifestyle. Its adherents believe in the possibility and the necessity of sanctification, understood as a work of the Holy Spirit distinct from justification. By **justification**, a person is forgiven for past sin and placed in a new relationship with God. By **sanctification**, that new relationship becomes more and more evident in the person's life as the Holy Spirit continues to bring about growth in grace. Other people are likely to be made aware of someone's membership in a holiness church by their lifestyle, which reflects, in ways that vary somewhat from church to church, their understanding of how a sanctified life is to be lived.

When it began, the **holiness movement** in the United States took many of its cues from John Wesley's teaching about Christian perfection. Wesley, you remember, was the founder of Methodism in England. When Methodism came to the United States, it brought Wesley's emphasis on sanctification and perfection with it. Originally, Methodists had many of the characteristics that have come to be associated with the holiness movement. As Methodism grew in numbers and wealth and became more a religion of the middle class, outward holiness was downplayed. Groups that disagreed with this lessening of outward holiness broke away. They often referred to themselves as Wesleyans, in order to distinguish themselves from the Methodists and to express their loyalty to the original intention of John Wesley.

The rejection of that which is "of the world" in order to attain holiness brought with it disagreements over precisely what was to be rejected. Over time, these disagreements led to there being many divisions within the movement. There are now several holiness groups made up of many churches, as well as many independent communities of believers without ties outside their own group.

What, then, are some of the things that holiness Christians reject as being too much of the world? The use of alcohol, smoking tobacco, and illicit drugs are universally banned among such groups. They are very careful in their language, avoiding not only obvious swearing and blasphemy, but much of the common slang used in our culture. Gambling, too, is universally forbidden. Attending movie theaters and sometimes watching television are not permitted. Dancing is avoided by most. Swimming, or swimming in mixed groups of males and females, is sometimes disallowed. Children often do not participate in physical education classes that violate their standards, such as those involving folk dancing, or those that require girls to wear slacks or shorts. Some holiness students also ask to be excused from participating in regular classroom work that conflicts with their beliefs. Examples include the teaching of evolution in biology or botany classes, sex education in health classes, or when movies are shown in class.

It is especially important, according to holiness teaching, that women follow a virtuous lifestyle. Women's role in the home and in the rearing of children makes them the primary transmitters of holiness. Frequently, women are discouraged from cutting their hair, or at least from wearing it shorter than shoulder length. The use of cosmetics and the wearing of much jewelry is frowned upon. A simple wristwatch and a wedding band are often the only permissible jewelry. High-cut necklines and at least elbow-length sleeves are the norm, and dresses or skirts are worn, rather than slacks or shorts.

Those in search of holiness tend to socialize with like-minded people who reinforce their values and way of life and who support them in their difference from the world. Marriages usually take place within the group, and children are encouraged to find their playmates among church members' children. Families are often large, and divorce is strongly discouraged, if not forbidden. This pattern of socialization has the twofold effect of reinforcing the sense of community within the group and maintaining the separation between those who are "of the world" and those who are not.

There are many independent churches within this movement. There are also some groupings of churches. Some of the better-known groups include several in the Church of God family, the Churches of Christ in Christian Union, and some conservative Mennonite groups. Two of the largest are the Church of the Nazarene and the Wesleyan Church, both of which are especially strong in the Midwest. Perhaps the best known of all the holiness organizations, because it maintains the highest public profile, is the Salvation Army. While most people probably associate the Salvation Army with thrift shops and Christmas bell ringers, it is also a fully functioning church. In addition to the social programs for which it is best known, Army Citadels hold Sunday and midweek services for a membership of about 500,000. Their wholehearted identification with the poorest of the poor and the outcasts of society make them able to reach out to people who are likely to be overlooked by other churches. The United Pentecostal Church is a major holiness denomination that is also pentecostal.

Some of you may feel that the restrictions that holiness imposes amount to a program for avoiding life in the real world. It certainly is true that there are fewer worldly temptations for people who conscientiously follow this path. Consider, however, the burden of difference that these people take upon themselves for the sake of the higher goals they seek. Students who are not a part the ordinary round of school activities, and whose dress and behavior set them apart from other students, may be ridiculed, or at least misunderstood and socially isolated.

Acceptance by others comes slowly or not at all under these circumstances. Those of all ages voluntarily limit social contacts and activities taken for granted by the majority culture. It is a life of difficult choices, the final validation of which must of necessity wait until an unspecified time in the future.

Part of the variety in American religion stems from variations in the way that different communities of faith balance out their appeal to the intellect, the will, and the emotions. Some services of worship are calm and dignified and offer stimulation primarily to the intellect. Those that emphasize ethical behavior and social service appeal to the will. Some offer more in terms of emotional satisfaction.

The experience of highly emotional worship and religious ecstasy is the foundation of pentecostalism. It has been a part of American religion for many years in the form of traditional pentecostalism and has gained in acceptance and visibility in the charismatic renewal movement (Figure 9–3). Pentecostalism is also one of the fastest-growing forms of Christianity, both in the United States and around the world. Two of the American denominations showing the most rapid recent growth—the mostly white Assemblies of God (1.8 million) and the mostly black Church of God in Christ (5 million)—are pentecostal.

The word **pentecostalism** refers to an event recorded in the Christian New Testament, in the Book of Acts. The disciples were gathered together following the devastating events of Jesus' crucifixion and death. They must have been a discouraged and disheveled band of men. As the biblical account goes, the Holy Spirit came to the disciples in a new and powerful way, described as "tongues like flames of fire, dispersed among them and resting on each one" (Acts 2:3, New English translation). They began to speak in languages other than those they usually used, and everyone present heard in their own language. In the confusion that followed, Peter is said to have spoken, quoting the Hebrew prophet Joel (God is said to be speaking here): "This will happen in the last days: I will pour out upon everyone a portion of my spirit; and your sons and daughters shall prophesy; your young men shall see visions, and your old men shall dream dreams" (Joel 2:28, New English translation). Most Christian churches celebrate this event annually in the spring, on Pentecost Sunday, as the anniversary of the founding of the church. For some Christians, however, it has meant much more. Pentecostal Christians (whether traditional pentecostal or charismatic Christians[14]) believe that what God did at Pentecost continues to happen today. People can receive the Holy Spirit in the same way as did the disciples, according to the Book of Acts.

Pentecostals believe that certain phenomena accompany and give evidence of the work of the Holy Spirit. The principal evidence of this gift is usually said to be the ability to **speak in tongues**. This phenomenon is also called **glossolalia**. Speaking in tongues takes two forms. People may speak in a recognizable human language. On the other hand, some pentecostals say that their tongues are not

[14]The *charismatic renewal movement* is discussed in the next section.

Figure 9–3   Pentacostal worship is emotional and enthusiastic. (*Guy Gillette/Photo Researchers, Inc.*)

recognizable human languages, but a private language given by God. Linguists who have studied this type of glossolalia have found that, although it is not a known human language, it has the characteristics that identify it as distinctly human speech. Theologian Harvey Cox describes glossolalia as "an expression of a spiritual feeling—whether it's pain or aspiration—that breaks out of linguistic restrictions."[15]

Pentecostals make another distinction as well. For some, tongues are a prayer language between the individual and God and do not call for interpretation. Others believe that tongues are a way that God uses to communicate with an entire congregation. In these instances, an interpreter is required to "translate" the message. Interpretation also is thought to be a gift of the Spirit. Usually, the speaker and the interpreter are two different people.

Although speaking in tongues is regarded as the primary manifestation of the action of the Holy Spirit, other gifts of the Spirit are mentioned in the New Testament. Examples of such lists can be found in 1 Corinthians 12:8–10, 28, and 29–30. The healing of physical and psychological illnesses is considered second only to tongues by most pentecostals. Prophecy and the interpretation of tongues receive considerable attention. Preaching and administration in the church are considered gifts. Exorcism for the removal of unclean spirits is prac-

[15]Quoted in Don Lattin, "Touched by the Fire," *Common Boundary*, July/August 1995, pp. 31–35.

ticed by some. Wisdom and knowledge are gifts, as is the ability to distinguish good from evil spirits. A few pentecostals handle venomous snakes and drink poison in response to a statement attributed to Jesus in the Gospel of Mark, which says that believers can do these things without harm (Mark 16:17–18).

Traditional pentecostalism began in American in the late nineteenth and early twentieth centuries. It was an outgrowth of the holiness movement. Like holiness, traditional pentecostalism usually emphasizes the necessity of outward holiness. More important, pentecostals focus on what they call the baptism of the Holy Spirit (often referred to in these churches as the Holy Ghost). This is said to be an encounter with God that may precede or follow water baptism. The specific religious experiences believed to be associated with the gift of the Holy Ghost became more important than the lifestyle associated with the holiness movement.

Two people are especially associated with the early history of pentecostalism in the United States. Charles Fox Parham was a traveling ex-Methodist preacher who settled in Topeka, Kansas, and founded a Bible school called the College of Bethel. In December 1900, some thirty or forty of Parham's students received the gift of tongues after studying Acts 2. The key person behind the development of pentecostalism as a movement, however, was William Joseph Seymour, a former slave who was at one time a student of Parham's. After receiving the gift of tongues himself in 1906, Seymour rented a run down building on Azuza Street in Los Angeles, which became the site of the well-known Azuza Street Mission. Seymour held very enthusiastic religious revivals at Azuza Street, and many people received the various spiritual gifts under his leading. The mission was eventually renamed the Apostolic Faith Gospel Mission, developed a missionary program both at home and overseas, and published a monthly newsletter plus several other publications. A movement had been born.

Several of the early pentecostal churches still exist in the United States, including the Assemblies of God (the largest), the Church of God (Cleveland, Tennessee), the Church of God in Christ, the Pentecostal Holiness Church, the Foursquare Gospel Church, and the United Pentecostal Church. Many still retain at least some emphasis on holiness, as well. There are also numerous independent churches in the pentecostal category, which are more likely to require a holiness lifestyle in addition to clear-cut evidence of the spiritual gifts. Their membership tends to come from the lower socioeconomic classes. Many congregations, although certainly not all, are predominantly black. Although they are not limited to any one geographical area, their greatest strength is in the Midwest, the lower Midwest, and the South.

Although linked by their pentecostal experiences, the various pentecostal denominations also have differences. As noted above, some, such as members of the United Pentecostal Church, affirm a holiness lifestyle, while others, such as members of the large Assemblies of God, do not. The United Pentecostal Church is also the largest of the "Oneness Pentecostal" churches, affirming the oneness of God rather than belief that God is a trinity of three persons in one God. People are baptized in the name of Jesus only, rather than with the more usual "in the name of the Father, the Son, and the Holy Spirit." Father, Son, and Holy Spirit are different manifestations of the one God rather than distinct persons united into a single God. By contrast, the Assemblies of God is trinitarian.

Although pentecostalism began as an interracial movement, segregated congregations and denominations became the norm. At present, new efforts toward racial unity are occurring. The predominantly white Pentecostal Fellowship of America, which includes several pentecostal churches, is reorganizing to include black churches, including the rapidly growing Church of God in Christ. Interest in unity has come about in part due to the necessity to work together in inner-city ministries.[16]

Pentecostal worship is emotional and enthusiastic, marked by frequent outbursts of pentecostal phenomena and shouts of "Amen!" and "Praise Jesus!" from the congregation. It addresses the human need for religious experience very directly. Traditional pentecostalism is, in its own right, a significant aspect of American religion. It also forms the background against which we can better understand the modern-day charismatic renewal movement. This movement shares important characteristics with traditional pentecostalism and at the same time has significant differences. An Assemblies of God college professor and former president of the Society for Pentecostal Studies summarizes his tradition this way: "This is the experiential religion par excellence. It fills a vacuum for meaning in life and does so at the deepest levels of one's experience. But it also incorporates one into a movement and community larger than oneself."[17]

THE CHARISMATIC RENEWAL MOVEMENT

The intense emotional involvement that characterizes pentecostal worship was not a part of consensus religion prior to the charismatic renewal movement. Since the revivals of America's early history, there have been sharp differences of opinion about the appropriateness of such "manifestations of the Spirit." Most of the consensus churches either ignored the pentecostals or criticized their worship as undignified and excessively emotional. The **charismatic renewal movement** refers to a group of Christians who have had pentecostal experiences but who are not members of traditional pentecostal churches. The word **charismatic** is derived from a Greek word that means "gift" and refers to the gifts of the Holy Spirit enumerated in the Christian New Testament. The charismatic renewal movement began in the United States, as far as we know, in 1960. The reverend Dennis Bennett of Saint Mark's Episcopal Church in Van Nuys, California, his wife, and about seventy other members of his congregation received the gift of tongues during a prayer meeting. The phenomenon spread very rapidly and soon

---

[16] *Christianity Today*, April 25, 1994.
[17] Quoted in Lattin, "Touched by the Fire," p. 34.

had appeared in every major Protestant denomination as well as in the Roman Catholic Church.

Richard Quebedeaux, in his study of the charismatic renewal movement titled *The New Charismatics, II*, explains its importance this way: The consensus Christian churches typically teach that God is present with the faithful, that new life in Christ is possible now, and that the Holy Spirit is present in the church, but they fail to make this message believable. There is no experiential evidence that would enable people to know beyond doubt that the message was true, and that God was present to them personally. The charismatic renewal movement rejects both the "liberal, nonsupernatural god who really isn't there anyhow," and the "rational evangelical god of the intellect," whose specialty is propositional truth. It embraces a "God you can feel, respond to, and *love.*" He continues, "It is the knowledge of this God, given through the experience of his Holy Spirit, that has bound charismatics together."[18] Modern-day charismatics are not content to be told about the presence of God in their churches and the presence of the Holy Spirit in their hearts. They seek knowledge and certainty, the certainty provided by the religious experience of the charismatic renewal movement.

There are several characteristics of the charismatic renewal movement that set it apart from traditional pentecostalism. For the most part, there has been no large-scale exodus of charismatics from noncharismatic churches. Usually they meet together in small prayer groups in addition to remaining involved in other church activities. In addition, however, the movement has given rise to charismatic groups that include charismatics from all sorts of church backgrounds. The movement emphasizes experience rather than doctrine and has become thoroughly ecumenical, with people of different backgrounds and theologies united in a common bond of experience.

The largest of the ecumenical organizations is the **Full Gospel Businessmen's Fellowship, International**, founded in 1951. Although founded before the rise of the new charismatic movement, it attracts people who count themselves among the new charismatics. The organization has grown rapidly and now has male and female members from all walks of life, a women's group (Women's Aglow Fellowship), and teen and youth groups. Members usually meet for a meal and to share experiences and testimony. Groups of charismatic students meet regularly on most college campuses in the United States. The charismatic renewal movement also holds nationwide conferences yearly, one of the largest of which is at the Catholic Notre Dame University in north-central Indiana.

In contrast to the highly emotional outpourings of early pentecostalism, the charismatic renewal movement is quieter. This toning down clearly reflects the middle-class and upper-middle-class nature of the charismatic renewal movement, another feature in which it differs from traditional pentecostalism. Most charismatics say that they receive the Holy Spirit in quiet prayer with a small group of other Christians. Those who have already had such experiences gather

[18]Richard Quebedeaux, *The New Charismatics, II* (New York: Harper & Row, 1983), pp. xiii–xv.

around people who are seeking the experience, pray with them, and place their hands on the seekers' heads. There is an incident recorded in the Book of Acts in which Paul is said to have laid his hands on some of the disciples. When he did, "the Holy Spirit came on them, and they spoke in tongues and prophesied" (Acts 19:6, New International Version). The initial experience of tongues is usually followed by continuing to speak in tongues and receiving other spiritual gifts. Because it is ecumenical and experiential, it is theologically diverse as well, with very little commonly held theology. Charismatics (who are also called *neopentecostals*, or *new pentecostals*) are bound together by their experience and by their belief in that experience.

The lifestyles of contemporary charismatic Christians differ little from the lifestyles of other people in their culture. The requirements of outward holiness that often mark traditional pentecostalism are absent. Charismatics share with evangelicals the desire to share the faith and joy they have found, and many actively witness to their experiences. For all their differences, though, modern-day charismatics are one with traditional pentecostals in their belief that God works experientially in the lives of believers now.

Both traditional pentecostalism and charismatic renewal offer people who participate in them the assurance that their God is present with them. Belief is superseded by evidence. Those outside the movement often wonder how those inside it can be sure that what they experience is in fact the work of the Holy Spirit. Nonparticipants often believe that phenomena such as speaking in tongues are the result of self-induced hysteria. There is a middle ground between the uncritical acceptance of the believer and the skepticism of the nonbeliever. When viewed from the empathic perspective of the academic study of religion, the heart of pentecostal religion, old or new, is seen to be both the experience itself and the **meaning** that it has for those who are a part of it. Whatever the explanation for the experience, it is clear that its meaning to those who are the recipients of it is religious and provides the certainty that they seek.

QUESTIONS AND ACTIVITIES FOR REVIEW, DISCUSSION, AND WRITING

1. What might be the advantages and disadvantages of the "separatist" position taken by the fundamentalists described in this chapter?
2. Has anyone ever "witnessed" to you? How did you feel, and why? If you yourself "witness" to other people, reflect on what doing so means to you.
3. Do you think that you would like or dislike being a member of a "megachurch," and why?
4. What is your response to the views of the religious-political right? Be sure that you can state the reasons for your response.
5. Do you think that the Christian Reconstruction Movement is a good thing or a bad thing for the United States? Why?
6. If you are able to get cable television, or if you can get religious television on a commercial channel: Watch two different programs and write an essay in which you reflect on what you observe.

7. If you are not a holiness Christian yourself, how would your life be different if you were? Try to see both positive and negative possibilities. If you are, reflect on what being a holiness Christian means to you.

8. If you are not a pentecostal or charismatic Christian yourself, discuss with friends or classmates who are what that experience means to them. If you are, reflect on what it means to you.

9. If possible, attend a pentecostal or charismatic worship service and write an essay in which you reflect on what you observed and experienced. **Women:** If you attend a traditional pentecostal service, remember that many of these churches do have a dress code for women. You may want to call first and inquire.

FOR FURTHER READING

Abelman, Robert, and Stewart Hoover, eds., *Religious Television: Conflicts and Controversies.* New York: Ablex Publishing Company, 1991. A collection of essays, both descriptive and analytic, that covers every facet of the subject.

Baumer, Randall, *Mine Eyes Have Seen the Glory: A Journey into the Evangelical Subculture in America.* New York: Oxford University Press, 1992. The strength of Baumer's work lies in its portrayal of specific groups and personalities.

Conover, Pamela Johnston, and Virginia Gray, *Feminism and the New Right: Conflict over the American Family.* New York: Praeger Publishers, 1983. Still an excellent study of the new right's positions on family issues, along with a feminist critique of that position.

Cox, Harvey, *Fire From Heaven: The Rise of Pentecostal Spirituality and the Reshaping of Religion in the Twenty-First Century.* Reading, MA: Addison-Wesley Publishers, 1995. One of the United States' most versatile commentators on religion and culture puts pentecostalism in an international cultural context. Fascinating comparison of pentecostalism with the New Age movement.

Dayton, Donald W., and Robert K. Johnston, eds., *The Variety of American Evangelicalism.* Knoxville, TN: University of Tennessee Press, 1991. The main focus of this book is a comparison of evangelicalism with traditions that are close to it, but different, such as fundamentalism, pentecostalism, black religion, and several others. In the process, the essays provide usually good definitions of the other traditions themselves.

Jorstad, Erling. *Popular Religion in America: The Evangelical Voice.* Westport, CT: Greenwood Press, 1993. Relationship of evangelical religion to several important issues such as family and economic values, and the interaction of popular evangelicalism with the media. Jorstad sees a new diversity emerging in the evangelical movement as a range of individual churches find their places under what has become a rather large umbrella.

Sherrill, John L., *They Speak with Other Tongues.* New York: Pyramid Books, 1964. Although this is an older book, it can be highly recommended. Sherrill is a reporter who was assigned to do a story on the charismatic renewal movement and became a part of it as a result. His account is fascinating, and provides a unique look at his journey from skeptical outsider to convinced insider.

10

Religio-Ethnic Christianity

THE CONCEPT OF A RELIGIO-ETHNIC GROUP

Religio-ethnic communities of faith are groups of people whose religion and ethnic, racial, or national identities are inextricably linked together. Eastern Orthodox Christians and black Christians in traditional black churches and black independent congregations are the two major representatives of religio-ethnic Christianity in the United States.[1] Although both of these groups include converts whose ethnic heritage differs from that most closely identified with the group—Eastern Orthodox of non-Eastern European descent and whites who are members of black churches—the ethnic identity of the group as a whole remains clear and important in its self-understanding. There are other religio-ethnic links that are much weaker: Irish-, Italian-, and Polish-Americans have historically been predominantly Catholic. People from Scandinavian and German backgrounds are frequently Lutherans, and at least some of British ancestry are Episcopalians. Now, however, these links are not as intense as those that follow. They are breaking down because of the greater assimilation of these groups into American culture.

These religious groups are important carriers of ethnic and cultural identity. For Eastern Orthodox Christians, the church often provides not only a place for worship, but a place in which native dress, language, food, and other cultural customs are preserved, understood, and appreciated. The church and its members become the primary social center for the group. Churches may also sponsor cultural festivals that help to bring the native culture of their members to the larger community. The church helps provide a link to "the old country," allow-

[1]In the next chapter, we will take up other religio-ethnic communities of faith.

ing its members to be both American and distinctively ethnic. By doing so, it plays an important role in easing the transition for new immigrants and in helping to keep the ethnic heritage from becoming lost in succeeding generations.

As you will learn, the black church played a central role in helping blacks become an integral part of American culture. At the same time, it helped to keep alive the traditions of distinctively black worship and religious life. It continues to do so today. To be accepted into our white-dominated culture, blacks often have to become "white people with black skins." The black churches provide a place in which black heritage and pride in blackness can be nurtured. They also provide resources to help blacks advance in the predominantly white culture.

The ways in which religion and ethnicity are interrelated are too complex for full exploration here. Three important points can be noted, however, in addition to what has already been said. Religion is an important source of stability and comfort among immigrants and others who are not fully at home in American culture. Immigration—whether forced or undertaken by choice—means the loss of the familiar. Often it entails separation from not only friends but family as well. Although for many, coming to the United States has meant the hope of a new beginning, it has brought with it grief and a sense of loss. In the midst of such feelings, religion offers something of "home" that can come with the immigrant.

Another point at which religion and ethnicity intersect is in the role of religious leaders. The religious leaders are usually among the better-educated members of the ethnic community and have tended to be respected in this country simply because they are religious leaders. This puts them in an excellent position to serve as spokespersons for the ethnic, national, or racial group in question. This has been particularly evident in the role of articulate black ministers in the civil rights movement.

Another reason for the importance of religion in this context is that religion has tended to be more acceptable in this country than has ethnic, national, or racial consciousness. Despite heightened ethnic consciousness and awareness of "multiculturalism," assimilation remains the dominant trend among ethnic Americans. "Religiosity has always been a much-admired trait in this country, but 'foreignness' and 'foreign loyalties,' as defined by a variety of standard makers, have been discouraged by formal and informal devices throughout American history."[2] Thus, religion has provided a "safe"—or at least "safer"—way to retain important dimensions of personal identity. Even this has occasionally backfired. During the Persian Gulf War in 1991, and later in the wake of the bombing of the World Trade Center in New York, there was a national tendency to regard all people of Muslim faith with suspicion, if not as outright enemies. Repeated media use of the phrase "Muslim terrorists" made the words synonymous in far too many peoples' minds.

---

[2] Laura L. Becker, "Ethnicity and Religion" in *Encyclopedia of the American Religious Experience: Studies of Traditions and Movements*, vol. 3, ed. Charles H. Lippy and Peter W. Williams (New York: Charles Scribner's Sons, 1988), pp. 1477–91.

Recent research[3] indicates that links between religion and ethnicity in the United States will continue to decline in the next millennium, for several reasons. (1) Both religion and ethnicity are declining in social significance, although some individuals continue to assign great importance to one or both. What is important is that this is now a matter of choice, in most instances. (2) Both religion and ethnicity are also declining in "inheritability." What this means is that "genes may be inherited, but the social meaning of those genes" increasingly is not. (3) While intermarriage, increasingly common, need not weaken either set of ties, it often does. To sum up, "as religion becomes more and more a matter of individual choice, and as persons become increasingly selective in making that choice, ethnicity, along with other background characteristics, will have a declining effect in determining religious identity."[4] This trend could significantly increase the cultural diversity of America's congregations over time. If it does so, becoming genuinely multicultural communities of faith will almost certainly challenge those congregations in ways that cannot yet be fathomed.

EASTERN ORTHODOX CHRISTIANITY

Some of you reading this book are undoubtedly Eastern Orthodox Christians. The majority of you are not. For those of you who are, this chapter is an invitation to see your church in a new way, from the point of view of the academic study of religion. For those of you who are not, I invite you to imagine yourselves in the world of an Eastern Orthodox service of worship. Bearded priests dressed in ornate vestments (Figure 10–1) lead an impressive procession to the front of the church. The air is heavy with the smell of incense. Around the church are many icons—paintings of Jesus, Mary, and the saints done in glowing colors, embellished with gold. The priest and the people chant responsively in Greek, its measured cadences seeming to belong to the time that the Christian New Testament was written. An air of mystery makes you catch your breath.

The **Eastern Orthodox churches** are a group of churches whose members follow the teachings and practices of Christianity as it was in the major cities of the Eastern Roman Empire in the first centuries of the Common Era. They include the Greek and Russian Orthodox Churches and churches with national ties to the former Yugoslavia, Ukraine, Serbia, Croatia, Armenia, and Romania.

The word **orthodox** means "correct" or "right," and Orthodox believers understand the rightness of their religion in three ways. It is right belief, continuing an unbroken tradition that reaches back to the time of Jesus himself. It is also right worship, which is the key to the unity of these churches. Right worship is at the very heart of their lives. It also means right organization, maintaining the

[3]Phillip E. Hammond and Kee Warner, "Religion and Ethnicity in Late-Twentieth-Century America," in *Religion in the Nineties, The Annals of the American Academy of Political and Social Science*, vol. 527, ed. Wade Clark Roof (Newbury Park, CA: Sage Publications, 1993), pp. 55–66.
[4]Hammond and Warner, "Religion and Ethnicity," p. 66.

Figure 10–1   The vestments of Orthodox Christian priests are ornately symbolic. (*Audrey Gottlieb/Monkmeyer Press.*)

forms of church government that were common in the earliest centuries of Christianity, closest to the time of Jesus. We will explore each of these dimensions in turn. The **Eastern** in Eastern Orthodox Churches means fidelity to the faith and tradition of the early church that was centered in and around Jerusalem, Antioch, Alexandria, and Constantinople. It also refers to the locations of the seven ecumenical councils of Christianity. Two were at Nicea, three at Constantinople, and one apiece at Ephesus and Chalcedon. The Eastern Orthodox churches accept these seven councils as authoritative.

History

For the first ten centuries of its existence, the Christian church was essentially one and undivided, although there were certainly differences between various geographical locations. Within a few years of the beginning of Christianity, there were communities of believers in all the major cities of the Roman Empire, one body of Christians with a diversity of beliefs and practices. There was as yet no central leadership. Leadership was shared among the leaders in the different cities.

Political, cultural, and economic differences contributed to a growing division of Christianity into East and West. The western church, centered at Rome, grew in power. Because Saint Peter had been a Bishop of Rome, Rome had an honor that the other cities did not. Recall here the passage in Matthew's gospel in which it is said that Jesus gave Peter the keys of the kingdom of heaven, cited in the chapter on Catholicism. As Rome gained greater power and authority, however, the East grew uneasy.

It is not necessary to trace the intricate political and religious differences that led up to the final division between Christianity in the West and in the East in order to understand American Orthodoxy. The political factors were at least as important in bringing about the final division as were the religious ones. In 1054 C.E., an emissary of the Bishop of Rome excommunicated the Bishop of Constantinople, who, in turn, excommunicated the Bishop of Rome, making formal and official a division that had been growing for centuries.

The first Orthodox church in the United States was a Greek Orthodox church in New Orleans in 1864. There had been a colony of Greek Orthodox people at New Smyrna, Florida, a century earlier. Orthodox immigration into the United States came relatively late. The first significantly large numbers were not present until the nineteenth and twentieth centuries. The first archdiocese (a church governmental unit, usually a metropolitan center, headed by an archbishop) in the United States was the Orthodox Archdiocese of North and South America, incorporated in New York in 1921. Large numbers of Greek immigrants arrived in the United States at the turn of the century, bringing their Orthodoxy with them. Large numbers of Russians arrived after 1917, when the Bolshevik Revolution began in Russia.

Two other events played significant roles in Orthodox history in the United States. First, missionaries from the Russian Orthodox Church established missions in Alaska as early as 1794, providing a base from which Orthodoxy could enter the United States. The large number of Orthodox Christians in Alaska meant that when Alaska became a state in 1959, the number of Russian Orthodox in this country rose dramatically. Second, thousands of Orthodox immigrants came from Greece, Asia Minor, Russia, and Eastern Europe between the Civil War and World War I.

In spite of the close national connections of the Orthodox churches, early archdioceses often included all the national churches, because the total numbers were small. Such archdioceses were incorporated in New Orleans in 1864, in San Francisco in 1867, and in New York City in 1870. As the numbers increased, national churches were organized. A Serbian Orthodox Church was incorporated in 1926, a Romanian church in 1935, Antiochene and Ukrainian churches in 1937, and a Bulgarian church in 1938. These churches still have a strong national consciousness that plays a major role in keeping them apart organizationally.

Eastern Orthodox Christianity in the United States

There are approximately 1 million Orthodox Christians in the United States. About 1 percent of Americans are members of Orthodox churches. Most are members of either the Greek or Russian churches. There are several monasteries, two schools of theology, a college, and several other institutions.

Belief

People of Orthodox Christian faith believe and practice in ways that are both like and unlike those of their Protestant and Catholic neighbors. Orthodox belief is based on the Bible and on the official teachings of the **seven ecumenical ("of the**

whole church") **councils** of the Christian church, which took place during the first 1,000 years of its history. Like Catholics but unlike Protestants, Orthodox Christians accept both the Bible and the church's tradition as genuine sources of revelation. Tradition is not found in a single document, but in many. The Nicene Creed is the principal creed. The creeds of the other councils are also believed to be true expressions of God's revelation. The Divine Liturgy (the principal act of worship) itself is an authoritative part of the tradition, as are the teachings of the early church Fathers. So is the Orthodox Churches' long history of **iconography**, the depiction of religious figures in special paintings. The veneration of icons will be discussed in the section on ritual.

As do most other Christians, Orthodox believers affirm that **God is a trinity**. This is emphasized in Orthodoxy, and God is understood as three persons who have one coeternal essence. God the Father is believed to be the Creator of all that ever was, is, and ever shall be. God the Son was sent for the salvation of humankind, and the Holy Spirit is God present always and everywhere to guide the church. **Great honor is given to Mary as the Mother of God.** Although she is not God, Orthodoxy teaches that at one time she contained God in the person of Jesus. She is referred to as **Theotokos.**[5] Jesus is believed to have been both fully human and fully divine during his earthly life. As do the great majority of Christians, Orthodox believers hold that Jesus as the Christ plays the essential role in the drama of human sin and redemption.

God, according to Orthodox thought, remains **shrouded in holy mystery** and cannot be comprehended by human beings. Orthodox Christians believe that, since God is "absolutely incomprehensible and unknowable" (Saint John of Damascus, c. 675–749 C.E.), all that people can say about God is what God is not. Thus, God is *in*corporeal, *in*visible, and *in*tangible.

Like those of Catholic faith, Orthodox Christians believe that the grace of God is a divine, saving power available to persons through the sacraments of the church. **Divine grace requires human cooperation.** Salvation is not based on grace alone, as most Protestants affirm, but on both grace and human cooperation, another belief that the Orthodox share with their Catholic counterparts.

Orthodox Christians believe that the image of God in humanity is distorted and tarnished as a result of the disobedience of Adam and Eve that is recorded in Genesis. This ancestral sin continues to be transmitted to all people. **Although the image of God is in each person, sin distorts it and makes it unclear.** Orthodox Christians believe that by means of the cooperation between divine grace and human effort, the image of God can become clearer and clearer. By participating in the church as a worshipping community, human beings can become more and more like God. Although this process stops short of a full deification of humanity, the accent on the divine potential of human beings certainly tends in that direction in Orthodox thought, and is an image of hope for all who follow it. **God did not become human to satisfy the demands of divine**

---

[5] *Theotokos* is Greek and means "Bearer of God."

justice, according to Orthodoxy, but to enable other human beings to become like God. As people grow in God's grace, the image of God shines ever more brightly.

Death means the separation of the soul or spirit from the body. Orthodox Christians believe that people immediately begin to experience something of heaven or hell—of being in communion with God or not. They also believe that there will be a final judgment. Based on the character of people's lives, their "resurrected existence will then live eternally in heaven in communion with God, or eternally in hell, out of communion with God."[6]

Ritual

Eastern Orthodox Christianity puts its greatest emphasis on worship and other **ritual**. Proper worship defines what it means to be Orthodox and links the various national churches together in close communion. The central act of worship is called the **Divine Liturgy**. It is a solemn yet joyful act that is stylized and highly liturgical. Originally, the language of the Divine Liturgy was Greek. In most churches now, the custom is to use the language of the people for most of the service, or to use a combination of the two. The Sunday morning liturgy is usually based on an order of worship developed by Saint John Chrysostom (347–407 C.E.), or on one developed by St. Basil the Great (c. 330–379 C.E.). All of its parts intend to express the holy mystery of God while maintaining it. God is present precisely as mystery. In worship, God is not so much to be understood as to be experienced and adored in mysterious holiness. The liturgy takes place in a church that is usually designed in the form of a cross, the arms of which project equally from the center, over which a dome is built (Figure 10–2). The Eastern arm of the cross is set apart by a richly decorated screen, the **iconostasis**, behind which the priest enacts the holy mysteries, shielded from the view of the congregation.

There are **three parts of the liturgy**. The first, sometimes called the **Morning Service**, includes the preparation of the communion elements and recalls Jesus' birth and God's incarnation. The second, the **Processions**, consists of responsive prayers, Bible readings, the sermon, and the Great Procession, in which the prepared communion elements are brought out. This symbolizes Jesus' coming to humankind to teach and to heal. The third part is the **Communion** service itself. The priest goes behind the iconostasis, consecrates the elements, and places the bread into the chalice of wine.[7] The chalice is carried among the people and all those who desire to do so partake. This third part of the liturgy symbolizes Christ's sacrifice for humankind. As do Catholic Christians, the Eastern Orthodox believe that the bread and wine actually become the body and blood

---

[6]Stanley S. Harakas, *The Orthodox Church: 455 Questions and Answers* (Minneapolis, MN: Light and Life Publishing Company, 1988), p. 97.

[7]A *chalice* is a special cup or glass, often stemmed, used to hold the wine used in the Eucharist.

Figure 10–2 This Greek Orthodox Church near Chicago incorporates the traditional domed roof over the sanctuary into distinctively modern architecture. (*Photo by the author.*)

of Christ. The entire service may last up to three hours. Not everyone attends for the full service, and it is not uncommon for people to leave the church and return during the service. It is customary for families to worship together, with even the youngest children present for much of the service. Orthodox Christians believe that it is beneficial even for children who are too young to grasp its meaning to be present for the Divine Liturgy.

In addition to the majestic Divine Liturgy on Sunday morning, there are **various services throughout the day**, marking out the passage of time into a holy cycle. The Orthodox believe that the day begins with sunset, so the nighttime services are the first of the day. Morning services take as their theme the coming of the true light of God and express thanksgiving for God's protection during the night that has ended. Midmorning commemorates the descent of the Holy Spirit at Pentecost. The noon service recalls the passion and crucifixion, and mid-afternoon, Jesus' death and burial. Evening services give thanks for the day past and seeks forgiveness for wrongs committed during the day. It also seeks God's protection for the coming hours of darkness. Most people, of course, do not participate in all these services, but in the monasteries, these rites pace the monks throughout the day and night.

The Orthodox Churches celebrate the seven traditional sacraments, which they call **Holy Mysteries**. The sacraments are believed to convey grace by the presence of the Holy Spirit within them. "God touches, purifies, illumines, sanctifies and deifies human life through the mysteries. . . . In them, we encounter Christ in order to be Christ."[8] People are **baptized by triple immersion**, sym-

[8]Alciviadis C. Calivas, "Orthodox Worship," in *A Companion to the Greek Orthodox Church*, ed. Fotios K. Litsas, (New York: Department of Communication, Greek Orthodox Archdiocese of North and South America, 1984), pp. 31–32.

bolizing both the three persons of the Trinity and the three days Jesus is said to have lain in the tomb. Infant baptism is the usual practice, in which case baptism may involve only partial immersion. Confirmation, or **chrismation**, in which the person is anointed with oil that has been blessed for that purpose, follows immediately. Newly baptized people, infants or adults, then receive their first communion.

Leavened bread and wine are used as the **communion** elements. As noted above, Orthodox Christians believe that the elements become the body and blood of Christ. It is expected that all Orthodox Christians who are baptized and confirmed will partake regularly, and participants often fast from the evening meal prior to the service. Only Orthodox Christians who are in good standing with the Church may receive communion. The laity usually receive the bread and the wine together in a small spoon made for that purpose; priests receive the elements separately.

The rite of **penance** as practiced in Orthodoxy reflects a number of themes that have already been mentioned. Baptism is only the beginning of a lifelong process of healing and restoring the damaged image of God within each person. This process is carried out in part through the sacrament of penance. The priest stands with the penitent, approaching God on the penitent's behalf and pronouncing God's forgiveness. Penance, writes one Greek Orthodox scholar, "is essentially a healing mystery, since sin is viewed primarily as a disease that needs to be healed, rather than a crime that needs to be punished."[9] The Orthodox are not altogether different from their Protestant and Catholic neighbors in this interpretation. Non-Orthodox Christians emphasize a juridical interpretation of sin and forgiveness. The Orthodox focus on healing the separation between people and God and the restoration of the divine image in people.

The sacrament of **ordination** sets men apart for the priesthood. Married men may be ordained as priests, but priests are not permitted to marry after they are ordained. Bishops and other leaders in the hierarchy are always drawn from the ranks of the celibate monks. Priesthood is limited to men, since the ministry of Christ is carried out in the Church by the priests who are in Christ's image. Through the priest, Christ is present in and to the Church.

Marriage reflects the union of Christ with the faithful, of Christ and the Church. It is believed to be for life. However, because marriage involves human free will, there is always the possibility that a mistake will be made. When divorce happens, the Church usually holds that a true marriage did not occur. The marriage did not show its necessarily eternal character. The laity may have up to three attempts to establish a true and valid marriage. A fourth marriage is absolutely forbidden. The rites for marriages other than the first are subdued and have a penitential character. Clergy may marry only once, because they are expected to set as good an example as possible for the laity.

Customs surrounding Orthodox weddings vary from group to group, but two are widespread. At one point in the ceremony, crowns are placed on the heads

[9]Calivas, "Orthodox Worship," p. 48.

of the bride and groom. The crowns are sometimes linked together with a ribbon. Although there are several meanings associated with the crowns, primarily they signify the new status of the couple as the King and Queen of a new Christian household. Orthodox Christians traditionally wear their wedding rings on their right, rather than their left, hands. The rings signify the couple's solemn pledge to each other, and the right hand is associated with strength and authority.[10]

The **sick are anointed** with blessed oil. Like the Catholic sacrament for the sick, this special service is intended to assist in recovery if that be God's will or to ease the passage from earthly to eternal life if that is to be the outcome.

Because the Orthodox churches follow the Julian rather than the Gregorian calendar, the **dates of the major festivals differ from those celebrated by other Christians.** For example, Holy Week (Palm Sunday through Easter) was a week later for Eastern than for Western Christians in 1995.

Orthodox ritual life, both in the church and in the home, is marked by the use of icons. **Icons** are special paintings that function as windows through which the sacred, without compromising its mystery, becomes visible. The painting of an icon is a devotional act carried out by a monk whose commitment to his work is not only artistic, but spiritual. According to Orthodox belief, icons are not to be worshipped; to do so is idolatry. Orthodox Christians worship only God, as do other Christians. But Orthodox Christians affirm the **veneration** of icons. In becoming human in Jesus, God accepted everything pertaining to humanity, including "being depictable." Thus, "to refuse to venerate an icon is . . . to deny the reality of the Incarnation."[11] Icons are carried in procession and venerated by bowing in front of them, kissing them, and lighting candles before them.

Lifestyle

The lifestyles of Eastern Orthodox Christians are determined as much by their national heritage and the extent of their accommodation to American culture as by their faith. Except for the celibate priests, Eastern Orthodox Christians do not separate themselves from life in the secular world.

Marriage and family life are highly honored and respected. Deviations from this pattern, such as premarital or extramarital sex or active homosexuality, are regarded as inconsistent with a Christian life. Sexually abusive behavior is explicitly condemned.

Orthodox Christians may not marry non-Christians in the Church, but they may marry baptized non-Orthodox Christians. If married outside the Church, they may not participate in the Eucharist, nor may they serve as a godparent for an Orthodox infant, or as a sponsor at an Orthodox wedding.

Abortion is not permissible except in cases in which the pregnancy or birth

---

[10]Harakas, *The Orthodox Church*, pp. 198–99.
[11]Paul D. Garrett, "Eastern Christianity," in *Encyclopedia of the American Religious Experience*, ed. Lippy and Williams, vol. I, p. 328.

of the baby would gravely endanger the life of the mother. Although children are valued and seen as an important part of marriage, conception and birth are not regarded as the only reason for physical intimacy. Therefore, birth control is left up to the conscience of the couple.

Eastern Orthodox Christians are encouraged by their church to uphold all just laws. They may in good conscience break an unjust law. Orthodox Christians, for example, participated in nonviolent civil disobedience during the civil rights marches of the 1960s. Involvement in public life is encouraged. Orthodox Christians support full human rights for all persons. Most churches officially supported the Equal Rights Amendment while simultaneously emphasizing the importance of the family. They remain, however, adamantly opposed to women being ordained to the priesthood, for the reasons noted in our discussion of ordination.

Organization

Organizationally, each of the nationally associated Orthodox churches is independent (the preferred word for this among the Orthodox is **autocephalous,** "self-headed"). Patriarchs lead the churches in each of the four ancient centers of Orthodoxy: Constantinople, Antioch, Alexandria, and Jerusalem. Among these four, the **Patriarch of Constantinople** is said to have primacy of honor and spiritual leadership. He is called "first among equals" but has no more authority than the rest. In addition to these four patriarchates, each of which has divisions within it, there are other major autonomous bodies of believers, such as those of Russia, Greece, and Serbia. Although they are independent in their organizational structure, they are united on important liturgical and theological points.

The Pope has no authority for Orthodox Christians. They believe that the original Christian church was governed by bishops who presided over limited geographic areas. There was no one central authority. The Orthodox interpret the "rock" referred to in Matthew 16:18 ("upon this rock I will build my church") as Peter's faith rather than Peter himself, thus undercutting the primacy that the Catholic Church ascribes to the Bishop of Rome. This style of government has been maintained to the present time. Within each autonomous Church, government is hierarchical.

Some Orthodox churches in the United States remain formally linked with their countries of origin. In practice, the American churches operate with considerable autonomy. National consciousness notwithstanding, there is a degree of unity among Orthodox Christians in the United States. Particularly in the United States, most Orthodox Christians long for greater unity:

> The more deeply the Orthodox strike roots in North America, the more they lament the ethnic foliage that conceals a united confession of faith. Immigration history, not theology, separates the Orthodox people. And in general they long for and anticipate their union in one organically Orthodox fellowship."[12]

[12]Anthony Ugolnik, "An Ecumenical Estrangement: Orthodoxy in America," *The Christian Century*, 109, no. 20 (June 17–24, 1992), p. 611.

The **Standing Conference of Orthodox Bishops in America** is one voice for American Orthodoxy. There are two views of how Orthodox unity in North America might come about.

The **Orthodox Church in America** was formed in 1970 by the merger of several Russian churches. Its goal is to unite the Orthodox churches of the United States into a single body. It is headed by an archbishop who has the title, "Archbishop of Washington [D.C.], Metropolitan of All America and Canada." The fact that Russians were the first Orthodox Christians in the United States leads the Russian Orthodox Church to the belief that they have precedence in the United States.

Greek Orthodox Christians, who far outnumber the Russians, however, have been reluctant to accept the Russian-founded group as representative. The **Greek Orthodox Archdiocese of North and South America** has become the center of the Greek point of view that holds that all Orthodox Christians owe allegiance to the Patriarch of Constantinople (now Istanbul, in Turkey). The Greek archbishop officially represents the Patriarch in North America, and Archbishop Iakovos (who is also the head of the Standing Conference) has done much to encourage support of this view.[13]

Saint Vladimir's Seminary (Russian) in New York State has become a training center for Orthodox clergy of many national backgrounds. There is also a Greek Orthodox seminary in the United States, the Holy Cross Greek Orthodox School of Theology in Boston. There is also an Orthodox Theological Society of America, which includes members of all groups, and an Orthodox Inter-Seminary Movement. In worship, pan-Orthodox liturgies on the first Sunday of Lent have become an American tradition.

Eastern Orthodoxy is an embodiment of Christian faith centered in a rich liturgical life that vibrates with the resonances of a tradition as old as the Christian Church itself. For a significant number of American citizens, it is the faith that provides the sacred meanings that make life good. It relates the passage of time throughout the year and the passage of life through its various stages to God, providing a context of holy mystery that transfigures the mundane world.

BLACK CHRISTIANITY

If you worship or have worshipped in a predominantly black congregation, you have an idea about what black religion is. If you have not experienced it directly, you may not know much about it. In that case, have you seen black religion depicted in the movies or on television? How is it portrayed? In either case, what comes to mind when you think of black religion and worship?

---

[13]Ugolnik, "An Ecumenical Estrangement," pp. 611–12.

The Christian Churches and the Civil War

Religion figured prominently in the events that led up to the Civil War, in the war itself, and in the various attempts at interpreting its meaning that followed it. Slavery was the main issue that divided some of the young nation's largest communities of faith. The Methodists, Baptists, and Presbyterians were all divided in the mid-1800s. While there were other differences involved, disagreement between pro- and antislavery factions was the main cause. Some communities of faith, of which the Disciples of Christ is the best example, were so thoroughly congregational in their organization that there was nothing for the slavery question to divide except local congregations. Some, such as the Unitarians, Universalists, and Congregationalists, were largely northern churches and actively supported the northern call for abolition. The Lutheran, Episcopal, and Catholic churches remained undivided until the South withdrew from the Union, even though each had significant numbers of members in both North and South, and each had vocal pro- and antislavery groups. Reform Judaism had grown significantly in both North and South by the time war loomed on the horizon. The combination of its congregational organization and its determination to fit into the life of the culture in which it was located meant that Jewish congregations tended to take on the prevailing view of the gentile majority, be it pro- or antislavery. In spite of that, Judaism's strong sense of being the one house of Israel prevented any sharp divisions.

Both North and South looked to their faith, their churches, and their religious leaders to justify their position on the matter of slavery and to sustain them in the terrible bloodshed that pitted American against American and kin against kin. Both were certain that God was on their side, that theirs was the righteous cause, and that God would help them to prevail over their opposition. Both attempted to demonstrate support from the Christian scriptures. And, in both South and North, religious people sought to minister to those caught up in the war. There were chaplains with both armies, and aid societies assisted them in their work by providing reading materials, visitation, and facilitating communication between soldiers and the families they had left behind. It fell to these volunteers to deal as best they could with the grief of those from whom the war had taken family members, friends, and neighbors. The accounts of their work, along with that of the chaplains and medical personnel, are a stirring record of humanity amidst the inhumanity of war.

Religious perspectives gave rise to some of the most memorable literary and artistic responses to slavery and to the Civil War. Harriet Beecher Stowe's staunch and thoughtful Congregationalism led to her writing *Uncle Tom's Cabin*. James Russell Lowell's stirring "Once to Every Man and Nation," familiar to most Protestant churchgoers, reminds us of the prophets of the Hebrews when they called on their people to make a decisive, once-and-for-all choice between good and evil. And, Julia Ward Howe's "The Battle Hymn of the Republic," although it became an anthem of the North, spoke eloquently of God's judgment on any people who made the wrong choice in that decision.

After the guns of battle were stacked and silent, the religious categories of divine wrath and punishment and the religious overtones of sacrifice were brought into play by both sides to interpret the meaning of the war and of victory gained or defeat suffered. Others, keenly aware of the ambiguous nature of the entire situation, called for repentance on both sides and reconciliation of hearts as well as governments.

The Free Black Church

A major shift came with emancipation and the development of black religion in the context of official freedom coupled with social repression and oppression that continued long after the Emancipation Proclamation was signed. The Emancipation Proclamation was a statement issued by President Abraham Lincoln on New Year's Day, 1863, that ended slavery throughout most of the South.

The **Baptist** and **Methodist** churches carried out the most vigorous and successful work among the blacks after emancipation. The vast majority of freed blacks were a part of one of these two communities of faith. A smaller, yet significant, number, especially in Maryland and Louisiana, were Catholic. Following the war years, the black church grew rapidly. Rejection or segregation of black members by historically white denominations (such as the Baptists' and Methodists' insistence on separate seating) led to the growth of all-black congregations within these denominations as well as to the formation of a number of black denominations. It was in these black denominations and in the all-black congregations within predominantly white denominations that black religion continued to evolve its distinctive style and message.

The black churches played a unique role in the developing black community, in the North and South, in rural areas and cities, to which increasingly large numbers of blacks were moving in search of work. The black churches were much, much more than simply religious institutions, although their primary identification as religious institutions influenced everything else in which they were involved.

> The black church has no challenger as the cultural womb of the black community. Not only did it give birth to new institutions such as schools, banks, insurance companies, and low income housing, it also provided an academy and an arena for political activities, and it nurtured young talent for musical, dramatic, and artistic development . . . in addition to the traditional concerns of worship, moral nurture, education, and social control. Much of black culture is heavily indebted to the black religious tradition, including most forms of black music, drama, literature, storytelling, and even humor.[14]

---

[14]C. Eric Lincoln and Lawrence H. Mamiya, *The Black Church in the African American Experience* (Durham, NC: Duke University Press, 1991), p. 8.

As historian Sydney Ahlstrom points out, black churches also served as a "surrogate for nationality" that substituted religious identification for the tribal identity that had been left behind.[15]

The Christian ministry was the only profession open to blacks and the black churches were the only institution controlled by blacks. As such, they served as schools for leadership training and development. Most of the black political leaders in the United States trace their roots back to the church, and many to the ministry itself. Frequently in the history of the black church, the minister, who was the most highly educated member of the black community, served as the liaison between the black community and that of the dominant whites. This function remains important, even though blacks have joined the ranks of the educated and the professionals in increasing numbers.

The Reverend Jesse Jackson's 1984 and 1988 political campaigns for the Democratic presidential nomination illustrate both of these last two points. He was able to use the black churches to organize voter registration drives and political support, thereby transforming black religion into political power. His campaign speeches were reminiscent of some of the speeches of Martin Luther King, Jr., and they clearly reflected his training and experience as a black Christian minister. At the same time, particularly in the 1988 campaign, he became a spokesperson to the white voting community on behalf of, not only blacks, but of other poor and disadvantaged groups as well. His effectiveness in doing so is reflected in the support he had from white voters.

The Black Church and Civil Rights

Black religion was at the heart of the civil rights movement. It had helped the slaves maintain some sense of humanity and peoplehood. It had provided structure and organization in the years following emancipation. And, it provided a framework in which hopes for civil rights could become political realities.

The **civil rights movement** became an integral part of black religion. Most of the significant events of the civil rights movement occurred in the period that is centered on the turbulent decade of the 1960s and extends for a few years on either side of it. The black churches, their people, and their leaders were intimately involved.

It can be said that the civil rights movement began in May 1954 with a U.S. Supreme Court decision. In *Plessy* v. *Ferguson* (1896), the Court had ruled that segregated facilities, such as schools and accommodations, were permissible as long as the facilities provided were of equal quality. In *Brown* v. *Board of Education of Topeka, Kansas* (1954), the justices ruled that separate-but-equal education was not allowable under the Constitution and ordered that schools proceed

---

[15]Sydney E. Ahlstrom, *A Religious History of the American People* (New Haven, CT: Yale University Press, 1973), p. 710.

with integration as quickly as possible. Celebration of this victory in the black community was short-lived, since it soon became apparent that noncompliance and massive resistance to the Court's instructions were the rule. Discontent in the black community continued to rise, made sharper by hopes that had been raised only to be dashed again.

In this tension-charged atmosphere, an event occurred in December 1955 in Montgomery, Alabama, that brought the civil rights movement into national prominence. Rosa Parks, a domestic worker returning home after a long and tiring day, took a seat on a bus directly behind the driver. When a white person boarded the bus and demanded her seat, the driver, as was customary, demanded that Mrs. Parks move to the back of the bus, where blacks were required to sit. When she refused, she was arrested and jailed. In response to Mrs. Parks' arrest, the leaders of the black community in Montgomery, more than half of whom were ministers, organized what came to be known as the Montgomery bus boycott, a steadfast refusal of blacks to ride the city buses. This protest continued for a year. It was announced from church pulpits, and churches were responsible for printing leaflets. Churches served as information centers, set up alternative means of transportation, and were pickup points for carpools. They were the sites of encouragement rallies that raised the people's determination as the boycott wore on.

By popular vote of his fellow clergy, a young black minister who had recently come to the Dexter Avenue Baptist Church was thrust into leadership of the bus boycott. This was **Dr. Martin Luther King, Jr.** King soon became the undisputed leader of the civil rights movement. He brought to the task his lifelong experience of the black church, the moving preaching style of the black minister, and a social conscience informed by the liberal Protestantism he had learned while obtaining his doctorate at Boston University. King advocated **nonviolent protest.** His reading of the lives and teachings of Jesus and of Mohandas Gandhi, the Indian Hindu politician, convinced him that nonviolence was the morally right way to deal with the situation in which blacks found themselves. Nonviolence meant **civil disobedience** in the spirit of Christian love rather than hatred and revenge against whites. *Civil disobedience* meant deliberately breaking laws that were unjust but being willing to endure verbal and even physical abuse without fighting back and to go to jail if necessary for one's actions. It meant working for reconciliation, not encouraging separatism.

Within a few years, many blacks, especially students, had used King's nonviolent methods in sit-ins at segregated lunch counters throughout the South. Freedom rides began to protest segregation in interstate commerce facilities. Many blacks rode interstate buses and entered facilities such as eating areas and restrooms that were reserved for whites. Such segregation was by that time illegal, but the laws were not enforced.

In January 1957, the **Southern Christian Leadership Conference** (popularly, SCLC) was formed, with Martin Luther King, Jr., as its founder. It proved to be one of the most effective black organizations throughout the 1960s and early 1970s. Protests in Birmingham, Alabama, were among the largest organized by the SCLC. King's "**Letter from Birmingham Jail**," a classic of the movement, was written while he was jailed in Birmingham as a result of his participation in these efforts. In it, King distinguished between a just law and an unjust law. A just law is one that squares with the moral law or the law of God. An unjust law does not. Unjust laws also legalize inequality and difference and are inflicted upon a minority who, by reason of not being allowed to vote, had nothing to say about their passage. People should obey just laws. Unjust laws, on the other hand, should be broken, but in the spirit of nonviolence and love already indicated.[16]

In the late summer of 1963, a massive demonstration in Washington, D.C., focused on segregation in accommodations. The following summer, the **Civil Rights Act** was passed. This piece of legislation received strong support in Congress from leaders of Protestantism, Catholicism, Eastern Orthodoxy, and Judaism, and from blacks and whites alike.

March 1965 saw the well-known march from Selma to Montgomery, Alabama. With King's able leadership, clergy and laity from all the major branches of Christendom and Judaism, along with humanists and free thinkers marched and sang together in protest. Many went to jail. In August of the same year, the **Voting Rights Act** was passed. When Martin Luther King, Jr., was assassinated in the spring of 1968, many of the goals of the early civil rights movement had been met. But there was yet more to do.

Black Christian Militancy and Black Power

Gradually, the mood of the civil rights movement changed. Leaders arose who felt that the methods of Martin Luther King, Jr., worked too slowly. They believed he was too willing to compromise, too moderate, too willing to work with whites. Why the change in mood? Black Presbyterian theologian Gayraud S. Wilmore puts it this way: By the mid-1960s, "many believed that following King meant to give more attention to loving the enemy than to doing something about the suffering of brothers and sisters."[17] In most respects, King was a moderate among Christian ministers. For many blacks, patience with moderation had worn thin. When it had been formed, the Student Nonviolent Coordinating Committee (SNCC) had been committed to King's nonviolent methods, but its early commitment to nonviolence had lessened. Its leaders and rank-and-file members alike were willing to accept and condone violence in the service of righting the wrongs of previous centuries. The passage of the Voting Rights Act in the summer of 1965 sparked an incident that drew national

---

[16]Martin Luther King, Jr., "Letter from Birmingham Jail," in *Why We Can't Wait* (New York: Harper & Row, Publishers, 1963).

[17]Gayraud S. Wilmore and James H. Cone, eds., *Black Theology: A Documentary History, 1966–1979* (Maryknoll, NY: Orbis Books, 1979), p. 16.

attention, and, in some quarters, outrage. There was a week of bloody and destructive race riots in several major American cities. The week of uprisings highlighted the great frustration of the black community and showed both whites and more moderate blacks how far the militants were willing to go to meet their goals.

In the summer of 1966, **James Meredith** was shot and wounded while leading a 220-mile voting rights walk from Memphis, Tennessee, to Jackson, Mississippi. **Stokely Carmichael** and others who took over leadership on that march led the marchers in chants of "black power!" with clenched fists raised in what would become a nationally recognized symbol. The chants of "black power" were often led by church people and they were accompanied by talk of God's judgment upon America for the injustices done to blacks and of coming retribution for oppression.

In 1967, the National Committee of Negro Churchmen became the National Committee of Black Churchmen. In 1969, the committee sponsored a conference on black economic development. Most of the key leaders of the black religious community had long since come to recognize that economic freedom was one of the main keys to ending oppression, a key without which no amount of good intention was enough. At that conference, James Forman read the "**Black Manifesto.**" It is a document that "burns with anger and despair," as Forman said his brothers and sisters did. It made demands, demands that white Christian churches and Jewish synagogues pay reparations that would begin to offset the damage done by economic oppression. It explicitly accused these communities of faith of conscious and willing participation in the processes of slavery and oppression and of not moving nearly rapidly enough to bring about change. Specifically, it demanded $500 million. The money was to be spent in a variety of ways. Loans for land and homes were a main goal. Publishing, printing, and television networks were to be established. Training and skills centers were to be built. A National Black Labor Strike and Defense Fund was to be established. A black university was to be established in the South.

On May 4, 1969, Forman read the Manifesto, uninvited, to the assembled congregation of New York's prestigious Riverside Church. The white churches and synagogues strongly resisted paying any money for reparations. Those that did discuss it seriously often found their congregations split. The Manifesto was an effective tool for drawing national attention to the economic problems that had not been solved. It also illustrated the distance that the civil rights movement had moved from King's style of leadership. No longer willing to work with white religious groups, the supporters of the Manifesto drew clear battle lines.

Not all black churches supported the black power movement, and the movement itself drew support from people and groups not associated with the churches. Nevertheless, the growing consciousness of Jesus as Liberator that would highlight black religious thought gave support and religious legitimation to a powerful new thrust in the ongoing struggle of the black community.

Since the Civil Rights Movement

Five important changes have taken place in the black church since the era of the civil rights movement. First, denominations are less important as a part of black Christian identity than they were. Second, the women's movement has increased tensions in black churches, as women have pressed for and gained greater leadership. This has alienated some black males. Third, blacks are less likely than before to accept a "white Jesus," preferring more culturally relevant symbols. Fourth, the emphasis on dealing constructively with inner-city problems has increased greatly. Finally, preaching focuses more on Bible stories than previously, and some preachers are taking on a more educational role in their preaching.[18]

The Black Church at Worship

The black church's worship is distinctive, with links back to the African and slave experiences of its members. It is worship in which the Holy Spirit is encountered by the worshippers as an experiential reality, in which they are transformed by the presence of their God. Theologian James Cone has noted the **six main elements in black worship** wherever it takes place. They are "preaching, singing, shouting, conversion, prayer, and testimony."[19]

Preaching is the most important, because the preacher speaks the word of God to the people. The black churches emphasize that preachers must be called by God to preach; it is not their decision, but an answer to God's call. It is customary to give an account of this call to the congregation. The sermon is not a lecture; it is enacted, using the rhythms of body movement and voice to give life to the message in response to the Spirit's leading. The people in the congregation participate by their shouts or more subdued responses of "Yes, Jesus," "Say it, Brother," "Amen!" and the like. This congregational responsiveness pulls preacher and listeners together in a common act of worship (Figure 10–3).

After preaching, **singing** is next in importance, because it prepares for, and then intensifies, the experience of the Spirit. It sets the mood, although it cannot force the Spirit to come. It is said that good singing can overcome poor preaching, and that, while there can be church without preaching, there must be singing. Some black churches, especially the larger ones, have regular choirs, but congregational involvement in singing is the rule. For white Christians accustomed to two or at most three hymns during a worship service, the sheer number of hymns and religious songs in a black church service, as well as the hand-clapping, hand-waving enthusiasm with which they are sung, may come as a surprise.

Shouting and **conversion** are closely related. Shouting, sometimes referred to as "getting happy," is understood in the black church as a response to the ac-

---

[18] *National Christian Reporter*, February 25, 1994.
[19] James H. Cone, *Speaking the Truth* (Grand Rapids, MI: William B. Eerdmans Publishing Company, 1986), p. 22.

Figure 10–3   Easter Sunday service at Ebenezer Baptist Church, Poughkeepsie, NY. (*Kathy McLaughlin/The Image Works.*)

tion of the Holy Spirit, a form of religious ecstasy. It is not the same as similar phenomena in white pentecostal churches, because it grows out of an altogether different sociopolitical background and set of life experiences. The white pentecostal is a member of the dominant race, whereas the black is oppressed. As black theologian James Cone writes very pointedly, it is "absurd . . . to contend that the Ku Klux Klansman and the black person who escaped him are shouting for the same or similar reasons."[20] Blacks shout in joy over the authentic personhood given by Jesus and participation in his life and liberation, experienced as a present, here-and-now alternative to oppression and depersonalization. Shouting usually accompanies and is evidence of conversion, and recurs when that experience is renewed. The gaining of authentic identity *is* conversion, something so radical that the metaphor of dying and rising fits it. Conversion is, on the one hand, a one-time event, but on the other hand, it is an ongoing experience and process, and both events are signaled by shouting.

Prayer, free and spontaneous rather than read from a book, is understood as communication with Jesus. Like so much else in black worship, it is rhythmic, echoing the rhythms of the African past.

Finally, during **testimony**, people speak in front of the congregation about their determination to stay with their lives in Christ and in the church in spite of difficulties. They believe that they are called by God and testify to their intention to be worthy of that call. It is an encouragement both to the person tes-

---

[20]Cone, *Speaking the Truth,* p. 27.

tifying and to those who hear it. The congregational responses of "Yes, Sister" or "Tell it, Brother" let the speakers know that the rest of the congregation is with them against the temptations that arise.

Black Religious Thought

Theologically, black Christianity is conservative and traditional, in both thought and practice. Black Christians affirm the traditional beliefs of the church, with minimal modification. For the average person in the pew, especially, "keeping the faith" is much more important than modernization.

Historically, the black church has been a place to which people could retreat from the dehumanization of white oppression. It has preached and sung that "You're somebody in God's eyes even if you're nobody here." Black churches still offer their people this sort of message. But even when its message has been otherworldly and has promised heavenly freedom instead of struggling for earthly freedom, it has been a place of healing, a place that helped people remain sane in the midst of the insanity of slavery and the problems of newly freed blacks. Being a somebody in God's eyes was a powerful incentive to work toward a society in which there are no longer any nobodies.

The distinctive contribution of the black churches to the American theological enterprise is **black theology**. Black theology is **not simply traditional Christian theology**, which has been overwhelmingly white, European, and male, **overlaid with the experience of blackness**. It is guided and informed by the experience of blackness right from the outset. The experience of blackness sets the agenda for this way of doing theology. This approach became self-conscious and came to public attention during the tumultuous 1960s, as a part of the civil rights movement. It is also **thoroughly Christian**, taking as its starting point and focus the Christian New Testament, especially the gospels of Matthew, Mark, and Luke, that tell the story of Jesus' life, death, and resurrection. It is also part of the larger category of theologies called liberation theologies. Liberation theologies all deal with the message of the Gospels for an oppressed group, be it Third World, black, or female.

There are a number of themes upon which nearly all black theologians would agree. The theme of **freedom** is central. Black religious thought draws on both the Christian Old Testament and the Christian New Testament in this respect. As a recent study of the black church put it, "the Old Testament notion of God as an avenging, conquering, liberating paladin remains a formidable anchor of faith in most black churches." However, **Jesus as the liberator** of the poor and oppressed is unquestionably the controlling theme of black theology. The suffering of black people throughout their history finds "immediate resonance with the incarnational view of the suffering, humiliation, death, and eventual triumph of Jesus in the resurrection."[21]

[21]Lincoln and Mamiya, *The Black Church*, pp. 3–4.

Jesus as the liberator means liberation now, in this world, in terms of voting rights, jobs, equal access to good education, and adequate housing. The liberation that Jesus offers certainly includes freedom from the eternal punishment of unforgiven sin. It certainly includes a hoped-for future in which oppression and pain of every kind shall cease. But first and foremost, Jesus means liberation now, sociopolitical and economic liberation. He means full humanity for people who have never had full humanity.

God is a God of justice, especially concerned for the fate of the oppressed. God is believed to be on the side of the oppressed and against the oppressor. God does not support the ruling class and the status quo but instead supports the attempt to change that status quo to bring about a more just and equal society. This, too, reflects the importance of the Christian Old Testament in black religious thought. In a similar vein, the Kingdom of God is seen in terms of justice and equality in this world. People, with God's help and guidance, are responsible for bringing it about. While it may not come in its fullness until God intervenes decisively in human history, it can be greatly advanced. Black theology is a theology of political action; concepts such as the Kingdom of God are politicized and translated into concrete changes in how people live.

Black religious thought is **thoroughly contextual**. Theology has usually been done by and for the privileged classes—in the United States, white men. It has usually been assumed that there was but one theology, and the problem was to get that one correct. Contextual theology recognizes that, although Christians believe that there is only one God, there are a vast number of ways that people may understand God, based on their own time and culture. Theology is a circular process in which the current situation and the Bible interpret and reinterpret each other. For black theology, the beginning point is the experience of slavery and oppression. Any theology that does not take that experience into account and does not ring true to people whose identity is marked by that experience cannot be valid.

In the United States, black theology was the first of the contextual, liberation-oriented theologies to come to national attention. It set the stage for other attempts to interpret the Christian message in terms of a particular people's history. The pioneering work of the black theologians helped all theologians in the United States to realize how much their social and cultural settings influenced their theologies. It made it much more difficult to justify doing theology as if time and place do not matter.

Descriptive Data

About 80 percent of blacks in the United States are Protestant. Not quite 10 percent are Catholic. Less than 1 percent are Jewish, and about 5 percent each claim no religious preference or claim some other religious preference. This 5 percent includes Black Muslims. Among the Protestants, two-thirds are Baptist and about 10 percent are Methodist. About 1 percent each are Lutheran, Presbyterian, and Episcopalian; about 15 percent indicate some other preference, and about 5 percent are nondenominational. Looked at from another perspective, about 30 percent of all Baptists are black, as are about 10 percent of all Methodists. All together, there are approximately 65,000 black Christian congregations, with about 24 million members.

Approximately 80 percent of religiously affiliated blacks in the United States are members of one of the **seven major historically black denominations:**

> National Baptist Convention, USA, Incorporated
> National Baptist Convention of America, Unincorporated
> Progressive National Baptist Convention
> African Methodist Episcopal Church
> African Methodist Episcopal Zion Church
> Christian Methodist Episcopal Church
> Church of God in Christ

The list clearly reflects the success that Baptist and Methodist missionaries had among the slaves and later among the free blacks, both north and south. The first black church in the United States was Baptist, and the first black denomination was Methodist.[22] Both black worship and black theology have developed most fully in the historically black churches, although both are found elsewhere as well.

The **black pentecostal denominations, of which the Church of God in Christ (COGIC) is by far the largest,** have shown the greatest growth among black churches in the twentieth century. The founder of COGIC, Charles Harrison Mason, had been a part of the Azuza Street revival in the early 1900s. Pentecostalism is growing more rapidly among blacks than among others in the United States.

There are also a number of black or nearly all black congregations in Christian denominations that are predominantly white, such as the American and Southern Baptists, United Methodists, Presbyterians, Episcopalians, and Roman Catholics. These black congregations worship in a style that is closer to that of comparable white congregations. As Cone points out, however, although the forms may be different, the white denomination's style of worship is not the central self-identification of the black congregations. They did not participate in the creation of those traditions of worship and cannot affirm them wholeheartedly. Their primary identification is with the experience of blackness, of suffering and oppression, and the word of liberation in the gospel of Jesus as Liberator.[23]

Black congregations reflect the same sort of social stratification as their white counterparts. For example, as affluence and education rise, they are more likely to have a formal service, with a robed choir, a highly educated minister, and a director of religious education. In other words, the black congregations become more like the white congregations. Many would say that they become less true to authentic black religious experience.

---

[22]Lincoln and Mamiya, *The Black Church*, pp. 23 and 47.
[23]Cone, *Speaking the Truth*, p. 129.

Data from surveys that include questions about frequency of attendance at worship, private prayer and Bible reading, strength of religious preference, and religious commitment typically show that blacks participate in both public worship and private religious acts more frequently than their white counterparts. Their religious preference and commitment are stronger. They are more likely to consider religion a very important part of life and are more likely to believe that it can solve most or all of today's problems. Blacks are much more likely to be fundamentalist in their religious outlook, by about three to two, and are half as likely to be liberal.

Women in the Black Church[24]

As with predominantly white Christian churches, black Christian churches have historically had a majority of female members and an almost exclusively male pastorate. This pattern continues in black churches, for the most part, into the present. Women do have many other leadership roles in the black churches, such as evangelists, deaconesses, lay readers, Sunday School teachers, counselors, and the like. Women are also "mothers of the church,"

> . . . an honorific title usually reserved for the wife of the founder or for the oldest and most respected members. . . . The phenomenon of the "church mother" has no parallel in white churches; it is derived from the kinship network found within black churches and black communities.[25]

It is clear that these women have positions of great power within their congregations. Some women, barred from ordination, also went out to found their own churches, becoming powerful preachers and leaders in their own right.

The black Methodist denominations were the first to ordain women as pastors. Congregational polity among the Baptist groups has limited the development of consistent policies on the ordination of women, but the tendency is for fewer women to be ordained there. While policy usually does not explicitly prohibit it, tradition does. Pentecostals remain firmly against it. Overall, the reluctance to grant full ordination to women has come under increasing criticism in the last two or three decades, and changes are coming about slowly.

QUESTIONS AND ACTIVITIES FOR REVIEW, DISCUSSION, AND WRITING

1. What seem to you to be the advantages and disadvantages of religion and ethnic, national, or racial consciousness being interrelated in these communities of faith?
2. If there is an Eastern Orthodox church where you live or where you go to school, try to make an appointment to visit the church during the week. Notice particularly the

---

[24]Most of the material in this section is summarized from Lincoln and Mamiya, *The Black Church*, chap. 10.
[25]Lincoln and Mamiya, *The Black Church*, p. 275.

architecture of the building, the icons, and the iconostasis. Most priests will be glad to have you visit and will be quite willing to answer your questions. You might also want to consider attending the Divine Liturgy on Sunday morning.

3. If you are accustomed to worshipping in a white congregation, attend a worship service at one of the historically black churches. If you worship in a mostly black congregation, attend a service in a mostly white congregation. Reflect on the differences you observe.

4. Get your class together in integrated groups of black and white students and discuss your perceptions of each other's worship.

5. In your opinion, what are the advantages and disadvantages of the nonviolent methods of Martin Luther King, Jr.?

6. Read and report on James Baldwin's autobiographical novel, *Go Tell It on the Mountain*.

7. If you can get a videotape of the movie, *The Long Road Home*, with Whoopi Goldberg, view it and write a brief essay on the roles that the black church played in the civil rights movement, as depicted in the film.

FOR FURTHER READING

Cone, James H., *Martin and Malcolm and America: A Dream or a Nightmare*. Maryknoll, NY: Orbis Books, 1995. Explores the role and influence of Martin Luther King, Jr., and Malcolm X, undoubtedly the two most influential black religious leaders in the history of the United States.

Cone, James H., and Gayraud S. Wilmore, eds., *Black Theology: A Documentary History*. Maryknoll, NY: Orbis Books, 1995. Two volumes cover the years 1966–79 and the years 1980–92. The first volume is completely revised and updated from an earlier work, while the material in the second is all new. The definitive source for tracing the development of black theology in the United States.

Harakas, Stanley S., *The Orthodox Church: 455 Questions and Answers*. Brookline, MA: Holy Cross Orthodox Press, 1988. A concise but comprehensive handbook. Emphasizes Greek Orthodoxy but includes more general entries as well.

Lincoln, C. Eric, and Lawrence H. Mamiya, *The Black Church in the African American Experience*. Durham, NC: Duke University Press, 1991. Based on extensive survey and field interview data. Also has good historical material. The current definitive study.

Litsas, Fotios K., ed., *A Companion to the Greek Orthodox Church*. New York: Department of Communication, Greek Orthodox Archdiocese of North and South America, 1984. A good basic introduction to Eastern Orthodoxy in general.

Matsuoka, Fumitaka, *Out of Silence: Emerging Themes in Asian American Churches*. Cleveland, OH: United Church Press, 1995. Based on a study of four Asian American Protestant congregations. Little has been written so far about Asian American Christianity, and this is a pioneering work. Several themes that are important in black theology emerge here as well.

Paris, Peter J., *The Social Teachings of the Black Churches*. Philadelphia: Fortress Press, 1985. Thorough study of social ethics, based on the official records of the African Methodist Episcopal Church and the National Baptist Convention, USA. Highlights the "constellation of religious and moral values" that are a part of the black Christian tradition.

Stewart, Maria W., et al., with an Introduction by Sue E. Houchins, *Spiritual Narratives*. New York: Oxford University Press, 1991. Autobiographical narratives by Stewart, Jarena Lee, Julia A. J. Foote, and Virginia W. Broughton, four black women who preached despite their having been denied formal ordination.

11

Other Religio-
Ethnic Religions

If you are not clear about what a religio-ethnic group is, you should reread the introductory material in the preceding chapter. People of all the major religions of the world live in the United States. Many of these religions fit our definition of religio-ethnic groups. In this chapter, we will look at three of the larger and better-known world religions whose members live in this country. The first, Islam, began in the same general geographic area as did Judaism and Christianity, and has much in common with them. The second and third, Hinduism and Buddhism, began in India, and are in many ways very different from the Semitic religions. I have kept the use of unfamiliar words to a minimum, instead using more familiar equivalents that convey the sense of what is meant. I have used less familiar terms when doing so seemed warranted because (1) they are used often in discussing a particular religion, (2) you would be likely to encounter them in your other reading or experience, or (3) they are often used and/or greatly preferred by followers of the religions.

A new immigration bill passed in fall 1991 allows a greater diversity of religious workers from foreign countries to enter the United States. The bill liberalizes the qualifications for "religious workers" to include lay workers as well as religious professionals. The bill states that the applicant must be a member of a recognized United States denomination. However, most religious groups now have at least small numbers in the United States, with some sort of organization. The bill will also ease conflict between immigration officials and applicants from religious groups whose leadership does not necessarily fit the pattern established by American clergy. For example, Hindu and Buddhist religious teachers often do not do many of the things that American clergy do, and this has made it difficult for them to be recognized as religious professionals by the Immigration and Naturalization Service.

ISLAM

Islam is the third of the Semitic monotheistic religions, along with Judaism and Christianity. **Semitic** in a general term that refers to people and religions of Middle Eastern origin, and so includes Judaism, Christianity, and Islam, as well as others. **Monotheism**, as you probably remember, means the belief in and worship of only one God. People who are followers of Islam are properly called **Muslims**. The word **Islam** has connotations of both "submission" and "peace"; it is the peace of one who submits wholly to God (or **Allah**, an Arabic name for God). A *Muslim* is one who submits to Allah. You may have heard Muslims referred to as "Muhammadans" or a similar term. This is incorrect and very offensive to Muslims, because they are followers of Allah, not of Muhammad.

Before you read further, think about what your own opinion of Muslims and of Islam is. Do you know any Muslims personally? What kinds of things have you heard about Muslims, or about Islam as a religion?

Muhammad

The story of Islam begins with Muhammad, whom Muslims believe is the "Seal of the Prophets," the last and final prophet in a long line of prophets sent by Allah to bring God's truth to humankind. He was born about 570 C.E. Forty years later, in 610, while meditating alone, Muhammad had an experience in which he believed that the angel Gabriel spoke to him, conveying the actual words of Allah himself. He was told that he had been chosen as a prophet, and that the words that he would be given he must repeat to all who would listen. The revelations continued until shortly before Muhammad's death in 632. Islam began as an oral tradition, passed from Muhammad to a few close associates and, finally, to the world.

Although Muhammad is regarded as the founder of Islam, Muslims also claim Abraham as their ancestor, as do Jews and Christians. According to both Tanakh and the Muslim sacred scripture, Abraham had two sons. Ishmael, his son with Hagar, Sarah's maid, was his firstborn. Ishmael became the ancestor of the Muslims. Isaac, Abraham and Sarah's son, became the ancestor of the Jews.

Muhammad, the Prophet, was a human being, no more than that. The Christian identification of the person Jesus of Nazareth with God is blasphemous to Muslims because making a human being God's equal does not recognize the incomparable greatness and oneness of Allah. Muhammad is, however, regarded as the model for what an ideal person is, and the stories about his life are a source of inspiration for his followers. What Muhammad said and did, as recorded by his companions in the tradition (**Hadith**), provide a blueprint for the interpretation and application of the Quran[1] to the various situations of life. Poetry in

---

[1]The *Quran* is the Muslims' sacred scripture.

praise of the Prophet and his life exists in virtually every language spoken by Muslims, and love for him and for his family marks Muslim devotion. Standards for Muslim belief and action come not only from the Quran, but from its application exemplified in the life and sayings of Muhammad.

Muslims believe that religious truth is to be found in the revelation of God to the other "peoples of the Book," Jews and Christians. That truth had become corrupted, making it necessary for Allah to send Muhammad to correct and complete it.

The Quran

The sacred scripture of Islam is called the **Quran,** or the **Holy Quran** (sometimes spelled "Qur'an"). It was originally written in Arabic, and most Muslims believe that it is fully authentic only in that language. Islam is a missionary religion like Christianity, however, and the Quran has been translated into many languages, including English.

The first chapter is recited at the beginning of prayers. It summarizes many of the principal themes of Islam (author's paraphrase):

> In the name of Allah
> Most gracious and most merciful.
> Praise be to Allah,
> The cherisher and sustainer of the worlds;
> Most gracious and most merciful;
> Master of the Day of Judgment.
> We worship only You,
> And we seek Your aid.
> Show us the straight way,
> The way of those to whom You give Your grace,
> Those whose portion is not wrath,
> And who do not go astray.

Allah commanded that Muhammad **cry** or **recite** the Quran, and reciting still plays an important part in Muslim devotion. The words themselves, since they are believed to be the very words of Allah, have power:

> Recitation of the Qur'an is thought to have a healing, soothing effect, but can also bring protection, miraculous signs, knowledge, and destruction, according to Muslim tradition. It is critical that one recite the Qur'an only in a purified state, for the words are so powerful that the one who recites it takes on a great responsibility. Ideally, one learns the Qur'an as a child, when memorization is easiest and when the power of the words will help to shape one's life.[2]

---

[2]Mary Pat Fisher and Robert Luyster, *Living Religions* (Englewood Cliffs, NJ: Prentice Hall, Inc., 1991), p. 275.

Beliefs

The core beliefs of Islam, from which all others arise, are the oneness and unity of Allah and the prophethood of Muhammad. There are two primary subgroups within Islam, the **Sunni** Muslims (by far the larger subgroup) and the **Shia** Muslims. There is an nucleus of beliefs that is widely shared among Muslims in North America, and these form the basis for our discussion here.

Muslims, as stated above, believe in **the oneness of Allah.** "Oneness" here is not primarily a matter of arithmetic, of there being numerically only one God. Rather the emphasis is on the utter incomparability of Allah, there being nothing as great as Allah. It is also not simply an intellectual matter, but requires trust in Allah, submission to the will of Allah, and reliance upon Allah for everything in life.

They also believe in the **angels of Allah.** Angels are spiritual beings whose entire role is to serve Allah. Each has a specific duty to perform. This belief arises from the prior belief that knowledge cannot be limited to what can be perceived with the senses, that there are in fact things that exist that we cannot know through the senses (Quran 16:49–50 and 21:19–20).

Muslims also believe in **all the books of Allah,** including the sacred writings of Judaism and Christianity, culminating in the Quran. There are specific references in the Quran to God's having given Tanakh to the House of Israel and the Bible to Christians. The Quran is the standard by which the others are judged. Insofar as they agree with it, they are true and are to be accepted. When they differ from the Quran, it has precedence.

As a result of this, Muslims also believe in **all the prophets of Allah.** There are approving references to many of the Hebrew prophets (Abraham, Moses, and David among them) as well as to John the Baptist and Jesus. Each age and each nation is believed to have had its messenger from Allah. The Quran says (2:136, author's paraphrase)

> Say: We believe in Allah, and in the revelation given to us, and to Abraham, Ishmael, Isaac, Jacob and the Tribes; and that which was given to Moses and Jesus, and that which was given to all the prophets from their Lord. We do not differentiate between them, and we bow to Allah in submission.

Muhammad, as stated before, **is the last and final Prophet.** Allah entrusted him with the prophecy that completes and corrects those that have gone before.

Those of Islamic faith also affirm **life after death.** The Quran paints vivid pictures of both Paradise and Hell, as well as of a Day of Judgment in which all people will be called to account for their lives. Muslims believe that Allah keeps an accurate account of everything people do and think. Good deeds will be rewarded and evil ones punished.

The requirements of **Muslim ethical or moral behavior** are very similar to those of Christianity and Judaism. Marriage and family are very important; marriage is considered a duty and is based on a legal contract to which both husband and wife agree. Sexual relations outside marriage are strictly forbidden. Divorce is permitted, but strongly discouraged. Anything injurious to oneself or to others—mentally, physically, or morally—is forbidden. Respect and care for the elderly is considered very important, and people are expected to care for their parents in their later years. The equality of all persons and dealing with others with respect and total honesty is a fundamental moral value.

Thinking about Muslim morality brings up a much-misunderstood concept, **jihad**. *Jihad* is often translated "Holy War," and this has given rise to the popular misconception of Islam as a fanatical and war-hungry religion. The basic meaning of jihad is otherwise: It means the continual, inner spiritual struggle for submission to Allah, in which all people must engage daily. It is a mistake to think that all Muslims are religious fanatics bent on terrorism. All religions, including those better known in the United States, have given rise to fanaticism at times. But we don't identify Judaism and Christianity with their fanatic representatives. We should extend the same courtesy and moderation to our Muslim neighbors.

The Five Pillars of Islam

The Five Pillars are **five specific acts required of all faithful Muslims**. Although they are classified as "required," their actual observance varies from one person to another, even in traditionally Muslim countries. There is tension between those who support strict observance as the only way to be a "good Muslim" and those who accept a wider range of observance. This tension, it should be noted, is not unique to Islam, but exists in all religions. The first pillar is **faith, shown in the repetition of the creed** (*Shahadah*): "There is no God but Allah, and Muhammad is the Prophet of Allah." Devout Muslims repeat this affirmation of faith daily. Doing so helps keep the major principles of their faith at the center of their lives. These are often the first words spoken to a newborn Muslim baby, and the last words spoken or heard by one who is dying. While saying the Shahadah is important, the faith which it expresses is the central concern.

The second pillar is **prayer five times daily**. Ritual cleansing precedes the prayers, and each prayer is accompanied by specific ritual actions such as sitting, standing, and prostrating oneself with the forehead touching the floor or ground. Muslims pray facing Mecca, the Holy City of Islam, located in what is now Saudi Arabia. These are set, formal prayers. In addition, Muslims are encouraged to repeat these prayers more times than is required and to add their own personal prayers to the required ones. Prayers are to be said at dawn, at midday, midafternoon, dusk, and at night. There is some flexibility in the exact times; the idea is to have the prayers paced throughout the day. Doing so helps keep Muslims continually aware of Allah and of the need for submission to him. Those who can are encouraged to attend the **mosque (masjid)**, the Islamic place of worship (Fig-

Figure 11–1 The *Masjid,* or mosque, Islamic Center of Toledo, Ohio. The presence of Muslims, Hindus, Buddhists, and others of the less familiar religions in the United States expands the range of religious architecture, as well as of religious beliefs and practices. (*Photo courtesy of Richard J. Fears.*)

ure 11–1) for the midday prayers on Fridays. Islam does not have a weekly Sabbath, but the community of faith gathers to pray these prayers together and usually to hear the Quran read and explained in a talk by the **imam** or prayer leader.

As you can imagine, the required prayers can be difficult for Muslims in the United States. Prayer times may conflict with work times, and there may not always be an appropriate place to pray in the workplace. Employers may not always want to make the slight accommodation necessary to allow time for prayers, and the curiosity of fellow workers can be embarrassing. On the other side, many Muslims appreciate the opportunity it gives for them to express their faith to non-Muslims.

The third pillar is the **giving of alms** to help those in need. This is not simply charity. It is more like a religious tax in that it is required. It amounts to about 2 percent, based on a person's net worth. Muslims in the United States select a Muslim organization to which they will pay the alms; for many, it is the Muslim Student Association. They are encouraged to make other charitable contributions, as they are able. Muslims do not look down on wealth, as long as it is gotten honestly; the honest earning of money and wise management of it is a tribute to Allah. But Allah must also be worshipped through one's wealth, and this is the point of almsgiving.

Fourth is **fasting during the month of Ramadan.** The Islamic religious calendar differs from the civil calendar, so Ramadan occurs at different times in different years. Ramadan is the month in which tradition holds that the revelation to Muhammad began. Fasting, in this instance, means complete abstention from eating, drinking, smoking, and sexual activity from just before sunrise until just after sunset. A meal is eaten immediately before and immediately following the hours of fasting. This activity helps unite Muslims around the world, encourages empathy for those who are hungry or otherwise lacking, and reinforces submission to the will of Allah. Ramadan is also a time of increased spiritual awareness, when Muslims often spend extra time in reading and studying the Quran and in prayer. Fasting is not required of young children, women who are pregnant or menstruating, travelers, the elderly and those who are ill or frail, as well as others on whom it would impose an unreasonable burden.

The fast is followed by the Festival of Fast-Breaking. This is a joyous time in which families and friends gather together to rejoice in the end of this strenuous time and to celebrate the spiritual benefits gained from it.

The last of the pillars is the **hajj, or pilgrimage to Mecca,** a journey that Muslims are required to make at least once in their lives, as long as they are mentally, physically, and financially capable of doing so. Hajj brings Muslims from around the world together for a series of religious rituals in and around Mecca. Its center is the Grand Mosque and the Kabah, a large stone building that Muslims believe was built by Abraham and Ishmael for the worship of Allah. Most pilgrims also visit Medina, the city in which Muhammad found shelter after he was forced to flee Mecca because people there would not accept his teaching. After the Meccan tribes were defeated, Muhammad made a pilgrimage back to Mecca in 629. The rites that he performed then are the prototype for those carried out by Muslims today.

Muslims in the United States

Estimates of the number of Muslims in the United States vary considerably. It is not necessary to be a member of a mosque to be a Muslim. Too, some Muslims remain hesitant to identify themselves as Muslims because prejudice still exists. A recent random sample survey of 113,000 people, commissioned by the Graduate School of the City University of New York, found the following: Muslims account for about 0.5 percent of the population, or less than a half-million people. This is below previous estimates that had ranged from 3 to 8 million people. One possible source of difference is "Christians from Arab countries who identify culturally with the Muslim community, but not religiously." The same survey revealed that about 40 percent of Muslims are black, although this accounts for only about 2 percent of the black population in the United States. It is also one of the fastest growing religions in the United States, as well as worldwide. Most Arab Americans, however, are Christians, perhaps because Christians tend to emigrate to the United States from Muslim countries in greater numbers than do non-Christians.[3]

Muslims have come to the United States from virtually all of the Middle Eastern countries in which Islam is common, as well as from India, Pakistan, China, the former Soviet Union, and elsewhere. There have been Muslims in the United States for many generations, as well as a steady influx of recent immigrants. There are also American converts to Islam. Thus, on the one hand, there is an Islamic *community* here: a group of people united by a common religion. On the other hand, there are several communit*ies* of Muslims here: American-born, descendants of immigrants, and recent immigrants, as well as Muslims of various national and ethnic backgrounds.

Their experience in the United States poses both potential and peril for Muslims:

> American Muslims are experiencing both exhilaration at the opportunity to increase their numbers and develop their institutions and frustration and dismay as they continue to experience prejudice, intimidation, discrimination, misunderstanding, and even hatred. . . . [Muslims in the United States] have unprecedented freedom to experiment with forms and structures for the separation of religion and state away from the watchful eyes of wary governments and the criticism of traditionalists. At the same time, this freedom is fraught with the danger of innovation and deviance; the great range of options available in the American context carries the threat of sectarian division and fragmentation.[4]

Like members of most other religious groups, Muslims in the United States range from liberals who seek accommodation with the surrounding culture to the very conservative who seek to preserve the inherited tradition and advocate separation from those who do not agree. There are also differences of opinion between Muslims who want to convert non-Muslims and those who do not.

The Muslim **mosque** (*masjid* **is being used increasingly**) has changed character in the United States. In most traditionally Muslim countries, the mosque is simply a place in which the community of the faithful gathers for the Friday midday prayers. The **imam**, or prayer leader, is a member of the community who is skilled in Quranic recitation and perhaps exposition. There is no professional clergy in Islam, and usually the imam holds another job. In the United States, the mosque has become much more like a church or synagogue, and the imam has become a professional clergyman, in most instances. Mosques offer a full range of activities, both religious and cultural, for the Muslim community. Be-

---

[3]*New York Times National,* April 10, 1991, p. 1.
[4]Yvonne Yazbeck Haddad, "Introduction: The Muslims of America," in *The Muslims of America,* ed. Yvonne Yazbeck Haddad (New York: Oxford University Press, 1991), pp. 3 and 5.

sides the traditional prayer service, there will often be women's groups, classes for all ages and both genders, social activities, and day care. The imam is expected to function as the leader of the congregation, a counselor, an administrator, and as the representative of the Muslim community to the surrounding culture.

As traditionally interpreted, Islamic law covers every aspect of life for Muslims: religious and secular (a distinction that is itself alien to Islam), private and public, extraordinary and mundane. Muslims who live in a non-Muslim culture must decide the extent to which full adherence to Islamic law is possible or desirable. As you might expect, individual Muslims vary in how carefully they keep all the details of Islamic law. There are two sources of variation: (1) different aspects of observance receive different attention, and (2) different Muslim subpopulations vary in their observance.

In the first place, some regulations are kept much more fully than others. For example, Muslim law forbids the payment or receiving of interest on money. Using the American banking system makes this extremely difficult. Most Muslims in the United States do have bank accounts and do use credit when necessary. Muslim law also forbids the consumption of pork, pork products, and alcohol. The great majority of Muslims does not knowingly consume pork or pork products, and most Muslims make a conscientious effort to find out if prepared foods contain them. Fewer adhere absolutely to the alcohol prohibition, although a majority does. Whether or not Muslims themselves choose to use alcohol, they must decide whether to offer it to non-Muslim guests in their homes. Some do and some do not.

Muslims are also discouraged or forbidden from dating as it is practiced in the United States. Youth meet prospective mates through their families and at activities at the mosque. Social interaction takes place only in a well-chaperoned group setting. Marriages are usually arranged. Women especially, but men also, are discouraged from marrying outside the faith. If they do, they may marry only a Jew or a Christian (other "peoples of the Book"). This makes finding a suitable partner within such a small population difficult. Muslim magazines often carry matrimonial ads in which families invite correspondence from potential partners for a daughter, sister, son, or brother.

There is no consensus among Muslims in the United States about the application of Muslim laws and values. There is no doubt that observance declines with a number of factors. Less strict observance is associated with being in the United States for a longer time, with interacting with non-Muslim Americans, and "apparently as a general result of living in American culture."[5]

There are a number of Muslim organizations in the United States. I will mention only a few of them. Most of you who are reading this book are college students. Many of you are members of or active in campus religious organizations sponsored by your community of faith. The **Muslim Student Association**

---

[5]Yvonne Yazbeck Haddad and Adair T. Lummis, *Islamic Values in the United States: A Comparative Study* (New York: Oxford University Press, 1987), chaps. 3, 4, and 5.

was organized in the 1960s. It offers religious and social events for Muslim college students, and provides opportunities for non-Muslim students to learn about Islam. The Muslim Student Association is one of the constituent groups of **The Islamic Society of North America**, an umbrella organization of several groups. It is generally considered to be the primary national Muslim organization, especially by immigrant Muslims. It publishes a journal, *Islamic Horizons*. The **American Muslim Mission** is the largest organization of American-born Muslims. It publishes *The Muslim Journal.*

Recall that in the discussion of Muslim beliefs, we distinguished between Sunni and Shia Muslims. There is a third group of Muslims in the United States, the **Sufi Muslims**, or simply, **Sufis.** Sufism is the **mystical branch of Islam**, comparable in that respect to Hasidic Judaism. Sufism first came to the United States in 1910 with an Indian musician named Pir Hazrat Inayat Khan. There are now organizations throughout the United States. Their beliefs focus on the essential unity of all religions. They affirm that there is one God, one holy book ("the sacred manuscript of nature"), one religion, one law, one human brotherhood, one moral principle, one truth, and one path.[6] Meditation and ecstatic dancing facilitate communion with God. The Order accepts initiates as individual students, sponsors worship as the Universal Worship of the Church of All, and also has a Healing Order that works with group healing rituals.

Women in Islam and Muslim Women in America

It is clear that under Quranic law, women received more equal treatment than was otherwise common in Muhammad's lifetime. Religiously and legally, women and men were considered as equals. It is also the case that, while having equal standing before Allah and before the law, women and men were thought to be different from each other, with different primary spheres of responsibility. Even if she were active in the public realm, a woman's primary responsibility was in the home, while a man's primary area of influence was the public arena.

Most Muslims in the United States approve of a married woman's working outside the home if she chooses. Even more approve if financial circumstances require it. Traditional Muslim dress requires that women cover most of their bodies when outside the home. Most Muslim women feel free to adopt American clothing styles, while often avoiding the less modest ways of dressing that are common here. More are either required or choose to wear more traditional dress in the prayer room of the mosque. Some wear traditional clothing as a way of identifying with the Muslim community and expressing their commitment to its values. It should be noted here that the Quran specifically enjoins modesty in clothing for *both* sexes (Quran, 24:30–31), a fact that is often overlooked in discussions of women's dress codes.

Traditionally, whatever else women's roles outside the home have been,

6"Sufi Thoughts," Sufi Order, Lebanon Springs, NY, n.d.

women have had almost no opportunity to participate in the leadership of the mosque. In many Islamic countries, women rarely even attend the mosque. In the United States, women may or may not attend Friday prayers; most likely, they do not. Nonetheless, women do play an active role in most mosques, in fund-raising, teaching, supporting its social life, and in both formal and informal influence on decision making. Many believe that women should be eligible for any lay leadership position, including the presidency of the mosque. Women do not serve as imams.

Muslim thought about the appropriate roles of women, and the American understanding of the Muslim view both vary:

> Contemporary Islam is subject to several different currents, each strong and with articulate advocates. While some reaffirm the necessity of women remaining in the home to maintain [traditionally Islamic] values for the sake of Islamic society, others stress the importance of full female participation in the public life of the Islamic community. The latter perceive the traditional position of women vis-à-vis men as alien to Islam and argue for equal rights in the workplace as well as equal participation in the outward manifestations of Islam.
>
> These various strands of thought, along with the legacy of misunderstanding of Islam on the part of many Westerners, make it difficult for Americans to fully appreciate the position of women in Muslim society. Many . . . [Muslims feel] that Americans in general do not understand the role of women in Islam and their own conviction that the Muslim women does, in fact, have a better situation than women in other religious traditions.[7]

Islam and Black Americans

Black Americans were attracted to Islam by its message of complete racial equality. Muslim tradition holds that a daughter of Muhammad married a black man. Islam also offered belief in one God and a strong ethical code, as did Christianity, but it was not identified as clearly with the white oppressors. The story of Islam as it relates to the struggle for black freedom and self-definition is complex. It is clear that Islam offered American blacks an opportunity for a more positive self-identification:

> Although very few references explain how ideas about Islam became available in the black community, it is clear that this religion promised a new identity, a feeling of "somebodiness" denied by the dominant culture, a liberation from . . . relegation to insignificance. The new adherents shed Christianity, which they perceived as the root of their oppression in its glorification of suffering and promise of redemption in the hereafter.[8]

---

[7]Haddad and Lummis, *Islamic Values in the United States*, pp. 125–26.
[8]Beverly Thomas McCloud, "African-American Muslim Women," in *The Muslims of America*, ed. Haddad, p. 178.

The history of the Black Muslims in the United States is complex. Muslims estimate that about 10 percent of the slaves who were brought from Africa were Muslims. Timothy Drew (1866–1929) was the founder and leader of a group called the Moorish Science Temple of America. Upon his death, Wallace D. Fard (also known as Farrad Mohammad or Wali Fard) gathered a group around himself to continue Drew's work. The group soon became too large to meet in homes and rented a meeting hall, which they named the Temple of Islam. Within three years, the Temple had grown to be a large organization. Within the Temple, Elijah Muhammad became an influential leader, and, when Fard disappeared in 1934, Muhammad emerged as the leader of what was then called the Nation of Islam.

Almost from the beginning, there was a group within the Nation of Islam who did not fully agree with Muhammad. This group was led by Malcolm X (born Malcolm Little in 1925). Especially later in his life, Malcolm X and his followers wanted to move the Nation closer to traditional Islam and away from complete separation from whites. They founded the Muslim Mosque, Incorporated, in 1964.

The Muslims had carried out an effective prison ministry for some time, and it was while in prison that Malcolm X converted to Islam. He was attracted to it, as his autobiography tells, by its promise of a more structured life centered on traditional family values. After a pilgrimage to Mecca, he founded the Organization of Afro-American Unity, a nonsectarian and racially integrated group.[9] Meanwhile, the Black Muslim movement had come to symbolize black power. Many of Malcolm X's teachings were incorporated into the secular themes of black power, such as pride in blackness, the importance of knowing black history, separatism, and the importance of being black and separate before trying to be black and integrated. He also advocated black unity and black control of the institutions affecting the black community. Black Muslims emphasized the ethical teachings of Islam. Occupational stability and a quiet, restrained lifestyle marked by modesty in all things was the rule. The Islamic ethics encouraged and required by the organization most associated with black separatism thus had an ironic effect: They helped move blacks closer to the white mainstream of society.

In 1975, Elijah Muhammad died and his son, W. D. Muhammad (b. 1933) assumed control of the Nation of Islam. Under his leadership, the Nation moved closer to the viewpoint of the Muslim Mosque. People who were dissatisfied with this approach came together around Louis Farrakhan in a movement to return to the separatist views and policies of the old Nation. Farrakhan's followers have remained an outspoken minority among American Muslims.

It is Malcolm X who has retained, even after his death, a hold on the imagination of American blacks, Muslim and non-Muslim alike. A poll done at the time that Spike Lee's controversial movie, *Malcolm X*, came out indicated that although only about half of American blacks really understood what Malcolm X

---

[9] Malcolm X, *The Autobiography of Malcolm X* (as told to Alex Haley) (New York: Ballantine Books, 1973).

stood for, a majority consider him a hero. Most rank him second only to Martin Luther King, Jr., in importance to contemporary blacks.[10]

Although the themes of black power and separatism have been muted among black Muslims, Islam remains a viable alternative for American blacks. It shares much with Christianity without being identified with slavery and oppression.

Christians and Muslims in the United States

There are not a lot of data on the response of the predominant Christian community of faith to Muslims in the United States, but one author has identified three relatively clear patterns of response. (1) Some accept Muslims as a part of the pluralistic American religious landscape, respecting their values and beliefs and including them as an equal part of the religious community. The differences are not ignored, but respected. The goal is to develop "a common life, in which all can share equally, where religious identity is not blurred by syncretism or a superficial romanticism about similarities, and within which all can be faithful to their particular religious calling." Many of the consensus Christian churches have taken this position.

(2) Some Christians view Muslims as an opportunity for making converts. The overall view here can be summarized this way: "For this category of church people the most important issue in their relationships with people of other faiths remains conversion." Some in this category take a very negative approach to those of other faiths and to Islam in particular (World Vision is an example). Others show a genuine sensitivity to other communities of faith (Southern Baptist literature falls into this category). In either case, the object is conversion.

(3) A third category is in between the other two. People and churches in this category try to take seriously both the claims that American religious pluralism makes and the exclusive claims that their religion makes against competing claims. Rather than discount either, they have chosen to live with the tension between the competing claims. The Reformed Church in America and some Lutherans illustrate this position.[11]

All but the first of these positions involves at least some unwillingness to admit non-Christians to full participation in the human family of faith. The second sees non-Christians only as objects for conversion, whether the approach is "hard" or "soft." The third is much more open, but retains its exclusive emphasis in the end. In either case, those who are outside the Christian community of faith are not allowed to be fully neighbors in the community of religions. This does not apply to Muslims alone. The same pattern of response applies whatever the non-Christian group or individual is.

---

[10]*Newsweek*, November 16, 1992, p. 68.

[11]Byron L. Haines, "Perspectives of American Churches on Islam and the Muslim Community in the United States: An Analysis of Some Official and Unofficial Statements," in *The Muslims of America*, ed. Haddad, pp. 39–52.

HINDUISM

What we now call Hinduism began in India, sometime between 2000 and 1500 years before the lifetime of Jesus. Unlike the religions you have studied so far, it has no single founder. The word **Hinduism** is an umbrella term for a vast collection of religious beliefs and practices that nonetheless have enough in common to warrant grouping them together. Indians themselves often use the term **Sanatana Dharma** for their religion. It means "original religion," since Indians believe that theirs is a form of religion that has existed since the dawn of humanity. Hinduism is, however, quite different from the religions that have been discussed thus far. One author, commenting on the challenges of teaching about Hinduism, calls it the "ism that isn't." He continues,

> Hindus . . . have little interest in specifying a single line of teaching authority that ought to be embraced by all. . . . Hinduism has no central authority, no unifying scripture, no verbal formula to which all its adherents give regular assent. . . . Yet . . . it still has a coherence that separates Hindus from other religious people.[12]

In what follows, you will learn the basic outlines of the Hindu worldview and then be introduced to some of the Hindu groups in the United States.

As noted above, there is no single sacred writing that all Hindus regard as equally central. The **Vedas**, however, are the oldest of the sacred writings and have influenced the entire development of Hinduism. The **Bhagavad-Gita** is an important devotional classic, and is the best known and best loved sacred writing among Hindus.

The Hindu Worldview

Whereas the Semitic religions distinguish clearly between God as Creat*or* and everything else as creat*ion*, Hindus do not use this distinction. Rather, **every living thing is a manifestation of the sacred**. The divine can be seen and known in everything that is, and everything that is can be seen as a part of the divine. This also means that, fundamentally, there can be no sharp separation between things—between the divine and the human, or between people and all other beings.

Another distinctive feature of Hinduism is the related concepts of reincarnation and karma. **Reincarnation** means (1) that a person's present life was preceded by other lives, and will likewise be followed by other lives. It also means (2) that these lifetimes do not happen randomly, but are connected. The way that life is lived in one lifetime determines the quality of the next incarnation. **Karma** is the moral law of cause and effect that links lifetimes together. The principle of karma states that every action has a reaction. In our own culture, even if

---

[12]John Stratton Hawley, "Teaching the Hindu Tradition," in *Teaching the Introductory Course in Religious Studies: A Sourcebook*, ed. Mark Juergensmeyer (Atlanta, GA: Scholars Press, 1991), pp. 37–38.

we ourselves are not a part of the Judeo-Christian-Islamic tradition, most of us are accustomed to thinking in terms of rewards and punishments: good deeds will be rewarded and evil ones punished. Karma, by contrast, is a moral law that operates analogously to natural laws such as gravity. Certain results inevitably follow certain actions. As described in one of Hinduism's sacred writings,

> According as one acts, according as one conducts himself, so does he become. . . . As is his desire, such is his resolve; as is his resolve, such the action he performs; what action he performs, that he procures for himself.[13]

I often tell students in my classes that if they spend Friday night in the "Chug" (a local bar that caters mainly to students), the way they feel on Saturday is karma. Their roommates' reaction, however, may be punishment!

Belief in reincarnation brings up the question of what it means to be a person, according to Hindus. First, we must **distinguish between our empirical self and our Real Self**. Our **empirical self** is what we think we are, what ordinary experience tells us we are. For most of us, it probably includes our physical body, our mind and personality, and our subconscious. All these aspects of us are individual and personal: they pertain to us as individuals, and as personal beings. The **Real Self**, on the other hand, is that of the divine within each and every person. It is not personal, nor is it individual. The Real Self is what moves from lifetime to lifetime throughout successive incarnations:

> Just as a person, having cast off old garments, puts on other, new ones, even so does the embodied One [i.e., Real Self], having cast off old bodies, take on other, new ones. . . . For, to one who is born, death is certain, and certain is birth to one who has died. . . . As in this body, there are for the embodied One childhood, youth, and old age, even so is there the taking on of another body.[14]
>
> As a goldsmith, taking a piece of gold, reduces it to another, more beautiful form, just so the Real Self, striking down this body and dispelling its ignorance, makes for itself another and more beautiful form.[15]

The human problem, as it is expressed by Hindus, is not sin and disobedience (as in Judaism, Christianity, and Islam), but **ignorance and illusion**. We fail to understand the real nature of reality and of ourselves, and, in that misunderstanding, act in ways that reinforce the illusion of separateness. As long as we think and act as though we *are* our empirical selves, as long as we think and act as though we are separate from other beings and from the universe itself, we remain trapped in the cycle of death and rebirth.

The goal of human life is escape from the cycle of death and rebirth. Throughout however many lifetimes it requires, a person comes increasingly

---

[13] *Brihadaranyaka Upanishad.*
[14] *Bhagavad-Gita.*
[15] *Brihadaranyaka Upanishad.*

closer to grasping the unity of all things, including the Real Self, in the divine. Eventually, when that unity is fully grasped, incarnation ceases and the Real Self is reunited with the divine, which, of course, it never really left. Most Hindus describe this as an unbroken communion between the Real Self and the divine, in which the distinction between the two is preserved while the separation is overcome. Others, however, prefer to picture it as a complete merger between the Real Self and the divine, in which both separation and distinction are overcome.

A final feature of Hinduism that deserves mention here is its recognition of the **validity of all religious paths**. As there are any number of ways to climb a mountain, say most Hindus, so there are many paths to reunion with the divine.

Three Hindu Ways of Liberation

Within itself as well, Hinduism offers people more than one way to seek release and liberation. These ways are not exclusive; people usually follow more than one, accenting one over the others and perhaps changing throughout a lifetime. People differ in their personalities, in their stage and station in life, and one method will not be best for all.

One very popular way is **devotion to a god or goddess**. By increasingly identifying with their chosen god or goddess, people increase their intuitive grasp of the oneness of themselves and the divine. Many Hindus worship **Shiva**, and many others are devotees of **Krishna** or **Vishnu**, gods whose concern for human beings is paramount. Others are devotees of the **Great Goddess**, who takes many forms. Deities are worshipped by prayer and offerings to their images at home altars and in temples. Deity worship personalizes the divine, giving the devotee the opportunity for a warmly emotional relationship with the sacred.

Hindu religious art abounds with images of deities, both pictures and statues. Statues are especially important. It may be difficult for you to understand the role that images of gods and goddesses play in Hinduism. For Hindus, *seeing* the divine is a basic way of experiencing communion with the sacred. The divine is present precisely *as* the image, giving itself for worship. These are not idols. The clay or the brass of the statue is not worshipped, but the deity whom it portrays and makes present to the devotee is who is worshipped.

Another very popular way to seek liberation is through **duty**, **work**, or **action**. To follow this way means to do what is called for by one's position in life, without allowing oneself to become attached to the results of the action. Scripture says that people have a right to their actions, but not to the fruits of those actions. Attachment to the results of what we do binds us in the cycle of reincarnation. To whatever extent we can give up attachment to the results of our actions, we can lessen the grip of karma, according to Hindu belief.

Dharma is an important concept here. Dharma refers to the underlying order of the universe and also to the way that a person must live in order to fit into that order. In India, the caste system plays a central role in determining a person's dharma. It is not nearly as much of a consideration among Hindus in the

United States. Nonetheless, the basic idea that each person has a particular place in the overall scheme of things remains. Lessening karma's grip, then, is a matter of becoming aware of one's dharma and following it to the best of one's ability.

Most Hindus focus on devotion and appropriate action as ways to liberation. In addition, liberation can be won through **intuitive knowledge and insight** gained through study and meditation. The scriptures are studied, not with the goal of intellectual knowledge but with the goal that their message will become the truth of the Hindu's entire being. The study and contemplation of the meaning of sacred texts is accompanied by **yoga**, a discipline that works through the body and mind to enable the adept to realize the sought-for unity. Yoga begins with bodily postures and progresses through control of breathing and several deepening stages of concentration and meditation. This approach to gaining liberation requires time, discipline, and the capability to deal with difficult texts. It is clearly not for everyone. At the same time, many Hindus do incorporate elements of yogic practice into their daily routine.

Women in Hinduism

Hinduism's attitude toward women has always been highly ambivalent. On the one hand, great attention is paid to the Great Goddess in all her manifestations. The major gods have their female consorts. Female energy is important in the attainment of liberation in certain approaches to meditation. In Vedic times, women were educated, participated in religious rituals, and were recognized as scholars, poets, and teachers.

On the other hand, the particular way in which the female and male principles are related in the sacred makes it clear that the "male principle is necessary if the female principle is to be fertile and good. Alone, the female principle tends to be evil and dangerous." Further, docility and service to one's husband are honored above all else. Arranged marriages often took place when a girl was very young, even before puberty. In the classical period, the "most concise index of women's place . . . is the traditional common belief that no woman of any caste could gain salvation, except in a future life, when she had been reborn as a man."[16] The horrifying practice of a widow's burning herself on her husband's funeral pyre (now outlawed in India) highlights the dreadful situation of a woman without a man.

Hindu women in the United States in the 1990s are primarily cosmopolitan and educated. They move in social circles that include professionals, administrators, and managers. Their lives are less determined by the Hindu tradition regarding women than by their position in American society. Temple leadership is usually limited to male priests, with women having a role to play as teachers of children. Typically, women are the ones who maintain the tradition of worship at a home altar for the benefit of their families.

---

[16]Denise Lardner Carmody, *Women and World Religions* (Nashville, TN: Abingdon Press, 1979), chap. 4.

Hindu Life and Worship

In many ways, we have already been discussing Hindu life. Distinctions between religion and the rest of life are alien to Hinduism, so that the pathways to liberation described above are also descriptions of the lifestyles of Hindu people. Here, I want to concentrate on the ethical dimension of Hinduism and then on Hindu worship.

The **moral life** is one that coincides with the natural order of the universe, the dharma. What it means to live by the dharma differs, depending on a person's place in the society, stage in life, and gender. There are also ethical prescriptions and proscriptions that are constant.

One listing of what it means to live a good life includes **self-restraint, giving or self-sacrifice**, and **compassion**. Narrow self-interest should be set aside for the good of the whole. Having set aside self-interest, a person will not be blown about by the winds of emotion. Such a person is described in the *Bhagavad-Gita* as one who is "without hatred of any creature, friendly and compassionate without possessiveness and self-pride, equable in happiness and unhappiness alike . . . dependent upon nothing, disinterested and unworried . . . who neither hates nor rejoices, does not mourn or desire, and gives up both good and evil" (12:13–17).

Compassion for all beings on the Earth is a central value. To feel compassion is not enough; people must act with compassion and seek the good of all. The *Mahabharata* says that the person will be happy who "abstains from injuring others, is truthful in speech, is honest with all creatures, who practices forgiveness, and who is never heedless."

Nonviolence in all thoughts and actions is another central value. Many Hindus are vegetarians who eat no meat, and some avoid eggs as well. Hinduism is probably best known in this regard from the teachings of Mohandas Gandhi, whose commitment to nonviolence and the power of truth helped to gain India's independence from British rule. Gandhi's teachings, in turn, profoundly influenced Dr. Martin Luther King, Jr. and the practice of civil disobedience in the civil rights movement and similar movements that followed it. As embodied in Gandhi and later in King, nonviolence means more than just abstention from acts of violence. It means more even than avoiding violent thoughts. Violence as part of solutions to problems must be replaced with a positive commitment to problem solving without violence in thought, speech, or action.

Other moral values include **truthfulness, chastity, not being greedy, contentment, the study of sacred texts, and care in diet**. These are among the "moral preliminaries" required of those who practice yoga and have become part of the broader Hindu ethical tradition. Marriage and family are very important.

Hindu worship life revolves around the **home altar** that is an important part of most Hindus' homes. The altar will probably have a statue or statues of the chosen deity or deities. After ceremonial cleansing, people make offerings of fruit, incense, or flowers to their deities. They see the deity in the image and in return are seen by the deity. The food offered to the deity may then be eaten by the worshipper as a part of the deity's blessing. Some people perform this ritual, or **puja**, twice daily, while some perform it only in the mornings. While approximately 75 percent of Hindu women perform daily devotions for the benefit of their families, only about half of Hindu men do so. Puja is also performed in **temples**, where it is more elaborate.

Each god and goddess has a festival day, and these are celebrated with worship at the temple. Other **religious holidays** are celebrated as well. Often, weekly worship is also held, usually fitted into the common Sunday morning time period. It resembles worship at the home altar, with the addition of readings from sacred texts, a sermon or lecture, and devotional songs. Many temples in the United States have become social centers for the Indian community, as well, and sponsor a number of social events, in addition to holding classes for children and adults. The priest associated with the temple—who may hold another job as well—also performs **life-cycle rites** such as birth rituals, weddings, and funerals for Hindu families. Hindus who do not live close enough to attend a temple regularly can request that puja or other services be performed at a distant temple in return for a financial contribution. While most temples in India are dedicated to one primary deity, those in the United States are often dedicated to several.

Hindus may accommodate to United States religious culture in other ways, as well. Some Hindus celebrate a five-day festival of Ganesha's Gift Giving on December 21–25. *Ganesha* is a deity, usually depicted with the head of an elephant, who is regarded as a remover of obstacles. Families may build a shrine to Ganesha in their homes and decorate it with pine boughs, ornaments, tinsel, and lights. Christmas trees, Santa Claus, and other religious and secular symbols are not supposed to be used. Gifts are placed before the shrine daily and worship is offered to Ganesha. After the final puja on December 25th, the gifts are opened with great festivity and celebration. Gifts are also given to employees and employers, as well as friends.[17]

Hindus in the United States

There has been much less detailed research done on Hindus in the United States than there has been on Muslims. The number of Hindus remains quite small—less than 0.5 percent of the population. Nearly all Hindus are either immigrants or descendants of immigrants from Hindu countries; fewer Westerners have become Hindus than have embraced either Islam or Buddhism. As you saw with Arab Americans, most Asian Americans are Christians. With a few exceptions, Hindus have not sought converts. Most live in urban areas. The largest concentrations are in the Los Angeles, San Francisco, New York City, and Chicago metropolitan areas. Many Hindus now living in the United States are professionals, intellectuals, and upper-level management personnel.

There are a number of Hindu groups in the United States, many of

---

[17]*Hinduism Today*, 14, no. 12 (December 1992), p. 16.

which are quite small. The three discussed represent different emphases in Hinduism.

The **Vedanta Society** was founded in 1894 by Swami Vivekananda. It was the first Hindu organization in the United States, and is arguably the most influential on an intellectual level, although it is neither the largest nor the best known. Each Vedanta Center in the United States is a branch of the Ramakrishna Order, the monastic organization that Vivekananda founded in India.

Vedanta seeks to incorporate the methods and ideals of all Hindu movements. It describes itself as "a federation of faiths and a commonwealth of spiritual concepts." It supports all the pathways to liberation that were described above. Vedanta teaches four basic principles:

1. Truth is one, although known by many names. Likewise, God is One, although worshipped in many forms.
2. People in their essential nature are divine.
3. The goal of human life is to realize this divinity.
4. There are innumerable ways to realize this divinity.

The Vedanta Society of New York summarizes Vedanta this way:

Vedanta is a way of living and realizing. It gives full freedom to each individual to evolve morally and spiritually according to his or her own faith and conviction. It includes various truths found in all religions of the world, including the teachings of the worlds great saints and sages. In Vedanta is found a reconciliation of religion with science, of faith with reason. A Vedantin is a seeker of truth who accepts and respects all religions as paths to the same goal.[18]

Vedanta Centers offer weekly worship that is similar to that already described for Hindu temples. They usually offer classes in various aspects of Hinduism as well. The leader, or *swami*, who is invited by a local Board of Trustees to come from the Ramakrishna Order in India, also gives private instruction to students. The organization also operates Vedanta Press, a source for Hindu religious literature and other relevant books.

The primary embodiment of Hindu devotionalism in the United States is the daily and weekly worship that Hindus perform in their homes and in temples. The **International Society for Krishna Consciousness (also known as ISKCON or the Hare Krishna Movement)** is an organizational embodiment of Hindu devotionalism. It was founded in the United States by His Divine Grace A. C. Bhaktivedanta Swami Prabhupada (1896–1977) in 1965. Its Indian origins go back to a Bengali saint named Caitanya Mahaprabhu (1486–1533). Caitanya taught an interpretation of Hinduism that made Vishnu the one high god and Krishna his supreme incarnation. The Krishna Consciousness movement emphasizes union with the divine attained through ecstatic devotion to Krishna.

---

[18]"What Is Vedanta?" Vedanta Society of New York, n.d.

The Movement describes its mission as

> to promote the well being of society by teaching the science of Krishna con-
> sciousness according to the *Bhagavad-Gita* and other ancient Vedic scriptures of
> India.[19]

Members follow five rules of conduct: (1) No meat, fish, or eggs may be
eaten. (2) No intoxicating drinks or plants may be used, including tobacco, alcohol, coffee and tea. (3) There must be no gambling. (4) Illicit sexual activity
(defined as any sexual activity between people who are not married to each other,
or marital sex except for procreation) is also prohibited. Finally, (5) the name of
Krishna is to be chanted daily in a prescribed ritual.

Devotees who choose to devote full time to the movement and live in the
temples follow a rigid schedule of devotion and work. There are also opportunities for those who cannot or do not wish to enter this fully into the community.
Devotees, whether living in the temple or not, give very high priority to *sankir-
tan*, daily chanting of the **mantra**. Mantra chanting has been a part of Hindu religious practice since its earliest times. *Mantras*—spiritual phrases—help to focus the mind and are believed to have power in and of themselves to align the
devotee's consciousness with the deity. Temples are always open to visitors, who
are welcomed into a world that may make them feel as if they have been magi-
cally transported to India itself (Figure 11–2).

The following beliefs are affirmed by nearly all Krishna devotees:

1. By sincere spiritual practice, we can be free of anxiety and experience the bliss of
   pure consciousness in this lifetime.
2. We are our eternal souls, not our perishable bodies, and since Krishna is our common father, all are brothers and sisters.
3. Krishna is the Godhead, the energy that sustains the whole of the universe. He is
   eternal, all-knowing, omnipresent, all-powerful, and all-attractive Personality of
   the Godhead.
4. The absolute truth can be found in the scriptures of all the world's great religions.
   The *Bhagavad-Gita* ("Song of the Lord Krishna") is regarded as the oldest revealed
   scripture and as the actual words of God.
5. Vedic knowledge must be learned from a true, unselfish spiritual master.
6. Food is to be prepared for and offered to Krishna before we eat. The acts of pre-
   paring and consuming food thus become worship.
7. All actions are to be performed as offerings to the Lord Krishna, with nothing being done merely for sense gratification.
8. The recommended means for attaining consciousness of and union with the godhead in this age is the chanting of the holy names of the Lord. The Hare Krishna
   mantra, a song of praise to the Lord Krishna, is the best way for most people to do
   this. It goes like this:

---

[19]"International Society for Krishna Consciousness Fact Sheet," 1990.

Figure 11–2 Congregational members of the International Society for Krishna Consciousness live and work in the general community, practicing Krishna consciousness in their own homes and attending the temple on a regular basis. (*Photo courtesy of the International Society for Krishna Consciousness.*)

Hare Krishna, Hare Krishna (Praise to Krishna, Praise to Krishna)
Krishna Krishna, Hare Hare (Krishna, Krishna, Praise, Praise).
Hare Rama, Hare Rama (Praise to Rama, Praise to Rama)
Rama Rama, Hare Hare! (Rama, Rama, Praise, Praise)

The *a* in Rama is soft, as *ah*, and *hare* is pronounced *ha-ray*. *Rama* is one of Vishnu's incarnations, the hero of the epic poem the *Ramayana*. The Krishna Consciousness Movement teaches that this one mantra is the mantra for everyone in this present age, rather than following the more traditional practice that requires that mantras be given individually by gurus[20] and be kept secret.

According to the founder, chanting the name of Krishna using this mantra conveys all the benefits of the other Hindu practices, and much more rapidly: "Simply by chanting the holy name of God, one can attain that perfect self-realization which was attained by the yoga system. . . . by performance of great sacrifices . . . and by large-scale temple worship."[21]

There are about fifty ISKCON temples in the United States, as well as six farm communities and six vegetarian restaurants. The organization claims about

[20]*Guru* is an Indian word that means a religious teacher and mentor.
[21]A. C. Bhaktivendanta Swami Prabhupada, *Krsna Consciousness* (New York: The Macmillan Publishing Company, 1970), p. 12.

3,000 fully initiated members and an additional 500,000 lay members who participate in temple activities at least monthly. The number of Indian participants has increased, and the number of non-Indian devotees has dropped considerably.[22]

Besides the temples, farm communities, and restaurants, the Society operates the Bhaktivedanta Book Trust for the publication of literature on Indian philosophy and religion. It also publishes *Back To Godhead: The Magazine of the Hare Krishna Movement*. Its "Food for Life" program distributes meals at no cost to those who need food. This program is an outgrowth of the custom of sponsoring a free meal every Sunday at the temples, which began in the very early days of the movement.

The rigorous monastic life and the sometimes aggressive solicitation of Krishna's American devotees have marked them off as distinctive and unusual. Their way of life is a small slice of India in a very non-Indian culture. There can be little doubt, however, about the sincerity and devotion of these followers of an Indian deity whose main attribute is his desire to help struggling human beings attain release from spiritual suffering.

There are many different Hindu groups in the United States that are based on some form of yoga. **The Self-Realization Fellowship** is typical of these. It was founded by a Bengali Indian, Paramahansa Yogananda, in 1925. Yogananda (1893–1952) taught in this country for more than thirty years.

Yogananda taught the classical form of yogic meditation outlined in the *Yoga Sutras* of Patanjali. His teaching and the practices that he developed are based on the traditional Hindu belief that the divine is within each person and can be experienced directly through meditation. Having experienced it in meditation, people can come to manifest it increasingly in everyday life. According to the Self-Realization Fellowship:

> The science of Yoga offers a direct means of stilling the natural turbulence of thoughts and restlessness of body which prevent us from knowing what we really are. By practicing the step-by-step methods of Yoga . . . we come to know our oneness with the Infinite Intelligence, Power, and Joy which gives life to all and which is the essence of our own Self. . . . [The] inner fulfillment we seek *does* exist and *can* be attained. In actuality, all the knowledge, creativity, love, joy, and peace we are looking for are right within us, the very essence of our beings. All we have to do is realize this.[23]

The Self-Realization Fellowship emphasizes that the techniques they teach and practice do not have to be accepted on authority or faith, but can be tested in the life of each person. These techniques also accord with the discoveries of

[22]J. Gordon Melton, *The Encyclopedic Handbook of Cults in America: Revised and Updated Edition* (New York: Garland Publishing, Inc., 1992), pp. 237–38.

[23]*Undreamed-of Possibilities: An Introduction to Self-Realization: The Teachings of Paramahansa Yogananda* (Los Angeles: Self-Realization Fellowship, 1982), pp. 5 and 3.

Western science. It is a scientific method for self-discovery and realization. Awareness and consciousness, energy, are withdrawn from outward concerns and redirected inward toward the goal of self-realization. Yogananda taught, and the Fellowship he founded continues to teach, the essential unity of all paths to liberation—wisdom, action, yoga, and devotion. He also taught that all religions are valid pathways to the same goal.

There are eight temples and about 150 smaller centers in the United States, as well as a program of correspondence study. The centers offer classes, workshops, and weekly devotional experiences. Members frequently greet one another with the traditional Hindu greeting, **Namaste**, which means "the deity in me greets the deity in you." Besides laypeople who participate in the Centers' activities, there are "renunciants" who have chosen to pursue liberation more arduously and remain celibate, spending quite a lot of time in meditation and study.

BUDDHISM

The Buddhist story begins with a Hindu, **Siddhartha Gautama** (563–483 B.C.E.). His followers came to call him "**the Buddha**," meaning "**the Enlightened One**." As a young man, Gautama became very distressed over the inevitable suffering of human life—aging, sickness, and death, among other things. Although born to a noble life, he renounced privilege and set out in search of a resolution to the spiritual unrest that plagued him. According to Buddhist tradition, he found what he sought during meditation, discovering the way to release from the burden of suffering (Figure 11–3). He then went about teaching what he had learned to other people and founding an organization around his teachings.

Figure 11–3 Statues of the Buddha show him in serene meditation.

Like Hinduism, Buddhism has a number of different sacred writings. The **Pali Canon** records what Buddhists take to be the teachings of the Buddha himself after his Enlightenment. Its importance is agreed upon by the great majority of Buddhists. Beyond that, various Buddhist subgroups accept other scriptures as valid.

Basic Buddhist Teachings

The Buddhist worldview is different than that of Hinduism in some important respects, although there are similarities as well. As do Hindus, Buddhists affirm that the principles of **reincarnation** and **karma** operate in every human life. Where Buddhists and Hindus differ is that Buddhists do not believe that there is a Real Self that reincarnates. Rather than seeing the universe as myriad manifestations of an eternal, unchanging spiritual reality, Buddhists see it as a vast, interconnected process. Buddhists also teach that **there is an intrinsic, moral order of the universe**, akin to the Hindu concept of dharma.

Dependent arising and impermanence are central attributes of everything that is. **Dependent arising** (sometimes "dependent co-arising") simply means that everything that is arises from something else. Nothing exists in and of itself, without connections to other things. One thing leads to another in an unbroken chain. **Impermanence** points to the Buddhist belief that everything changes. Everything in the universe, including ourselves, is part of this vast, interconnected process. What underlies the universe as we observe it is not the sacred absolute of Hinduism, but constant change, constant becoming.

Buddhists believe that there is no eternal, unchanging Real Self. If we pay close attention to ourselves, Buddhists say, we will discover that **we are a constantly changing collection of attributes**, such as consciousness, perceptions, feelings, physical matter, and impulses to act in certain ways. There is no Real Self that can be found underlying this change.

This leads to a **reinterpretation of reincarnation**, because *nothing* goes through the rebirth process. Buddhists simply say that each lifetime is connected to the ones before it and will be connected to those that come after it in a **chain of causation**. The analogy of lighting the wick of one candle from the flame on another is often used. Nothing is transmitted from candle to candle, but the flame of the second is unarguably connected to the flame of the first.

A basic statement of Buddhist belief, attributed to the Buddha himself, is the **Four Noble Truths**. It is an application of the foregoing interpretation of the world to human life and the human problem. We'll take the Truths one at a time.

1.   **All of life is marked by suffering**. The Buddha was not, and Buddhists are not, long-faced pessimists without joy and happiness. Quite the contrary! What Gautama had in mind here is that, no matter how good life is, there is always an element of dissatisfaction, suffering, or basic "out-of-whackness" about it. Birth and death, he said, cause suffering on either end of the life cycle. In between, there is illness, having to deal with things we do not like and being sepa-

rated from things that we do like. There is wanting more than we have, or wanting something different than what we have. Think about the ways that this is true in your own life, remembering that the Buddha's analysis applies to all people, not just to Buddhists.

2. **This suffering or dissatisfaction comes from self-centered, inappropriate clinging.** In a world of constant change and impermanence, anything that we try to cling to will slip out of our grasp, or change, and we ourselves will change. There is nothing that will support the weight of our clinging.

When we want other than what we have, or expect someone to be different than they are, we illustrate what Buddhists feel is inappropriate attachment. Examples are easy to come by. We cling to images of ourselves that are outdated or that weren't ever really accurate. We cling to the image we have of someone close to us, and then they disappoint us when they don't conform to that image.

3. **To stop the suffering, then, stop the inappropriate clinging.** By eliminating the cause, the effect is eliminated. When we stop thinking and acting as if there were anything that we could reasonably expect to sustain our clinging, the dissatisfaction that comes from frustrated desire stops too. When we cling and act in other ways that are self-centered, we act as though we are separate selves trying to hang onto other separate beings. Since everything is already interconnected, Buddhism teaches, there is no need for clinging.

4. The Buddha proposed a method for accomplishing this goal. Buddhists call it the **Noble Eightfold Path.** Because the Buddha became enlightened by his own efforts, traditional Buddhists teach that people are responsible for bringing about their own liberation from suffering. The first two steps on the path refer to **wisdom**: right understanding and right motivation. Right understanding means increasing our ability to see things as they really are, changing and impermanent. Right motivation means sincere desire to work on bringing about change, steady effort, and determination. The next several steps have to do with **morality**. Right speech means to speak truthfully and compassionately, without exaggeration, harshness, or rudeness of speech. Right action means observing the basics of Buddhist morality. Beyond that, it means acting with a balance of wisdom and compassion, always seeking the good. Right occupation means that one's occupation (which takes up a significant part of one's time) should not involve violating the moral precepts, and should be such that it encourages peace and harmony, again striving for the good of all beings. Right effort means steady attention to weeding out negative and unhelpful ways of thinking and acting and replacing them with positive and helpful ways. The emphasis here is on constancy; the Path is a map for minute-by-minute existence, not for occasional use. The last two steps have to do with **meditation**. Right mindfulness means being aware in every moment. Right meditation deals directly with meditation techniques. Buddhists do not practice meditation as a way of going inward to find a Real Self (which, remember, does not exist, according to Buddhism). Different schools of thought teach different techniques. What unites them is that meditation is used as a way of being fully aware in every moment,

then letting that moment go, as a way of calming and focusing the mind and bringing home the fleeting nature of everything.

Buddhists believe that there can be an end to the cycle of death and rebirth. This is the ultimate goal of the Eightfold Path. The Buddhist word for that goal is **Nirvana**, a word that refers to the extinction of a flame from lack of fuel. The painful fire of suffering can be extinguished by withdrawing the fuel of attachment upon which it feeds. The Buddha did not speak very much about Nirvana, believing that doing so was not useful in the search for liberation. For a person who finds Nirvana in this lifetime, it certainly means living without dissatisfaction, living with nonattachment and thus with complete peace. It means the elimination of anything that separates the individual from the interconnectedness of all that is, the end of the illusion of isolated existence. When someone who has reached this advanced state of spiritual awareness dies, he or she escapes from reincarnation.

Another summary of what is of central importance in Buddhism is the **Three Treasures** (also, **Three Refuges**, or **Three Jewels**). Although there is no affirmation of faith that is required to become a Buddhist nor any set formula that makes a person a Buddhist, the Refuges may be said to define what being a Buddhist means. "**I take refuge in the Buddha.**" *To take refuge in the Buddha* means to place one's trust and confidence in the Buddha having become the Enlightened One. For traditional Buddhists, especially, the Buddha is a human being, nothing more. Thus, the fact that he, through his own effort and determination, was able to achieve liberation means that *any* person can do so, provided they are willing to make the effort. The Buddha's humanity also means that the Buddha nature is to be found in all persons, as well as other beings. Following the way mapped out by Siddhartha Gautama is a means to realize one's own Buddha nature more fully. "**I take refuge in the Dharma.**" Buddhists use the word *Dharma* to refer primarily to the Buddha's teaching. *To take refuge in the Dharma*, then, means to have confidence in the Buddha's teachings as a true analysis of reality and as the way to accomplish what he accomplished. "**I take refuge in the Sangha.**" *Sangha* has two levels of meaning. Narrowly, it is the community of Buddhist monks. For traditional Buddhists, liberation is possible only after one has become a monk. Monks work for liberation full time, and they symbolize the goal of Buddhists. On a broader level, the *sangha* means the entire community of people, living and dead, who have walked the path to enlightenment mapped out by Gautama. Buddhists live in the certainty that they are not alone in their quest for enlightenment. Others have been this way before them.

There are three major divisions within world Buddhism. **Theravada** is traditional Buddhism, believed by its adherents to be the closest to the actual teachings of the Buddha. It is most common in Southeast Asian countries. This approach to Buddhist life places the greatest emphasis on the role of self-effort in gaining enlightenment. As a result, it also values full-time monastic life over lay practice. **Mahayana** places more emphasis on lay Buddhism. Mahayanists also teach that **Bodhisattvas** are beings whose own achievements could enable them to enter Nirvana and escape the round of death and rebirth. However, they have chosen not to do so, remaining in an earthly body to help others attain liberation. Mahayana is the most common form of Buddhism in China and Japan. Tibetan, or **Vajrayana**, Buddhism makes use of visualization, chanting, sacred drawings, and various types of meditation to enable the realization of the Buddha nature within each person.

Buddhist Morality and Worship

Buddhist morality has already been mentioned as one of the steps on the Eightfold Path. I want to enlarge on that point. One standard statement of Buddhist morality is the **Five Precepts:**

1. **Do not kill.** Buddhists expand this precept to include not harming any living being, insofar as it is possible to avoid such harm. Positively, it means doing all that one can for the good of all beings on the earth. Nonviolence and noninjury are central in any Buddhist system of ethics.

2. **Do not steal.** Again, Buddhists understand this as going beyond outright stealing. It also means not taking advantage, not appropriating anything in any way that does not belong to you. Avoiding paying legitimate taxes is another example, as is borrowing and not returning an item.

3. **Refrain from wrongful sexual behavior.** Complete abstinence outside of marriage is the rule. Sexual activity is regarded as appropriate only for married couples. Wrongful sexual behavior includes any behavior that degrades another person, as well as sexual behavior that might spread disease.

4. **Do not lie.** Expanded, this includes refraining from saying anything that is hurtful, such as slander and gossip, rude and harsh speech, impolite language, running down other people, as well as idle chatter when silence would be better.

5. Finally, Buddhists are told to **avoid the use of intoxicants** of all kinds, such as alcohol and intoxicating drugs. Using them clouds a person's mind and also increases the likelihood that other ethical principles will be violated.

Buddhists link **wisdom and compassion** together in determining which actions are good. The same word is used for "mind" as for "heart." Wisdom without compassion becomes cold, sterile rationality; compassion without the wisdom to use it skillfully becomes ineffective.

Buddhism presses home the importance of cultivating proper attitudes and a proper frame of mind, so that outward actions flow freely from internal dispositions. Four attitudes are especially valued. People ought to have an attitude of **friendship** toward all beings. This will then lead to **kindness**, the resolve to remember the kindness of others and to increase the kindness with which we deal with others. **Compassion** is the will to always work for the happiness of other beings. Compassion is not pity. *Pity* is a condescending attitude, whereas *compassion* regards all beings as equals. Finally, **impartiality** means that we will have these attitudes toward all, equally, without basing our attitudes on qualities that we like or dislike in others.

These attitudes are summed up in the **Six Paramitas**, another statement of how Buddhists try to live. The first, **giving**, encourages an unselfish spirit toward all beings, without regard for whether one thinks of them as friends, enemies, or strangers. **Morality** means acting in ways that manifest the Buddha nature that is within. **Patience** encourages calmness and patience in the face of life's troubles, maintaining a good spirit in spite of difficulties. **Joyful effort** means the maintenance of steady effort in meditation and in the other Paramitas, avoiding indolence and changeability. **Meditation** means taking time daily for meditation. It goes beyond the time devoted specifically to meditation, however, in that it includes being mindful and fully aware of whatever one does, being wholly "in the present moment." Finally, **wisdom** points to the importance of a sound rational understanding of the basic truths of Buddhism.

Like Hindus, Buddhists often have a small **altar or shrine in their homes**. A Buddha statue represents the historical Buddha and helps devotees focus on the Buddha nature within themselves, as well. Other statues may represent specific aspects of the Buddha. There is often a bodhisattva statue, too. Flowers symbolize enlightenment and a candle or altar light symbolizes the light of wisdom. Incense is often offered in gratitude for the Three Refuges and other blessings. An offering of water represents cleansing and a food offering represents giving and the willingness to share what one has with other beings.

Buddhists who live where they can go to a **temple** participate in activities that center around the natural rhythms of the lunar calendar. The holy days occur at the new moon, the full moon, and eight days after each, making them about a week apart. Attendance at the temple is not required, and some Buddhists participate much more than others. There is a religious new year festival in the spring, and the Buddha's birthday is widely celebrated. Temples also offer classes, special rituals for the passages of life, and serve as social centers.

Like Hindus and other non-Christians in the United States, Buddhists may accommodate to the major Christian religious holidays that are part of the culture. For example, Shasta Abbey in California (Zen Buddhist) celebrates December 24 as the Festival of the Eve of the Buddha's Enlightenment and December 25 as the Festival of the Buddha's Enlightenment.

Women and Buddhism

Traditional ideas about women and women's capabilities persisted in Buddhism even as in Hinduism. At the same time, Buddhism allowed for the establishment of orders of nuns. The rules established for female sanghas, however, guaranteed submission of nuns to monks, and ensured that the number of nuns would remain small. That they existed, and continue to exist, however, is significant. Although men controlled the writing and codification of sacred texts (as in all the world's religions), the question of the legitimacy of women's quest for nirvana and full participation in religion arises again and again.

One of the ways that Buddhism has changed as it has come West has been that greater gender equality in the West has forced the issue within the Buddhist community. American women have been and continue to be interested in Buddhism, and there is evidence that their increased participation, especially in leadership positions, is contributing distinctive accents to the practice of American Buddhism. These include

(1) minimizing power differences and bringing warmth to all relationships, (2) working with emotions and the body, (3) group activity that promotes sharing experiences and open communication; "effort" and "striving" are being replaced by "healing" and "openness," and (4) an activist orientation based on a vision that the essential fact about the universe is interrelatedness.[24]

The influence of women in American Buddhism leads to changes in Buddhist thought, as well. Buddhist theologian Rita Gross enumerates four changes that she foresees in Buddhist thought as a result of the increasing presence of trained and respected female leaders and thinkers in the United States:

Greater emphasis on Buddhism as a path to freedom within the world rather than escape from the world: Rather than freedom from rebirth (world-denying), Buddhism offers freedom from suffering within worldly life. Impermanent, conditioned existence itself is not the problem, but the problem is our attitude toward it.

Deeper appreciation of the centrality of the sangha: The sangha is traditionally seen as less important than the Buddha or the Dharma. Rethinking Buddhism along lines suggested by feminism makes the community the "indispensable matrix of spiritual existence," essential for spiritual life and growth.

Seeing everyday life and work as practice: The ordinary *is* the sacred, not necessarily sacred but made so by mindful awareness. The life of the householder cannot be thought less spiritual than that of a nun or monk.

Rethinking the role and necessity of meditation as spiritual discipline: Meditation is necessary, but it cannot be regarded as the only valuable human activity, nor as the only valuable religious activity. Taken to extremes, it becomes world-devaluing.[25]

Asian Buddhists in the United States

Less than 0.5 percent of the population of the United States is Buddhist. Like Hindus, Buddhists are found primarily in major metropolitan areas. Buddhists have come to the United States from every Buddhist country in the world and have tended to remain clustered in national groups. Buddhists came from China as early as the 1800s to work in the mines during the Gold Rush. Japanese Buddhists arrived later, but their impact has been greater. Even later, Buddhists came from Vietnam, Cambodia, Thailand, and Laos. Buddhists also came here from Tibet when the Chinese Maoist regime attempted to destroy Buddhism there. We will discuss representative Buddhist groups in each immigrant community to convey the scope of Asian Buddhism in the United States.

[24]Joseph B. Tamney, *American Society in the Buddhist Mirror* (New York: Garland Publishing, Inc., 1992), p. 95.
[25]Rita Gross, "Buddhism after Patriarchy?" in *After Patriarchy: Feminist Transformations of the World Religions*, ed. Paula M. Cooey, William R. Eakin, and Jay B. McDaniel (Maryknoll, NY: Orbis Books, 1991), pp. 65–86.

Theravada Buddhists came to the United States in the wake of the Khmer Rouge regime's attack on Cambodian Buddhists in the 1970s. Theravadins also came here from Laos, Sri Lanka, Thailand, and Vietnam, especially following the Vietnam War. There are a greater number of Vietnamese Buddhists in the United States than those from other Southeast Asian countries. They are spread more widely across the country, as well, due to efforts to resettle the large numbers of Vietnamese refugees. The majority of Vietnamese in the United States are Buddhists, although a significant minority are Christians.

The **International Buddhist Meditation Center** in Los Angeles, California, is the largest of the Vietnamese Buddhist organizations. Although Vietnamese Buddhism is almost exclusively Theravada, the Center blends various Buddhist schools of thought and practice. Buddhist leaders and teachers from a variety of backgrounds teach there and many groups use the facilities. Ordination for monks borrows from a number of traditions as well. Worship services feature chanting of the scriptures in several languages, including English. You may have heard of **Thich Nhat Hanh**, a Vietnamese monk who is known as a strong and articulate advocate of peace. In 1991, the International Buddhist Meditation Center had about 300 members in the one center, which is staffed by four priests.

The largest **Japanese** Buddhist organization in the United States is the **Buddhist Churches of America**, which has about 100,000 members in the United States. It is considered to be a mission outpost of the Japanese church, which is the largest Japanese Buddhist group. There are about 130 temples or branches. As with all the Mahayana schools of thought, life as a Buddhist layperson is emphasized:

> The principal aim in following [these teachings] is to achieve harmony between life as a religious follower of the Buddha Dharma and life as a secular layperson. . . . [The] very essence of its tradition addresses the difficulties of practicing the Dharma in a secular world of human relationships.[26]

This form of Buddhism teaches that faith in **Amida Buddha**, the Buddha of Infinite Wisdom and Compassion, will bring liberation and rebirth in the Pure Land, a state of complete enlightenment. Rebirth in the Pure Land means becoming a Bodhisattva, dedicated to returning to earthly existence to assist the liberation of all beings.

In its "church" type of organization and focus on the importance of regular participation in the activities of the church, BCA has adapted Buddhism to its American context. Its teaching about the importance of reliance on Amida Buddha to bring about liberation reflects its Mahayana roots. Because this is similar to Protestant Christians' reliance on the power of faith in Jesus as the Christ, it has not appeared completely alien to American religious sensibilities and has provided an important vehicle for the acculturation of Japanese Buddhists. It has

---

[26] "Buddhist Churches of America: Jodo Shinshu Hongwanji-ha" (San Francisco, CA: Buddhist Churches of America, 1990).

also attracted some American converts and offers an outreach membership program for those who live far from any BCA church.

Zen, probably the form of Buddhism best known in the United States, also came here from Japan. There are two principal schools of Zen, *Soto* and *Rinzai*. While some American Zen centers focus on one or the other, many teach both. One of the largest Zen centers is in Los Angeles, California. It has branched out into centers throughout the United States. Zen followers concentrate on meditation, practicing daily meditation and participating in periodic retreats in which many hours daily can be devoted to *zazen*, Zen "sitting meditation." The awareness developed during meditation is also practiced in everyday life. ZCLA offers daily zazen for practitioners, classes, regular talks and discussions, weekend retreats, and longer retreats. It also offers *sesshin*, the opportunity for practitioners to discuss their practice with leading monks.

Shasta Abbey is the headquarters of the **Order of Buddhist Contemplatives**, a Zen organization that consciously adapts traditional Zen practice to Western culture. It was founded in 1970 by a British-born Buddhist nun, the reverend Jiyu-Kennett-Roshi. Its main focus is training women and men for the Zen Buddhist priesthood in the United states. The daily Order of the monastery can serve as a good example of life in a Zen monastery in the United States (Figure 11–4). The schedule is intended to provide variety while keeping the partic-

Figure 11–4

TYPICAL DAILY SCHEDULE OF THE MOUNT SHASTA ABBEY

5:55 Rising
6:15 Meditation
6:55 Morning Service
7:25 Temple Cleanup
8:40 Breakfast
9:15 Work
10:45 Meditation (three periods)
12:30 Spiritual Reading Period
1:10 Lunch
1:40 Rest
2:45 Work
3:45 Midday Service/Meditation
4:30 Class
6:05 Dinner
6:35 Rest
7:30 Meditation/Walking Meditation
8:10 Meditation/Evening Office
10:00 Lights Out

ipants' attention focused on spiritual pursuits and ensuring a minimum of distractions. Meals are vegetarian. Participants are expected to conduct themselves mindfully, keeping in mind the spiritual purpose of their being there and the need to respect that same purpose in others.

The largest organizational representation of Chinese Buddhism in the United States is the **Dharma Realm Buddhist Association**, founded in 1959. Although based on Zen Buddhism, it teaches all five major schools of Chinese Buddhism. As well as attracting Chinese Americans, it has a following among American Buddhists as well. Its emphasis on monastic Buddhism with strict discipline makes it unique among Buddhist organizations in the United States. Its Dharma Realm Buddhist University was the first Buddhist university established in the West.

Tibetan Buddhists fleeing the Maoist regime's purge of Buddhism in Tibet brought **Vajrayana** Buddhism to the United States. **Vajradhatu**, headquartered in Boulder, Colorado, is the largest of several such organizations in the United States, with about 4,000 members. It sponsors a full range of ritual and educational activities and serves as a focus for the Tibetan Buddhist community in the United States. It also sponsors the **Naropa Institute**, one of the better-known Buddhist educational facilities in the United States. Its **Shambhala Press** is one of the major publishers of Buddhist literature in the United States.

Americans and Buddhism

People in the United States became Buddhists in far greater numbers than they became Hindus, and there may well be more non-Asian Buddhists than Asian Buddhists here now. Americans who have become Buddhists are almost uniformly white, middle-class, well-educated people between twenty-five and forty-five years old.[27]

European-Americans have been interested in Buddhism at different times for different reasons. Sociologist Joseph Tamney divides the American interest in Buddhism into four clearly definable phases:

> First, during the years 1800–1880, roughly, there emerged a serious interest among intellectuals in Eastern religions. The Transcendentalists incorporated Eastern ideas into their religious world view. Soon after, Theosophy was invented; this new religion was more Asian than European. The second period, 1880–1950, was the time when Buddhist institutions catering to European-Americans were established in the United States. For the first time, a significant number of Americans became Buddhists. The third period was 1950–1975, i.e., the years during which Buddhist institutions grew rapidly and Buddhism entered popular culture. "Beat Zen" was invented. The final phase, 1975 to the present, has been a time when Buddhist ideas and practices have been coopted by various professional groups as well as by those in the New Age movement.[28]

[27]Charles S. Prebish, "Buddhism," in *Encyclopedia of the American Religious Experience: Studies of Traditions and Movements*, ed. Charles H. Lippy and Peter W. Williams (New York: Charles Scribner's Sons, 1988), p. 676.

[28]Tamney, *American Society in the Buddhist Mirror*, p. xviii.

In the process, Buddhism has been changed as it has interacted with American culture. We have seen this (to a lesser extent) in Islam and Hinduism as well. Such change is inevitable when a religion comes from one culture and enters into the life of a very different culture. Tamney's summary of the changes that Buddhism has undergone in its American context provides a good summary of the current situation of Buddhism in the United States:

> First, the monastic life is not considered the ideal; American monks find it necessary to develop a Buddhism that does not make the laity second-class practitioners. Second, Americans favor an eclectic approach borrowing from all Buddhist traditions. Third, participatory democracy is being applied to Buddhist organizations. Fourth, what it means to be a Buddhist is being defined in terms of both contemplation and social action, especially in regard to peace and ecological issues.[29]

A BRIEF NOTE ABOUT ORTHODOX AND HASIDIC JUDAISM

In many ways, Orthodox and Hasidic Judaism both fit the profile of religio-ethnic religions. They are closely, although not exclusively, associated with a particular national or ethnic group. They maintain a distinctive culture within their groups (Figure 11–5). They tend to regard themselves as separate from the larger American culture. In light of their keen national and ethnic consciousness, they certainly could have been included in this chapter. I decided to include them along with other varieties of Judaism as a part of the religious consensus in recog-

Figure 11–5   Hasidic Jews have a distinctive way of being Jewish and a distinctive culture, as well. (*Bettye Lane/Photo Researchers, Inc.*)

---

[29]Tamney, *American Society in the Buddhist Mirror*, p. 90.

nition of the extent to which Jews as a group have become a part of that consensus.

QUESTIONS AND ACTIVITIES FOR REVIEW, DISCUSSION, AND WRITING

1. If you live or attend school close to an Islamic mosque (look in the Yellow Pages under "Religious Organizations," or perhaps "Churches"), make arrangements to attend the Friday midday prayer. Non-Muslims are welcome at mosques. There may be some dress restrictions for women; inquire before you attend.
2. Especially if this is not possible, try to arrange for a Muslim student who attends your college or university to come and speak to your class.
3. If you are not a Muslim, pick one on the Five Pillars of Islam and discuss what it might mean to you if you were. You may want to do some additional reading on the Pillar that you choose. If you are a Muslim, discuss what one of the Pillars means to you.
4. If you are fortunate enough to live or attend school close to a Hindu or Buddhist temple, arrange to visit and write an essay on what you observe and your response to it.
5. Especially if # 4 is not possible, try to secure a guest speaker for your class from one or both of these Indian religions.
6. If your library subscribes to any periodicals published by United States Muslims, Hindus, or Buddhists, read through two or three issues and write about what impression you form of the religion.
7. Yoga as a form of physical exercise and relaxation is taught in many physical education departments. If your school has such a class, invite the instructor to demonstrate some of the basic postures with class participation.
8. Discuss with a group of your classmates the ways in which the Four Noble Truths apply in (1) your own lives and (2) American culture in general.
9. What are some practical, concrete applications of the Hindu and Buddhist ideal of noninjury or nonviolence in our own culture? How could you as an individual put this ideal into practice?
10. How do you think you would respond to the daily routine of the Shasta Abbey?
11. The three ways that Christians relate to Muslims do not apply only to these two groups. They describe the basis on which members of any two communities of faith can relate to each other. What is your response to each as a "model" for interfaith relations?

FOR FURTHER READING

Carmody, Denise Lardner, *Religious Woman: Contemporary Reflections on Eastern Texts.* New York: Crossroad, 1991. A feminist analysis of Islamic, Hindu, and Buddhist sacred texts dealing with women, as well as sacred writings from Japanese and Chinese sources.

Ellwood, Robert S., and Harry B. Partin, *Religious and Spiritual Groups in Modern America,* 2nd ed. Englewood Cliffs, NJ: Prentice Hall, Inc., 1988. There are good sections on Hinduism, Buddhism, and other Indian religions. Additionally, a vast multitude of other religious alternatives are described. Highly recommended.

Haddad, Yvonne Yazbeck, ed., *Muslims of America.* New York: Oxford University Press, 1991. A collection of essays that deals with nearly all aspects of Muslim life in the United States and Canada. Especially good sections on the perception of Muslims in the United States and on Muslim women.

Haddad, Yvonne Yazbeck, and Adair T. Lummis, *Islamic Values in the United States: A Comparative Study.* New York: Oxford University Press, 1987. A very thorough and engaging discussion of how Islamic values do, and do not, fit into American culture, and what Muslim people do in response.

Jackson, Carl T. *Vedanta for the West: The Ramakrishna Movement in the United States.* Bloomington, IN: Indiana University Press, 1994. Valuable as a study of the Vedanta Movement itself, Jackson's book also focuses on the transformations undergone by Eastern religions when they come West.

Shinn, Larry D., *The Dark Lord: Cult Images and the Hare Krishnas in America.* Philadelphia: Westminster Press, 1987. Good descriptions of the lives and values of Krishna Consciousness members, contrasted with common perception of them.

Tamney, Joseph B., *American Society in the Buddhist Mirror.* New York: Garland Publishing, Inc., 1992. Tamney's theses, which he ably supports, is that Americans have been interested in Buddhism at various times for various reasons, as Buddhism helped to compensate for characteristics of American culture. The author's method provides a good example of the benefits of studying religion in relationship to the larger culture.

Young, William A., *The World's Religions: Worldviews and Contemporary Issues.* Englewood Cliffs, NJ: Prentice Hall, Inc., 1995. This is an excellent introduction to the world's religions, written from a perspective that is compatible with that taken in this book. Covers all the basics and includes a section on each religion's response to contemporary ethical issues.

12

How Religion Can Become a Problem

Religion can become a problem for individuals, or for society as a whole, when it leads to violence, terrorism, addiction, or other dysfunctional behaviors. It is important to note two things at the outset: (1) Religions are not the only organizations that may become a problem in these ways. Virtually any organization has this potential. (2) The great majority of the time, religions *do not* lead their followers to violence or other criminal activity, nor into addictive behavior.

Consider, however, the following: At a rural school corporation in the Midwest, a group of concerned parents meets with the elementary school principal following a basketball game. The issue? They want to place an armed guard around the school during the times that the children arrive at and leave the school. Threats that their daughters will be kidnapped and used in rituals by alleged Satanists have them very worried. Rumor has it that, in the woods nearby, dead cats and dogs have been found, the gory remains of magical rites. In the South, a county sheriff goes on the local radio station, urging parents to keep their children indoors after dark, because "Devil worshippers are looking for young kids to kidnap."

Or this: On a large college campus, several students sit late at night, talking quietly with one of the residence hall staff people. A friend of theirs has become involved with a religious group that actively recruits students for membership. The group seems to take up all her time, and she has made it very clear that she is no longer a friend of theirs; she claims that they do not know the truth. One of the students recalls, "Yeah. You know, I remember a kid in my high school who got into some group like that. He decided that it wasn't for him, and he wanted to leave. The group wouldn't let him. His folks finally got some sort of court order to get him away from them."

In another small midwestern town, a three-year-old dies from a lung infection that would have responded easily to medical treatment. Her parents are members of a group that does not believe in medical care. The parents are now in jail on charges of criminal child neglect. These stories are all true. There are religious groups in the United States that frighten a lot of people. They have beliefs and practices that seem strange in our culture. Many people call them *cults*.

The word **cult** has strongly negative associations. Despite our cultural affirmation of religious pluralism and the legal right of a variety religious groups to exist within the law, there is a definite bias that also exists. Even when we support the idea of religious freedom and pluralism, we are often uneasy when confronted with communities of faith that depart too far from the usual or average ways of being religious.

The mass murder-suicide episode that occurred at Jonestown, Guyana, in November 1978 in the People's Temple group created near-panic reactions wherever nonconventional religions were mentioned. To a greater or lesser extent, those feelings continue today. Jonestown again captured public attention on the occasion of its tenth anniversary in 1988. The People's Temple tragedy certainly served to remind all of us that things labeled "religion" could at times be dangerous.

Similar questions and fears were raised yet again in the spring of 1993 when a violent confrontation between federal Alcohol, Tobacco, and Firearms agents and members of the Branch Davidian religious group led to a fifty-one day standoff that ended as the group's compound outside Waco, Texas burned, a conflagration in which about eighty people, including a number of children, died. A year after the devastation at Waco, five Davidians had been convicted of voluntary manslaughter, two more on weapons charges, and four had been acquitted of any responsibility in the deaths of the four Alcohol, Tobacco, and Firearms agents who died when they stormed the compound. The appropriateness of the government's actions is still being debated.

These events raise difficult questions in a pluralistic culture that prides itself on its religious freedom, especially in light of the distinction between freedom of religious belief and freedom of action motivated by religion. The Supreme Court's decision in the *Reynolds* case (discussed in Chapter 2) meant that matters of religious belief are beyond the concern of the government. What people believe may not be restricted. However, when that belief is translated into specific actions, the government may intervene to stop actions that are held to be very damaging to society or repulsive to commonly agreed upon moral standards.

THE WORD *CULT:* DEFINITIONAL PROBLEMS

In looking at the word itself from the standpoint of definition, we should first note that **cult is always an outsider's word.** People use it to describe a religious group with which they disagree, of which they are suspicious or frightened, or toward which they feel hostile. No one describes their own religion as a cult!

Beyond this, however, there is simply no agreed-upon definition of the word, and different individuals and groups use it to mean very different things. There are **three major types of definitions**.

1.   **Social scientists** typically divide religious organizations into "churches," "sects," and "cults." Each of these classifications has a very specific meaning within sociological literature. The sociological meaning of the word cult focuses on religious innovation within a culture; cults are the locus of innovation and religious change within the culture. When sociologists use the word in a sociological context, they intend it to be neutral, neither favoring nor maligning the religions. It simply identifies what type of religious group it is.

2.   The second type of definition is theological, usually from a **Christian** perspective. A cult is defined as a deviation from Christianity, based on the assumption that Christianity is the only true religion. On these terms, a cult is heretical, follows false beliefs, and is a distortion or perversion of biblical Christianity. This applies to both alternative interpretations of Christianity (Latter-day Saints and Seventh-day Adventists, for example) and to religions that have no connection with Christianity (Islam, Hinduism, and Buddhism, for example).

3.   The third approach to definition came about with the **secular anticult movement** in the 1970s. It grew out of the disappointment, fear, and anger of parents whose daughters and sons had abandoned family traditions and parental hopes in favor of a new and often radically different religion and the lifestyle that went with it. This definition emphasizes a variety of characteristics that are judged to be destructive, such as secrecy, authoritarian leadership, thought control, deception, and financial misdealing.

A type of definition that differs from the three above is that used by William Whalen in *Strange Gods: Contemporary Religious Cults in America*.[1] Whalen defines a cult simply as a group whose beliefs and/or practices differ greatly from those that are common in the rest of the culture. This definition has the advantage of pointing to what most people think of when they hear the word. It does, however, have at least two problems. On the face of it, at least, it is not pejorative. However, there is often a lurking idea, whether implicit or explicit, that what is *usual* is also *normal* or *right*. In that case, definitions based on a group's similarity to or difference from the prevailing culture have the same sorts of problems associated with the second and third definitions mentioned above. The second problem with such definitions is that they permit the inclusion of a wide variety of groups, beliefs, and practices which are very different from each other. Whalen, for example, includes groups as diverse as the Unification Church, Children of God, Jehovah's Witnesses, the Way, and the Unitarian Universalists.

In my opinion, the word *cult* no longer has any place in the description and discussion of religious groups and people in the United States (or elsewhere). Its definitions are too varied and the emotional responses that it evokes are too strong and unreflective. As a recent essay summarizes well,

---

[1] William J. Whalen, *Strange Gods: Contemporary Religious Cults in America* (Huntington, IN: Our Sunday Visitor, 1981).

In current popular usage. . . , the term [cult] is applied to a disparate array of groups and has no clear and consensual denotation. It does, however, have the sensational *connotation* of an authoritarian, mind-controlling movement in which convert-victims are mentally enslaved and can be made to perpetrate violence and crime as ordained by a charismatic prophet or guru. A label possessing an unclear denotation but a sharp negative connotation becomes primarily an emotive vehicle for conferring a stigma.[2]

As the authors go on to note, however, there is quite possibly "no fully adequate alternative" yet, a judgment with which I would agree. In what follows, *nonconventional religion* will be used to denote these groups.

VIEWS ON NONCONVENTIONAL RELIGIONS

Whatever they may be called, nonconventional religions are the subject of ongoing controversy. There is no clear agreement on just how much of a threat nonconventional religions pose, nor on what to do about them. The following are representative of some of the positions taken.

Researchers do not agree on something as basic as the number of such groups active in the United States. The Cult Awareness Network (CAN, a leading secular anticult[3] organization) claims there are about 2,500 and the number is growing. On the other hand, the Institute for the Study of American Religion, headed by J. Gordon Melton, cites approximately 700.[4] Clearly, the threat, if such exists, increases as the number increases. At the same time, it is easy enough to understand the variation in these estimates. Many of these groups are small, and, because of the threat of retribution, tend to maintain a very low profile. Some groups form and disintegrate rather quickly or are reborn with a new name. Anticult organizations have a vested interest in claiming a large number of groups and adherents, whereas those who want to downplay the problem have a similarly vested interest in claiming the opposite. Lack of agreement on what groups to include adds to the problem.

Anticult organizations portray nonconventional religions as a new and radically different aspect of American religion, usually beginning in the 1960s. Others point out that "new religious groups, far from being new to the American social landscape, have been one of its most perennial features. . . . Religious diversity and the flowering of new religious groups are actually hallmarks of American history."[5]

There is a tendency to lump all new and unusual religious groups together and portray them as exercising near-total control over every aspect of their mem-

[2]Thomas Robbins and Dick Anthony, "'Cults,' 'Mind Control,' and the State," in *From the Ashes: Making Sense of Waco*, ed. James R. Lewis (Lanham, MD: Rowman & Littlefield Publishers, Inc., 1994), pp. 125–35.
[3]The word *anticult* is used extensively by these organizations themselves, and will be used here.
[4]"Cults in America," *CQ Researcher*, 3, no. 17 (May 7, 1993), p. 387.
[5]David G. Bromley, "The Mythology of Cults," in *From the Ashes: Making Sense of Waco*, ed. James R. Lewis, pp. 121–36.

bers' lives and thoughts. In reality, there is, as you would expect on further reflection, a wide range in the degree of control exercised.

Scholars also do not fully agree on the extent and exact nature of "mind control," undoubtedly the characteristic most associated with the term *cult* in the minds of many people. One model holds that people completely lose their capacity for independent action, becoming "puppets" or "robots," with no free will whatsoever. Usually included in this model is the idea that the "brainwashing" tactics of an experienced recruiter are virtually irresistible, and the convert a hapless victim. This explanation has not held up to scientific investigation, which has shown that there are no techniques capable of completely overwhelming free will under conditions which pertain in the United States. This theory is still *accepted*, however, and has important legal ramifications. If the members of these groups have had their freedom of choice totally disabled, then tactics such as "kidnapping" them and deprogramming them to free them from the influence of the group are likely to be regarded as appropriate and even necessary techniques. Court-ordered conservatorships and guardianships for legal adults can easily be justified in these circumstances. It has also been noted that this "explanation" of someone's involvement with a group, deemed unacceptable by the member's family, explains it in terms that put no stigma on either the family or the group member, thus freeing them from any hint of self-blame.[6] This view also supports the corollary that members have in effect had their money "stolen" from them by the group when they made contributions or turned over assets to the group.

The second model does not assert that free will has been lost in any legally or ethically defensible sense that would support and even require dramatic intervention. The responsibility for behavior remains with the member of the group, who continues to be seen as a functional adult.[7] This view is substantiated by the fact that the majority of people who become part of such a group do eventually leave it; the defection rate would be much lower if the thought control were as effective as the first model claims. And, although many and perhaps most people in the United States would feel that turning over all of one's assets to such a group is an unwise choice, it remains a choice, freely made, on this model.

The issue of thought control is related to the question of how people join religious groups. It is helpful to have an historical perspective on how the process of religious conversion has been described. The standard way of interpreting what happens in conversion has been based on the model provided by the biblical accounts of Paul's conversion on the road to Damascus. It was sudden, highly dramatic and emotional, and it was said to result from God's action. Paul had little control over the process (Acts 9:1–18). When this model of conversion is used

[6]David G. Bromley and Anson D. Shupe, Jr., "The Future of the Anticult Movement," in *The Future of New Religious Movements*, ed. David G. Bromley and Phillip E. Hammond (Macon, GA: Mercer University Press, 1987), p. 224.

[7]Thomas Robbins and Dick Anthony, "'Cults,' 'Mind Control,' and the State," in *From the Ashes*, ed. James R. Lewis, pp. 125–37.

to interpret conversion to an unusual religious group, God's intervention in Paul's life is replaced by devious tactics of brainwashing, hypnotism, and coercive persuasion applied against helpless and passive people without their control or consent. There is a newer model of conversion that is much more accurate. In a highly pluralistic culture such as ours, conversion is frequently not a one-time event. Most people join and leave several groups, religious and nonreligious, over the course of their lifetimes. Only a small number of people who have some initial contact actually join, and few of those who do remain for very long. Those who do join often have serious reservations about the group and their membership in it. Their participation is an experiment. People often behave as group members for a time, trying out a new role and way of life, while changing their beliefs and values very little. Participating in a group and accepting its teachings are not the same thing. On this model, affiliation with a religious group is seen along the same lines as affiliation with other groups, as a part of the human search for fellowship and identity. In other words, it is a normal, even necessary, process, one that cannot be taken as evidence of mental incapacity. Potential members and converts are active participants in the process, not passive victims of some deceptive and mysterious mental blackmail.[8]

Like other groups that actively recruit members, nonconventional religions have developed ways of attracting people to their causes. When the Bill of Rights was added to the Constitution, and religion became a matter for voluntary association rather than birth, religious groups had to seek converts. They had to make their particular way of being religious attractive to people. In line with the accepted style of consensus religion, most of this competing for members in the United States is rather low key. Some communities of faith have sought members more aggressively and more visibly, and have been criticized for using a "hard sell" approach. The Latter-day Saints and Jehovah's Witnesses have concentrated on door-to-door solicitation of members. Other groups have chosen instead to focus on recruitment through existing friendship patterns, in which people who are already members invite their friends. They also seek new members in public places such as airports and bus terminals. Some seek members on college campuses.

Some groups *have* used deceptive techniques, not revealing the true identity of the group when approaching a prospective member. People have become involved in weekend retreats and longer conferences without full disclosure of what they would be doing once they arrived. There have been instances in which isolation and dependence upon the group leaders for transportation made leaving in the middle of such events difficult. Seeking to build group spirit quickly and firmly, leaders have at times overlooked or denied participants' legitimate needs for privacy and time to reflect on what was happening. Many people re-

---

[8]David G. Bromley and James T. Richardson, *The Brainwashing-Deprogramming Controversy: Psychological, Legal, and Historical Perspectives* (New York: Edwin Mellen Press, 1983), pp. 3–4. Other relevant studies include those reported in David G. Bromley and Anson D. Shupe, Jr., *Strange Gods: The Great American Cult Scare* (Boston: Beacon Press, 1981), and Larry D. Shinn, *The Dark Lord: Cult Images and the Hare Krishnas in America* (Philadelphia: Westminster Press, 1987).

gard these sorts of practices as unacceptable and inappropriate. However, the evidence does not support the accusations of brainwashing that have routinely been leveled against these groups.

One of the most common allegations about socially unacceptable religious groups is that there is a great deal of sexual abuse, including abuse of children, that takes place within the walls of the usually communal living arrangements. Leaders are charged with taking advantage of members and with encouraging sexual abuse among the members themselves. However, other scholars point out that there are actually *fewer* serious accusations of sexual misconduct than against "mainline" priests and ministers.[9]

Those who fear the impact of nonconventional religions advocate constant vigilance and sometimes government intervention to "control the menace." One prominent spokesperson for the anticult movement states that these groups pose "very real threats to public health, mental health, political power, and democratic freedoms—as well as growing concerns over consumer issues—that become apparent as we learn how these manipulative and often unethical groups have spread into . . . the major sectors and institutions of our society."[10] Another observer of new religions worries that the coming millennium will encourage the rise of groups such as the Branch Davidians.[11]

Others fear the abridgement of constitutionally guaranteed freedoms at least as much as they fear the religions that provoke them. A representative of the Christian Legal Society writes that "the government is forbidden from interfering or abridging individual or organizational religious liberties. The anticonversion legislation proposed by various states does in fact intrude upon the very core of individual liberties and religious freedom."[12] According to a national survey carried out by People for the American Way, more than 50 percent of the attempts to censor school and public library books and public school textbooks now involve books that contain material that the would-be censors believe to be Satanic or occult.[13]

WHO JOINS, AND WHY

Most research on nonconventional religions shows a common set of demographic traits among members. The vast majority are between the ages of eighteen and twenty-five. They are middle-class, reasonably intelligent people with

[9]J. Gordon Melton, *Encyclopedic Handbook of Cults in America, Revised and Updated Edition.* (New York: Garland Publishing, Inc., 1992), p. 189.

[10]Margaret Thaler Singer, with Janja Lalich, *Cults in Our Midst.* (San Francisco: Jossey-Bass Publishers, 1995), p. 5.

[11]Hal Mansfield, quoted in "Doomsday Cults: Only the Beginning," *Newsweek*, April 3, 1995, p. 40.

[12]Thomas S. Brandon, Jr., *New Religions, Conversions, and Deprogramming: New Frontiers of Religious Liberty.* (Oak Park, IL: The Center for Law & Religious Freedom, 1982), p. 1.

[13]Jeffrey S. Victor, *Satanic Panic: The Creation of a Contemporary Legend.* (Chicago, IL: Open Court, 1993), p. 156.

some college education, although not usually college graduates. They are male and female in approximately equal numbers. Most are white. Most come from intact homes. All segments of the religious population of the United States are represented. Although most come from homes in which religion was a part of life, few were themselves active as teenagers. Many more people with these same demographic characteristics *do not* become members of nonconventional religions. Why some people and not others?

The age range of eighteen to twenty-five helps to point us to some—not all—of the answers to the question about why people may join nonconventional religions. This is a time of passage, a time of transition in most Americans' lives. It may be a time of uncertainty. It is most definitely a time when forging our own identities as people different from our parents is of great psychological importance. It is a time of vulnerability for many. Having left the security of home or the college environment, people search for new sources of stability and security. Having left old friendships and groups that answered the need for human fellowship and intimacy that we all share, people seek new connections. It is a time when they may see their old lives and views as very outmoded and no longer useful, and a time when new patterns of living and values need to be acquired.

Other factors may influence a person's decision to join a religious group very different from the one in which they were raised, or to join a religious group for the first time. When we are confronted with a host of new choices, choices that, once made, will influence the rest of our lives, choice fatigue may set in. We are confronted daily with more choices than our grandparents could even imagine. In this situation, the promise of "six simple steps to love and acceptance now and salvation in the future" is alluring. In the present climate of uncertainty and doubt, many people are sincerely looking for an authority. They want a person or a philosophy of life that says with conviction, "This is it!" Some religions provide a comprehensive environment that reaches into every corner of life and offers an answer to every question. Once the major choice to join is made, other choices are sharply reduced. This comes as a welcome relief to the person suffering from choice fatigue.

Religions that are outside the cultural consensus offer an alternative, often something that seems much simpler. Many of those to whom such groups are attractive are sincerely seeking something better. Some people join such a group in search of answers to the dissatisfactions with everyday life that we all experience from time to time.

Others of those who join are engaged in a genuine spiritual quest and a search for an understanding of life's meaning that they can call their own. Many have found the more ordinary religions, the ones they and their friends grew up with, to be lacking in religious experience. Consensus religion has tended to devalue religious experience. Many of the nonconventional religions, especially those that developed in the East, emphasize techniques of spiritual experience, such as meditation, visualization and chanting.

Specific psychological or emotional predispositions may lead people to join. Those with an unusually low tolerance for ambiguity may be drawn in by the promise of certainty. Those who have stronger-than-average needs for dependency may see the highly authoritarian structure of some religious groups as a good way of meeting this need. Those with an usually strong need for approval from others will be susceptible to the "instant friendship" and acceptance sometimes offered. For some, the assurance of being in a group that believes itself to be the only true religion provides a bulwark against insecurity.

In other words, people choose membership in a nonconventional community of faith as a way of meeting needs that most people in the culture find met in consensus religions. These are important needs that we all have, simply because we're human beings. The emotional need for love and acceptance, the intellectual need for understanding and a framework of beliefs and values within which we can make sense of our world and our lives, and the moral need for a sense of purpose and direction all give rise to questions for which all of us search for answers. In many ways, the members of these communities of faith are no different from those of you who are reading this book. They may be somewhat more vulnerable because of their life circumstances or emotional makeup, or they may be experiencing an uncomfortable transition in their lives. They may have found ordinary answers unsatisfactory. They are people very like ourselves, with similar needs, hopes, and fears. They are persons who have chosen a different way of answering life's questions. Factors similar to these influence people to change their political party identification, switch from one consensus religion to another, make drastic changes in lifestyle, or even have cosmetic surgery. In other words, the influence of these factors is not restricted to people's decisions to join unusual religious groups.

An interesting perspective on the similarity of those who do and those who don't join nonconventional religions is provided by a psychiatrist who asserts that the experience of childhood itself lays the groundwork for "cult behavior" in us all. He offers the following easily-recognizable examples of such actions:

> speaking of outsiders to one's own group or of adversaries as if they were all the same, and characterizing them by negative traits alone, while not being interested in or trying to obtain accurate information about them
> not being willing to consider the possible validity of an adversary's viewpoint, while not looking critically at one's own point of view
> in groups, devaluing those who dissent, regarding dissent as a problem
> self-righteousness.[14]

---

[14]Arthur J. Deikman, M.D., *The Wrong Way Home: Uncovering the Patterns of Cult Behavior in American Society.* (Boston: Beacon Press, 1990), pp. 149–54.

RELIGIOUS ADDICTION AND
NONCONVENTIONAL RELIGIONS

Recent literature on religious addiction gives us one way to understand how it is that religion sometimes becomes a problem in an individual's life or in the life of a society. *All* religions, without exception, are subject to being used in an addictive way. However, some, by their structure and the types of beliefs and lifestyle they advocate, may be more prone than others to being used in this way.

Like drugs, food, or personal relationships, religion can be addictive. Here, *addiction* means using

> . . . something outside to escape from and control something we're afraid of inside. . . . [We] can use religion or religious things in exactly the same way as drugs or alcohol, to escape from what is real within. Religious addiction attempts to control painful inner reality through a rigid religious belief system. . . . What better drug of choice than a perfect, all-powerful, all-knowing God out there who controls everything and everybody?[15]

Other religious "drugs of choice" can include a powerful, charismatic religious leader, ritual practices, and religious beliefs.

The painful feeling from which addicts (religious or not) seek escape is most often *shame*. Shame is not the same thing as guilt. Shame, as it is being used here, is "a toxic, debilitating core sense of being unlovable and inferior as a person. . . . Guilt says I *made* a mistake; shame says I *am* a mistake."[16] Hurts that people receive as children and adults may lead to feelings of inadequacy and shame, and to an unwillingness to risk more hurt and shame. When strong, these feelings can cause people to unconsciously assume an attitude of "don't trust, don't talk, don't think, don't feel." When people are told often enough that their own reality is wrong, they learn to mistrust their sense of reality itself. This, then, makes people unwilling and indeed unable to question what they are told in the name of religion.[17] This may make religious groups and leaders that discourage questioning more attractive than they otherwise would be. It can also lead to the use of religious practices such as prayer and chanting as a way to escape and shut off the hurtful feelings.

There is no sure way to identify when religion is being used addictively. What is healthy for one person, at one stage of their life's development, may signal addiction for someone else. We also need to keep in mind that passionate

---

[15]Matthew Linn, S. J., Sheila Fabricant Linn, and Dennis Linn, *Healing Spiritual Abuse and Religious Addiction* (New York and Mahwah, NJ: Paulist Press, 1994), pp. 2–13. The Linns' book deals only with Christianity, but the basic dynamics of religious addiction that they describe apply to any religion.

[16]Linn, et al., *Healing Spiritual Abuse*, p. 43 (emphasis added).

[17]Linn, et al., *Healing Spiritual Abuse*, p. 118.

commitment to one's religion is *not* the same as addiction, even when that commitment exceeds what other people might consider "reasonable."

An important corollary of this view is that when religious addicts become religious leaders, they become spiritual abusers. Spiritual abusers perpetuate the heritage of shame. When a religious leader, doctrine, ritual, or writing makes us

> ... feel ashamed of our feelings, our desires, our call in life, or any other aspect of our real self, then we are [encountering] it with blinders of spiritual abuse. We need to stop and question ... how [religion] is being interpreted to us.[18]

Religion challenges us, calls us to examine our lives in the light of the best in the religious tradition and the experience of the community of faith, but it should not shame us.

One implication of this research on religious addiction is that "nonconventional religions" and "consensus religions" are not two entirely separable things. The leaders and the followers of nonconventional religions are not all that different from those who follow more conventional religions. Everyone has the potential to turn to religion in an addictive way, and every religion has the potential for abuse. This said, it is also the case that religions which require unquestioning loyalty to the leader, the teachings, and the community, and those that require followers to spend great amounts of time in ritual practices, seem to invite the addictive use and abuse of religion by those so inclined. This becomes even more likely if shame and other negative means of social control are used.

The results of research on religious addiction mean that in evaluating the harmful potential of a religious group, or of *any* group, we need to look not only at the characteristics of the group, but at how *we* relate to the group, what our purposes and motives are for being involved in it. Harmfulness is at least as much a function of the relationship of a follower to the group, as a characteristic of the group.

NONCONVENTIONAL RELIGIONS AND COLLEGE STUDENTS: TWO VIEWS

As we noted above, many college students are at a stage in psychosocial and faith development that is quite challenging and often threatening. According to some researchers, this makes college students especially vulnerable to recruiters for nonconventional religions, and campuses particularly fertile sites for such recruiting. One college official describes them as "a major threat to the welfare, human rights, and indeed the very futures" of college students.[19] Nonconven-

---

[18]Linn, et al., *Healing Spiritual Abuse*, pp. 129–30.
[19]Carl J. Rheins, "Why This Book?" in *Cults on Campus: Continuing Challenge*, ed. Marcia R. Rudin (New York: American Family Foundation, 1991), p. 1.

tional religions, he alleges, "lay siege to" college campuses and "prey upon students." Further, he argues, unlike the more commonly accepted religious groups on campuses, which "support the spiritual life of students and assist them in their college endeavors, cult groups seek students to assist only the cult organization."[20]

Those who see nonconventional religions as a special threat to college students also point out that their effects go against what colleges try to do. "Cults, through the conversion process, close off and break down the logical faculties of the mind by narrowing the attention span of their members, robbing them of freedom of thought, intellectual growth, and personal development. . . . There is no question that destructive religious cults rob students of the very things we have joined together in universities to teach."[21]

In contrast to this approach, others point out that nonconventional religions, like other groups, have the legal right to be where they are. Students have a constitutionally guaranteed right to practice their faith, whatever that faith may be. They have as much right to organize for religious purposes as for any other purpose. Student religious groups have the same rights and responsibilities as other student groups. Ministers and other religious advisors have the right to work with college students. "The only restrictions which the college places on these advisors are those dictated by fair play for each other and by consideration for the orderly processes of the college."[22]

According to this view, the way to deal with whatever problems exist from the presence of nonconventional religions on college campuses is not suppression or repression. Universities and colleges should be centers of openness to variant perspectives—all perspectives. They should be centers for the free expression of ideas—all ideas. Limiting access or forcing it into rigidly structured, narrow boundaries often causes more problems than it solves, and runs the risk of violating students' constitutional rights. Forcing any group into covert activity increases the likelihood that it will come to be a threat. When freedom of speech prevails, "cult leaders can be heard and their beliefs and practices openly challenged and debated by the educational community."[23] This approach helps to diffuse anxiety about the little-known, may keep groups from "going underground," and facilitates exposure to new and controversial ideas, thus enhancing the educational process.

---

[20]Gregory S. Blimling, "The Involvement of College Students in Totalistic Groups: Causes, Concerns, Legal Issues, and Policy Considerations," in *Cults on Campus*, ed. Rudin, pp. 33–59. (When the word *cult* occurs in a direct quote, I have retained it.)

[21]Gregory S. Blimling, "Cults, College Students, and Campus Policies," in *Cultism on Campus: Commentaries and Guidelines for College and University Administrators.* ed. Robert E. Schecter and Wendy L. Noyes (New York: American Family Foundation and The National Association of Student Personnel Administration, 1987), pp. 5–20.

[22]George W. Jones, "Students and the Practice of Religion on Campus," in *Cultism on Campus*, ed. Schechter and Noyes, pp. 71–80.

[23]Blimling, "The Involvement of College Students in Totalistic Groups," p. 55.

RECOGNIZING THE POTENTIAL FOR HARM

The radical pluralism that characterizes religion in the United States today means that we live in an "open market" in which many groups, religious and secular, mostly benign but some potentially destructive, compete for our attention, time, and money. Part of becoming an "educated consumer" of group membership is making intentional choices rather than drifting unreflectively into participation. It does not come within the purview of the academic study of religion to evaluate religions, nonconventional or otherwise. Many groups—both religious and secular—offer lists of the characteristics of potentially damaging groups, each from its own point of view. What follows are but a few examples that suggest the variety in these lists. Each of them reflects the values of the group that is proposing the list.

One of the most brief comes from a book concerning nonconventional religions and college students. It includes three characteristics that can apply to religious and secular groups:

> Exclusivity: groups that claim or imply that only they have the right answers
> Totalitarianism: organizations that force complete conformity with what the group prescribes
> Psychologically damaging to members or their families: especially separating members from family.[24]

A second approach is somewhat more complicated. It lists a number of questions to encourage "critical reasoning" in the sorting-out process:

> Does the leader or group charge money for membership? Obligatory payments—distinguished from voluntary donations—are a danger signal.
> Does the leader have high moral standards? Spiritual attainment leads to higher-than-average moral conduct, not attempts to justify immorality.
> Does the leader claim special spiritual development, powers or attainments? Such claims are always suspect. Humility is universally regarded as a virtue.
> Does the group seek new converts vigorously? Groups that are "out to save the world" are divisive forces that potentially do more harm than good.
> Who appointed the leader or teacher or master? True spiritual leaders are confirmed by outside sources, rather than being self-styled prophets.
> Are the teachings "trans-rational" or "pre-rational"? "Mythic logic, group-think, dogma, obedience without insight, and so forth" should make us cautious.
> What daily results does your participation have? Positive effects should be readily apparent to friends and family.

Most groups or teachers will score both positive and negative on this list, requiring the potential follower to weigh the results carefully. Far from being an

---

[24]Robert C. Fellows, MTS, "When You're Asked about Cults," in *Cults on Campus*, ed. Rudin, pp. 102–4.

easy refuge for the lazy, "following a spiritual master or path requires a tremendous amount of maturity, self-control, and discrimination."[25]

A longer and more complicated approach is taken by neo-pagan P.E.I. Bonewits—himself a leader of a nonconventional religion—who proposes a list of fifteen traits and suggests scoring the group from a low of one to a high of ten on each. The higher the score, the more potential for danger. The fifteen characteristics are: (1) amount of internal control, (2) infallibility claimed by leadership, (3) trust placed by followers in leadership decisions, (4) rigidity of dogma, (5) emphasis on recruiting, (6) number of subsidiary groups not clearly identified with main group, (7) wealth, (8) political power, (9) sexual manipulation, (10) censorship of access to outside opinions and information, (11) dropout control, (12) endorsement of violence, (13) paranoia, (14) grimness, and (15) surrender of will.[26] The scoring continuum makes this list more flexible than most, but also more complicated. The fifteen attributes will vary in their importance for different people, and it is important to remember that not all local groups within a larger group are likely to be identical in how they function.

FEAR OF NONCONVENTIONAL RELIGIONS AND THE QUESTION OF VIOLENCE

Why do we fear and mistrust alternative religious movements? Part of it is simply fear of the unknown, the unfamiliar. Part of it is the real potential for violence and abuse that exists, although there is less of this than media attention would lead us to believe. Part of it is the horrifying image of the Branch Davidian compound engulfed in flames. Two other perspectives deserve our attention, as well, for they are thought-provoking and help us to set the discussion in the context of the larger role of religion in American culture.

The first is provided by Jeffrey Victor, a New York sociologist whose own son was wrongly labeled a "Satanist" because of his preferred taste in clothing. This personal encounter with the public reaction to Satanism led Victor to employ his sociologist's training in the attempt to understand what was going on with what he came to call the "Satanic panic" in the United States.

Briefly, the claim of a "Satanic conspiracy" in the United States asserts

> . . . that there exists a secret organization, or network, of criminals who worship Satan and who are engaged in the pornography business, forced prostitution, and drug dealing. These criminals also engage in the sexual abuse and torture of children. . . . kill and sacrifice infants, and sometimes adults, and commit cannibalism with the body parts. . . . kidnap children for ritual sacrifice and commit random murders of indigents. . . . Satanists have infiltrated all the institutions of so-

[25]David Christopher Lane, *Exposing Cults: When the Skeptical Mind Confronts the Mystical.* (New York: Garland Publishing, Inc., 1994), pp. 225–41.

[26]P.E.I. Bonewits, *Real Magic* (Berkeley, CA: Creative Arts Book Co., 1971), p. 215.

ciety in order to subvert society, create chaos, and thus promote their beliefs in Satan worship.[27]

While there certainly have been crimes committed by people who claimed to have committed them in the name of Satan, and while people draw and wear symbols associated with Satan and sometimes leave these symbols at the site of ritualistic activities, there is "no reliable evidence" of the avowed conspiracy.

In that case, what's going on here? Victor explains it this way. The Satanic conspiracy scare is symptomatic of something deeper, the collective perception of a moral crisis in American society. There is

> . . . a loss of faith in the moral order . . . , a perception of the rapid decline in traditional moral values. People are saying, in essence, that "our world is falling apart, because all things good and decent are under attack by evil forces beyond our control."[28]

The precipitating factors include economic decline, uncertainty and the stress that accompanies it, and family disintegration, which has been endemic in the United States in recent history. There is little agreement about whether such a moral decline actually exists or how severe it is, if it does exist. What is crucial here is the *perception* that it exists, because it is the shared perception that has behavioral consequences.

Many of the factors underlying the Satanic scare are believed to have a particularly strong impact on children. Parents fear for the welfare of their children, not only from economic uncertainty and family problems, but from "child molesters and drug dealers, violent teenage gangs, and teen suicide." Even more, parents' "deepest fear is that their children may 'go wrong' due to 'outside influences' over which parents have little control: influences from their children's peer group, teachers, and the mass media."[29]

Victor's thesis is that Satanists involved in a huge Satanic conspiracy have been culturally invented as "scapegoat deviants for the social stresses and internal social conflicts which currently beset American society." Satan proves to be an ideal metaphor with which to express the collective perception of serious moral decay. The conspiracy theory arises "from people's socially constructed predisposition to find Satanism in many unrelated incidents and activities." In the face of cultural conflict of the magnitude people experience today, it is socially necessary to find a scapegoat upon which to focus the conflict in order to prevent the conflict from tearing the culture asunder. In a time of widespread disagreement over what constitutes moral conduct, *Satanists* have been culturally defined as

---

[27]Victor, *Satanic Panic*, pp. 3–4.
[28]Victor, *Satanic Panic*, p. 55.
[29]Victor, *Satanic Panic*, pp. 155–56.

. . . traitors to, or deviant from, the over-arching moral values of the United States. When moral values are in dispute in a society, a witch hunt for moral subversives serves the purpose of clarifying and redefining the limits of moral conduct.[30]

Victor points out (it seems to me, correctly) that scapegoating as a general pattern has increased in the United States in recent years. Targets have included homosexuals, blacks, Jews, immigrants from a variety of places but most notably Hispanics and Haitians, feminists, and environmentalists. Not only alleged Satanists but followers of nonconventional religions in general get caught up in this trend.

A very different sort of explanation comes from Dean M. Kelley, Counselor on Religious Liberty to the National Council of Churches. Kelley's reflections on the topic emerged in response to the Waco tragedy. Kelley's point is that as a culture, we tend to distrust and misunderstand religions that elicit great personal investment from their followers, and we question the sanity of those followers. Kelley writes,

> Few people invest themselves fully in anything. . . . But new religious movements can often attract and enlist higher levels of energy for longer periods of time in commitment to their spiritual vision than any other form of human endeavor. They seek to harness every waking thought and action of their adherents for the advancement and enhancement of their cause. This can be very threatening to their neighbors. . . . But this highly structured high-energy phenomenon can be very attracting to people with intense needs for ultimate meaning. . . . These high-energy movements are the forms of religious behavior at the same time most in need of legal protection and least likely to receive it.[31]

Stephen Carter makes a similar point in his recent and very popular book, *The Culture of Disbelief.* Religion, Carter asserts, has come to be trivialized and regarded as a "hobby" in American culture. Through "all of this trivializing rhetoric runs the subtle but unmistakable message: pray if you like, worship if you must, but whatever you do, do not on any account take your religion seriously."[32]

As you learned in Chapter 3, the presence of both points of view—religion as a very intense, all-consuming experience that sets its members apart from the rest of society and religion seen as one part of life without comprehensive claims on its members—have been present in the United States since the beginning. The passionately religious were a small minority then, and they remain so today. They often incurred the mistrust and persecution of the more moderate then, as they do now. It is worth noting as well that we tend to mistrust and devalue passion

---

[30]Victor, *Satanic Panic*, p. 194–98.
[31]Dean M. Kelley, "Was Religious Liberty Violated at Waco?" *ACRM Info*, American Conference on Religious Movements (April 1994), pp. 8–9.
[32]Stephen L. Carter, *The Culture of Disbelief: How American Law and Politics Trivialize Religious Devotion* (New York: HarperCollins Publishers, Inc., 1993), p. 15.

and radical commitment in general, not just in the religious sphere. Put-down terms such as "tree-huggers" and "feminazis" come to mind. Passionate commitment to causes, people, and ideals is "messy." It doesn't fit in well with our image of a smoothly flowing society. And, it may lead people to rash actions. It challenges our spoken affirmations of a pluralistic culture in which all points of view can find a home in a community of dialogue.

At the same time, as Carter also points out, the passionately religiously committed may not want to engage in dialogue on the terms usually set by modern culture. When individuals seek to engage in dialogue or to influence public policy in the "public square," goes this line of thought, their views must be justified and justifiable in secular terms, no matter how they arrive at those views. It is precisely these terms that the passionately committed are often unlikely to accept as the fundamental rules of the game.[33]

How is it that the canons of public discourse have come to be defined in secular terms in a nation in which over 90 percent of people claim belief in God or a higher power? Survey research on religious commitment sheds light on this apparent contradiction. When religious commitment is measured on the basis of standards drawn from within religion itself, the vast majority of Americans are found to be "effectively secular." These standards include such things as attendance, membership, personal devotional activity, religious salience, and the importance of religion to the respondent. The "committed" report at least some activity on all five of the above indicators. This category includes about one-fifth of the adult population. People with limited religious commitment have attitudes and views that are much closer to those with no religious commitment than they do to their committed peers. They are in effect, "functional secularists."[34] A further factor is that those involved with entertainment and media—the opinion setters and gate keepers—demonstrate a higher degree of secularism than does the general population. Secularism is more prevalent among the highly educated, as well, who are more likely to be in leadership positions in the culture.

Both Kelley and Carter provide additional perspectives on the matter of religion and violence. Kelley raises the question whether the Branch Davidians were acting as "outlaws" or "non-laws." Having noted that many people feel that religious groups cannot be put "above the law," he notes that, while all citizens are bound by law, not all laws are enforced or enforced equally; police officers in fact use considerable discretion in what laws will be enforced and against whom. (To make this point salient, try observing the speed at which the majority of people drive and compare it with the speed limit!) In this situation of differential and partial enforcement, enforcement decisions become a matter of priorities. Which violations will be selected? And, which perpetrators?

In this situation, Kelley argues that religious groups should, by-and-large,

[33]Carter, *The Culture of Disbelief,* pp. 53–6.
[34]Lyman A. Kellstedt, John C. Green, James L. Guth, and Corwin E. Smidt, "Religious Traditions and Religious Commitments in the USA." Paper presented to the XXIIth International Conference of the International Society for the Sociology of Religion, Budapest, Hungary, July 1993.

be let alone. They are, at most, usually "non-laws" rather than "outlaws." For an offense to be punishable as a criminal infraction, there must be *criminal intent.* Religious people and groups who act rashly in the service of their beliefs "are not **outlaws,** in the sense of trying to rip off the rest of society for their own aggrandizement, like a drug-running gang or a racketeering mob. They are at most **"non-laws,"** in the sense of being preoccupied with the safeguarding and promulgation of their own spiritual vision to the exclusion of everything else." When the law conflicts with their sense of religious obligation, they take on the role of "rebels."[35]

Carter, commenting on the Branch Davidian tragedy, writes that

> People to whom religion truly matters, people who believe they have found the answers to the ultimate questions, or are very close to finding them, will often respond to incentives other than those that motivate more secularized citizens. In particular, the threat of death . . . will mean less to some religionists. . . . The lesson of history is that the very religious, when threatened by overwhelming secular force, will often prefer suicide to surrender."[36]

He goes on to point out that everything the Davidians did has also been done by secular people (and more often). Their crimes, if proven, must not be confused with their religiosity. "In other words, we must not assume that it is *the fact of believing deeply* that made the Davidians dangerous, even if it is true that *what they believed deeply* made them dangerous."[37] We must, as a predominantly secular society with a secular legal system, be careful to distinguish the content of belief from its source in belief. Violence or other criminal activity committed with religious motivation is no different than that done out of secular motives.

CURRENT CONCERNS

There is an almost countless number of religious groups that have been, or are, called "cults" by their detractors. The list has varied throughout history. Currently, the two groups, or better, groups of groups, that seem to be of greatest concern are Satanism and the Christian Identity movement. Those who characterize themselves as religious conservatives tend to be more concerned about Satanism. Those who consider themselves religious, political, and social liberals are more likely to voice concerns about Identity Christians. Because these two groups are prominent now, they are discussed extensively here. For a much more exhaustive discussion of nonconventional religions, see J. Gordon Melton's *Encyclopedic Handbook of Cults in America: Revised and Updated Edition.*[38]

[35]Kelley, "Was Religious Liberty Violated at Waco?" pp. 1–10.
[36]Carter, *The Culture of Disbelief,* pp. 275–76.
[37]Carter, *The Culture of Disbelief,* p. 277.
[38]New York: Garland Publishing, Inc., 1992.

Satanism

Satanism has received a lot of negative publicity in recent years, especially in some areas of the country. We can distinguish between two types of Satanism. Anton LaVey (b. 1930) founded the **Church of Satan** in 1966. He collected standard occult and magical teachings around the motif of the worship of Satan. The thrust of **magick** (spelled with a "k" to distinguish it from stage magic) in general is the use of ritual to tap into the power of the universe and use that power to control what happens in one's life. In addition, these forces are believed to manipulate and control people; unless they are the control*lers*, people are the control*led*. There are no other options, according to this worldview. Secrecy is part and parcel of this perspective. It is a defense against hostility and misunderstanding, as well as against curious people who might become involved for shallow reasons (e.g., the chance to participate in an orgy). More important, believers in magick feel that most people simply are not ready for the knowledge that they themselves possess.

The Church of Satan teaches that those things that Christianity has usually condemned as sins (such as pleasure seeking, vengeance, and pride), are actually virtues. Logically, the Church of Satan is dependent on Christianity; it is a reaction to it. LaVey's teachings are contained in three books: *The Satanic Bible* (1969), *The Compleat Witch* (1970), and *The Satanic Rituals* (1972). A list of Nine Satanic Statements at the beginning of *The Satanic Bible* summarizes LaVey's teachings:

1. Satan means indulgence, not abstinence.
2. Satan means living fully now, not vague spiritual aspirations for a future life.
3. Satan means self-knowledge, not hypocrisy and self-deceit.
4. Satan stands for kindness to those who deserve it, not love for the unworthy.
5. Satan stands for vengeance, not forgiveness.
6. Satan means responsibility for those who are responsible, not misplaced concern for "psychic vampires."
7. Satanism teaches that humans are simply animals, animals whose intellectual and spiritual development can make them more vicious than the other animals.
8. Satan encourages gratification of physical and mental desires.
9. "Satan has been the best friend the church has ever had, as he has kept it in business all these years!"

The Church of Satan, in other words, encourages individuals to seek the greatest gratification of their desires and feel free to practice "selfish virtues." The followers of Satan developed a religious framework for a pleasure-seeking life, without violating laws. For the most part, they maintain a very low profile in society. The shock value of something that calls itself Satanism has made its members the target of persecution. At the same time, it has been an ideal vehicle for those who wish to rebel against the predominant culture. (Remember that one of the characteristics attributed to Satan is that he is the arch-rebel.) Although membership figures are not made public and members are often understandably reluctant to reveal their affiliation, membership in the Church of Satan is not widespread.

The individual's birthday is the most important holiday celebrated. Walpurgisnacht (April 30) marks the rebirth of nature in the spring, and Halloween is celebrated as well. Various other magickal and celebratory rituals round out the ritual calendar. In line with its orientation to magick, ritual is the central focus of Satanism in any of its forms.

The second form of Satanism consists of **ritual magick groups**. These small and loosely organized groups believe that people can use the power attributed to Satan to enhance their own power. These groups are responsible for much of the animal sacrifice, sexual rituals, desecration of graves, and human sacrifice that are attributed to Satanism. They are not connected with the Church of Satan. Members of the Church of Satan have sometimes assisted law enforcement officers in investigating such incidents.

Participating in these groups is often a way that their members act out psychological and emotional disturbances. It is important to distinguish cause and effect here. One model depicts Satanism itself as leading to violent, criminal, and antisocial behavior. Another, more accurate, model posits a prior cause—anger and rage, alienation, social maladaptation—that leads both to membership in a Satanic group and to the violent, criminal, and antisocial behavior.

There are a seemingly endless number of stories that circulate concerning the havoc and violence wreaked by Satanists, whose numbers are said to be increasing dramatically. Very few of these reports have been corroborated by outside sources or hard evidence. The attack on Satanism has come largely from evangelical Christianity which, understandably enough, sees Satanism as a pervasive threat. Mike Warnke, author of the best-selling *The Satan Sellers*, has long been a standard on the talk show and lecture circuit. Recently, an investigation carried out by the evangelical Christian community itself discredited Warnke. His claimed "insider" view as a former Satanist and Satanic priest was demonstrated to be a fiction.[39] His work had been responsible for a great deal of the popular opinion of Satanism. This development may well accelerate the call for objective corroboration of stories of this type.

The Christian Identity Movement

"Soldiers of the far right are engaged in a struggle for the hearts, minds and souls of men and women across the Pacific Northwest."[40] The **Christian Identity movement** is a coalition of groups with two primary interests: (1) They have developed their own interpretation of the Bible to justify and encourage racism and

[39] *Religion Watch*, September/October 1992.
[40] Don Duncan, "Thunder on the Far Right," *Grapevine*, July 1987 (New York: Joint Strategy and Action Committee of the National Council of Churches), p. 1.

violence against all people other than whites of European descent. Blacks and Jews are especially targeted. (2) They emphasize the importance of paramilitary training, so that members are prepared to defend themselves in the collapse of order that the organization believes will soon occur. Christian Identity includes several different groups, many of which have ties to the Ku Klux Klan. Among them are the following:

> The **Christian Conservative Churches of America**, which teach the coming collapse of the United States government and encourage members to band together for their survival and the survival of the white race. Associated organizations include **The Christian-Patriots Defense League**, "dedicated to preserving Anglo-Saxon culture against any form of miscegenation" [mixing of the races, especially through interracial marriage] and **The Citizen's Emergency Defense System**, a private military force ready to be activated should the situation demand it.
> **Church of Jesus Christ Christian, Aryan Nation**, a "white racial theo-political movement whose aim is the establishment of white Aryan sovereignty over the lands of Aryan settlement and occupation."
> **The Covenant, the Sword, and the Arm of the Lord**, perhaps the most militant of the groups that comprise the movement. "It fully expects a major internal war in which white Christians will be set against Jews, blacks, homosexuals, witches, and Satanists, as well as foreign enemies."[41]

There are similar organizations in Britain and Canada.

This movement believes that it is the birthright of white Europeans (whom they call Israelites) to be the wealthiest, most powerful nations on earth and to dominate other countries in all ways, using whatever force is necessary to accomplish that goal. The basis is not the covenant that is so important in Judaism, in which the people of God are pledged to obedience and brought into being as a nation by God's choice. The basis is race.

The biblical interpretation that serves as a theological backing for their views is complex and idiosyncratic. According to Christian Identity, when the Lost Tribes of Israel were carried off into captivity, they did not remain in Assyria. They escaped in several waves and moved westward, across Asia Minor, into Europe, the Scandinavian countries, and the British Isles. This identity of the Lost Tribes with modern-day British/German/Celtic countries, including the United States, is the key to their understanding of their role. Jews are believed to be the offspring of Satan. Blacks and other people of color are referred to as pre-Adamic, that is, a lower form of life than whites. Pluralism of any sort is seen as a great evil.

Christian Identity uses its view of the end of history to justify its paramilitary activity. Many Christians believe that Christ will return to Earth, accompanied by both a period of upheaval and conflict and a period of peace and blessedness, "when the lion will lie down with the lamb." Christian Identity

---

[41]Melton, *Encyclopedic Handbook of Cults in America*, pp. 71–6.

teaches that the time of trial and upheaval will precede the return of Christ. There will be no "rapture," in which the faithful are rescued from the Earth before it is wrapped in conflict. Rather, the faithful are expected to remain and help fight the battle as God's agents and soldiers. Identity followers claim that humankind has already entered the period of tribulation. They teach that it is of great importance to be ready to take up arms in God's cause. Being ready to fight for the coming Kingdom means being racist and anti-Semitic in the Identity interpretation of Christianity. In Idaho, for example, pop-up targets bearing the Star of David symbol have been seized.[42]

Many Americans feel threatened by the problems that confront us all: inadequate health care funding, AIDS, the threats inherent in nuclear proliferation, problems in the farm economy, unemployment and underemployment, homelessness, and discipline problems among youth, to name but a few. In this situation, it is easy to look for a scapegoat. Christian Identity focuses this scapegoating and gives it a violent edge, at the same time assuring its followers that they are the only ones who are truly doing God's will.

The movement has been criticized on several grounds. Biblical scholars point out that its theology cannot be supported from any evidence. More pointed criticism has been directed against the racial views and policies of its constituent groups. Because the movement's theology inherently contains the potential for violence, its activities are closely monitored in areas where groups exist. Some members have been indicted on charges ranging from murder to burglary and conspiracy, with some convictions resulting from the charges.

THE WAY, FAITH ASSEMBLY, AND THE UNIFICATION CHURCH

The following three nonconventional religions are less extreme in their views than is either Satanism or the Christian Identity movement. They are important examples of less controversial nonconventional religions.

The Way, International was founded in 1942 by a former minister of the Evangelical and Reformed Church (now a part of the United Church of Christ), Victor Paul Wierwille (1916–1985). He gave the organization its present name in 1974. Headquarters are near New Knoxville, Ohio, and colleges are maintained near Rome City, Indiana (Figure 12–1), Emporia, Kansas, and at other sites. They are quite active on some college campuses. The group's beliefs are stated in the language of traditional Christianity. While these beliefs agree with those of more traditional Christians on many points, some are distinctively different.

1. The Old and New Testaments are held to be inspired by God and perfect as originally given. The various books are said to pertain to different periods in God's re-

---

[42]Duncan, "Thunder on the Far Right," p. 3.

Figure 12–1 The Way, International, has an extensive training program for its members. (*Photo by the author.*)

lationship with humankind. The Way uses its own translation of the Bible and emphasizes the books of Ephesians, Colossians, Philippians, and Galatians.
2. Belief in God, Jesus, and the Holy Spirit is affirmed, but Jesus is not believed to be God and is not considered divine. The Spirit is the power of God, and is impersonal, rather than personal.
3. The Way is pentecostal, believing in the gifts of the Holy Spirit such as speaking in tongues, healing, and prophecy.
4. They believe in one baptism, that of the Holy Spirit, and reject water baptism.
5. The organization of The Way reflects the way in which they believe that the earliest Christian church was organized.

The Way offers a thirty-three hour tape and film course called **Power for Abundant Living**. With further instruction people may become members of The Way Corps, which is a leadership program, or the worldwide missions program, **Word Over the World**. The **American Christian Press** publishes its written materials, including *The Way Magazine*.

The Way has often been the target of deprogrammers when parents have charged that their daughters and sons were being held by the group against the children's will. It has also been criticized for its financial policies, and in 1985 its tax-exempt status was revoked by the Internal Revenue Service. The revocation was overturned by the Supreme Court in 1990.

Faith Assembly was founded near Warsaw, Indiana, by Hobart Freeman. Its headquarters are now in Wilmot, Indiana. There are now Faith Assembly branches in all forty-eight connecting states and at least six foreign countries. Freeman, a former professor at Grace Theological Seminary, had begun collecting a group of devoted followers around him even before he lost his teaching position because his views were no longer acceptable to his colleagues and his church. He then devoted all his time to developing the point of view that he had begun to believe while at Grace, and to gathering an even larger band of followers.

The new church existed for some time without attracting much public attention. Then a public health nurse noticed that the infant mortality rate and the death rate for women in childbirth were much higher for Faith Assembly members than for the population at large. The investigation that followed thrust the Faith Assembly into the public eye. Controversy followed as newspapers, especially the Fort Wayne *News-Sentinel*, published reports of more deaths, along with rigid control over members by Freeman and a "Gestapo-like" mentality within the leadership ranks. The unsolved murders of an editor of the *News-Sentinel* and his family added to the controversy.

Freeman taught the complete avoidance of all conventional medical care, and reliance upon prayer to Jesus for all healing. He told those who listened to him that if they died, or if their children died, it was because their faith was deficient. Adequate faith, coupled with the positive confession of that faith, guaranteed results. One of Freeman's own daughters and her husband left the group after their baby died. Freeman himself died in 1986, and leadership passed to his remaining son-in-law. Under his leadership, the group's views moderated somewhat. While they continued to teach and practice reliance on religious healing, they became less opposed to medical care, especially for children. This came about in part, because the deaths of children led to several court cases and a number of convictions on charges ranging from child neglect or abuse to manslaughter.

The charges and convictions arising from Faith Assembly cases raise the thorny question of the relationship between religious belief and practice in a nation that declares itself to be on the side of religious freedom. It is clear that if an adult wishes to abstain from traditional medical care for religious reasons, that is not the concern of the government. It has become clear in the Faith Assembly cases that it *is* the government's concern when a minor child is deprived of medical care that could have saved its life. In these instances, the state has charged, and the courts have agreed, that the state does have a compelling interest in protecting the lives of helpless children, an interest that overrides the parents' freedom of religion.

The **Unification Church** is a Korean import that has worked very hard at attaining greater acceptance in American culture. The Unification Church (also known as the Holy Spirit Association for the Unification of World Christianity) was organized in 1954 by the Korean Sun Myung Moon ("Shining Sun and Moon"). Its members are frequently called Moonies, usually a derogatory term. According to Unification Church teaching, Adam and Eve were created by God, sinless, and could therefore have been the parents of a perfect human race. However, as the story in Genesis portrays it, Eve was led astray by the devil (in the form of the snake), and then led Adam astray also. Thus, sin and death came into the world.

Seeking to restore humanity to fellowship with God, God sent Jesus as the Messiah, the savior. Jesus was not able to complete his mission and bring about salvation that was both physical and spiritual, however. According to the Christian Bible, Jesus did not marry, and thus could not provide the foundation for the beginning of a new and perfected humanity. Another messiah was needed. This messiah must be male, to reflect God's masculine nature, must marry a wife who reflects God's feminine nature, and together they will produce the children that will be the beginning of the perfected race. The key role of perfected, sinless families in bringing about a restored world order is the reason for the mass weddings for which Moon became famous.

The key text for Unification theology is *Divine Principle*. It is an interpretation of the Christian Bible that is said to clarify the divine principle that Unification followers believe the Bible contains. All of the group's teachings are drawn from this book and others that enlarge upon its principles.

The church carries out a complex program of activities in the United States. Many of its organizations take different names. Some of these are the International Cultural Foundation, the Conference on the Unity of the Sciences, Professors World Peace Academy, Washington Institute for Values in Public Policy, National Council for the Church and Social Action (CAUSA, an anti-communist group), Paragon Press, Rose of Sharon Press, and CARP (Collegiate Association for the Research of Principle, its college evangelism branch). National headquarters are now in New York City. There are about 5,000 members in the United States, with more in Japan and Korea.

Moon spent thirteen months in prison for tax evasion in 1984–85. While this event hindered the group's quest for acceptance, it should be noted that many organizations and individuals within the framework of consensus religion came to Moon's defense, on the basis that the government's interference in the internal affairs of any religious group was a threat to all religious groups.

It is too early to determine if the Unification Church's bid for acceptance will be successful. Its American followers have a clean-cut "all-American" quality about them that will certainly help their search for a place in the mainstream. The church's outspoken support for causes such as the antiabortion movement, anticommunism, and government noninterference in church-operated schools has lessened antagonism from conservative Christians, to whom these issues are very important. Many of their leaders have been trained in theology at some of our leading graduate schools of religion. Their conferences are instrumental in bringing together scholars from many areas. The church's beliefs differ considerably from the average, as do some of their practices. Yet they have had at least limited initial success in forging links with other religious groups. They may move into a position in society parallel to that occupied by the Latter-day Saints. They will be accepted or tolerated by the consensus, without actually being admitted as a part of it.

Nonconventional religions have been a part of the religious scene in the United States almost since its beginning. They will continue to be present, probably in increasing diversity. The approach of the year 2000 seems certain to give rise to new millennial, apocalyptic groups. In this situation, it seems important to maintain a balance between naive, uncritical acceptance of everything that wears the label *religion*, and unreflective negative reaction to everything that appears to be *nonconventional* religion.

QUESTIONS AND ACTIVITIES FOR REVIEW, DISCUSSION, AND WRITING

1. Think about how you would feel if you had joined a community of faith that meant a lot to you and then you were forcibly removed from it and deprogrammed.
2. Think about how you would feel if someone you loved joined a particular religious group and refused to see you anymore. If, on the other hand, they were willing to help you, would you be eager to try to understand their new community of faith and what it meant to them?
3. Find out if any nonconventional religions are represented in your community. If so, try to arrange to visit them, and, if possible, talk with some of the members about what their participation means to them. Instead of visiting, you might invite one of their members to speak with your class.
4. For both Satanism and Christian Identity, write a paragraph in which you discuss what you think are the main reasons for their appeal to people today.
5. Write brief essays in which you respond to the views of (1) Jeffrey Victor concerning Satanism and scapegoating and (2) Dean M. Kelley and Stephen L. Carter concerning passionate religious commitment and our cultural response to it.

FOR FURTHER READING

Deikman, Arthur J., M.D., *The Wrong Way Home: Uncovering the Patterns of Cult Behavior in American Society*. Boston: Beacon Press, 1990. The author's thesis is that "cult behavior" is something in which all people may engage, not just those is specific religious groups. He builds a convincing case and offers suggestions for lessening such behavior in the culture.

Lewis, James R., ed., *From the Ashes: Making Sense of Waco*. Lanham, MD: Rowman & Littlefield Publishers Inc., 1994. Essays from a variety of perspectives in response to the Branch Davidian tragedy. Usually critical of how the situation was handled.

Melton, J. Gordon, *The Encyclopedic Handbook of Cults in America: Revised and Updated Edition*. New York: Garland Publishing, Inc., 1992. Undoubtedly the single best reference on this topic. In spite of the author's continued use of the outdated word *cult*, Melton maintains a thoroughly even handed approach throughout. Good references in each chapter.

Singer, Margaret Thaler, with Janja Lalich, *Cults in Our Midst*. San Francisco: Jossey-Bass Publishers, 1995. Deals with what nonconventional religions are, how they work, and helping "survivors recover." Singer is one of the leading spokespersons for the contemporary anticult movement, and writes from that perspective.

13

Alternative Religion in the Popular Mode

In addition to the vast variety and sheer number of *institutional* alternative religions that we find in the United States, there is a wide range of alternative *popular* religious attitudes and practices. There are institutional manifestations connected with these, but the **focus is on individual and small group involvement apart from ecclesiastical settings such as churches, synagogues, and temples.** I have selected four of these alternatives to review in this chapter. These certainly are not the only ones, but they are representative. The first three—the New Age movement, feminist spiritualities, and twelve-step and self-help programs—overlap at several points. The fourth—agnosticism and atheism—is substantially different.

THE NEW AGE MOVEMENT

The **New Age Movement** is difficult to pin down, because it is not a specific group but a very loose network (a favorite New Age word) of groups, organizations, and individuals with a common set of concerns. There are authors, psychologists, teachers, leaders, body workers, and the like who are well known to most New Agers. There is, however, no single authority. There are well-known and widely accepted books, but no single authoritative text. There are several common beliefs and practices, yet no absolutely definitive belief or practice.

The near-total lack of organization and the flexibility of definition make it difficult to estimate the number of people involved in the New Age movement.

There is also a problem about who, exactly, to count. Are only members of organizations identified with the New Age to be included? Or, should we include anyone who likes to listen to New Age music? These two estimates would result in wildly different numbers. One recent survey indicates that adherents of the New Age movement add up to under 30,000.[1] It has been called the "most popular and widely publicized new religion in recent years."[2]

Its origin in the United States is often traced to the 1960s. Similar ideas, however, have been present throughout American history. The 1960s were a time of discontent with many of the values of the West, especially its spiritual values. At the same time, there was an increased interest in the religious and spiritual values of the East. Courses in world religions and Eastern religions became popular on college campuses. An influx of immigrants from the East brought many Americans into direct contact with ancient Eastern spiritual disciplines and teachings. At the same time, interest grew in the "alternative tradition" of metaphysical, occult knowledge, and practices that has been a part of the history of the West itself.

The key theme which unites New Age followers is one that links them with much of what has gone before in religion in the United States: "The New Age Movement," writes one observer, "can be defined by its primal experience of transformation. New Agers have either experienced or are diligently seeking a profound personal transformation from an old, unacceptable life to a new, exciting future."[3] Although in many ways very different, this same spirit animated the Puritans, those moved by the great revivals of the late 1700s and 1800s, and those who today experience being born again. It also informs the extensive secular self-help movement.

Beliefs

The teachings and practices of the New Age Movement are diverse. There are, however, several major themes that stand out because they recur frequently in New Age literature. We can begin with the major beliefs and attitudes that characterize New Age thinking.

One emphasis is the **need to overcome the dualism that has characterized much of Western thought**. Many of these dualistic ways of thinking have become part of how we view the world and ourselves: sacred or divine/profane or ordinary, religion/science, spirit/matter, mind/body, male/female, thinking/feeling. Virtually without exception, New Age thinkers believe that these dualism must be replaced with a **holistic vision** of the world and ourselves that overcomes dualism while including legitimate differences.

[1] *The New York Times National*, April 10, 1991, p. 1.
[2] Ruth A. Tucker, *Alternative Religions and the New Age Movement* (Grand Rapids, MI: Zondervan Publishing House, 1989), p. 319.
[3] J. Gordon Melton, Jerome Clark and Aidan A. Kelly, *New Age Encyclopedia* (Detroit, MI: Gale Research, Inc., 1990), p. xiii.

An important corollary of this view is the belief in the **immanence of the divine within all things**. Western culture has traditionally taken its cues from a "three-level" view. At the highest level is a God who stands outside the created world and is very different from and vastly superior to it. In the middle are people, created by this God and thus most emphatically not God, yet at the same time, thought to be higher than the rest of creation. The nonhuman world makes up the third level, different from both God and human beings.

In contrast to this understanding, New Agers believe that there is a single life force that is inherent in all living things. The New Age philosophy is **monistic**.[4] The same universal energy animates everything that is. This energy is usually thought of as psychic or mental in nature rather than physical.

Another important corollary of this view is that **all things are intimately interrelated**. The entire universe is a seamless web of life. Nothing happens in isolation, and anything that happens has an impact on the whole.

This leads directly to a great **concern for planet Earth and an interest in ecology**. Since all things are interrelated, the fate of all hinges upon the fate of each. Everyone is responsible for the preservation of the Earth's resources and species. "Think globally, act locally" is an often-repeated phrase.

The **present time is a time of dramatic, far-reaching change**. Some see this change coming in abrupt, cataclysmic fashion. Others see it more in terms of gradual, yet sweeping change. Either way, the accent is on the present time as the beginning point for change at every level of being, from the individual through the entire universe.

The **transformation of self will lead to a transformation of the culture and the planet**. Almost without exception, New Agers believe that the changes that are coming about begin with individual transformation and radiate outward. Individuals have a responsibility to work to transform themselves in order to bring about planetary transformation. No one is exempt from this responsibility, and everyone can do something about the fate of the whole by working on themselves. Most of those who identify themselves as a part of the New Age share a nearly boundless optimism about the possibilities for both personal and communal transformation.

However, self-transformation is but one aspect of what the New Age calls upon individuals to do. **Compassionate service to individual people, to one's community, and on wider levels** is a prominent theme, although one that receives relatively little attention from outside the movement. Through such service, people can bring about startling transformation.

The **underlying unity of all religions** is also a central belief. Although religion takes many forms in different cultures, beneath the differences is a universal religion that will eventually be recognized by all people. This universal religion is grounded in the cycle of the changing seasons and the cycle of human

---

[4]*Monism* is a philosophical and religious view that holds that underneath the apparent diversity of life, there is but one reality.

lifetime. It understands life as a continual process of transformation through which people grow into greater consciousness. Inner exploration, psychic development, and self-awareness are valued highly.

This is but one dimension of the belief that the **development of a planetary culture is both possible and desirable.** This worldwide (and some would say, universe-wide) culture will not replace the distinctive cultures that now exist. It will complement them, both enhancing them and being enriched by them. Legitimate differences will remain. New Age believers look forward to a time when there will be one world government and a world language that is spoken and understood by all, facilitating communication and greater understanding among nations. Some favor the development of a worldwide monetary system to facilitate trade and a world court system as well.

This very large worldwide or planetary goal is echoed in the **development of the communal lifestyles** that have attracted some, bringing into being, in a small and local way, the type of organization that is foreseen on a much wider scale. Such communities are believed to provide the best context for personal transformation, for working toward greater transformation, and for demonstrating that these ideas can work.

Cooperation is more important than competition, and much more to be desired. This relates back to the belief in the interconnectedness of everything. If everything is indeed interconnected, competition is simply the various parts working against the whole. Cooperation benefits the whole by eliminating conflicting actions of the parts.

Most followers of the New Age believe in some form of the Eastern teachings of **karma** and **reincarnation.** They often emphasize the karmic effects of actions in the present lifetime. One way in which the New Age belief in reincarnation differs from most classical Indian teaching on the subject is that New Agers often believe that people can become aware of past lives through meditation, hypnosis, or past-life regression therapy. Doing so is held to be an important way of resolving present problems.

Rituals and Lifestyle

Several key practices are shared by many within the New Age movement. **Being on a spiritual path of some sort is important to most New Age believers.** For some, this means choosing a path and staying with it for a lifetime. For others, it means sampling a variety of spiritual disciplines. The path may be taken from Hindu or Buddhist practice. For some Americans, the importance of finding a compatible spiritual path has led to the study and practice of Native American (Indian) spirituality. Whatever path or paths are chosen, the goals are awareness of the life force and self-development. The goal of union with the mysterious reality that is both within and beyond can be attained more quickly if a deliberate path is taken, rather than leaving it to chance.

The most important religious act is getting in touch with this life force through **ritual** and **meditation**. New Age believers seek communion with sacred reality. They believe that it is both within themselves and within the depths of all that is. Aligning oneself with the flow of the universe is both the goal and the means to the goal. Such alignment is said to produce physical and psychic healing, can bring about parapsychological experiences, and leads to strong feelings of well being and peace of mind.

People **meditate** for many reasons and by many specific means. Meditators seek to quiet and focus their minds. Doing so is said to bring a sense of peace and focus to all of life, a kind of heightened awareness and perspective that extends beyond the time spent in meditation, so that it infuses all activities and relationships. Many people believe that it also has significant health benefits. It is a primary way of being in touch with the sacred. It is a way to reenergize and replenish the energy spent in transformation.

There are nearly as many ways to meditate as there are people who meditate. Many people focus on their breathing, counting to a specific number and then starting over, being aware of how their breathing feels. This helps them stay focused on the present. Some may focus on other objects such as a statue of a deity, a candle flame, or a flower. Some use music for a focus. In mantra meditation, a word or phrase is used. By focusing on one thing with complete concentration, distractions are kept to a minimum.

Rituals of many kinds are also important elements of New Age practice. Meditation is itself a ritual. Rituals may be done to celebrate the changing seasons and the phases of the moon. The New Age movement offers the opportunity for people to construct their own rituals to mark events and occasions for which the larger culture does not have rituals, or to develop creative, more personalized rituals to be used instead of more common ones. *Affirmations* seek to replace negative thoughts with positive ones. *Visualization* encourages people to "see" mentally and spiritually the goals they seek, believing that such seeing helps to bring them into being.

Holistic health and alternative healing are important dimensions of life for many people involved in the New Age movement. The underlying philosophical and religious assumptions of the movement lead people both to question standard medicine and to seek out alternatives to it. Chiropractic, herbal medicine, traditional systems of healing such as those of China and India, and nutritional approaches to healing are all part of the New Age healing repertoire. So are many kinds of body work and massage, done to benefit body, mind, and spirit. Aromatherapy makes use of the effects attributed to specific scents, and color therapy does the same with color. Healing through the use of crystals is popular among some. As with nearly everything in the New Age movement, there is a wide-ranging pragmatism in its approach to healing. Try it and see if it works. Different things work for different people and in different situations. Nontraditional health care practitioners treat many New Age followers who are disillusioned by allopathic medicine and want therapies that are usually less invasive and that attend to the entire person, not just the disease.

Many advocates of the New Age try to follow what they describe as a **simple, natural** lifestyle. This means different things to different people but often includes a preference for clothing made from natural fibers such as cotton and wool over synthetics, natural cosmetics and household products, organic food and growing food at home, and limitation of participation in America's consumer-based culture.

These themes are not new; most, if not all, of them can be found in various earlier groups and movements in the United States. But the New Age movement as it exists in the United States (as well as elsewhere) in the 1990s does have two characteristics that distinguish it from its predecessors and give it a distinctively "modern" flair: First, the basic ideas and themes of the New Age are being applied to distinctly contemporary issues, including world peace, nuclear war, ecological concerns, AIDS, hunger, and homelessness. Second, the very important concept of the immanence of the sacred has been cut loose from its moorings in Eastern religious thought so that it can be espoused by those whose basic religious orientation is in the Judeo-Christian-Islamic tradition.[5]

Organization

There is vast diversity within the New Age movement. Beliefs, and, especially, practices range from the serious and thoughtful to the frivolous and mercenary. Prominent New Age author David Spangler helps us distinguish the serious from the less serious. Merchants have discovered that New Age sells and do not hesitate to take advantage of that fact. Most of the publicity surrounding the New Age movement has focused on many highly publicized teachers and adepts, a renewed interest in angels, channelers, popular self-help books and tapes, and occurrences such as the harmonic convergence of the late 1980s. The requirement for inclusion at this level seems to be that some "glitzy" aspect of the movement catches public interest.

Some followers of the New Age movement are committed to dramatic change in themselves and in their culture. Economics, politics, social institutions, education, and technology are all involved and are all changed to support planetary goals. People with this perspective speak about becoming able to see everything as holy, a reintegration of the human with the sacred, and with the earth conceived as a living being. In Spangler's words, it is "a deepening into the sacramental nature of everyday life, an awakening of the consciousness that can celebrate divinity within the ordinary and, in this celebration, bring to life a sacred civilization."[6]

A number of **organizations** are involved to a greater or lesser degree with the New Age. At the same time, there is no single New Age organization, nor

[5]Mary Ferrell Bednarowski, *New Religions and the Theological Imagination in America* (Bloomington, IN: Indiana University Press, 1989), pp. 17–18.
[6]David Spangler, *Emergence: The Rebirth of the Sacred* (New York: Dell Publishing Company, 1984).

even a cluster of them. There are **centers** that teach the various mystical, occult, and Eastern religions. **Yoga teachers** can be found in most cities. **Health-food stores and restaurants** have at least some relationship to the movement, since many practitioners are vegetarians, and most, if not all, emphasize the importance of natural, chemical-free food. **Bookstores** provide books dealing with New Age subjects, and sell tapes and records of New Age music. Research into **parapsychology** (extrasensory perception studies and near-death experiences, for example) is also part of the New Age movement. Interest in psychic development has led to the production and distribution of audiotapes, videotapes, and tapes with **subliminal**[7] messages designed to assist in self-development. There are also scientists involved in studying the relationships between physics, biology, other sciences, and the Eastern teachings of the New Age. A group of **journals and magazines** makes new information available and facilitates communication among New Age believers. Titles include *East/West Journal, Yoga Journal, Common Boundary,* and *New Age Journal.*

New Age followers are a diverse group of people for whom an authentic spiritual search has led generally eastward and inward. Their affiliation with the movement varies from being at its center to barely touching its edges. They are among those whose religious needs have not been met in the more usual religions. New Age believers do not meet in church buildings or have an organized hierarchy of leadership. It is a religion, however, in that it provides for its followers the four elements of belief, lifestyle, ritual, and organizations in a way that helps to make life meaningful and good.

How can we summarize such a diverse movement and perhaps locate it within the larger sweep of American culture? A review of several New Age books does so this way:

> It is not all that clear . . . what role the New Age movement plays in American culture. It functions in many ways. It can certainly be seen as another blossoming of the persistent metaphysical tradition in America. It is an arena in which people in a secular culture can ask and answer theological questions in nondoctrinal terms and outside the parameters of established religious institutions. It generates alternative perspectives on a variety of social issues, pollution and nuclear warfare among the most central. It provides insights into some of the effects of religious pluralism in American culture—in part, perhaps, the coming to fruition of popular knowledge about non-Western religious traditions. It offers a forum in which both experts and amateurs speculate about the relationships among religion, the physical sciences, and the social sciences. And it demonstrates the vitality of grass-roots religion and what might even be called "grass-roots science" in American culture.[8]

When it is described in this way, we can see that the New Age movement is not something alien to its American context. It integrates themes and basic

---

[7] *Subliminal* means below the level of conscious awareness.
[8] Mary Ferrell Bednarowski, "Literature of the New Age: A Review of Representative Sources," in *Religious Studies Review,* 17, no. 3 (July 1991), p. 216.

ways of approaching religion that have been a part of the culture almost from the beginning.

TWELVE-STEP AND THE SELF-HELP MOVEMENT

Twelve-step programs such as Alcoholics Anonymous are only part of a larger movement that we can call the self-help movement. However, the founding of **Alcoholics Anonymous** marked the beginning of a new era in self-help movements as well. Its twelve steps to recovery provide the blueprint for many such programs today.

A.A., as it is most commonly known, began in Los Angeles, California, in 1935. It was founded by a layman, William G. Wilson, and a doctor, Robert Smith (usually referred to as "Bill W." and "Dr. Bob," since anonymity is a cornerstone of group procedure). These two men, along with a third individual, began talking together about how to overcome their struggles with alcohol, and the organization was born out of their experience together.

Much of the basic philosophy of A.A. initially came from the Oxford Groups or Moral Re-Armament Movement, a fairly conservative Christian movement that had begun in England in the early 1920s. Stated briefly, the movement held that

> God could become real to anyone who was willing to believe. . . . Estrangement from God is . . . caused by moral compromise. People needed to examine their lives against the standards of absolute purity, unselfishness, and love. . . . [The movement] emphasized the need for sharing and guidance. Sharing consists of confession of one's sins and failures to another member of the group.[9]

At first, the members of "The Way Out" (as the group for recovering alcoholics was first named), remained part of Moral Re-Armament. However, the rather evangelical Christian bent of that group became a problem as interest in their approach to alcoholism spread to include people of other faiths and no faith at all. The group revised its approach so that a very clear spiritual element remained, without its being linked to any particular religion. In its essence, A.A. and its offshoots offer people

> . . . a nondenominational, nonpolitical approach to spirituality as the foundation for developing a positive self-image and arresting the illness that was manifesting itself in compulsive behaviors. These Twelve-Step Programs . . . [offer] the individual the opportunity to develop his or her own conception of a Higher Power,

[9]J. Gordon Melton, *The Encyclopedia of American Religions*, 3rd ed. (Detroit: Gale Research, Inc., 1989), p. 964.

to build personal relationships, and to make a guided self-assessment so that major life changes could be made.[10]

The approach that A.A. takes to recovery from alcoholism is that alcoholism is a disease that has physical, mental, and spiritual dimensions. It can be best treated through its spiritual dimension. When alcoholics work on their spiritual lives, physical and mental recovery will follow as well. This is best done, say A.A. members, in the context of supportive groups of fellow sufferers. The strategy is summarized in the famous Twelve Steps.[11]

1.   We admitted that we were powerless over alcohol, that our lives had become unmanageable.

2.   We came to believe that a power greater than ourselves could restore us to sanity.

3.   We made a decision to turn our will and lives over to the care of God as we understood him. A.A. regards the admission of one's inability to deal with the problem on one's own as the necessary starting point. It echoes the Christian belief in people's powerlessness apart from God. "As we understood him" is central to the spiritual view of A.A. People do not have to accept a particular belief in God or a Higher Power, but are left free to conceptualize their Higher Power as they will. For some, however, this remains a stumbling block, and there have been a few groups formed that follow a similar approach to that of A.A. but without the overtly religious overtones. The largest of these self-consciously secular sobriety groups is S.O.S., or Secular Organizations for Sobriety (also, Save Our Selves).

Women and black people, especially, have questioned this approach, feeling that neither needs to have their sense of oppression and powerlessness reinforced, since that is often part of the problem. They have also asked if it simply substitutes one kind of dependency—albeit perhaps a less destructive one—for another.

4.   We made a searching and fearless moral inventory of ourselves.

5.   We admitted to God, to ourselves, and to another human being the exact nature of our wrongs. These two steps clearly reflect the movement's roots in Moral Re-Armament. They also reinforce the distinctive spiritual or religious nature of A.A.'s technique. Self-examination and confession to God and to another person are important dimensions in many religious groups.

6.   We became entirely willing to have God remove our defects of character.

7.   We humbly asked him to remove our shortcomings. Willingness to be helped is understood to be a necessary precondition of being helped. Again, this belief is a feature of many religions, as well.

---

[10]Sandra Sizer Frankiel, "California and the Southwest," in *Encyclopedia of the American Religious Experience: Studies of Traditions and Movements*, ed. Charles H. Lippy and Peter W. Williams (New York: Charles Scribner's Sons, 1988), p. 1520.

[11]The Twelve Steps are listed in nearly every Alcoholics' Anonymous publication. The steps are in italic type. I have added comments to some of them.

8.   We made a list of all persons we had harmed, and became willing to make amends to them all.

9.   We made direct amends to such persons whenever possible, except when to do so would injure them or others. You may remember that the Jewish practice of repentance includes making amends to people who have been wronged. Buddhists, as well, believe that direct amends should be made whenever possible and whenever no further injury will result from doing so. The same is true of some other religions.

10.   We continued to take a daily inventory, and when we were wrong promptly admitted it. Commitment to consistency and regular, mindful self-examination is also a feature of many religions. It was practiced, for example, by the Puritans who were in the New World from the earliest days of the colonies.

11.   We sought through prayer and meditation to improve our conscious contact with God, praying only for knowledge of his will for us and the power to carry that out. The spiritual dimension of this step is obvious. It carries forward the theme of surrender of self-will to the will of a higher power.

12.   Having had a spiritual awakening as a result of these steps, we tried to carry this message to other alcoholics and to practice these principles in all our affairs. Three of the major religions of the world—Christianity, Islam, and Buddhism—are missionary religions, carrying the message of spiritual awakening to other people. "Spreading the Gospel" has been an important feature of Christianity in the United States, as well as elsewhere.

This analysis of the twelve steps clearly delineates the spiritual character of the movement. Like organized religions, twelve-step and other self-help programs offer their followers something from each of the four dimensions of religion. Perhaps the most important **belief** is that human beings *can* transform their lives. Even when the situation appears hopeless—or most of all when it appears hopeless—people have the capacity to make a better life for themselves. Some programs, like A.A., advocate reliance on a power outside oneself. Other programs focus on self-effort. Certainly the reliance on "other power" is more in tune with the predominance of Christianity in this country. Reliance on self-effort, however, echoes a theme as old as the beginning of the United States: the self-reliant frontiersman or frontierswoman setting out to conquer the wilderness. Self-effort and individualism, although not always highlighted in American religion, are significant parts of the larger American cultural story. The importance of "working on oneself" and bettering oneself goes back as far as the Puritans, for whom growth in personal character was a highly prized goal. Taking responsibility for one's actions and their results is also a theme that is written large in both religion and secular culture in the United States.

There is yet another presupposition of the self-help movement that draws on an important feature of American religion. In self-help groups, people are aided in their own efforts by their peers. While a few groups have a professional leader or counselor, many do not. Even in those that do, the professional is there primarily as a facilitator, not as "the person whose responsibility it is to fix everything." Democracy in government in the United States has spilled over into many areas of life. We noted that even those communities of faith that are primarily hierarchical in their organization are usually less so in their American embodiments. There is a tendency to see the leaders as leading their congregations in ministry, rather than being the only ones involved in ministry. Many alternative popular spiritual groups are very democratic in their structure. Especially in recent years, we have become a nation of individuals who seek to take responsibility for our own lives, whether in terms of religion, health, education, or automobile repair. "Let a professional take care of it" is no longer thought of as the only or the best solution.

Alcoholics Anonymous teaches the importance of changing one's **lifestyle** if one is to stay sober. Lasting sobriety is not likely to be achieved if recovering alcoholics continue to go to bars, socialize with former drinking buddies, and engage in whatever other behaviors were associated with their drinking. Most self-help groups emphasize changes in lifestyle. The details of these changes depend upon the goal of the particular group, but lifestyle is a focus for nearly all. New habits must replace old, and new rewards must supplant old, negative ones. This reflects the importance that lifestyle and morality in general have for American religion. As a general rule, people's religious *beliefs* are not of great concern to most people, as long as those who hold the beliefs conform to the accepted canons of behavior.

The **ritual** dimension is there as well. Meeting together for mutual support and fellowship is central for the self-help movement. It is customarily believed that the best context for making important changes is a fairly small, supportive group of people who know what each other are going through because they're "all in the same boat." Some groups help people develop rituals to mark important changes of life, recognizing that rituals simply do not exist for many contemporary occasions that nonetheless need rituals.

Certainly the **organizational** dimension is present. Alcoholics Anonymous itself spawned a number of other organizations such as Al-Anon (for families of alcoholics) and Alateen (specifically for teenagers), and, most recently, groups for adult children of alcoholics. Twelve-step groups have been formed to help people recover from other compulsive behaviors, including drug addiction, gambling, overeating, uncontrolled spending, and spouse and child abuse. These organizations have then developed groups for spouses and other family members of the recovering person. A nearly limitless number of other kinds of support groups have formed, all based on the premise that the best support in a crisis comes from other people who have been through similar experiences. Some direct all their energies toward helping the people involved. Weight Watchers is but one example. There are also support groups for people with cancer (and for their families and friends), and those who are divorcing, chronically ill, or in chronic pain. Your campus may have a variety of support groups for students. Groups for students who suffer test anxiety is but one example.

Other support groups have also developed a "political" dimension that complements their supportive function. Mothers Against Drunk Driving (MADD) began as a support group for parents whose child had been killed or injured in an alcohol-related accident. They soon began working actively to reduce the number of such accidents. Support groups for people who are HIV-positive or who have AIDS (and their families and friends) often undertake political activity on behalf of affected people.

As we have seen, the self-help movement, exemplified by Alcoholics Anonymous and other similar groups, is clearly a spiritual movement. For some people, it is an adjunct to participation in a community of faith. For others, it is a substitute for such participation. The specific format, and certainly the proliferation of these groups, is relatively new on the American scene. On the other hand, as we have seen, some of the themes and presuppositions are as old as the United States itself.

FEMINIST SPIRITUALITIES

Most—although not all—of the religious groups and organizations in the United States share at least some of the patriarchal viewpoints and practices that continue to mark American culture in general. This has created concern for many women in these communities of faith. We can describe the responses that women make to this situation in terms of a continuum. At one end are those **many women for whom traditional structures, views, and rituals are meaningful and fulfilling**. Survey data strongly indicate that women are more traditionally religious than are men. Many women, perhaps the majority, are not disturbed by references to God as "He" and to humanity as "man." These women can and do remain within their traditional communities of faith and find meaning there, without seeking or desiring change. Some may feel threatened by people who *are* bothered by the questions and issues that do not bother them and who do seek change. The religious right has made upholding women's traditional roles a central theme.

Some women elect to remain within their communities of faith without actively seeking change, even though they are dissatisfied with things as they are. They simply do not see themselves as agents of change, or do not want to "rock the boat" in ways that may threaten the stability of their lives. They are content to see change come slowly, if it comes at all.

Further along this continuum are those **women who actively work for change within their churches, temples, and synagogues**. It is among these women that one form of **feminist theology and feminist spirituality** has emerged. These women, and men who are sympathetic with their cause, work to change religion in all of its dimensions to make it more inclusive of women and women's views and experience. You learned about some of these changes in Chapter 3.

There are also **women who cannot find anything within their tradition to** sustain their religious lives. Some of these women abandon religion altogether and **become secularists or secular humanists.** For at least some of them, the women's movement itself comes to serve many of the functions that religion plays in people's lives. It helps to provide a worldview, sometimes provides rituals, supports a relatively well-defined lifestyle, and provides organizational structures within which to work and find fellowship with like-minded people. Others have **turned to Eastern religions** in the hope of finding space there in which their feminism and their religion could exist side by side. Often hope has turned to disappointment when the chosen religion was found to embody many of the same attitudes as did the religion they had left.

Other women have **founded or joined groups specifically based on women's spirituality.** This is the response that I will focus on in this section. More specifically, I want to look at **goddess worship and the Wiccan tradition** as it relates to feminist spirituality.

Women and men who consider themselves to be followers of the types of religion described below also do not agree completely on how the religion should be named. Some prefer **Wicca** (practitioners are **Wiccans**), a word meaning "Wise Ones." It has the same root as our word "wisdom." Some of its advocates believe that using this less familiar word helps overcome the negative connotations often associated with the word "witch." Others deliberately use **Witchcraft** and **Witch** in a bold move to reclaim the word from its detractors. Others prefer **the Craft**, with its emphasis on the ritual work that Wiccans do. For still others, **the old religion** signifies the ancient roots of this worldview. I will use these terms interchangeably.

Attempts to develop an agreed-upon statement of Wiccan belief have fallen far short of universal acceptance among actual Wiccans. Decentralization and the autonomy of individuals and groups is a primary organizing principle. However, it is possible to describe certain basic beliefs that are widely shared among Wiccans. In a similar fashion, I will describe common ritual practices.

Wicca is one form of a larger world view, that of **magick.** Magick was described in the preceding chapter. You will recall that the basis of this view is that there are unseen, although completely natural, forces within the world that can control and manipulate people if people do not learn to control them. Sybil Leek, a contemporary American Witch, defines magick as "the art of producing a desired effect or result through the use of various techniques such as incantations and presumably assuring human control of supernatural agencies or the forces of nature."[12] Ritual provides the primary tool for working with these forces. In a nation in love with technology (although perhaps less enamored of its promises than we once were), Witchcraft offers a "spiritual technology" with which to interact with unseen forces. At the same time, it runs against the primary grain of American thought about the divine. The Judeo-Christian tradition that has had

---

[12]Sybil Leek, *Diary of a Witch* (Englewood Cliffs, NJ: Prentice Hall, Inc., 1968), p. 4.

the greatest influence on American religious ideas emphasizes that God cannot be manipulated nor controlled by human beings.

Most Wicca in the United States traces its roots back to British author and lecturer Gerald B. Gardner (1884–1964) and therefore it is called "Gardnerian Wicca." Although there are various accounts of exactly how Gardner developed his religious thought and practice, it blended together elements from Western occult and magickal traditions with various pieces of Eastern religions that he picked up while living in India and Southeast Asia. The Gardnerian tradition came to the United States with Raymond and Rosemary Buckland in the mid-1960s. The Bucklands formed a coven on Long Island, and Gardnerian thought and practice spread from there. Although there are many variations within the American Wiccan community, most of them retain at least the outlines of Gardner's world view and ritual. Among the most closely related schools is the Alexandrian, formed by Alexander Sanders (1926–1988).

Beliefs

The way in which the sacred or holy is thought about and spoken about, addressed in prayer and celebration, is one of the most central beliefs in any religion. In response to the traditional habit of thinking and speaking of God in the Judeo-Christian-Islamic tradition as if God were male, some women have turned to belief in and worship of the Goddess instead. Goddess worshippers believe in a female creator, often paired with a god as the male principle. Although it came to public attention in the 1970s, goddess worship had been explored much earlier by women in the Victorian period.[13] Followers of the goddess look back to religions that predate Judaism and Christianity, in which the goddess was very important. Worshipping both a god and a goddess, with the emphasis placed on the goddess, restores a balanced view of ultimate reality or the holy for these people, in ways that simply altering traditional language cannot. Not all followers of the Goddess are Wiccans, but virtually all Wiccans are worshippers of the Goddess.

According to one feminist scholar, women need the goddess for four main reasons. (1) Her most basic meaning is the acknowledgement of female power as good and as independent of anything or anyone else. She provides a way that female power can be called forth in ritual and prayer. (2) She affirms the female body and the life cycles inherent in it that are also inherent in the earth. She appears in the roles of maiden, mother, and crone, affirming virginity, motherhood, and old age. (3) The goddess encourages women to affirm that the will of the female can be effective in the world and to work to make it so. Through the goddess, women can believe in the female will as valid and not subordinate to the will of males. (4) The goddess is a revelation of female bonding, especially the

---

[13]Rosemary Radford Ruether and Rosemary Skinner Keller, *Women and Religion in America, Volume III: 1900–1968* (San Francisco: Harper & Row, Publishers, 1986), p. xiv.

mother-daughter bond, as opposed to the patriarchal heritage in which women's bonds are with men. The goddess helps women to affirm and celebrate "female power, the female body, the female will, and women's bonds and heritage."[14]

One practicing Wiccan woman puts it this way: Images of deity as Goddess "inspire us to see ourselves as divine, our bodies as healthy, the changing phases of our lives as holy, our anger as purifying, and our power to nurture and create, but also to limit and destroy when necessary, as the very force that sustains all life."[15]

For many goddess worshippers, the goddess is a way to the recognition and celebration of the divinity within themselves. They experience the entire world as one divine whole and see themselves as a part of it. To address and celebrate the goddess is but a step on the way to "reclaiming [their] own divinity as part of the vastness of the natural world."[16]

Wiccans usually worship the Goddess in her threefold form, sometimes referred to as the **Triple Goddess**. She is **Maiden, Mother,** and **Crone,**[17] signifying the various ages of woman. She is frequently symbolized by the phases of the moon—the waxing or rising crescent, the full moon, and the waning or subsiding moon. Wiccans draw on the goddess traditions of many times and cultures, believing that all the names of the Goddess are equally valid. She is invoked by many names in ritual:

> Isis, Astarte, Diana, Hecate, Demeter, Kali, Inanna. . . . Listen to the words of the Great Goddess, the Great Mother of the Universe—Gaia, Yemaya, Spider Woman, Ishtar, Ashtoreth, Mary, Inanna, Demeter—known by a thousand names across geography and time.[18]

Most also worship her consort, **Pan** or the **Horned God** of the fields. He, likewise, has had many names in many times and places.

Wiccans also affirm the **divinity and holiness of all living beings and of the Earth** itself (or, as many would put it, Herself). There is disagreement about the relationship between Wicca and the Pagan religious traditions, but they have at least this in common.

> In the Wiccan worldview, there is no warring dichotomy between Spirit and Nature. Rather, they are part and parcel of one another; the sacred permeates all as-

---

[14]Carol P. Christ, "Why Women Need the Goddess: Phenomenological, Psychological, and Political Reflections" in *Womanspirit Rising: A Feminist Reader in Religion,* ed. Carol P. Christ and Judith Plaskow (San Francisco: Harper & Row, Publishers, 1979), pp. 276–85.

[15]Starhawk (Miriam Samos), *The Spiral Dance: A Rebirth of the Ancient Religion of the Great Goddess* (San Francisco: Harper & Row, Publishers, 1979), p. 8.

[16]Hallie Inglehart, *Womanspirit: A Guide to Women's Wisdom* (San Francisco: Harper & Row, Publishers, 1983), p. 97.

[17]*Crone* is a term of respect that means "a wise old woman."

[18]The first listing of names is from a widely used chant, the origin of which is unknown at this time. The second is the beginning of the "Charge of the Goddess," cited in Nikki Bado, "Multiculturalism within the Women's Spirituality Movement: The Search for Female Deistic Images" (unpublished paper), p. 1.

pect of the cycle of life and death. Witchcraft takes its teachings primarily from Nature, in the cycle of the seasons, which we call the Wheel of the Year, we are inspired to see and experience the sacred dimension within the rhythms of life all around us. . . . Becoming aware of and in tune with the rhythms of Nature—the cycles of beginning, growth, and ending, learning how to work with these rhythms and not against them—these are the lessons of the Wheel of the Year.[19]

Witches believe that **people**, because we are conscious and have freedom of choice, **have a unique responsibility toward the environment**. It is up to people to live a lifestyle that reflects respect for Earth and to live in harmony with Nature. Often, Earth is revered as a manifestation of the Goddess.

Witches **do not worship Satan** or the Christian devil. The beginnings of Wicca predate Christianity, while Satanism relies on the development of the idea of Satan within the Christian tradition.

Nor do Witches try to put evil spells and curses or hexes on people. Such behavior is always considered unethical. Self-determination, personal freedom, and autonomy are central values in Wiccan ethics and morality. Most Witches feel that it is unethical even to work a spell for someone's benefit without their knowledge and agreement. There are two basic principles that guide behavior. One is the "Wiccan Rede," **An ye harm none, do what ye will.** *An* here is an ancient use of the word that means "as long as." The second is the principle that what people do returns to them. Many put this in terms of the **Threefold Law:** Whatever we do returns to us three times over, be it good or ill.

Practices

Witches often organize into **covens** or small groups of three to twenty people to perform rituals and enjoy fellowship. There are also *solitaries*, Witches who, through personal choice or circumstances, practice alone. Some covens are all female (and a few are all male) and some are mixed. Although there are traditional rituals that have been handed down, most feel very free to improvise and create new rituals as occasions call for them.

"**Casting a circle**" is a fundamental ritual. The circle thus marked off becomes a sacred space. Wherever it is, indoors or out, city or farm, it becomes a place in which the sacred can be contacted and interacted with. Ritual purification of the circle removes negative energy from it, protects those within it, and helps to concentrate their own spiritual energies on the task at hand. This is most often done using the traditional elements of air, earth, fire, and water. Often, gods and goddesses are called upon to be present alongside the human participants.

The circle having been cast and purified, participants often **raise a cone of power**. This is done by chanting or dancing (or both) or running around the circle. The "cone of power" is really the combined wills of the group, intensified

---

[19]Nikki Bado, "Changing the Face of the Sacred: Women Who Walk the Path of the Goddess," in *Explorations: Journal for Adventurous Thought*, 8, no. 1 (Fall 1989), p. 7.

through ritual and meditative techniques, focused on an end collectively agreed upon.[20]

The focus can be any of a number of things. Healing, both physical and emotional, is a common focus. Healing can be directed toward individuals (within the circle or outside it), groups, or Earth itself. Sometimes the focus is simply to raise positive energy. Coven work often centers around directing positive energy toward the goals of the members and others—be it finding a job, a love relationship, overcoming a crisis, or simply living with grace and joy in everyday life. This type of work is done in **esbats**, coven meetings that are held traditionally at the time of the full and new moons, although they may be held at other times as well. Some covens, for example, meet weekly. The ritual work is most often followed by sharing a meal or at least refreshments and a time of fellowship.

There is also a series of **seasonal festivals or Sabbats** that reflect the natural cycle of the seasons and the positions of the Sun and Earth relative to each other. There are four **Great Sabbats**: (1) **Samhain** or the Celtic New Year on October 31; (2) **Candlemas** on February 2, a Winter festival that focuses on purification and the beginning of Spring; (3) **Beltane**, May 1, the great Spring festival of fertility and renewal symbolized by the marriage of the god and goddess; and (4) **Lughnasadh** (in some accounts, **Lammas**), the August 1 festival of the first fruits of harvest that also looks toward the seasonal decline of Winter. The four **Lesser Sabbats** celebrate the Summer and Winter solstices (June and December) and the Spring and Fall equinoxes (March and September).

Initiation is an important ritual for individual Witches. Although some Witches believe that a person must be initiated by another Witch, others support self-initiation, especially if the opportunity for initiation by a practicing Witch is not available. However it is carried out, it is a rite of beginning, of accepting and celebrating one's status, and of becoming a part of the Wiccan community of faith and agreeing to live by its norms.

Organizations

When we try to estimate the number of people who are Wiccans, we encounter problems similar to those involved in counting New Agers. We also confront a different problem. Because of the negative associations that many people bring to Witchcraft, many Wiccans are understandably reluctant to reveal their participation. Groups do not report membership figures. One recent survey puts the number of Wiccans in the United States at under 50,000.[21]

Most Wiccan covens are small, and there is no central organization. Those that I describe below are intended to be examples of some of the better-known

[20]Margot Adler, *Drawing Down the Moon: Witches, Druids, Goddess-Worshippers and Other Pagans in America Today*, 2nd. ed. (Boston: Beacon Press, 1986), p. 109.
[21]*New York Times National,* April 10, 1991, p. 1.

ones. The **Church and School of Wicca** in New Bern, North Carolina, is one of the most accessible of the Witchcraft groups. Its twelve-lesson home study course is widely advertised. Its members have campaigned energetically to promote what they believe is a correct understanding of the meaning of the Craft and to help overcome centuries of prejudice and misunderstanding.

The **Church of Circle Wicca** is located in Mount Horeb, Wisconsin. Like the Church and School of Wicca, it has maintained a much higher public profile than have most Wiccan groups. It is believed to be the largest network for such groups, and its Circle Sanctuary is the site of many intergroup conferences and celebrations.

The **Covenant of the Goddess** is in Berkeley, California. It is a national organization that encourages cooperation between various covens and traditions within American Wicca. Its members also work for the legal recognition of Wicca as a religion. Such recognition would make the same benefits available to Wiccan groups that are enjoyed by other communities of faith, such as tax exemption.

Dianic Wicca, exemplified by the Susan B. Anthony Coven Number One, is a collective term for covens that have developed a strongly feminist emphasis. They consider themselves completely separate from the Gardnerian lineage. Dianic Witches worship the ancient goddess **Diana** (identified with the Greek goddess Artemis). Diana was a deity of woods and forests and the special patron of women and childbirth. She is a virgin, and her virginity symbolizes female independence from males. Since its organization beginning in the early 1970s, Dianic Wicca has been recognized as an important dimension of American Wicca. Its followers unite in Dianic covens or participate in non-Dianic covens.

Our Lady of Enchantment, Church of the Old Religion also sponsors correspondence courses. Its center near Nashua, New Hampshire, includes a bookstore, library, museum and a seminary for training priestesses and priests in the Wiccan tradition. Some members live at the center itself. Members and nonmembers, residents and sympathetic nonresidents, may participate in the ritual and educational life of the community and share in its fellowship.

What are we to make of Wicca? What does it offer its adherents? It seems to me that there are several things. (1) As a part of the magickal tradition, it offers people techniques for dealing with the mystery of the divine in constructive ways that people believe allow them to benefit from sacred forces. (2) It offers an alternative to the patriarchalism of the prevailing Western and most Eastern religions. (3) It teaches the immanence of the divine in all things and thus seems to many to be more "Earth-friendly" than the monotheistic religions. Its seasonally-based ritual calendar gives people ways to celebrate their closeness to the natural world. (4) Similarly, its emphasis on the sacred within every person suggests new ways of understanding what is to be a human being. (5) For many women, Wicca provides a way to affirm and celebrate being a woman in a culture that has not always valued women as highly as males.

AGNOSTICISM AND ATHEISM

Before you read further, stop and ask yourself what might lead someone to be an atheist or agnostic. Do those views seem to you to be reasonable ones for someone to hold, whether or not you, yourself, do?

We'll begin with a brief definition of each word. **Atheism** is most often defined as not believing in any deity. In the United States, atheism usually means not believing in God as God is thought of in the Judeo-Christian-Islamic tradition. However, many atheists think that this definition is inadequate. While acknowledging that the word **atheist** is used to mean a person who *denies* the existence of God, they press for a distinction:

> Even an atheist would agree that *some* atheists (a small minority) would fit this definition. However, most atheists . . . would hold that an atheist is a person *without* belief in God. The distinction is small but important. Denying something means that you have knowledge of what it is that you are being asked to affirm, but that you have rejected that particular concept. To be *without* belief in God merely means the term "God" has no importance or possibly no meaning to you.[22]

Having said that, however, it is necessary to note that, usually, in the United States, most people use the words *atheism* and *atheist* with the meaning of not believing in God.

A typical definition, and one from a trustworthy source, is as follows:

> [A]theism is the doctrine that God does not exist, that belief in the existence of God is a false belief. The word *God* here refers to a divine being regarded as the independent creator of the world, a being superlatively powerful, wise, and good.[23]

Agnostics (those whose position is **agnosticism**) are people who do not think that we have enough evidence to say with any certainty if God exists or if God does not exist. Some agnostics believe that, even if we can say with some degree of certainty that God does exist, we can have absolutely no knowledge of the nature or character of that God.

Atheism, agnosticism, and various other types of "free thought" that are not in accord with the Judeo-Christian perspective have been a part of the religious and cultural perspective ever since Europeans came to the New World. Atheism and agnosticism were included in the plurality of religious views held by the early colonists and by the framers of the Constitution. Current survey data indicate that between five and ten percent of the population does not believe in some higher power.

---

[22]Gordon Stein, "Introduction," in *An Anthology of Atheism and Rationalism*, ed. Gordon Stein (Buffalo, NY: Prometheus Books, 1980), p. 3.

[23]George Alfred James, "Atheism," in *The Encyclopedia of Religion, Vol. 1*, ed. Mircea Eliade (New York: Macmillan Publishing Company, 1987), pp. 479–80.

There are a number of different themes that appear repeatedly in people's reasons for disavowing belief in a supreme being or higher power. One study of the phenomenon lists seven such themes.[24] Some people believe that **the being whom people call God is a projection of human needs, wants, and hopes.** Following psychiatrist Sigmund Freud, for example, some atheists say that we as human beings want a father figure to protect us, to punish us when we deserve to be punished, and to reward us when we have been good. We want, in other words, to remain in a childlike relationship with a powerful father. Since our earthly fathers inevitably die—and also fail to meet our expectations while they are alive—we create a God who is an omnipotent, all-knowing father. Alternatively, following Marx, people who are oppressed and mistreated project a God who will reward them in the future for present suffering and deprivation. This, then, invites abuse by the privileged and ruling classes, who can promise those they oppress future rewards in Heaven for compliance and punishments in Hell for disobedience. This dynamic was at work in some of the uses made of Christianity by slave holders.

A third alternative of this type is more sociological. Following sociologist Émile Durkheim, this view holds that a society (rather than individuals) projects a God as the source of its dearest values and social norms. The social norms and cultural values gain authority and sanction by being attributed to the deity. A very similar dynamic can be seen when proponents of various (and often opposing!) social positions claim that "God is on their side," as has been done by both sides in the abortion rights debate and the homosexual rights debate.

A second argument atheism espouses is that **faith in God is simply not consistent with the scientific view of reality and the methods that such a view entails.** In other words, "God" cannot be proven by the methods of science, especially as refined and practiced by the natural sciences. Furthermore, the concept of God may be used to fill in where knowledge does not exist, as a substitute for knowledge, thus hindering the furtherance of knowledge. This is sometimes called a "God of the gaps" theology. "God" is brought in to explain that for which there is no other explanation. Thus, as human knowledge grows, God must necessarily shrink. Although most theologians do not support this view, it is fairly common among believers generally.

Third, some people think that there is a language problem where God is concerned. **The word *God* simply does not have a clear, unambiguous meaning.** Statements about God cannot be verified or falsified in the usual ways.

A fourth view, one that is particularly troublesome for many people, is that **the existence of God cannot be reconciled with the presence of so much human suffering.** Catastrophic disasters, pain and suffering endured by innocent populations, and horrifying illnesses that afflict apparently "good" people all have

---

[24]S. Paul Schilling, *God in an Age of Atheism* (Nashville, TN: Abingdon Press, 1969), chap. 3. The basic list is Schilling's; the comments are mine.

led to questions about God's existence. Even if they do not question God's existence, people may question God's simultaneous goodness and power (cornerstones of the Judeo-Christian-Islamic view). If God is both all-good and all-powerful, the argument runs, why does God allow things like this to happen? These questions run the gamut from individuals asking "Why?" after the death of a parent, child, or spouse, to those of Jewish faith who asked, and continue to ask "Why?" after the Holocaust.

A fifth argument that atheists make against God's existence is that such a view is **incompatible with the recognition of the autonomy and worth of humankind.** The Christian insistence that people need a savior, or the Jewish and Muslim avowal that people need the guidance of God to live truly good lives seems to some people to contradict human autonomy, freedom, and worth.

Sixth, some people feel that **belief in God leads to people not working actively for change in the social order.** In some instances, this is a response to the perceived social conservatism of religion, religion's tendency to maintain the status quo rather than support change. As you have seen, some women feel very strongly that their churches and synagogues have been on the side of female oppression rather than on the side of women's rights. In other cases, this view stems from the shift in focus that sometimes goes along with belief in God and life after death. For some, although certainly not for most, believers, life in this present world is greatly devalued compared with eternal life with God. This devaluation then undercuts any attempt to better this life.

Finally, some people simply point to the fact that, **the world around, many people, including many who espouse very high ideals, do not believe.** If the whole experience of humankind is taken into account, there are just too many people for whom God is not a fact of their experience.

While several of these views are most likely to lead a person to atheism, at least three of them might also lead to agnosticism. Many agnostics simply feel that there is not enough evidence either for or against God's existence to warrant certainty. Some are disturbed by the ambiguity and lack of clarity that surrounds our use of the word *God.* And certainly some do wonder about how well people get along without such belief. Fewer agnostics than atheists tend to be militant about their position. For the most part, their "unknowing" makes them reluctant to try to make converts.

One of the sharpest statements of a militantly atheistic view comes from a pamphlet entitled "A Secular Humanist Declaration." In the Introduction, the authors state, "Regrettably, we are today faced with a variety of antisecularist trends." They then list a wide variety of manifestations of religion that they consider to be "dogmatic authoritarian . . . fundamentalist, literalist, and doctrinaire," choosing their examples from both the United States and around the world, and including aspects of virtually all religions. They continue

These religious activists not only are responsible for much of the terror and violence in the world today but stand in the way of solutions to the world's most serious problems. . . . [We] find that traditional views of the existence of God either are meaningless, have not yet been demonstrated to be true, or are tyrannically exploitive.[25]

This secularist attack on religion is every bit as immoderate as many secularists accuse religion of being in its attacks on secularism.

There are few **atheist organizations** in the United States, and, for most people, atheism is a matter of private belief and conviction. Probably the best-known American atheist was **Madalyn Murray O'Hair**, the twentieth century atheist whose name became for a time nearly synonymous with atheism itself. She founded **American Atheists, Incorporated**. The following list of principles comes from that organization. Although it begins with an emphatic denial of the existence of any deity, its basic tone is a positive consideration of human responsibility in light of that denial.

1. There is no heavenly father. Man must protect the orphans and foundlings, or they will not be protected.
2. There is no god to answer prayer. Man must hear and help man.
3. There is no hell. We have no vindictive god or devil to fear or imitate.
4. There is no atonement or salvation by faith. We must face the consequences of our acts.
5. There is no beneficent or malevolent intent in nature. Life is a struggle against preventable and unpreventable evils. The cooperation of man is the only hope of the world.
6. There is no chance after death to "do our bit." We must do it now or never.
7. There is no divine guardian of truth, goodness, beauty and liberty. These are attributes of man. Man must defend them or they will perish from the earth.[26]

Although some atheists are most concerned to persuade other people to take up their position as well, many do encourage this type of positive, humanistically based ethic alongside their denial of the God of the believers. Although they do not share the belief in God that most Americans have, they do share many of the same moral commitments.

These are some of the popular alternatives or supplements to participation in an organized community of faith. Woven into the tapestry of American religious life along with organized religion and the consensus alternatives, they help to make it a rich blend of colors and textures unrivaled anywhere else in the world.

---

[25]Paul Kurtz, ed., "A Secular Humanist Declaration," *Free Inquiry*, 1, no. 1 (Winter 1980), pp. 9 and 18. Kurtz drafted the Declaration, which was signed initially by 58 people, the majority of whom were from the United States.

[26]J. Gordon Melton, ed., *The Encyclopedia of American Religions: Religious Creeds* (Detroit: Gale Research Company, 1988), p. 636. The gender-exclusive language is in the original.

QUESTIONS AND ACTIVITIES FOR REVIEW, DISCUSSION, AND WRITING

1. If there is a New Age bookstore in your community, visit it and note the types of literature, music, and other items that are available. If you can, speak with the owner or manager or someone who works there about their clientele and the purpose that they believe the store serves.

2. What might be some advantages of overcoming the dualistic ways in which we usually think about ourselves and the world? What might be the disadvantages?

3. If you have been a part of a twelve-step or self-help group, reflect on the extent to which it was based on spiritual presuppositions or had a spiritual impact on you.

4. If you can locate one in your community, attend a Wiccan ritual or meeting. Write an essay on what you observe and how you respond to it. If this is not possible, try to find a Wiccan who is willing to come and speak to your class.

5. What effect do you think that ritual observance of the changing seasons and phases of the moon would have on you?

6. If possible, have an atheist and/or agnostic come and speak to your class. If they are willing to do so, ask them to discuss why they believe as they do, and whether or not they have encountered prejudice against their views.

7. If you yourself are atheist or agnostic, reflect on why you are. If you have friends and acquaintances who share your views, try to discuss this with a group.

8. Which of the reasons for being atheist or agnostic seems the most compelling to you? Why? Which seems the least compelling? Why?

FOR FURTHER READING

Anderson, Sherry Ruth, and Patricia Hopkins, *The Feminine Face of God: The Unfolding of the Sacred in Women.* New York: Bantam Books, 1991. Based heavily on interviews with "spiritually mature women in our time and culture" who describe "the unfolding of the sacred in their lives in their own words, in the language of their own hearts." Minimal commentary and a focus on the process rather than the result. A good read.

Eller, Cynthia, *Living in the Lap of the Goddess: New Feminist Spiritual Movements.* New York: Crossroad, 1992. A major effort at reporting on and analyzing the religions of goddess-worshipping feminists. Combines sociological analysis and reporting with material from interviews and description of rituals. Highly recommended.

Ferguson, Duncan S., ed., *New Age Spirituality: An Assessment.* Louisville, KY: Westminster/John Knox Press, 1995. A collection of essays assessing the meaning and impact of New Age spirituality, written both from within and outside the movement.

Lewis, James R. and J. Gordon Melton, eds. *Perspectives on the New Age.* Albany, NY: State University of New York Press, 1992. Begins with a thorough historical overview that relates the present movement to its historical predecessors. Covers various aspects of the movement and includes essays on the New Age in several foreign countries.

Melton, J. Gordon, with Jerome Clark and Aidan A. Kelly, *New Age Encyclopedia: A Guide to the Beliefs, Concepts, Terms, People, and Organizations That Make up the New Global Movement Toward Spiritual Development, Health and Healing, Higher Consciousness, and Related Subjects.* Detroit, MI: Gale Research, Inc., 1990. What can a reviewer add to the subtitle?! As with Melton's other encyclopedia works on religion in the United States, this is thorough, accurate, and very well indexed.

O'Hair, Madalyn Murray, *The Atheist World.* Austin, TX: American Atheist Press, 1991. Transcripts of radio interviews by America's best-known atheist spokesperson.

$\mathcal{E}$pilogue: Neighbors, not Strangers

I hope that this book has left you with a continuing interest in religion in the United States. Knowing our neighbors, religiously speaking, does not guarantee our appreciation of them. However, living in ignorance may well guarantee, or at least substantially contribute to, intolerance and lack of acceptance. Ignorance allows prejudice, preconceptions, and misunderstanding free rein. Strangers may easily become enemies.

I've been thinking a lot about values lately, mostly because the recent birth of our first grandchild has set me to reflecting on the kind of world in which I'd like her to grow up, the kind of woman I hope she will become. I'd like her to grow up in a *community of neighbors, not strangers*. Neighbors are people who are part of the same community. It is no accident that the words *community* and *communicate* stem from the same root. *Neighbors* are those who can and do communicate with each other. Communication in the community of neighbors must be based on several things. There must be the *willingness* to communicate—to share ideas, beliefs, and feelings openly. There must be openness to receive what is shared. This requires an open space, as it were, free of prejudice and preconceptions. There must be accurate information, in order for communication to be meaningful. And, there must be difference. The community of neighbors, not strangers, is not based on sameness, on uniformity. It is based on respect for differences. It cannot be based on an attitude of weighing differences to see who is right and who is wrong. People in the community of neighbors, although committed to their own communities of faith and the values they uphold, are also committed to the larger endeavor of understanding and appreciation, not to judgment.

John Witte, Director of the Law and Religion progam at Emory University in Atlanta, says that "the notion that we have to develop golden rules of religious liberty—treating everyone in a manner in which we would like to have ourselves treated as religious people—is something that has only recently caught on."[1] The idea of treating others as we ourselves wish to be treated (which is affirmed in all of the major religions of the world), *if actually lived out*, would go a long way toward bringing about a climate in which strangers can become neighbors.

[1]Quoted in *Islamic Horizons*, November/December 1994, pp. 14–15.

Index